BERLIN

Author

Gordon McLachlan is from Scotland and his career in publishing has involved constant traveling. He began in the field of sales before transferring to writing six years ago. He has authored and coauthored guides to Germany and Poland.

Photographer

Helka Ahokas was born in Carelia, Finland, and brought up in Sweden. After studying Art, she went into the travel business and eventually came to Hong Kong, where she has lived for the last twelve years. She has photographed extensively in Asia and has a special regard for the Himalayan region. She is the photographer for the *Odyssey Illustrated Guide to Nepal*.

BERLIN

Gordon McLachlan

Photography by Helka Ahokas

PASSPORT BOOKS
a division of *NTC Publishing Group*
Lincolnwood, Illinois USA

Published by Passport Books in conjunction with
The Guidebook Company Ltd

This edition first published in 1995 by Passport Books, a division of NTC Publishing Group, 4255
W. Touhy Avenue, Lincolnwood (Chicago), Illinois 60646-1975, USA. Originally published by
The Guidebook Company Ltd © The Guidebook Company Ltd. All rights reserved.

ISBN: 0-8442-9674-0
Library of Congress Catalog Card Number: 93-86167

Grateful acknowledgment is made to the following authors and publishers for permissions
granted:

Walter-Verlag AG for
Berlin Alexanderplatz by Alfred Döblin

Oxford University Press for
The Golden Pot and Other Tales by ETA Hoffmann, translated by Ritchie Robertson © 1992

Simon & Schuster Inc for
Little Man, What Now? by Hans Fallada, translated by Eric Sutton, © 1933, 1961

Rowohlt Verlag GmbH, Reinbek bei Hamburg, for
A Small Yes and a Big No by George Grosz © 1955 by George Grosz, translated by Arnold J Pomerans ©
1982 by Allison & Busby Ltd. Original published under the title *Ein Kleines ja und Ein Grosses Nein*, and
Germany? Germany! by Kurt Tucholsky © 1960, translated by Harry Zohn

Random House Inc for
Mephisto by Klaus Mann, translated by Robin Smith © 1977

Penguin Books Ltd and Viking Penguin for
Goodbye to Berlin by Christopher Isherwood

Angel Books for
Cécile by Theodor Fontaine © 1992

Luchterhand Literaturverlag, Martin Secker & Warburg Ltd (permission applied) for
Local Anaesthetic by Günter Grass © 1969, translation © 1970

Luchterhand Verlag and Allison & Busby Ltd (permission applied) for
The Wall Jumper by Peter Schneider © 1982, translation © 1983

Weidenfeld & Nicholson and Pan Books Ltd (permission applied) for
A Legacy by Sybille Bedford © 1956

Methuen and Suhrkamp Verlag (permission applied) for
Short Stories by Berthhold Brecht © by Stefan S Brecht 1956

Editor and Series Editor: Anna Claridge
Illustrations Editor: Caroline Robertson
Design: De•Style Studio
Maps: Tom Le Bas and Bai Yiliang

Photography by Helka Ahokas
Additional photography courtesy of: Wolfgang Albrecht from the book "It Happened at the Wall",
Haus am Checkpoint Charlie 84–85, 231; Bauhaus-Archiv, Museum für Gestaltung, Berlin 172,
173; Bundesarchivs Koblenz 32–33; Deutsches Historisches Museum, Berlin, Germany 14–15, 16–
17, 95, 115; Forschungs- und Gedenkstätte Normannenstrasse 256; John Heartfield, Dacs 1994,
293; Käthe-Kollwitz-Museum, Berlin 160; Anthony Leicester 92, 93; Gordon W McLachlan 105;
Museum für Naturkunde 148; Stiftung Schlösser und Gärten Potsdam-Sanssouci 24–25; Verwal-
tung der Staatlichen Schlösser und Gärten Berlin 282, 285;

Production House: Twin Age Limited, Hong Kong
Printed in Hong Kong by Sing Cheong Printing Co Ltd

Sanssouci Palace, Potsdam

Contents

*see below for legend for these maps

Street Map Legend

▬▬ ▬▬ U-Bahn line	
▬▬▬▬▬ S-Bahn line	
● FRANZÖSISCHE STR. U-Bahn station	
● UNTER DEN LINDEN S-Bahn station	
Tiergarten Park or open space	

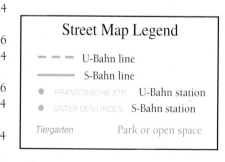

Poster for UFA-Revue (Babelsberg studios), Theater des Westens

Introduction

The intrinsic fascination of Berlin is very different from that of other major European capitals. It does not have the venerability of London, Paris or Vienna, let alone Athens or Rome. Indeed, much of it is broadly contemporary with the average North American city to which it yields nothing in the way of modernity. As long ago as 1929, Erich Kästner aptly characterized it in the children's classic *Emil and the Detectives* as a place where 'all the buildings stretched up and up into the sky', so fixing its image on the consciousness of generations of young readers.

Yet Berlin is also a city where the past seems omnipresent, where every surviving historic building illuminates a facet of its extraordinary and often disturbing past. It was here, far more than anywhere else, that the crucial events of the 20th century were enacted. As a culmination, there were the bitter decades of division when the city served as a microcosm of the Cold War, cleft down the middle by the Berlin Wall, the cruelest and most hated frontier the world has ever known.

Berlin presents the opportunity to witness history in the making as the city strives to shed its duality and become a fitting capital for Europe's strongest and richest nation. The task is a huge one, which, although begun as soon as the Wall fell in 1989, will continue for the rest of the century and beyond, leaving plenty of reminders of division in the interim. Hopefully, a unified, well-organized, dynamic and responsible city will emerge, with the ashes of two quite separate fantasies left in its wake. For, let there be no doubt, make-believe was a key component in the life of both parts of the divided city.

West Berlin was an artificially preserved enclave, a supposed paragon of the capitalist mode of life in the very heart of a Communist state. Yet the truth was that it owed its existence to its propaganda value alone and was utterly dependent on outside help, its apparent prosperity the direct result of huge external subsidies. In terminal decline from its earliest days, its constantly falling and aging population was boosted by continuous influxes of immigrants, chiefly from Turkey, and members of the young 'alternative' set, who were thereby able to dodge the draft. It was a city whose very status was puzzlingly ambiguous: although closely associated with the Federal Republic of Germany, it never became a constituent part of it, remaining under the perpetual and benevolent occupation of the Allied armies.

East Berlin was the capital of the German Democratic Republic, an inappropriately named rump state that never managed to fulfil its ambition of rivalling its Western neighbour. Nor could it realistically have hoped to do so: not only did it have a third of the area and population and a fraction of the natural resources, it had to bear the burden of occupation by a vast army of the Soviet Union, whose intentions were always cynically exploitative. Though the GDR seemed fixed and immutable until a few months before its sudden demise, the real puzzle is how such an inherently flawed state, purveyor of the greyest of grey lifestyles and propped up in later years by subsidies from its bitter German rival, ever managed to survive as long as it did.

This is but one of the many mysteries in the truly improbable story of Berlin. Founded in the 13th century, it is little more than a third of the age of such continuously prominent German cities as Cologne and Augsburg. It did not achieve the stunning early growth and development of other medieval foundations like Hamburg, Lubeck, Frankfurt or Nuremberg, all of which became powerful city-states; it was not even the capital of a substantial feudal duchy, as Munich was. Instead, it belatedly became the seat of the Margraves of Brandenburg, rulers of a marshland territory conquered from Slav tribes, and made up the eastern frontier district of the Holy Roman Empire of Germany. Until the latter half of the 17th century, it was little more than a village, which, for all the limitless ambition of the hereditary Margraves of the Hohenzollern dynasty, had played no significant part in German history.

There are but few reminders of medieval Berlin, mostly hidden amongst later structures. On the other hand, its period as capital of the Kingdom of Prussia—a self-appointed monarchy named after an exterminated Baltic tribe, which became the great predatory power of 18th- and 19th-century Europe—is vividly evoked in baroque, rococo and neoclassical showpieces, as well as in the bloated historicist extravaganzas erected after the Prussians finally forged a unified Germany in 1871.

It is the short interlude of the Weimar Republic, which followed the defeat of the German Empire in World War I, that has had the strongest impact on the English-language perception of Berlin, thanks to the stories of Christopher Isherwood. In many ways, the city they encapsulate—a city of seedy cabarets and nightclubs, of artistic freedoms and sexual decadence, of political passions and economic opportunism—belongs to the realm of myth. Yet more than the occasional echo of this heady epoch, the only period prior to 1989 when all of Berlin was governed on a democratic basis, can be found in the present-day city.

The collapse of this fragile society ushered in Adolf Hitler's Third Reich, a regime as evil as any in human history. Though not the birthplace of Nazism, the city was for twelve terrible years its capital. Had the vision of global domination come to pass, Berlin would have metamorphosed into a world capital named Germania, bisected by enormous highways and festooned with gargantuan edifices of a corrupted neoclassicism to the triumph of the Nazis. Thankfully, no more than a start was made to the project but there remain plenty of uncomfortable reminders of this inhuman epoch.

The forty years of Communist totalitarianism have left a considerably larger mark both on the cityscape and on the mentality of many of its citizens. Only time will tell how longlasting each of these will be, but for all the changes there have been in the past few years, it still requires minimal powers of observation to distinguish between the old East and West Berlin.

This is not a city to be seen in a hurry. It occupies a huge geographical area, with some of the far-flung corners ranking among the most rewarding. In terms of conventional sights, it is far richer than is often imagined, and complicated by the fact that, as a legacy of division, it still has two of almost every attraction, from the Antiquities Collection to the Zoological Gardens. Taken as a whole, its museums, in one of the more beneficial spin-offs of Prussian authoritarianism, are unsurpassed by those of any city in the world. A host of lakes, parks, gardens and forests provide ample respite from the pressure-cooker mentality of the city centre. The hotels, restaurants and shops, at least in the former West Berlin, are all that would be expected of a capital city. There is an enormous choice in music and theatre, while the nightlife really does pulsate all night every night. Above all, it is a city with a definite sense of place and, for the coming years, will undoubtedly maintain its reputation as one of the world's most exciting destinations.

Fragments of the Berlin Wall

The History of Berlin

Archaeological evidence shows that hunter-gatherers lived in the swamp that is the site of present-day Berlin as far back as 8000 BC. However, early settlement patterns were sporadic. The area fell outside the boundaries of the Roman Empire and was inhabited by a series of nomadic tribes of both Germanic and Slavic origin. Not until the 12th century did anyone attempt to establish permanent control over the territory. By this time, the German nation was established in the form of the Holy Roman Empire, a loose grouping of independent states allied to the Papacy with each side having a degree of influence in the other's affairs. The Empire's expansionist policy, manifest in the *Drang nach Osten* (drive to the east), was thus motivated not only by the desire to increase Germany's standing as a major European power but also to facilitate the spread of the Christian Gospel.

Early History

In 1157, an eastern frontier district of the Empire, designated as a Mark (March) or Margraviate, was established as a hereditary possession of Albert the Bear of the Ascanian dynasty. The area was called Brandenburg after an erstwhile Slav settlement, repopulated with Germans, that became its principal town. Albert quickly established control over the region, driving its previous settlers eastwards and making it a key bulwark of the Empire's defences.

Exactly when Berlin was founded remains unknown: its emblem of a bear clearly derives from Albert's nickname, though it is unlikely that the town existed in his lifetime. Spandau, now a Berlin suburb, is first documented in 1179; Berlin itself not until 1244, seven years after its twin settlement of Cölln, which faced it across the Spree at an easily fordable point. Cölln occupied an island site, the present-day Museumsinsel and Fischerinsel, the latter name being a reference to the fact that its population mainly comprised of fishermen. Berlin, not suffering the same restrictions of space, quickly outpaced its neighbour, growing outwards from its original location, today's Nikolaiviertel. It became essentially a trading town, a key staging post for merchants moving grain, hides, timber and fish between Russia and the great North Sea port of Hamburg at the mouth of the Elbe. They had to unload their goods at Berlin before continuing overland, or else via the Spree and the Havel to the latter's confluence with the Elbe.

Despite their proximity, Berlin and Cölln initially functioned as wholly separate towns grouped around their respective parish churches, though a partial move towards unity was made in 1307 with the building of a joint town hall. Twelve years later, the Ascanian dynasty died out, and with them the political stability of the Brandenburg Margraviate that had been a prerequisite for economic prosperity. The twin towns soon found themselves sucked into the conflict between Emperor Ludwig the Bavarian and the Papacy as central authority throughout the Empire began to break down. Despite joining the Hanseatic League of trading towns in 1359, for nearly a century Berlin and Cölln suffered from the disruption to honest trade by the robber barons who filled the political void.

In 1411, Emperor Sigismund appointed Friedrich von Hohenzollern to re-establish authority in Brandenburg. The Hohenzollerns were an enormously ambitious aristocratic family from the southern province of Swabia who had, until then, failed to make their cherished breakthrough into the small group of powerful dynasties who controlled most of Germany. Friedrich himself, in his previous capacity as Burgrave of Nuremberg, had failed in an audacious attempt to win power at the very heart of German affairs by trying to seize full control of that proud city-state, then the nation's *de facto* capital. Taking on the challenge of Germany's poorest and most lawless province seemed scant consolation and an unlikely way towards fulfilling the

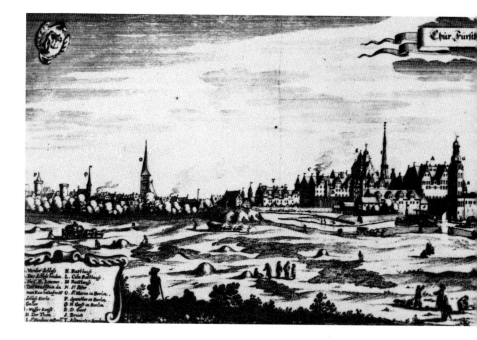

dynasty's ambitions. However, Friedrich's gamble quickly paid off. Within four years he had subdued the robber barons; his reward was the re-established Margraviate and with it the status of a hereditary Elector—one of the seven hugely powerful grandees who appointed the Holy Roman Emperor.

The advent of the Hohenzollerns was in every way fateful for Berlin and Cölln, which were formally merged in 1432. Although prosperity returned, this did not, as local people hoped, lead to the combined town gaining, like Hamburg and Nuremberg, the cherished status of a Free Imperial City—an independent city-state subject only to the emperor. By designating it as their capital, the Hohenzollerns ensured that it remained within their feudal domain. Elector Friedrich II, 'The Iron Tooth', began the construction of the town's first castle in 1451, thus giving very visible notice to the potentially rebellious burghers as to where true power lay. The establishment of a permanent court changed the character of the town; courtiers were encouraged to build themselves fine houses and a whole new range of trades sprang up to make the luxury goods now demanded.

In 1538, Elector Joachim II Hector began the transformation of the castle into a splendid new Renaissance palace. The following year, he embraced the Lutheran

The Electoral Residence City Berlin-Cölln by Caspar Merian (1627–86).
Drawn between 1646 and 1651, this early topographic view of Berlin was engraved in
Topographia Electoratus Brandenburgici in 1652.

BERLIN
soll von ALU
BERTO sugenant Ursus,
der Beer von
Anhalt Marg
graffen zu
Brandenbu:
erbauet sein u.
daher den Na:
men Berlin
überkomen ha
ben, da sie nu
zinlich zuge.
nomen hat sie
A:1380 eine gro.
se Feüersnoth
ausgestanden
ihr ist aber hers
nach gewaltig
wider aufgehol.
fen, u. mit meh
rern Privilegi
en begabet wor
den, da aber
A:1440. ihre
Burger des gut̄
Glücks halber
so sie in der
Kauffmanschaft
gehabt über.
muthig worde
u. sich an ihrē
Rath vergriffē
hat Marg
graff Fride
rich ihre Frey
heit beschnitē
u. ein Schlos
allhier gebauet
u. haben fol.
gends die Chur
fürsten zu Brā
denburg ihr
Hofflager all.
hier angestellet.
Sie ligt an dē
Flus Spree der
sich bey Span.
dau in die
Havel mit
derselben aber
beij Werben in
die Elbe er.
giefset
In der Closter
Gassen ist das
Hausworinnen
die Alte Chur
fürsten Hoff ge
halten, diese
Statt ist nicht
sonders gros,
hat 3 Thor u.
wird in 4. Kir
chē geprediget
Gegen Berlin
über dem Was
ser lieget die
Statt COLLN
allwo die Chur
fürstlich nu
Königliche

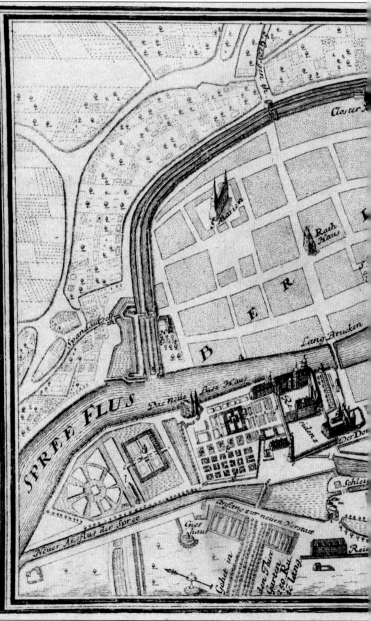

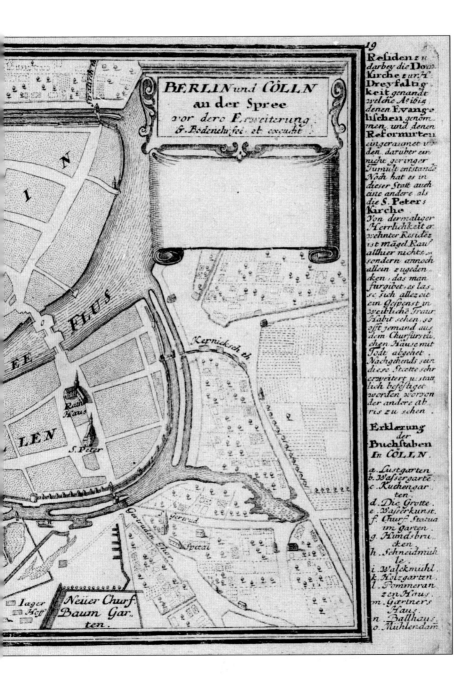

Map labels:

BERLIN und CÖLLN
an der Spree
vor dero Erweiterung
G. Bodenehr fec et excud.

LINI

FLUS

EE

LEN

Rath Haus

S. Peter

Kernicksch th.

Gertrud

Spital

Gertruden Thor

Jager Hof

Neüer Churf. Baum Gar. ten.

Residenz, darbey die Dom-Kirche zur H. Dreyfaltigkeit genandt welche Anno 1619. denen Evangelischen genommen, und denen Reformirten eingeraumet worden, daruber ein nicht geringer Tumult entstande. Noch hat es in dieser Statt auch eine andere als die S. Peters Kirche. Von dermaliger Herrlichkeit erwehnter Residez ist mägel. Rau allhier nichts, sondern annoch allein zugedencken, das man furgibet, es lasse sich allezeit ein Gespenst in weibliche Frauen Habit sehen, so offt jemand aus dem Churfürstlichen Hause mit Todt abgehet. Nachgehends seyn diese Stette sehr erweitert u. statt lich befestiget worden. worvon der andere abris zu sehen.

Erklerung der Buchstaben In CÖLLN.

a. Lustgarten
b. Wassergarte
c. Kuchengar ten.
d. Die Grotte.
e. Waserkunst.
f. Churf. Statua im garten.
g. Kindsbrücken
h. Schneidmühle
i. Walckmühl.
k. Holzgarten
l. Pommeran zen Haus.
m. Gartners Haus
n. Ballhaus.
o. Mühlendam.

Reformation, though this did not become the official state religion until 1563. Another important convert to Protestantism was his kinsman Albrecht von Hohenzollern, Grand Master of the Teutonic Knights, a crusading quasi-monastic order based in the distant Baltic province of Prussia. By abandoning the ties with Rome, he was able to secularize the order's holdings as an independent duchy nominally subject to the neighbouring Kingdom of Poland. This was to be a crucial development in Berlin's history, though its significance was not to become evident until 1618, when the Elector Johann Sigismund became heir to both family territories, which were united as Brandenburg-Prussia.

The same year saw the outbreak of the complicated series of dynastic and religious conflicts collectively known as the Thirty Years' War, which was mostly fought out on German soil. There was widespread devastation as well as depopulation through the spread of the plague as much as battlefield casualties. Berlin was occupied both by the Swedes, who intervened to support the Protestant states, and by imperial forces loyal to the Austrian-based Hapsburg emperors, who aimed to establish the same sort of centralized Catholic-influenced control over Germany as they had already achieved by alliances and dynastic marriages over much of Europe. Although the city's population fell from over 12,000 to under 6,000, the war was crucial to the city's future development into a great metropolis. By the Peace of Westphalia of 1648, the Holy Roman Empire collapsed in all but name, with authority left in the hands of the princes who controlled its constituent states. Of these, Brandenburg-Prussia was potentially one of the most powerful, having been aggrandized through the acquisition of part of Pomerania and a number of secularized bishoprics.

The Rise of a Metropolis

Friedrich Wilhelm, known as the Great Elector, acceded to the title in 1640. On the cessation of hostilities, he began the processes that were to determine the future character of both the state and its capital. Prominent among these was a distinct military tinge: a standing army was established, with a permanent garrison in Berlin, which in time came to number one in five of the population. In 1675, its worth was amply demonstrated in the defeat of the Swedes, until then Europe's leading military power, at the Battle of Fehrbellin.

The Great Elector was also keen to develop trade. In the 1660s, a canal link was built to the River Oder, making Berlin the hub of the European waterway system. Even more crucially, foreign refugees were encouraged to settle. First to come were fifty prosperous Jewish families from Vienna in 1671. The following year, Huguenots

(preceding pages) *Map of Berlin-Cölln, with selected buildings superimposed, drawn by Johann Gregor Memhardt.*

(French Calvinists) began arriving. Their numbers swelled with the Great Elector's Edict of Potsdam of 1685, a direct retort to the revocation of the Edict of Nantes, which had ended religious freedom in France. In the initial years some 5,000 settled in Berlin, constituting a quarter of the population. Not only did they make an indelible mark on its economy through the introduction of linen and silk manufacturing and skilled crafts such as jewellery, they also influenced the whole culture of the city—from the long-lasting Francophilia of the court to the evolution of a distinctive local dialect. The presence of the immigrants also influenced the rapid geographical expansion of the city westwards from its medieval core. This had begun in 1647 with the construction of the boulevard of Unter den Linden and continued with the establishment of the suburbs of Friedrichswerder to the southeast and Dorotheenstadt to the north.

Work on laying out a third new district, Friedrichstadt, was begun upon Elector Friedrich III's accession in 1688. Together with his wife, Sophie Charlotte, great-granddaughter of King James VI and I, the first monarch of the United Kingdom, Friedrich concentrated on turning Berlin into a showpiece capital and cultural centre worthy of the epithet 'The Athens on the Spree'. The Academy of Arts was founded in 1696 under the direction of the great architect-sculptor Andreas Schlüter, while the Academy of Sciences was established four years later with Gottfried Wilhelm Leibnitz, arguably the most versatile genius since Leonardo da Vinci, as its first director.

In 1701, by a purely arbitrary action with no historical legitimacy, the Elector had himself crowned King Friedrich I of Prussia in the Baltic province's capital of Königsberg. By this step, which craftily circumvented the still valid rule of the Holy Roman Empire forbidding its princes from promoting themselves to full monarchs, he achieved for the Hohenzollerns the leading place in the hierarchy of German dynasties after the Hapsburgs, who had effectively become the hereditary emperors. The name of Brandenburg was thereafter dropped from the official name of the state, though Berlin remained very much its overall capital. Many of the city's finest buildings date from immediately before and after its designation as a royal residence, among them the Zeughaus (Arsenal), Schloss Lietzenburg (now Charlottenburg) and the rebuilt (though now destroyed) Stadtschloss (City Palace). In 1709, the five districts of Berlin, Cölln, Friedrichswerder, Dorotheenstadt and Friedrichstadt were at last formally amalgamated to form a single municipality.

Friedrich I's profligacy on prestige projects meant that the state coffers were empty at the time of his death in 1713. It was therefore fortuitous that his successor, Friedrich Wilhelm I, was of a purely philistine cast of mind. Nicknamed the 'Soldier King' despite never having fought any actual wars, it was he who was responsible for changing Berlin's classical allusion from Athens to Sparta. He built up an army some 80,000 strong, of whom 20,000 were quartered, mainly in billets, in the capital, so preserving the traditional ratio of one soldier to every four civilians. Parks, including the Lustgarten facing the Stadtschloss, were transformed into vast parade grounds. Priceless works of art were traded with foreign rulers in return for recruits to the supposedly outstanding dragoon troop, the *Lange Kerls* (Tall Lads), which, as its name suggests, was made up entirely of giants. Further measures taken by Friedrich Wilhelm to increase Prussian efficiency were the rationalization of the civil administration and the introduction of compulsory schooling for those between the ages of five and twelve.

His son, Friedrich II, known throughout the English-speaking world as Frederick the Great, was a very different ruler, whose love of the arts was matched by an enthusiasm for actual as opposed to theoretical warfare so that Prussia could expand and take her place among the foremost nations of Europe. Soon after his accession in 1740, he launched a war against Austria for control of Silesia, a much disputed province that had originally been Polish before fragmenting into a series of independent duchies that were all gradually subsumed into Bohemia, which then became part of the Hapsburg domains. Using as his pretext a dubious claim the Electors of Brandenburg had once had on one of the Silesian duchies, he succeeded in wresting most of the province from Austrian control, though not before Berlin had suffered the igno-

Entrance gateway to Schloss Charlottenburg

miny of a day-long enemy occupation.

In retaliation, Austria launched the Seven Years' War in 1756 in alliance with France and Russia, with the aim of crushing Prussia as a future force. This coalition proved too powerful even for Frederick's highly disciplined army, which endured several defeats, with Berlin itself falling to the Russians in 1760. However, by a mixture of his own military genius and the extraordinary good fortune of the alliance partners falling out with each other, Frederick was able to win the war and establish Prussia above Austria as the premier German state. In 1772, he made further territorial gains by collaborating with his erstwhile enemies in the first stage of the carve-up of the by then virtually ungovernable Kingdom of Poland, which in due course was wiped off the map altogether.

Gendarmenmarkt, former Schauspielhaus

Under Frederick's rule, the classical allusion underpinning Berlin was changed once again, this time—fittingly enough, given the penchant for territorial expansion—to Rome, and the eastern end of Unter den Linden was transformed into a modern version of a Roman forum. However, the king himself preferred to live in nearby Potsdam and it was he who was primarily responsible for raising this hitherto sleepy community to the status of a full-scale royal residential town where he could indulge his Francophile cultural activities to the full.

Berlin meanwhile continued to grow steadily in population to around 150,000, though this was not accompanied by any geographical expansion. The city's textile industry developed as the largest on the continent and the Royal Porcelain Manufactory was established as a profit-making concern. While there was never any doubt about Frederick's adherence to the creed of Absolutism, he did temper this by a commitment to the ideals of the Enlightenment. Torture and censorship were abolished, the first newspapers were set up, and there was a climate of relative intellectual freedom.

THE HOUSE OF HOHENZOLLERN

ELECTORS OF BRANDENBURG

Friedrich I   1415–40
m. Elizabeth of Bavaria-Landshut

Friedrich II   1440–70
m. Katharina of Saxony

Albert III (Achilles)   1470–86
m. Margarete of Baden

Johann Cicero   1486–99
m. Margarete of Saxony

Joachim 1 (Nestor)   1499–1535
m. Elizabeth of Denmark

Joachim II (Hector)   1535–71
m. Magdalena of Saxe-Meissen;
Hedwig of Poland

Johann Georg   1571–98
m. Sophia of Liegnitz; Sabine of Ansbach;
Elizabeth of Anhalt

Joachim Friedrich   1598–1608
m. Katharina of Küstrin;
Eleanor of Prussia

Johann Sigismund   1608–19
m. Anna of Prussia

Georg Wilhelm   1619–40
m. Elizabeth Charlotte of the Palatinate

Friedrich Wilhelm, The Great Elector   1640–88
m. Louisa Henrietta of Orange-Nassau; Dorothea of Holstein-Glücksburg
Also Duke of Prussia   1647–88

KINGS OF PRUSSIA AND ELECTORS OF BRANDENBURG UNTIL 1806

Friedrich I (Elector as Friedrich III)   1688–1713
m. Elizabeth Henrietta of Hesse-Kassel;
Sophie Charlotte of Hanover; Sophia Louisa of Mecklenburg-Schwerin
King of Prussia   1701–13

Friedrich Wilhelm I, The Soldier King   1713–40
m. Sophia Dorothea of Hanover-Great Britain

Friedrich II, Frederick the Great   1740–86
m. Elizabeth of Brunswick-Bevern

Friedrich Wilhelm II   1786–97
m. Elizabeth Christine of Brunswick;
Frederika of Hesse-Darmstadt; Julie von Voss; Sophie Dönhoff;

Friedrich Wilhelm III   1797–1840
m. Luise of Mecklenburg-Strelitz; Augusta of Liegnitz

Friedrich Wilhelm IV   1840–61
m. Elizabeth of Bavaria

KINGS OF PRUSSIA AND EMPERORS OF GERMANY

Wilhelm I   1861–88
m. Augusta of Saxe-Weimar-Eisenach
Emperor of Germany   1871–88

Friedrich III   1888
m. Victoria of Great Britain

Wilhelm II   1888–1918
m. Augusta of Schleswig-Holstein; Hermine of Reuss

GRUNDRISS

von

Berlin

Aufgenommen und gezeichnet mit Genehmigung
der Königl. Academie der Wissenschaften
von
J. C. Selter.

Im Verlage bei Simon Schropp et Comp. 1845.

Decline and Revival

Soon after Frederick's death in 1786, the fortunes of Prussia and its capital suddenly went into decline for the first time in well over a century. The reign of his nephew and successor, Friedrich Wilhelm II, was notable mainly for the introduction of the neoclassical style of architecture that, as well as giving the city its symbol, the Brandenburger Tor, also determined its future face. However, the economy, the army and the state administrative apparatus all began to lose their much-vaunted efficiency. The consequences of this became evident under the rule of Friedrich Wilhelm III, whose initial reaction to the threat from revolutionary France was to remain aloof. When Prussia was drawn into the War of the Third Coalition in 1806, the results were disastrous: comprehensive defeat at the Battle of Jena led within days to a two-year-long occupation of Berlin and loss of half the country's area and population.

When the French occupiers departed in 1808, liberal elements came to the fore. A thoroughgoing shake-up of the administration was carried out by the chief minister, Baron vom und zum Stein; a university was established on the initiative of philosopher Wilhelm von Humboldt; while the army, so long the lynchpin of the state, was reformed by Gerhard von Scharnhorst and August Gneisenau. Prussia's humiliations proved to be short-lived: the French were defeated at Grossbeeren in 1812 and at Leipzig in 1813, as a result of which Napoleon was forced into exile. When he attempted his comeback two years later, it was the timely Prussian intervention at Waterloo, following a heroic fast march to the scene of the battle, that decisively turned the tables against the French, eliminating the Napoleonic threat forever.

Prussia was amply rewarded by the division of spoils at the Congress of Vienna, which was set up by the victors to determine the future map of Europe, gaining Westphalia and the Northern Rhineland. Berlin itself was seen as a vital hub in the future European defence network and now stood in the middle of a huge state that stretched, with only the odd interruption, all the way from its Baltic homeland to the French border. It was also the dominant partner in the German Confederation, the replacement for the Holy Roman Empire. In recognition of its new importance, the city centre was remodelled by Karl Friedrich Schinkel, the architect who, more than any other, was to determine Berlin's overall appearance.

Notwithstanding the key role that reformers had played in enabling Prussia to defeat Napoleon, the forces of reaction used the country's victory to regroup and put a stop to further liberalization. As a result, the bourgeoisie temporarily abandoned the political fight, complacently consoling themselves throughout the three decades known as the Biedermeier period with an increasingly comfortable home life and a spirit of cultural and intellectual freedom.

(preceding pages) *Plan of Berlin 1843, by J C Selter*

Meanwhile, more significant social forces were being unleashed by an unforeseen consequence of Prussia's aggrandizement. The country had at either end of its territory the two richest areas of mineral deposits in Europe: the Ruhr and Upper Silesia. It was thus perfectly placed to become the world's second industrial nation, closely following the British lead and able to learn from the pioneering country's mistakes. Berlin soon became the leading industrial city on the continent, with a population that soared to 400,000 by 1840. Purely working-class districts, such as Wedding and Moabit, grew up, characterized by multi-storey apartment blocks with cramped rented accommodation. The city acquired a municipal gasworks, a railway link with Potsdam and a public transport system of horse-drawn omnibuses. August Borsig, who established a company to manufacture steam locomotives, became the city's first industrial tycoon; his power and wealth were soon rivalled by the electrial engineer Werner Siemens, producer of the first telegraph equipment.

In Berlin, as elsewhere, the changes wrought by the Industrial Revolution led to social unrest, with the bourgeoisie yearning once again for political influence, the working-class for better pay and conditions. This culminated in spontaneous uprisings throughout Europe in 1848. King Friedrich Wilhelm IV went so far as to don the revolutionary tricolour himself, granting Prussia a parliament and permitting elections to the German Confederation's National Assembly in Frankfurt am Main. However, the liberals who dominated the latter proved wholly unequal to the task of moulding their dream of a united Germany stripped of its traditional authoritarian control. Their political impotence, coupled to a general breakdown in public order, enabled the army to intervene the following year, as a result of which the revolution simply petered out.

Berlin as an Imperial Capital

The failure of liberalism meant that only Prussia was strong enough to force the smaller states to accept German unity, a target that became increasingly desirable with the success of the Industrial Revolution, which needed a single market in which to function effectively. In 1862, King Wilhelm I, who had acceded to the throne the year before, appointed Otto von Bismarck to the top governmental post of chancellor. A member of the Junker class of rural landowners, Bismarck had previously been a career diplomat but proved himself a stunningly ruthless and successful political operator, able to manipulate opponents at home and abroad with apparent ease.

Domestic opposition was silenced by Bismarck's immediate commitment to national unity, which was achieved by a series of audacious foreign policy manoeuvres.

First, he formed an alliance with Austria in order to recover the duchies of Schleswig-Holstein, which had long been part of Denmark. He then picked a quarrel over the division of the spoils, leading to the Seven Weeks' War of 1864 which left Austria crushed as a potential rival for control over Germany. Prussia annexed not only the two duchies but also the Kingdom of Hannover and other states that had remained neutral. The German Confederation was dissolved and replaced by one covering the north half of the nation only, over which Prussia now enjoyed a virtual hegemony. In 1870, Bismarck completed the jigsaw by engineering a war with France over the succession to the Spanish throne, having gained the support of the southern German states in advance. When victory was sealed the following year, the Second Reich (Empire) was proclaimed, with Prussia its overwhelmingly dominant state and Austria excluded altogether. Wilhelm I was named its Kaiser (emperor) and Berlin its capital.

With its new role as the epicentre of an empire, the city's population, which then numbered just over 800,000, ballooned steadily, reaching 2,000,000 just after the turn of the century. Its whole physical appearance rapidly changed out of all recognition. Grandiose palaces were erected to house the new ministries and other national institutions. A new boulevard, the Kurfürstendamm, was laid out to link the centre with the Grunewald. In time it became a thriving commercial quarter. The bourgeoisie moved to new suburbs to the west and south, while further working-class districts appeared, principally to the north and east. Improved communications were therefore needed: in 1881, the first electrified trams were introduced, to be followed by the S-Bahn railway in 1882, the U-Bahn in 1897 and motorized buses in 1905. There was a vibrant cultural life: the university enjoyed an international reputation; the museums were filled with the fruits of excavations made by German archaeologists in the ancient world; while theatre, music, literature and the visual arts all flourished.

These years of bounty came crashing to an end with the advent of World War I. Kaiser Wilhelm II, a firm believer in the divine right of kings, had dismissed Bismarck in 1890, two years after his own succession, in the belief that the aged politician had outlasted his usefulness. Elsewhere, this move was compared to the dropping of a pilot from a ship, a metaphor that proved strikingly accurate, as no successor was ever found who remotely emulated Bismarck's sureness of touch. This was particularly fateful in the field of foreign policy where jealousy of the colonial empire controlled by Britain, Prussia's longstanding ally, was a major factor in fuelling a European-wide arms race, which divided the continent into two nervous alliances. The German Reich thereby found itself forced into partnership with its old enemy Austria, whose own eastern empire was on the verge of collapse under a wave of nationalist movements. Ranged against them was the 'iron ring' of France and Russia, with Britain waiting in the wings.

In 1914, the Kaiser and his generals put their 'first-strike' theory into effect, whereby they hoped to deliver quick knock-out blows against the French and Russians in turn, before facing the more exacting threat posed by the British. At first, they received almost universal support at home but it soon became clear that they had miscalculated badly: violation of Belgian neutrality brought Britain into the war immediately, while failure to penetrate into France meant that they found themselves bogged down in a war on two fronts that claimed casualties on a scale never before experienced. When it finally became clear in 1918 that the war was lost, the military leadership hit on the cynical idea of transferring power to democratic politicians, who would thereby have to take the responsibility, together with any blame, for the peace treaty, while the army would in the meantime be given a breathing space in which to regroup.

By this time, popular discontent was already so rife that a full-scale revolution was only averted by the division of the political left wing into three bitterly hostile camps. The main group of Social Democrats (SPD), who had supported the war and now embraced a constitutional monarchy and a bourgeois social order, were opposed by a radical splinter group of pacifists (USPD) and by the Spartakist League, a Marxist organization which aimed to seize power in Berlin in the way the Bolsheviks had so recently done in St Petersburg.

Friedrich Ebert, leader of the SPD, was installed as chancellor on the abdication of the Kaiser. On 9th November his lieutenant, Philipp Scheidemann, made an impromptu declaration of a Democratic republic from the Reichstag (Parliament) in response to a tip-off that Karl Liebknecht of the Spartakists was about to proclaim a Socialist republic from the occupied Stadtschloss. Two days later, an armistice was signed as Ebert realized that the threat of Bolshevism would lead to an Allied invasion. He formed an unholy alliance with the army, which duly crushed the Spartakist revolution the following Janaury, a last-ditch attempt at a Communist seizure of power before the elections scheduled for later that month. The army's brutality—Liebknecht and his co-leader, Rosa Luxemburg, were murdered and dumped in the Landwehr Canal—not only deepened the divisions on the political left but also served as a warning that old-style militarism was far from quelled by wartime defeat.

The Weimar Republic

The SPD duly won the most votes at the elections to the Reichstag; as a result, Ebert was made President, with Scheidemann as Chancellor. A new constitution, hailed as the most liberal and progressive in the world, was drawn up. Initially, the politicians convened in Weimar, the small county town that had seen the most glorious flower-

The White Spots

In the Dorotheenstrasse in Berlin stands a building that was formerly the Military Academy. At a man's height there is a granite border that runs around the house, slab after slab.

These slabs look peculiar: they have white spots; the brown granite is light in many places—what can it be?

White spots, is that what they are? They ought to be reddish ones. This is where the German casualty lists were posted in the 'great' years.

This is where those terrible sheets of paper were posted, new ones almost every day, those endless lists with names, names, names . . . I own a copy of Number One of these documents; on it the military units are still carefully noted, there are few dead on this first list; Number One was very brief. I don't know how many more appeared after it—but there were well over a thousand. Name after name—and each time it meant that a human life had been snuffed out or that a human being was 'missing', crossed out for the time being, or wounded, or maimed.

That's where they were posted, where these white spots are now. Hundreds of silent people crowded around them, people who had their dearest ones out there and who were trembling that they might read one name among all the thousands. What did they care about all the Müllers and Schulzes and Lehmanns who appeared on these lists! Let thousands upon thousands perish—as long as he wasn't among them. And it was on this mentality that the war battened. And it was because of this mentality that it could go on like this for four long years. Had we all risen—all as one man—who knows how long it would have lasted.

People have said that I don't know the way a German can die; I know it well enough. But I also know how a German woman can weep—and I know how she weeps today, now that she slowly, excruciatingly slowly, realizes what her man had died for. What he has died for . . .

Am I rubbing salt on wounds? I should like to burn the celestial fire into wounds. I should like to cry out to the mourners: He died for nothing, for a madness, for nothing, nothing, nothing!

In the course of the years these white spots will gradually be washed away by the rain and disappear. But those other spots cannot be effaced. There are traces engraved on our hearts that will not go away. And each time I pass the Military Academy, with its brown granite and white spots, I silently say to myself: Promise it to yourself. Make a vow. Be active. Work. Tell the people. Liberate them from national madness, you, with your small power. You owe it to the dead. The white spots cry out. Do you hear them? They cry: No more wars!

Kurt Tucholsky, 'The White Spots', Die Flecke, 1919

Kurt Tucholsky (1890–1935), a satirist of the Weimar years, was the most renowned practitioner of the fabled Berliner Schnauze *(Berlin wit). His work, much of which first appeared, under five different names, in the literary and theatrical magazine* Die Schaubühne, *has a profundity that belies its essentially miniaturist approach.*

A Jew who renounced Judaism, Tucholsky was seemingly blessed with second sight, reserving some of his strongest bile for the complacent reaction of the assimilated Jewish community towards the rise of Nazism. He himself moved to Sweden, where he committed suicide.

A collection of his shorter pieces can be found in Germany? Germany! *Those with a Berlin setting include 'Face of a German', 'Little Man Outside a Tavern' and 'The White Spots', while the pick of the witty monologues of a complacent Jewish businessman, Herr Wendriner, is the short story 'Under the Dictatorship'.*

(following pages) Official opening ceremony of the ironically titled exhibition Das Sowjetparadies *(The Soviet Paradise) in the Lustgarten on 8th May 1942*

ing of the German Enlightenment, in a direct snub to Berlin with its monarchical and militaristic associations. The Weimar Republic, however, got off to an inauspicious start even before the constitution was ratified by being forced to accede to the Treaty of Versailles, whose terms were much harsher than anticipated. Germany was stripped of valuable pieces of territory with East Prussia left cut off from the rest of the country. A hefty reparations bill was enforced with payments scheduled to last for more than half a century.

Hopes for a Social Democratic republic soon collapsed. The political right wing invented the 'stab-in-the-back legend', falsely maintaining that an undefeated army had been betrayed, and extremist groups made significant gains at elections the following year, prompting the SPD, though still the largest party, to abandon government to weak minority coalitions. There were attempted putsches such as that by the civil servant Wilhelm Kapp, who gained control of Berlin for several days, and high-profile political murders, notably that of the Jewish Foreign Minister, Walter Rathenau. The reparations bill crippled the economy to such an extent that payments were witheld. This prompted the French to occupy the Ruhr region in 1923, where they were met with a policy of passive resistance which triggered nationwide inflation on a scale never previously experienced in world history. The currency was rendered worthless and the entire middle class left financially ruined.

From this nadir the Weimar Republic made an astonishing comeback through the political skills of the new chancellor, Gustav Stresemann, who negotiated vast American loans and began the process of Germany's rehabilitation on the world stage. The political immaturity of the bulk of the population, however, was revealed at the 1925 presidential election necessitated by the death of Ebert. It was won by the 78-year-old Field Marshal Paul von Hindenburg, a wily operator basking in an undeserved military reputation, vocal exponent of the 'stab-in-the-back legend' and an embarrassing reminder of times past.

Nonetheless, the Weimar Republic appeared to be flourishing and the main beneficiary was Berlin, which, in 1920, had incorporated all the outlying towns and villages to become a metropolis of 4,000,000 people, the largest on the continent. Its 'Golden Twenties' were characterized by a cultural rebirth, in which new artistic forms such as jazz and cinema were particularly prominent. This was also the period when the city became associated with cabaret, nightclubs and sexual freedom, all of which were metaphors for a generally liberal and tolerant attitude to life.

The Wall Street crash of 1929, which came a few weeks after Stresemann's death, destroyed the society he had built up, leading to escalating inflation and unemployment with no ready-made cure. The elections the following year benefited extremist groups, in particular the National Socialist German Workers' Party (NSDAP or Nazis), which polled the largest number of votes after the SPD. This ragbag collection of misfits, led by Adolf Hitler, a former Austrian army corporal and failed artist, held, as its name suggests, a curious mixture of far-right and far-left views underpinned by fanatical nationalism and anti-Semitism. It had its own private army, the brown-shirted SA or Stormtroopers, which engaged in intimidatory violence and often fought pitched street battles with the Communists. Previously, it had been regarded as a national joke, whose few successes had been in ultrareactionary Bavaria. Since 1926, however, Berlin had been assiduously wooed by a local organization commanded by Josef Goebbels, the only member of the party hierarchy with the slightest intellectual pretensions.

Hitler was soundly beaten by the aged, half-senile Hindenburg in the 1932 presidential election, having only just managed to obtain German citizenship in time to take part. Later the same year, the Nazis became the largest party in the Reichstag but lost ground when further elections became necessary due to the impossibility of stitching together working parliamentary coalitions. Hindenburg was forced to rule by presidential decree, with power residing in a small clique of advisors. It was as a direct result of the internal intrigues of one of these advisors, Franz von Papen, that Hitler, whose accession to power was by no means inevitable, was appointed chancellor on 30th January 1933.

The Third Reich

Once in office Hitler acted quickly to make his position absolute and called new elections in which the state apparatus was used to back up the Nazis' normal methods of terror. On 28th February, the Reichstag burned down; a simple-minded Dutch Communist was arrested for the offence, which may, in fact, have been the work of the Nazis. Whatever the truth of the matter, it provided a pretext for gagging all political opponents and the Nazis duly won the election, but without quite achieving an overall majority. Following the arrest of Communists and some SPD deputies and the granting of concessions to other minority groups, the Nazis were able, with the support of the traditional right, to get the Reichstag to vote itself out of existence. The Weimar Republic was thereby abolished by legal means and replaced by the Third Reich. Other political parties were forced to dissolve and all institutions were Nazified as Germany became a centralized state for the first time in its history. Conformity was ensured by networks of informers under the control of the Gestapo, the secret police, and concentration camps were set up for the detention of political opponents.

In Berlin, Goebbels, now the Minister of Propaganda and Popular Enlightenment, instigated a boycott of Jewish businesses on 1st April, the first in a series of progressively more vicious anti-Semitic measures. The following month, he led a book-burning ceremony of the works of authors deemed to be degenerate, thus presaging the complete collapse of the city's famed cultural life, with most intellectuals forced into exile. A year later, hundreds of potential Nazi opponents were slaughtered in the Night of the Long Knives, in which the SA were supplanted by the blackshirted SS. When Hindenburg died soon afterwards, Hitler combined the offices of President and Chancellor into that of an all-powerful Führer.

The new face of Germany was presented to the world at the 1936 Olympic Games in Berlin. Nonetheless, Hitler was never wholly enamoured with the city, much of which he intended to raze in the creation of his new world capital, which would be known as Germania. His favourite architect, Albert Speer, drew up plans for this Babylonian project, but little of it—and none of the most megalomaniacal aspects—was actually built. One way in which the Nazis did manage to alter the physical appearance of the city, however, was in removing most of the Jewish monuments. This was carried out on the night of 9th November 1938, known as *Kristallnacht* (literally, the Night of Broken Glass), when 23 synagogues were destroyed.

In foreign policy, Hitler set about reversing the Treaty of Versailles: in 1938, he incorporated his native Austria into the Reich and wrested the German-speaking Sudetenland from Czechoslovakia with the help of shameful British and French connivance. The following year, he turned his attentions towards his cherished aim of the elimination of Poland, having first signed a non-aggression pact with the Soviet Union, which included a secret clause carving up the victim country between them. This time, his belief that the Western powers would show the same lack of resolve as in earlier crises proved mistaken, and so World War II began. At first, all went well for Germany, with Poland, the Low Countries and France all capitulating, leaving the British vulnerable to an invasion. However, in accordance with the Nazi obsession with aviation, he delayed in favour of an aerial strike. The result was the Battle of Britain, in which the *Luftwaffe* was defeated by the RAF.

Undeterred, Hitler switched his attention eastwards, overrunning the Balkans and preparing for the largest military operation in history—the invasion of the Soviet Union. This also marked the period of the worst concentration camps, in which Nazi racial theories were put into practice, with prisoners from occupied countries treated as slave labour. Following the 1942 Wannsee Conference authorizing the 'Final Solution' to the Jewish 'problem', trainloads of Jews were sent to these camps to be gassed to death, in the hope of achieving a systematic genocide.

Following the turning point of the war at Stalingrad in 1943, Berlin underwent an aerial battering at the hands of the British and Americans that reduced much of the city to rubble and left 1.5 million people homeless. Internal resistance to Hitler, particularly among the office cadre, gained momentum, and only a fluke saved the dictator from assassination in the July Bomb Plot of 1944. Early in 1945, the Red Army closed in on Berlin. Hitler, marooned in his bunker, committed suicide before the Soviets finally took the city after a battle which cost them over 300,000 lives, whereupon they set forth on an orgy of rape and looting. The city's population had by now fallen from its prewar figure of over 4 million to 2.8 million, with only 6,500 Jews left out of the 160,000 there had been before the Nazi takeover.

Berlin Divided

An official surrender took place on 8th May in the suburb of Karlshorst. Following a previous agreement to divide Berlin into sectors of occupation, the British, Americans and French moved into the western parts of the city in early July. Later that month, the Potsdam Conference formalized the division of both Berlin and Germany into occupied zones (see page 296). It also confiscated most of Germany's Eastern Territories, setting the new border at the Oder-Neisse line, only some 100 kilometres east of the capital.

At first, there was a great deal of co-operation among the wartime coalition partners and democratic political life was relaunched. On the right of the spectrum, there appeared a new moderate party, the Christian Democrats (CDU). On the left, the desire to present a strong united force was complicated by the legacy of bad blood that had existed throughout the Weimar Republic between the SPD and the Communists. In the Soviet zone, the two merged in March 1946 to form the Socialist Unity Party (SED). This union was not repeated in the Western zones and the SPD came close to achieving an absolute majority in the city-wide elections held in October the same year.

Strains inevitably developed among the erstwhile allies as each moulded its zone in its own image. Matters finally broke down in 1948 with the introduction of currency reform in the West. The Soviets retaliated with the Berlin Blockade, cutting off all road and rail links to the Western parts of the divided city. Another world war might well have ensued but the blockade was defeated within a year by a massive operation of airlifts, which, at its peak, saw a plane loaded with supplies touch down every thirty seconds.

By this time two different societies were emerging on German soil. In May 1949, the Western allies amalgamated their zones of occupation, other than Berlin, into the Federal Republic of Germany; four months later, the Soviets launched their territory as the German Democratic Republic (GDR). In spite of its name, the latter was structured on the Soviet model under the control of the SED, which had meanwhile transformed into a Politburo-led party. East Berlin was the obvious choice for its capital, despite the fact that the city as a whole remained under general Allied occupation. This arrangement left West Berlin as a stranded enclave within the GDR; it was ruled out as capital of the Federal Republic for logistical reasons, and the small university town of Bonn in the Rhineland was chosen to serve as the 'temporary' seat of government until the country could be unified again.

The two German states soon drifted apart, with the Federal Republic built up into a thriving mixed economy with the help of American aid while the GDR was subject not only to central planning but also to extensive Soviet asset-stripping. Notwithstanding its own division Berlin continued to function as a unit with a combined public transport system and free movement of labour across the city. Its position as a town straddling two very different societies became even more anomalous after 1952. Following Western rejection of Stalin's proposal to establish a united Germany on a democratic and neutral basis, the GDR's borders with the Federal Republic were sealed. It was hoped that this measure would halt the steady flow of emigration, particularly of professionals and skilled workers, to the West. Far from doing so, however, this continued apace through the loophole of Berlin.

Early indications that the Western Allies were impotent to influence events outside their part of the divided city came when they failed to save a number of historic monuments, notably the Stadtschloss, which were demolished on ideological grounds to make way for grandiose Stalinist planning schemes. Their impotence was shown up even more starkly in June 1953, when East Berlin was the setting for a revolt against the imposition of increased work norms—the first uprising in any of the new Soviet satellite states. When it was brutally suppressed by Red Army tanks, they could do no more than make a token protest. They were, nevertheless, able to take a stronger stand in 1958 by ignoring the ultimatum of Soviet leader Nikita Kruschchev for a combined Allied withdrawal from Berlin, which would thereby be demilitarized and handed over to the GDR.

The continued boom in the West German economy at this time brought about an ever-increasing demand for labour. Unskilled workers were recruited from Turkey, the Balkans and the Mediterranean countries; for skilled positions, the GDR provided the most ready source. By 1961, 1,500 people a day were moving permanently westwards via Berlin. Not only did this thwart Communist ambitions of achieving economic superiority over the West, in order to prove the Marxist-Leninist theory that capitalism was inevitably doomed, it also put the viability and thus continued existence of the GDR at stake.

The country's dictator, Walter Ulbricht, persuaded his Soviet masters that the solution to the problem was to seal off the border with West Berlin. On the night of 13th August 1961, a temporary barbed-wire frontier was thrown across the city and the combined public transport network disrupted by the closure of S-Bahn and U-Bahn stations that lay on cross-border lines. This was a prelude to the building of the concrete Berlin Wall, a highly sophisticated defensive system that was the first that had ever been built to keep its citizens in as opposed to an invader out (see page 86). Eventually, it was equipped with searchlights, landmines and automatic firing devices, patrolled by guard dogs and manned by armed frontier guards obliged to enforce a shoot-to-kill policy on would-be escapees. Cynically labelled the 'Anti-Fascist Protection Wall' throughout its history, its construction was justified as an act which prevented another war. In the first few days there were many daring escapes, but this became an increasingly dangerous and desperate option as the defences were strengthened.

Once again, the Western Allies found themselves powerless to act but were fortified in their determination to maintain West Berlin as a separate entity. Subsidies were poured in to present the half-city, less than honestly, as a showpiece of the capitalist way of life, while special business incentives and tax concessions were granted to encourage the existing population to remain there as well as to attract incomers to fill the jobs vacated by those now trapped in the East.

This situation prevailed until Willi Brandt, former Mayor of West Berlin, became Chancellor of the Federal Republic in 1969. His *Ostpolitik* (Eastern policy) aimed at normalizing relations between the two German states and abandoned the previous hardline approach whereby the Federal Republic had claimed to speak for all of Germany and refused to recognize the GDR's right to exist. In return, West Germans and West Berliners were allowed to travel to the GDR to visit friends and relatives, though only pensioners and the disabled were able to make reciprocal visits. In addition, West Berlin's special status was guaranteed by the Four Powers Agreement of 1972. A further consequence of *Ostpolitik* was the fall of the hardline Ulbricht, who wanted to drive a far harder bargain than suited the Soviets at the time. He was replaced by its protégé, Erich Honecker, who was regarded as a relative liberal despite his first having come to prominence as the authority on construction of the Berlin Wall.

These agreements formed the status quo in Berlin for the next decade and a half. When the city's 750th anniversary was celebrated in 1987 (with the first documentary reference of Cölln substituting for the unknown foundation date), there seemed no reason why the situation would not continue indefinitely. The two parts of the city had each received lavish grants for the celebrations. Many of East Berlin's historic buildings, which had lain bomb-damaged since the war, were restored in order that it should appear as much a showpiece of the Communist way of life as West Berlin was of the capitalist alternative. By this time the GDR seemed firmly established as a legitimate rival to the Federal Republic: it had gained a worldwide reputation for sporting prowess and had developed the most prosperous economy in the Soviet bloc. While it was true that secret subsidies were received from the West in return for humanitarian concessions and the offloading of dissidents, and that Honecker, far from fulfilling early expectations, had proved an authoritarian and unenlightened leader, the GDR seemed to have achieved a grudging respect.

Berlin Reunified

Events in other countries soon shook up this cozy complacency, ushering in the period the Germans refer to as *Die Wende* ('The Change'). The programmes of *glasnost* and *perestroika* launched by Soviet leader Mikhail Gorbachev were the first key step. Honecker defied his political masters for the first time in his life and refused to implement these reforms in the GDR on the grounds that the country was functioning perfectly well without them. This stance left him with little room for manoeuvre, as became all too clear in 1989.

By this time Hungary had taken the Gorbachev reforms several stages further and had begun demolishing the barbed-wire frontier with Austria, thus creating the first gap in the Iron Curtain since 1961. Many GDR holidaymakers took advantage of this to try to make their escape to the West. Although some were caught and sent back home, others were able to take refuge in the West German embassy in Budapest. Soon, the Hungarian government's line softened under cajoling from West Germany and the border was opened for those wishing to leave. The embassy route was subsequently also used by GDR citizens on vacation in Czechoslovakia and Poland, and again resulted in their being allowed to move to West Germany.

Within the GDR itself, opposition movements centred on Church and environmental groups began to gain in strength. Leaflets were distributed and people took to the streets in protest. At the much hyped anniversary celebrations to mark the fortieth birthday of the GDR on 7th October, Gorbachev, who was greeted as the country's saviour, publicly admonished Honecker. Massive street demonstrations against the regime were held in the following days in both East Berlin and Leipzig. As a consequence, Honecker was ousted by his own protégé, Egon Krenz, on 18th October. Despite abandoning his own longstanding hardline credentials, Krenz proved unable to stem the revolution sweeping the country, which on 4th November led to a demonstration on Alexanderplatz that attracted over a million people. By the time the Politburo resigned en masse on 8th November, 200,000 GDR citizens had already voted with their feet and fled the country.

The following evening it was suddenly announced that exit visas were henceforth available on demand. In practice, this meant that the Berlin Wall was now open, as incredulous East Berliners soon discovered by swarming to the nearest crossing point and indulging in impromptu celebrations. Over the following weekend a million GDR citizens visited West Berlin and were each given DM100 in 'welcome money'. Moves were quickly made to reinstate some of the severed public transport links, as the city prepared itself for a return to something approaching normality.

In December Krenz was forced out of office, while the SED was stripped of its all-powerful role and repackaged as the Party of Democratic Socialism (PDS). Free elections were promised for the following May, but such was the momentum of events that they were brought forward to March. The leading West German politicians quickly supplanted local opposition leaders as the main players in the election. Chancellor Helmut Kohl, who dreamed of becoming the second Bismarck, readily seized the advantage presented by his incumbency. Promising speedy unification in which no-one would lose out, he presided over a landslide victory for his CDU-led coalition.

Throughout 1990 most of the Berlin Wall was demolished and former communications links were restored. A full currency union was enacted in July, as a result of which GDR-made goods quickly disappeared from shops to be replaced by those from the West. The same month Gorbachev agreed to withdraw Soviet troops within the next four years and to allow a united Germany membership of NATO, with the proviso that no foreign troops or nuclear weapons be stationed on the territory of the former GDR. In September, the Two Plus Four negotiations led to the wartime Allies restoring full sovereignty to Germany and terminating their rights over Berlin.

Complete German union was achieved, amid huge popular rejoicing, on 3rd October. Nationwide elections a few weeks later duly rewarded Kohl for his role in the unification process by returning his coalition with a healthy majority; the CDU also triumphed in Berlin's municipal elections. Although Berlin had already been confirmed as the country's capital, it still remained to be seen where the government would be located. The campaign was vitriolic, with the Bonn lobby arguing that it should retain its position as its name was synonymous with the internationally recognized responsible and democratic face of Germany, in contrast to the long history of dictatorship associated with Berlin, which in any case was no longer sufficiently central. In return, Berliners mocked Bonn as a provincial Rhenish backwater, wholly inappropriate for the main task in hand—namely, the rebuilding of the shattered economy of the former GDR. Contrary to expectations, Chancellor Kohl, himself a Rhinelander, backed Berlin, which narrowly triumphed in the decisive parliamentary vote of June 1991.

Once the initial euphoria of unification had died down, problems began to mount and many have yet to be resolved. With economic union, much of the entire GDR economy collapsed, leading to high unemployment in the East and recession in the West as the strains of integration began to bite. This fanned right-wing extremism, itself a predictable consequence of the pent-up frustrations of the GDR years, and led to alarming incidents of racist violence. There have also been inter-German tensions, caused by Western feelings of smug superiority and Eastern dismay at the way unification has in practice meant a wholesale takeover. Berlin is having to learn to adapt to the abolition of the subsidies both its halves received in their days as rival showpieces of their respective systems, and to live with the disruptions necessitated by the construction programmes and other developments required to transform it into a major world capital for the twenty-first century.

A Train Journey Through Berlin

It had rained the previous night and the part of the town flanking the river which the train was just passing lay in a thin morning mist, just thin enough to afford our travellers a view of the rear façades of the houses and their bedroom windows, which for the most part stood open. Remarkable things were to be seen, but most remarkable of all were the summertime cafés and places of amusement which lay here and there at the foot of the high railway arches. Between smoke-blackened side-buildings there rose a number of robinia trees, six or eight of them, around which a similar number of green-painted tables stood, with garden chairs propped against them. A hand-cart with dog in harness stopped in front of a cellar opening, and baskets full of bottles being carried in, and then with just as many empty bottles in them being carried out again, were clearly to be seen. In one corner stood a waiter, yawning.

But soon they had passed this congestion of streets, and in their stead appeared broad ornamental ponds and public squares, behind which towered the Victory Column in half-ghostly fashion. The lady pointed to it with the tip of her umbrella, shaking her head, and then lowered the curtain over the open window, though only half-way.

Her companion meanwhile began to study a map marked with thick lines which showed the railway network in the immediate vicinity of Berlin. He did not get far with his orientation, however, and it was only when they skirted the edge of the Zoological Gardens that he seemed to get his bearings and said: 'Look, Cécile, there are the elephant houses.'

'Ah,' she said, in an attempted show of interest, but remained leaning back in her corner, and only sat upright when the train

arrived at Potsdam. Many military men were striding up and down the platform here, among them an old general who, catching sight of Cécile, paid his respects to their compartment with particular civility, but then immediately avoided coming anywhere into its proximity again. This did not escape her notice, nor that of the colonel.

The signal was now given and the journey continued over the Havel bridges, first Potsdam Bridge, then Werder. No-one spoke and only the curtain with the woven emblem M.H.E. fluttered merrily in the wind. Cécile stared at it as though seeking to divine the meaning of these signs, but the only result was an increase in the expression of lassitude in her features.

Theodor Fontane, Cécile, 1886

Theodor Fontane (1819–98) was born to a family of Huguenot descent. Although generally accepted as the greatest German novelist of the second half of the 19th century, he only turned to fiction in his mid-50s, having previously been a popular balladeer, theatre critic, war correspondent and writer of travelogues. His fictional début came with Before the Storm, *an epic about the Napoleonic Wars; most of his 16 subsequent novels are short and have a contemporary setting. Fontane showed particular empathy with the woman's predicament and, although a loyal and devoted Prussian, was the sharpest and most trenchant critic of his country's ethical standards.*

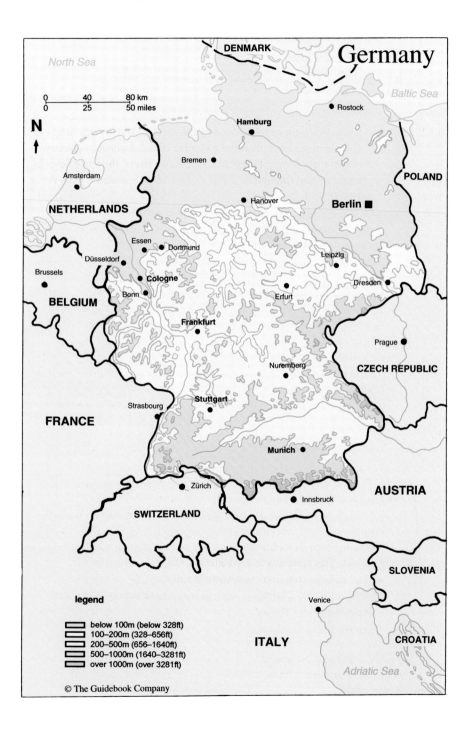

Geography

Berlin lies in the North German Plain at a latitude of 52.32 degrees and a longitude of 13.25 degrees in an environment largely shaped by the Ice Age. The average height of the land is 35 metres above sea level; there are a number of hills formed by glaciary drifts but the highest of these is only 115 metres. Of the two rivers, the Spree flows in a generally east–west direction through the heart of the city. At Spandau it joins the lake-strewn Havel, which flows north–south to Potsdam before changing course and joining the Elbe. The city occupies a total area of 883 square kilometres, stretching for a maximum of 45 kilometres from east to west and 38 kilometres from north to south. Within the boundaries are considerable areas of pine forest, which have taken root on the sandy soils deposited by terminal moraine. When parks and agricultural land are added, a total of about a third of the municipal area is green.

The city's position at the northeastern corner of the country is unusual for a capital, with the Polish border, which is far closer than the former one between East and West Germany, only an hour away by train or car. However, this is an anomaly created by territorial losses of 1945: prior to that, Germany stretched all the way along the Baltic as far as Memel in present-day Lithuania, and thus Berlin was quite centrally sited. The prewar population of over four million declined steadily throughout the years of partition, eventually dropping to three quarters of its previous level, though West Berlin remained the largest city in either state. Since German unification, the population figure has started to rise steeply and may well reach new heights by the end of the century. Nonetheless, the logistics of the Cold War years have bequeathed an unbalanced demographic make-up, with a fifth of the population of retirement age and a similar number aged twenty or less.

Currently, Berlin is one of the 16 *Länder* (states) that constitute the Federal Republic of Germany. This is a status shared with two other cities, Hamburg and Bremen, but whereas theirs is based on centuries-long civic independence, Berlin's is due entirely to the circumstances of its postwar division. In due course, it is likely that it will be reunited with its traditional heartland of Brandenburg, which surrounds it on all sides. This *Land* was revived after the fall of Communism, with Potsdam as its capital, but lacks cohesiveness without Berlin.

Berlin itself is divided into 23 districts, each of which is separately administered under the overall control of the unified city council. They are, in the order first mentioned in this guide:

Mitte: the city centre of what was East Berlin, made up of the original medieval core of Berlin and Cölln, together with its baroque and later extensions; location of most of the historic sights.

Charlottenburg: (here divided into Kurfürstendamm shopping area and Schloss Charlottenburg and its environs) formerly a separate city which grew up round a royal residence, it became the business and commercial heart of West Berlin, centred on the famous Ku'damm.

Tiergarten: named after its large wooded park, which supplanted the royal hunting grounds; also includes the arts complex of the Kulturforum, the world-renowned Zoo and the old working-class district of Moabit.

Spandau: an older town than Berlin itself and once a site of enormous strategic importance; now includes a large concentration of industry as well as stretches of farmland.

Reinickendorf: a federation of several old villages that has spawned Tegel Airport and modern housing developments.

Wedding: a solidly working-class inner suburb.

Wilmersdorf: predominantly a residential inner suburb, stretching from Ku'damm to Berlin's main forest, the Grunewald.

Schöneberg: best known as the hub of the raunchy prewar Berlin immortalized in Christopher Isherwood's novels, this inner suburb is now somewhat gentrified.

Kreuzberg: the most densely populated part of the city, with a large Turkish community; in Cold War days the hub of West Berlin's alternative subculture, but it has already moved upmarket.

Neukölln: another residential suburb created from the amalgamation of a number of villages.

Tempelhof: apart from the airport, a largely residential area, incorporating several old villages.

Steglitz: a middle-class residential suburb that includes the Botanical Gardens.

Zehlendorf: the poshest and least densely populated part of Berlin; within its boundaries are the southern half of the Grunewald, several lakes and the former village of Dahlem, now an important museum and academic quarter.

Pankow: a quiet suburb of 19th-century villas that was notorious as the favoured residential district of the GDR's élite.

Weissensee: the location of several early 20th-century model housing developments, but best known for its Jewish associations.

Hohenschönhausen, Marzahn and Hellersdorf: three suburbs of GDR-era concrete housing estate.

Prenzlauer Berg: a well-preserved quarter of 19th-century workers' tenements that served as the cradle of the 1989 revolution and has since become the favoured hang-out of bohemian intellectuals.

Friedrichshain: a small eastern extension of the Mitte district, with the most prominent Stalinist-style development in the city.

Lichtenberg: a densely populated eastern suburb, with the main civic cemetery.

Treptow: a working-class area of industrial concerns and housing schemes interspersed with parks.

Köpenick: Berlin's largest district, over half of which consists of lakes, hills and forests; there is also a historic core plus a large concentration of industry.

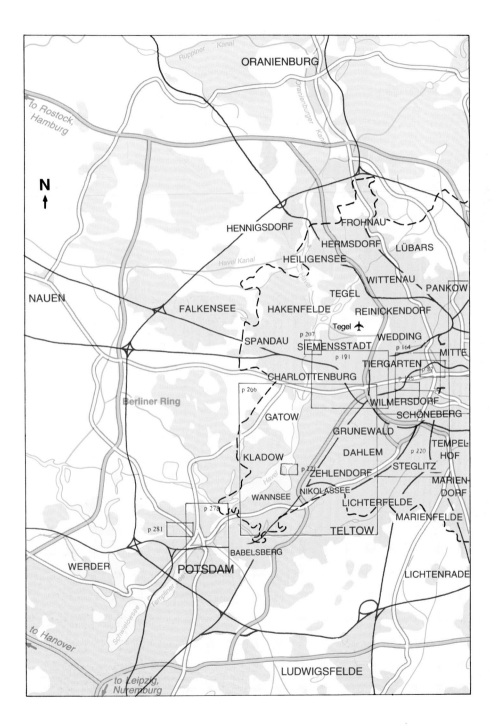

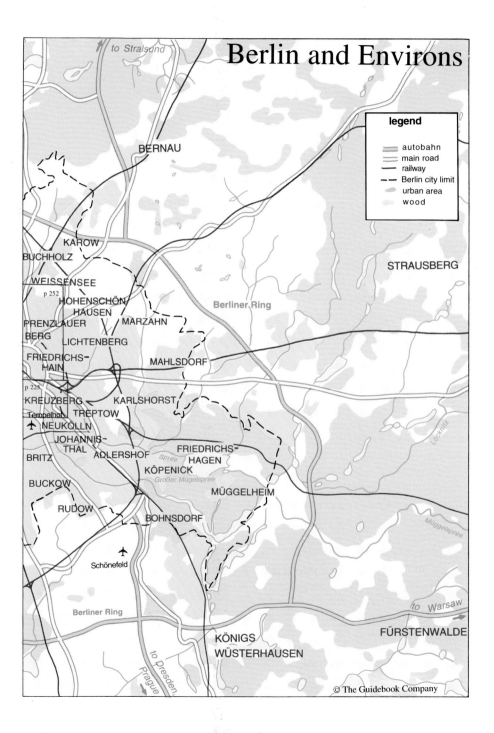

Berlin and Environs

to Stralsund

legend
- autobahn
- main road
- railway
- - - Berlin city limit
- urban area
- wood

BERNAU

KAROW
BUCHHOLZ

STRAUSBERG

WEISSENSEE
p 252
HOHENSCHÖN-
HAUSEN
Berliner Ring
PRENZLAUER   MARZAHN
BERG   LICHTENBERG
FRIEDRICHS-
HAIN   MAHLSDORF
p 225
KREUZBERG   KARLSHORST
Tempelhof   TREPTOW
Neukölln
JOHANNIS-
THAL   FRIEDRICHS-
BRITZ   ADLERSHOF   Spree   HAGEN
KÖPENICK
BUCKOW   Großer Müggelspree
MÜGGELHEIM
RUDOW
BOHNSDORF

Löcknitz

Schönefeld

Müggelspree

Berliner Ring

to Warsaw

KÖNIGS
WÜSTERHAUSEN   FÜRSTENWALDE

to Dresden,
Prague

© The Guidebook Company

Facts for the Traveller

Getting There

By Air

One legacy of Berlin's division is that, even though it has three airports, their combined volume of traffic is much less than that of Germany's premier airport, Frankfurt am Main. Long haul flights especially are far more likely to land at Frankfurt, leaving the option of continuing on to Berlin by a domestic flight on the German national airline Lufthansa (which runs up to 16 services a day), or else switching to the train. Nonetheless, there is an ever increasing number of direct international flights to Berlin, most of them to and from **Tegel** in the northwestern suburbs. British Airways fly three or four times daily from London and daily, except Saturdays, from Edinburgh via Birmingham. There are also daily non-direct links from Glasgow and Manchester via London or Düsseldorf. Lufthansa offer a daily link with London too, as do United Airlines. From the United States, Delta operate daily links with New York and Atlanta; American Airlines depart from Chicago, while TWA fly four times a week from New York.

Tegel is an efficiently run modern international airport with a huge horseshoe-shaped terminal. Its smooth operation is greatly aided by the provision of separate passport and customs controls at each gate. Facilities include a tourist office with a room-finding service, currency exchange bureaux, a left-luggage depository and desks for most of the major car rental firms. These are all generally open from early in the morning until late in the evening, but are not round-the-clock services: indeed, a peculiarity of Tegel is that it has no scheduled arrivals or departures between 9.30 pm and 6 am. Bus 109 links the airport with Bahnhof Zoo in the western centre of the city. Departures are every few minutes during normal working hours; the journey averages about half-an-hour but is subject to wide variations according to traffic conditions. As an alternative to going the whole way by bus, alight at Jakob-Kaiser-Platz and transfer to the U-Bahn network, on which the same ticket is valid.

The airport of former East Berlin is **Schönefeld**, situated at the extreme southeast of the city. With the demise of the state-run Interflug, this is mainly used by carriers from Eastern Europe, the Middle East and the Far East but is increasingly popular with charter operators and has definite potential for development. Singapore Airlines have a twice-a-week connection with Singapore, while Air Canada now offer a weekly run from Toronto. As yet, tourist facilities at the airport are rudimentary in comparison with Tegel, though there are money-changing and car-hire facilities. Bus 171 runs from the terminal building to the S-Bahn station Flughafen Schönefeld, from where trains run right through the eastern and western centres of the city, with the former reached in around half an hour. The same bus also continues to Rudow, where the U-Bahn network can be picked up.

Famed for its role in the air lifts that beat the Berlin Blockade, **Tempelhof** was used solely for military purposes following the construction of Tegel but is now enjoying a modest revival in the passenger market. As yet, this is confined to domestic services, with the exception of Conti-Flug's twice daily (except Saturdays) link with London City Airport. Just outside the terminal entrance is the U-Bahn station Platz der Luftbrücke, from which either the eastern or western city centre can be reached in ten to fifteen minutes.

In choosing a flight, it is well worth shopping around for the best deal in terms of price and flexibility. If flying from the UK, it is usually possible to find a flight for a similar or lower price than the equivalent rail fare. From elsewhere in the world, the cheapest option may be to fly to Frankfurt or Amsterdam and continue by train. Some useful contact addresses are given at the back of this book on page 317.

By Train
Berlin is linked by direct international trains to many European capital cities, including Amsterdam, Brussels, Paris, Copenhagen, Vienna, Prague, Budapest, Belgrade, Sofia, Bucharest, Warsaw, Moscow and Kiev. There are also direct services to London via the ferries at Ostend and Hook of Holland. Note that, with the increased availability of cut-price flights, these international trains seldom offer any saving in fares.

The internal German railway network benefits from heavy state subsidy and offers a regular, punctual and comprehensive range of services across the entire country. For the time being, it is administered by two separate companies: **Deutsche Reichsbahn** (DR) is responsible for former East Germany plus all of Berlin, **Deutsche Bundesbahn** (DB) for former West Germany. One potentially confusing feature is that Berlin, like London, has several railway terminals rather than a single main central station. Check carefully the station of arrival and departure though transfers from one to another are always included in the price of the ticket. Services from Western Europe generally stop first at **Wannsee** in the southwestern extremity of the city before continuing to their main point of arrival, **Bahnhof Zoo**, which is in the heart of what used to be West Berlin. Many of these trains continue on to **Friedrichstrasse**, the former border crossing point between East and West Berlin, and then to the inappropriately named **Hauptbahnhof** (Main Station), whose true function as the terminal for services to Poland and Russia was better conveyed by its pre-GDR title of Ostbahnhof (East Station). Further east is **Lichtenberg**, the main terminal for services to the Baltic coast and Central Europe, while **Schöneweide** to the south is the departure point for a number of domestic lines.

By Bus

With such a good railway network, long-distance bus travel has not caught on in Germany in the same way as in Britain or America. However, several services run to and from London and to Amsterdam and most of the larger German cities; all these offer substantial savings over the equivalent rail fares. They leave from the main bus station, the **Zentraler Omnibus-Bahnhof** (ZOB), located by the Funkturm to the west of the city centre, which can be reached by bus 147 or U-Bahn 7 from Kaiserdamm.

Passports and Formalities

UK citizens, in common with other EC nationals, need only a valid passport to enter Germany; a British Visitor's Passport, available from post offices, will also suffice. The official length of stay permitted is 90 days but in practice this is not enforced as EC passports are never date-stamped. Citizens of the United States, Canada, Australia and New Zealand can also stay 90 days. If intending to remain longer, it is advisable to apply for an extension from the German embassy before leaving home. In Berlin, extension applications should be made at the **Landeseinwohneramt**, Invalidenstrasse 57 (Tel 39 82 42 66). UK nationals intending to take up residence in Berlin can register here, or with the **Ausländeramt** at Friedrich-Krause-Ufer 24 (Tel 39 05 50). As Germans are themselves required to carry an ID card, which police and other public officials can request when they so wish, a visitor must retain a passport at all times.

Health and Insurance

All EC nationals can benefit from reciprocal health agreements with Germany if in possession of the form E111, which should be obtained from a Department of Social Security (DSS) office at least two weeks before departure. However, as it does not provide fully comprehensive cover, it is wise to take out a travel insurance to cover all eventualities, including protection against loss of money and belongings. Citizens of other countries do not qualify for any free treatment and should therefore carry comprehensive health insurance.

Most doctors, particularly in former West Berlin, speak some English; a list of recommended general practitioners is available from consulates (see Useful Addresses, page 317). Pharmacies (*Apotheken*), easily distinguished by a large red A, are spread throughout the city. They operate a round-the-clock service by rotation: outside normal hours, a sign in the door indicates the nearest one open.

Obelisk and Altes Rathaus with gilded statue of Atlas, Potsdam

Customs

Germany places no limit on currency import or export. There are general restrictions or bans on the import of meat products, fruit, flowers, plants and live animals. Otherwise, UK and other EC nationals over the age of 17 can import and export whatever goods they choose for their personal use, provided tax has been paid. For citizens of other countries and for duty-free purchases, the following limits apply:

50 grams of perfume	100 grams of tea
Other goods to the value of DM125	500 grams of coffee
200 cigarettes or 50 cigars or 250 grams of tobacco	
1 litre of spirits or 2 litres of wine (whether fortified, sparkling or still)	

Money

The German Mark (Deutschmark or DM), one of the hardest and most respected currencies in the world, comes in notes of DM5, which is gradually being phased out, DM10, DM20, DM50, DM100, DM200, DM500 and DM1000. There are coins for DM0.01 (one Pfennig), DM0.02, DM0.05, DM0.10, DM0.50, DM1, DM2 and DM5.

CURRENCY EXCHANGE

The safest way to carry money is to bring traveller's cheques. Whether bought in DMs or in the currency of the country of purchase, these are readily exchangeable throughout Berlin in banks or exchange offices (*Wechselstuben*), and can also be used in lieu of cash in the most upmarket stores. Eurocheques are also useful: they are readily accepted by a large number of shops, hotels and restaurants and can be used to obtain a cash advance from a bank. Given the consumer orientation of the society, it is surprising that the Germans are so unenamoured with credit cards. Although it is useful to carry one, particularly for obtaining cash advances, the opportunities for using it for purchases are far less frequent than in the UK or US. Exchange rates are roughly DM1.73 to the US$1, DM2.50 to the £1 and DM3 to French Fr10.

Standard banking hours are 9 am to noon and 1 to 3 pm or 2 to 6 pm; the procedures for changing money are somewhat protracted, with much form-filling. The *Wechselstuben* are generally a better bet for normal currency transactions, proceeding with a minimum of fuss and often at more favourable rates; they also give advances on Eurocheques and credit cards. A clutch of these, all open conveniently long hours, can be found around Bahnhof Zoo; the Deutsche Verkehrsbank at the front of the station is open Mondays to Saturdays 8 am to 9 pm, Sundays 10 am to 6 pm.

When to Go

Berlin is an attractive place to visit whatever the season. Paradoxically, July and August, in many respects the least desirable months, attract the most visitors. Apart from the inconvenience of tourist crowds at all the main sights, the weather is then at its clammiest and most of the theatres and concert halls are shut down. For those undeterred by the prospect of bad weather, the city is ideal for a winter break: the cultural scene is then in full swing; all but a handful of sights are kept open, with similar opening hours to those in the high summer; and the abundance of shops, museums and other indoor attractions offer ready-made escapes at times when it is uncomfortably cold to walk around. To enjoy everything Berlin has to offer, the best times to visit are from April to June and from September to October. The weather is usually at its most pleasant in these months and the parks, woods and gardens at their best, while all the aforementioned winter attractions are available as well as a wide choice of cruises on the lakes, rivers and canals.

What to Pack

What to pack depends not only on the time of year but also on the intended purpose of the trip. Berliners have a relaxed attitude towards clothing. Formal dress is still a common sight at expensive restaurants and in the opera houses, theatres and concert halls, particularly on opening nights. However, it is seldom *de rigeur*, and audiences at even the most highbrow venues generally range across the entire gamut of dress. Far from being frowned upon, eccentric or outlandish gear is generally accepted as a statement of personal preference in a city that has long prided itself in the catholicity of its tastes. Scanty summer wear for sightseeing is acceptable.

In winter, a heavy coat, scarf, gloves and thermal underwear are essential. Throughout the year, it is advisable to dress in layers to cope with likely temperature fluctuations. This is particularly true in winter when moving between the cold air of the streets and the often suffocating atmosphere of centrally-heated buildings. Given the fairly even distribution of rainfall throughout the year, waterproof clothing should be carried at all times. Footwear needs to be comfortable and sturdy, particularly for the cobbled streets of eastern Berlin, or if venturing into the forests.

Berlin's electricity supply runs on 220 volts with two-pin sockets. British equipment of 240 volts works fine with a change of plug or an adaptor, but American equipment of 110 volts requires a converter. Finally, Berlin is a world-renowned shopping centre so anything forgotten or lost can be easily replaced.

Climate

Berlin has a cross between a continental and a temperate climate, inclining more towards the former. Throughout the year, there can be sharp variations in temperature, not only on a day-to-day basis but also between the tightly built-up city centre and the wooded lakeland suburbs. Winters are generally bitterly cold, with plenty of snow and frozen lakes for weeks on end. Summers can be piercingly hot: the once famed *Berliner Luft* (Berlin air), celebrated in cabaret songs, offers little in the way of relief, its purity now annulled by industrial and traffic pollution. Transitions from one season to another are seldom obvious: it is not uncommon, for example, for a harsh winter to be followed by a sudden hot spell, only for this to be succeeded by cooler, more spring-like weather. Whenever it is unseasonably hot during the day, there is likely to be a sharp drop in temperature in the evening, with a further fall at night. Rainfall is fairly evenly distributed throughout the year but is heaviest at the height of summer, with July normally the wettest month.

Average monthly temperatures (Fahrenheit)

January	Min	27	Max	36	July	Min	57	Max	76
February	Min	27	Max	37	August	Min	56	Max	74
March	Min	32	Max	46	September	Min	50	Max	68
April	Min	40	Max	56	October	Min	44	Max	55
May	Min	46	Max	66	November	Min	36	Max	45
June	Min	54	Max	72	December	Min	29	Max	37

Time Zone

For all but a few weeks each autumn, Berlin, in common with the rest of Germany, is one hour ahead of Greenwich Mean Time and six hours ahead of Eastern Standard Time. Clocks advance an hour at the end of March and lose an hour in late September.

Getting Around

Berlin has an extensive and fully integrated public transport system (known by the acronym BVG), that consists of S-Bahn and U-Bahn trains, buses, trams and a few

City police show

ferries. The same tickets are valid for all forms of transport and there is no charge for transferring from one service to another in the course of a journey. Normal operating hours are from 4 am until 12.30 am (1.30 am at weekends), with a few night buses to span the interval when the rest of the network is shut down.

Although the complexity of the network can seem bewildering to a first-time visitor, the various route maps displayed within each station and in the shelters at bus stops help make journey planning relatively pain-free. The Schnellbahnnetz map, showing all the railway lines, is the most useful of these and is printed in this book on page 60. All bus and tram routes are also shown on the Liniennetz map, which can be purchased from station ticket windows. There is an absolute ban on smoking once inside all local public transport vehicles, but it is permitted on platforms.

By S-Bahn

The elevated railway lines crisscrossing Berlin are among its most distinctive and ubiquitous features. Most of the track belongs to the S-Bahn (*Stadtbahn* or City Railway), which is the fastest and most convenient means of transport for crossing the city. The S-Bahn has the added advantage of being linked up to Germany's mainline rail system; in the suburbs it runs at ground level, while it also has an underground stretch in the city centre. It suffered badly from underinvestment during Berlin's division, evident in the dilapidated condition of much of the rolling stock, with many ancient wooden bench carriages still in use. Extensive construction works will be necessary for several years yet to repair lines that were interrupted by the Wall and to provide much needed extensions, so delays and disruptions are to be expected.

Timetables are posted on the platform notice boards; normally services run at least every twenty minutes. Electronic departure boards indicate where the next service will terminate: note that this is not necessarily the terminus of the line itself.

By U-Bahn

The U-Bahn (*Untergrundbahn* or Underground Railway), which forms a slower-moving complement to the S-Bahn, is in much better shape than its counterpart, largely because it was less disrupted by the Wall. East Berlin's once famous ghost stations, which lay on lines starting and terminating in West Berlin, were reopened soon after the fall of the Wall, enabling a swift return to normality. Only the U-2 line was divided into east and west sectors by the Wall; it is hoped to join them up again soon. Confusingly, stretches of this and other lines are elevated like the S-Bahn.

Again, timetables are to be found on notice boards, but services are so frequent (every five minutes or so for much of the day) as to make them superfluous. Signs within stations always gave the name of the line and the terminus towards which it is travelling—they never indicate what direction this is.

By Bus and Tram

Berlin's bus network neatly complements that of the two railway systems, providing vital link-ups in the centre as well as a far more extensive coverage of the suburbs. Typically, station exits indicate the number and destination of the buses that leave from outside. Timetables posted at shelters show the exact time the bus reaches each of the stops along the route; in practice, these are adhered to with amazing accuracy.

West Berlin was almost the only city on the Continent to share the British penchant for double-decker buses, and these form the mainstay of the unified network. Entrance is always via the driver, exit by the rear door only; similarly, the front stairway to the upper deck is for ascent, the rear for descent. East Berlin favoured bendy-buses, and many remain in service. Usually, these have very few seats, the idea being to pack in as many standing passengers as possible. The same principle applies with the trams, which survive in East Berlin only. West Berlin was one of the few German cities to scrap them altogether, but a combination of logistical and environmental factors point towards a likely comeback.

Public Transport Tickets

There is a large range of ticket types:

Normal tariff (*Normaltarif*)—a single journey, including transfers, for one adult.

Reduced tariff (*Ermässigungstarif*)—a single journey, including transfers, for children between 6 and 14, students studying in Berlin and the unemployed.

Special tariff (*Sondertarif*)—applies only on selected bus routes, eg the stretch on Ku'damm between Rathenauplatz and Wittenbergplatz and the services through the suburban forests.

Short stretch (*Kurzstrecke*)—one continuous bus journey of no more than six stops, or one train journey, including transfer, covering no more than three stations.

Multiple tickets (*Sammelkarten*)—enables four journeys to be purchased in advance at a lower rate than buying them individually; available both for normal tariff and short stretch journeys.

Day ticket (*Tageskarte*)—unlimited travel over a 24-hour period for one adult accompanied by a child, a bicycle or a dog.

Family day ticket (*Familie-Tageskarte*)—unlimited travel, at weekends and on public holidays only, over a 24-hour period for an adult couple accompanied by any or all of their children.

Combined day ticket (*Kombi-Tageskarte*)—unlimited travel including the cruise ship services of *Stern und Kreisschiffahrt*, over a 24-hour period for one adult.

Six-day-ticket (*Sechs-Tage-Karte*)—unlimited travel, from Monday to Saturday inclusive, for one adult.

Monthly ticket (*Monatskarte*)—unlimited travel, from the first to the last day of a calendar month, for one adult.

Tickets can be bought from windows at S-Bahn and U-Bahn stations during normal working hours or from the orange-coloured automatic machines located on every platform and inside trams. Bus drivers sell single tickets only; those at the special tariff must be bought from them. Otherwise, single tickets are an expensive option and should be avoided wherever possible; in contrast, a monthly ticket can be a remarkable bargain: even during a two-week stay, it can pay for itself several times over. Single tickets are delivered time-stamped by the vending machines and are valid thereafter for two hours. Day tickets need to be validated in the cancelling apparatus located at the entrances to platforms and inside buses and trams; the same applies to each portion of a multiple ticket immediately before use.

When boarding a bus, it is standard practice to show the driver a valid ticket.

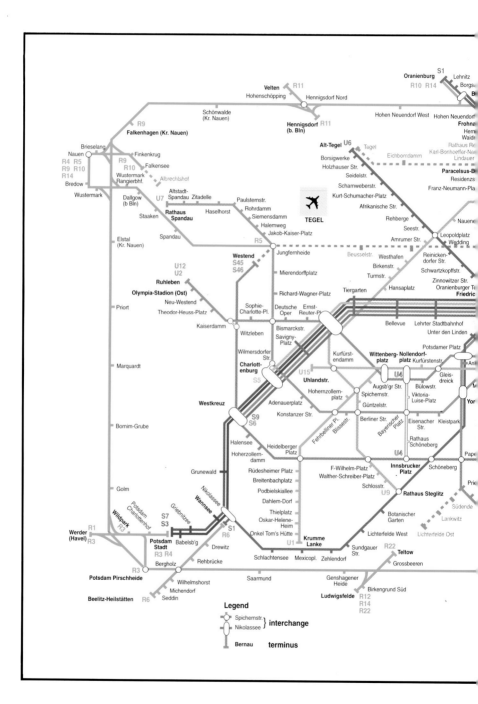

Legend

Spichernstr.
Nikolassee } interchange

Bernau   terminus

Berlin U-Bahn, S-Bahn and Regional Railways

Otherwise, the whole network functions on the honour system, with no formal controls and very infrequent spot-checks by plain-clothes inspectors, who automatically levy a hefty fine on anyone caught trying to ride for free.

BY TAXI

Unless in a group, taxis are an expensive way of travelling around Berlin, though prices are no higher than in other major European capitals. A further disadvantage is that they seldom save time on journeys that can be made by S-Bahn or U-Bahn, and this is particularly true with regard to long trips and during times of peak traffic. Taxis can be hailed from the street or picked up at the many ranks located outside stations, large department stores and hotels. Alternatively, radio taxis can be called on: 69 02, 96 44, 21 01 01/02 02, 24 00 24, 26 10 26, 69 10 01.

BY CAR

Cars can be hired from all the usual rental companies. However, the excellent public transport system makes a car superfluous for sightseeing purposes, quite apart from the problems of navigation and parking in a city which has not yet fully come to terms with the huge increase in vehicle ownership since the fall of Communism. Driving in former East Berlin presents several additional problems, notably the presence of a lot of inexperienced and often irresponsible drivers, and a large proportion of roads with potholes or uneven surfaces. Trams also present a special hazard: cars must give way at tram stops to enable passengers to cross the street in front of them; particular care must also be taken at junctions to avoid any possibility of colliding with a turning tram.

BY BOAT

Berlin's extensive waterways offer ample opportunities for a boat trip, though this is really only a means of relaxation and not a serious way of getting around. A variety of cruises is available between April to October, ranging from short canal trips through the centre to day-long excursions down the Havel and its lakes and on to Potsdam. The main jetties, from which several different companies often operate, are at Moabit, Tegel, Spandau, Wannsee and Treptow: see page 318 for more information.

ON FOOT

In any city, it is necessary to walk a bit in order to appreciate it to the full; this is particularly true of Berlin, whose parks and gardens are amongst its most attractive features. However, the sheer size of the place and the scattered nature of its historic sights mean that walking is a supplement and not an alternative to public transport.

As throughout Germany, pedestrians should beware of walking on the many paved cycle tracks. In the shopping streets, these are red and lie close to the kerb; in more outlying areas, they tend to be marked with the image of a cycle, with a corresponding one of a pedestrian in the other lane. Berlin is the only city in the country where jaywalking is encountered to any extent, but nonetheless the vast majority of people always wait patiently—even on a deserted street at night—for the green light to appear. Jaywalkers are unlikely to meet with anything worse than admonishment from law-abiding fellow pedestrians, though the police are entitled to levy an on-the-spot fine for the offence.

Information and Maps

Before leaving home, it is worth contacting the German National Tourist Office, which maintains branches in most foreign capitals (see Useful Addresses, page 317). In Berlin itself, the municipally run tourist offices (*Verkehrsämte*, also listed in Useful Addresses, page 317) are generally well organized and helpful. Staff are invariably fluent in English. By normal German standards, the supply of free promotional material is scanty, being confined to a basic map and a few leaflets. They do, however, produce the standard annual directory, complete with prices of hotels and guesthouses, and are able to book accommodation, either in advance or on arrival. Each month, they publish the *Berlin Programm*, with full listings of exhibitions, theatre, concerts, museums and art galleries, along with arrival and departure times of planes, trains and buses; there is also a small section devoted to Potsdam.

Available from newsagents are two well-established rival listings magazines, *Tip* and *Zitty*, which are the Berlin equivalents to London's *Time Out*. Each covers a fortnightly period, but they are published on alternate weeks from one another. There is also a recently founded monthly magazine in English, *Checkpoint*, aimed at the burgeoning English-speaking community in the city, as well as tourists. By far the best single map of Berlin is the *Falkplan*, available from newsagents or bookshops.

Communications

Telephones
The creation of a combined telephone system is one of the biggest headaches of German unification, and one that will not be completed for several years. At the root of the problem is the fact that, in total contrast to West Berlin's model modern network, that of East Berlin and the rest of the GDR was hopelessly underfunded, with relatively few subscribers, outdated technology and an absurd system of variable codes. Although the provision of telephones has increased enormously since the fall of

Communism, there is still an insufficient number of lines in the East, which can be harder to call from the West than almost anywhere in the world.

The city has a liberal supply of public telephone kiosks though many of those in the East do not function reliably. A large number of those in the West have recently been converted to accept magnetic cards only; these can be bought from post offices and some shops. Those operating with money accept DM0.10, DM1 and DM5 coins. Most phones can be used for international calls, the exceptions being those clearly marked *National*. Some kiosk are labelled *International*, with a ringing bell depicted alongside; this indicates it is possible to receive a call there. The cheapest times for phoning abroad are between 8 pm and 8 am on weekdays and all day at weekends.

To call Berlin from abroad, dial the international code (010 in the UK, 011 in the US, 001 in Hong Kong) followed by 49 30 and the desired number. To call abroad from Berlin, dial 00 followed by the country code (1 for US and Canada, 44 for UK, 353 for Ireland, 852 for Hong Kong, 61 for Australia, 63 for New Zealand), then the local code (omitting the initial zero), and finally the subscriber's number.

For emergency numbers in Berlin, see page 317.

POSTAL SERVICES

Mail between Berlin and the UK generally takes from two to four days; between Berlin and the US, from seven to ten days. It is best to attach an air-mail (*Luftpost*) sticker to anything mailed abroad. Prominent yellow postboxes are found throughout the city: these have two slits, one for mail within Berlin, the other for all other destinations (marked *Andere Richtungen*). The central post office, located within Bahnhof Zoo, has a limited 24-hour service. This is also the best place to have mail sent poste restante. Ask for letters to be addressed to: Postlagernde Sendungen, Postamt Bahnhof Zoo, 10623 Berlin. Fax and telex services are also available and at a cheaper rate than in most shops. Other post offices in the city are generally open Monday to Friday 8 am to 6 pm, Saturday 8 am to noon.

ADDRESSES

The street name always precedes the number. *Strasse* (street) is commonly abbreviated to *Str* and is often joined on to the end of the preceding word. Other terms, which again are sometimes tacked on to the previous word, include *Allee* (Avenue), *Brücke* (Bridge), *Damm* (embankment), *Platz* (square), *Ufer* (quay) and *Weg* (way). Because of the preponderance of tenements in Berlin, addresses are often qualified: VH (*Vorderhaus*) is the front part of the building, HH (*Hinterhof*) the rear, while EG (*Erdgeschoss*) refers to the ground floor, 1 OG (*Obergeschoss*) the first floor, 2 OG the second floor and so on. A new system of five-digit postcodes was introduced in 1993, replacing all previous ones.

Outdoor café in Kreuzberg

Etiquette

Berlin's belated rise to German dominance was due to the honing of administrative and military skills, and the culture of discipline and efficiency this brought is still much in evidence today. Fortuitously so, for the task of restoring a city divided so ruthlessly and artificially for such a long period is one that might otherwise have been insuperable. The downside of this tradition is that Berliners often appear too committed to serving as mere cogs in a great wheel.

To foreign visitors, their general attitude can seem standoffish and cool, if not downright cold. However, the sense of indifference towards visitors should not be interpreted as an expression of xenophobia. On the contrary, Berlin's tradition of welcoming immigrant communities, from the Huguenots in the 17th century to the Turks in recent decades, and as a place where all kinds of alternative subcultures can flourish, is evidence of a tolerance matched by few other European cities. Though racial tensions undoubtedly exist, they are far less serious than those of the average American city, despite the sensationalist press coverage given to the activities of neo-Nazi groups.

Berliners, nevertheless, like most Germans, are uncomfortable with the easy bonhomie so characteristic of the modern Anglo-Saxon world. Longstanding professional and business colleagues are prone to address each other by the formal *Sie*, instead of *du* (the literal translation of 'you'), and to eschew the use of Christian names. This formality never has overtones of either obsequiousness or condescension; even the youngest and most junior staff are given the courtesy title of *Herr* (Mr) and *Frau* (literally Mrs, but now taken by any adult woman). However, where the British have a snobbery about inherited titles, the Germans do about academic qualifications: anyone with a doctorate is addressed as *Herr Doktor* or *Frau Doktor*, to which the word *Professor* is appended for those holding university chairs.

When dealing with Berliners, try not to be overfamiliar. Always begin and end meetings with a handshake. In any encounter with bureaucracy, fill up preferred forms punctiliously; sloppiness is regarded as one of the worst vices. If able to speak in German, use only the formal forms of address unless asked to do otherwise. Trivial as it seems, the change to using *du* and Christian names is often regarded as a watershed development in a relationship, the change from acquaintance to true friendship.

Shopping Hours

The trading hours of shops in Berlin, as throughout Germany, are strictly curtailed by a law initially introduced to curb workaholic tendencies in the immediate postwar period. Although it has long lost any rationale and is in antithesis to longer opening times adopted in most other Western countries, an alliance of vested interests conspires to keep it in operation, despite a few recent modifications.

From Monday to Friday, stores may open no earlier than 9 am and must close by 6.30 pm, except on Thursdays when they may continue trading until 8.30 pm; in practice, many open later or shut earlier than these times. Normal opening hours on Saturdays are from 9 am until 2 pm, except on those designated *Langer Samstag* (the first Saturday of the month and each of the four preceding Christmas). Then trading is permitted until 4 pm from May to September and until 6 pm from October to April. On Sundays, only bakers are allowed to open, usually between 2 pm and 4 pm. The only shops which do not have to conform to any of the restrictions are those in or beside railway stations: in theory, they exist to serve bona fide travellers only, but no attempt is made to apply this restriction.

National Holidays

The following public holidays (*Feiertagen*) are observed in Berlin:

New Year's Day (1st January)
Good Friday (March/April)
Easter Monday (March/April)
May Day (1st May)
Ascension Day (April/May:
11 days before Whit Monday)
Whit Monday (May: 7th Monday
    after Easter)

Reunification Day (3rd October)
Day of Prayer and National Repentance
(3rd Wednesday in November)
Christmas Eve (24th December)
Christmas Day (25th December)
Boxing Day (26th December)

Virtually all shops are closed on these days, though many bars, cafés and restaurants remain open. Usually at least some museums can be visited, with the ones that do not observe the holiday taking the next day off instead.

Festivals and Annual Events

Whereas many parts of Germany, particularly the south and the Rhineland, are renowned for their popular festivals, the same cannot be said of Berlin: other than the stage-managed jamborees of the Nazi and Communist regimes, the city has kept faithful to its stolidly puritanical Prussian tradition. Such festivals as do exist, therefore, tend to have a serious bent.

January: Green Week—agricultural, gardening and nutritional show.

February: International Film Festival—second only to the Cannes Film Festival.

March: International Tourism Trade Fair—exhibitors from all over the world come to promote their countries' tourist attractions.
Musik Biennale (odd-numbered years)—features works by avant-garde composers.

April: Free Art Exhibition—displays the work of around 2,500 Berlin artists, both amateur and professional.

May: Drama Festival—brings together the best new productions from through out the German-speaking world.
German Open Tennis Championships—now one of the most important tournaments outside the four Grand Slam events.

June: Jazz in the Garden—with leading international artistes.
German–French Folk Festival—focuses on a different French city or region each year.

July: Bach Days—concerts of music by J S Bach and his contemporaries.
Midsummer Night's Dream—diverse series of concerts.
German–American Festival—high-spirited celebrations hosted by the US army.

August: International Electronics Exhibition (odd-numbered years)—brings together all the latest hi-tech equipment from around the world.

September: Festival Weeks—concerts and drama on a different artistic theme each year.
Medieval Fortress Festival—mock medieval events held at the Spandau Zitadelle.
Oktoberfest—small-scale replica of the famous beer festival of Munich.
German Touring Car Championships—held along the Wannsee autobahn.
Berlin Marathon—the third largest of its kind in the world.

October: International Film and Video Festival—featuring 'alternative' works in contrast to its glitzy February counterpart.

November: Jazz Festival—covering all varieties of jazz, with both German and foreign performers.

December: Christmas Markets—in many locations, including Marx-Engels-Platz, Breitscheidplatz and Spandau's Altstadt.
Menschen Tiere Sensation—circus that has been an annual event for over half a century.

More Cake?

Our appointment had not included the dog but Scherbaum brought the dachshund. The cold, sunny, windless January afternoon permitted us to carry little flags: our breaths. All those who passed us in the opposite direction, overtook us, or cut across our path sent up similar smoke signals: We live! We live!

The wide sidewalk at the corner of Kurfürstendamm and Fasanenstrasse presented itself. The pavement was bordered with black-rimmed piles of snow, which were marked with dog urine and excited Scherbaum's long-haired dachshund. (Order and merriment.) The terrace of Kempinski's was packed. Under the terrace roof infrared tubes glowed, providing an assembly of opulent stately ladies, who were spooning in pastry, with that upper warmth that makes for cold feet. Amid dwindling cakes, sugar shakers, cream pitchers, coffeepots, filter coffee and—as could be surmised—pots of Sanka stood cheek by jowl. Opulence was accentuated by fashionable clothes, tailor-made, or when ready-made from the best shops. Furs, mostly Persian lamb, but also a good deal of camel's hair, whose café-au-lait color went well with Sachertorte and with chocolate cream puffs, with paper-thin slices of Baumkuchen and the popular walnut layer cake. (Vero Lewand had called them cake-eating fur-bearing animals.) A few dogs, their leashes attached to chair legs, started tugging the moment we and Max located the spot chosen as the scene of the crime. Otherwise we attracted no attention because inevitably the ladies were used to tugging at their chair legs. Many dogs were led by. (In all there are 63,705 dogs in West Berlin, one dog to 32.8 inhabitants. The canine population has diminished: in 1963 71,607 dogs were kept, one dog to 29.1 inhabitants. That doesn't strike me as unduly many. Actually I expected there would be more. In all domains the same regressive tendency: the wasting away of Berlin. That's what I should have said to Scherbaum: 'Perfectly normal, Philipp: In the Kreuzberg section there is almost a shortage: only one dog to 40.6 inhabitants. To speak of a Berlin dog craze in the face of these figures is to foster a legend that has outlived itself.') We stared at the terrace which may have been interpreted as looking for a friend. Cake dwindled. New pastry was served. I began ironically, in order to divest our scene-of-the-crime inspection of any solemn, definitive quality: 'If we assume that a jelly doughnut contains two hundred calories, it becomes superfluous to ask how many calories are contained in a portion of Schwarzwald Kirsch Torte with whipped cream.'

(Vero Lewand's estimate had been correct: 'At least three pounds of jewelry apiece. And what do they talk about when they talk? Phew, about weight and dieting. Ugh!')

The ladies in hats glanced, ate, and spoke simultaneously. An unappetizing, much caricatured, yet innocent picture. In view of so much simultaneous and continuous gluttony, an outside observer, Scherbaum for instance with his preconceived opinion, was bound to infer a corresponding process: simultaneous and continuous bowel movements; for this obsessive abundance of apple strudel, almond crescents, cream kisses, and cheesecake could only be counterbalanced by a contrary image, by steaming excrement. I rose to new heights: 'You're right, Philipp. Colossal piggishness... Monumentally repulsive... And yet, we mustn't forget, it's only a partial aspect.'

Scherbaum said: 'There they sit.'

I said: 'It's worry that makes them stuff.'

Scherbaum: 'I know. They paste cake over everything.'

I: 'As long as they eat cake, they're happy.'

Scherbaum: 'It's got to stop.'

We stared for a while at the mechanism of the loading and unloading cake forks and registered innumerable little bites with detached and uplifted little finger. ('Pastry hour,' they call it.)

I tried to undermine Scherbaum's disgust (and my own): 'When you come right down to it, it's just funny.'

But Scherbaum saw interrelations: 'There you see adults. That's what they wanted and now they've got it. Freedom of choice and second helpings. That's what they mean by democracy.'

(Should I have countered his oversubtle comparison with a complicated disquisition on the pluralistic society? Well, Doc? What would you have done in my position?)

I tried to cheer him up: 'Imagine, Philipp, that those ladies in their overflowing plenitude are sitting there naked...'

'They won't shovel in any more cake. Afterwards, when they want to start in again, the image of Max, burning and writhing, will stand in their way.'

I said: 'Wrong. Here where you're standing they'll beat and kick you.

They'll kill you with umbrellas and heels. Just look at their fingernails. And other people, who were only out for a stroll, will form a circle, they'll push and shove, and end up arguing about whether that blob of humanity on the pavement burned a schnauzer, a terrier, a dachshund, or a pekinese. A few will read your sign, decipher the words 'gasoline' and 'napalm,' and say: 'What poor taste!' True, after you've been wiped out, most of the cake-eating ladies will pay up, complain to the management, and leave the terrace. But other ladies in similar furs and similar hats will take their places and order apple turn-over, cream kisses, and almond cake. They'll show each other with their cake forks where it happened. Here, right here where we're standing.'

Since Scherbaum said nothing but merely stood watching as the cake dwindled and a new generation of cake sprouted, I went on with my description of the consequences: 'They'll talk of inhuman barbarity and repeat the whole incident, savoring it along with their cream cakes and coffee, because your Max won't burn quietly, patiently, and quickly. I see him jumping and writhing. I hear him whimpering.'

Still Scherbaum said nothing. Max kept calm under my words. I let inspiration carry me. Talk, keep on talking to him. 'It would be perfectly reasonable, though, to try to reduce their cake consumption. But then you'd have to write the caloric values of the various tidbits on signs and parade back and forth on this sidewalk: For instance: A piece of raisin cake equals 424 calories. Then we'd need a breakdown into carbohydrates, proteins, and fats. That would be worthwhile, Philipp. A campaign of enlightenment against the society of superabundance...'

When I began listing the ingredients of Schwarzwald Kirsch Torte, Scherbaum vomited violently and in several gusts on the sidewalk outside the Kempinski terrace. The mechanism of a few cake forks stalled. Scherbaum retched. Nothing more would come. Before a circle could form—the pedestrian traffic had already come to a halt—I dragged Philipp and the whimpering Max across Fasanenstrasse into the crowd of afternoon strollers. (How quickly one can submerge.)

Günter Grass, Local Anaesthetic, 1969

Grass (b. 1927) has written poems, plays and essays and is an accomplished graphic artist. A veteran political campaigner for the Social Democratic Party, he is against the revival of a strong, unified Germany.

Food and Drink

Berlin's gastronomy ranks among its strongest points and, as befits a major international capital, a huge range of cuisines is available. The Turkish food here, thanks to the daily import of fresh ingredients by the large local ethnic community, is the best and most authentic outside Turkey. There are also plenty of Italian, Greek, Balkan, Chinese, Indian and other eateries. However, most visitors naturally gravitate towards traditional German fare, which, in spite of all the competition, maintains its overall dominance in the city's gastronomic life.

One very German peculiarity is that there is not the rigid distinction amongst eating and drinking establishments that exists in most other countries. The traditional inn (*Gaststätte* is the most common designation, though *Gasthof, Gasthaus, Brauhaus* and *Wirtschaft* are also used) not only serves full meals throughout the day, it also offers snacks and caters to those who wish only to drink, whether it be beer or a hot beverage. Similarly, most cafés offer far more than coffee and cake: they also sell alcoholic drinks and a wide range of food, often running to complete menus. Another point to note is that there are many more eateries in former West than former East Berlin, and that the overall standard is much higher in West Berlin. Hangovers of the GDR's culinary policy—an inadequate supply of state-owned places to eat, with a take-it-or-leave-it attitude towards customers—unfortunately still persist.

Breakfast (*Frühstück*) is normally, though not invariably, included in the price of a hotel room. In such cases, it is likely to fall midway between the spartan French start to the day and the elaborate Scandanavian spread. German breads include such specialities as *Pumpernickel*, the strongly flavoured black rye bread, and the salted *Bretzel*. Because of Berlin's 24-hour lifestyle, and above all because of its hectic nightlife, a large percentage of the population does not eat first thing in the morning. Consequently, many cafés serve breakfast meals through until late afternoon. These generally present a far wider and more imaginative choice than the usual hotel repast, typically in the form of all-inclusive deals centred on particular items such as cheeses, fruits or cereals. Foreign tastes are also well looked after: *Englischer Frühstück* is for those who cannot do without their bacon and eggs, *Französischer Frühstück* for devotees of coffee and croissants.

The *Café-Konditorei*, which combines the functions of café and bakery, is indelibly associated with Vienna but is also very much a Berlin institution, serving the mid-morning or mid-afternoon snack of coffee and cake (*Kaffee und Kuchen*). A downmarket but even more prevalent type of eatery is the *Imbiss* or snack bar, which serves hot savoury food throughout the day. Its staple fare is the sausage, boiled or grilled, with rolls or French fries as standard accompaniments. A popular preparation is chopped up and with a curry sauce—proof positive that the sausage occupies a rather less lofty culinary position than in many other German cities, where it is treated as a serious item of cuisine in even the best restaurants.

Berliners are very flexible about the main meal of the day. Many favour a heavy lunch (*Mittagessen*), eaten any time between 11.30 am and 2 pm, and therefore require only a light supper (*Abendbrot*, which literally means evening bread), usually at around 7 pm. Others, particularly office workers with only a short midday break, take a light lunch and a heavy dinner (*Abendessen*). All restaurants must by law display their menus and prices by the door, along with a note as to which, if any, day they are closed (*Ruhetag*). An increasing number offer a special daily menu (*Tageskarte*) of two or three courses at a bargain price: this is usually but not necessarily available at lunchtimes only. Despite the inroads made by *Neue Deutsche Küche*, the German version of *nouvelle cuisine*, most restaurants stick to the hearty traditional style known as *Gutbürgerliche Küche*. This is modelled on German home cooking and is thus reasonable in price, notwithstanding the penchant for generous portions.

Many soups are adaptations or direct copies of foreign models. Favourites include a liquidized form of the Hungarian goulash; a brown French onion soup with floating cheese and croutons; a spicy Serbian-inspired bean soup; and, in former East Berlin, a Ukrainian broth with sausages. Clear soups, usually made from chicken stock, are also popular; the tastiest are those with liver dumplings, though this is an import from Bavaria rather than an authentically Berlin dish. Most of the commonly encountered alternatives are vegetable-based, though bones and fat are often used in the cooking. Starters other than soups are fairly rudimentary: melon, salads, pâté and plates of cold cuts similar to those found on breakfast tables.

Main courses in most restaurants are overwhelmingly pork-based. This is less restricting than it might appear as virtually every part of the pig is used and prepared and garnished in a limitless number of ways, so that even a relentless diet of schnitzels, cutlets, steaks and chops can appear quite varied. The knuckle or trotter is the true Berlin speciality. The boiled version of this is the nearest there is to a civic dish, though its grilled counterpart brings out the taste of the abundant fat far better.

A number of secluded restaurants in woodland settings on the outskirts of the city specialize in game, with venison, hare, rabbit, duck, goose and pheasant likely to be on the menu—all at a price. Elsewhere, chicken is the only form of poultry commonly encountered and is usually the cheapest main course option. Fricassée on a bed of rice is the main alternative preparation to spit-roasting.

Berlin's inland position means that, other than in speciality restaurants, fish tends to be of the fresh-water rather than salt-water variety. By far the commonest is trout, while the more expensive carp, pike and pike-perch are also of excellent quality. Of those brought from the Baltic Sea, the rosefish outshines more familiar breeds such as sole, cod, haddock and plaice, though all these are available.

BEER

Germany is home to around 40 per cent of the world's breweries, whose products are second to none in quality. Standards are controlled by the *Reinheitsgebot* (Purity Law), first formulated in 1516 in Bavaria and now applied throughout the country. This provides strict rules for production, including the banning of chemical substitutes. Most German regions have their own highly distinctive brewing style, the products of which can be found in Berlin, though only a selection is likely to be available in any particular bar.

Weizenbier is a tart and refreshing brew made from wheat, predominantly in southern Germany. It is available either as *Kristall*, which is light and sparkling, or as *Hefe*, which has been given a strong yeast boost. Also from the south are *Münchener*, a brown-coloured lager from Munich, and *Rauchbier*, the aromatic smoky beer of Bamberg. *Bockbier*, a light or dark strong ale with a sweetish taste is made throughout Bavaria, but is chiefly associated with its original home, the Lower Saxon town of Einbeck. *Altbier* from Düsseldorf is a copper-coloured barley malt beer; *Kölsch* from Cologne is a pale, highly fermented beer served only in small glasses; while *Export* is a medium-strong premium beer primarily associated with Dortmund, Europe's largest beer-producing city. *Pils*, a bottom-fermented golden beer with a very high hop content, is made throughout the country; the brew from Jever in Lower Saxony is the bitterest in taste and is particularly popular with Berliners.

The price of a main course invariably includes vegetables, and often a mixed side salad as well. True to the cliché, cabbage, both hot and cold, takes pride of place. The red kind is normally stewed with apple or served cold with vinegar, while its green counterpart is pickled with juniper berries or made into a coleslaw salad. Potatoes are similarly ubiquitous, and appear on menus as French fries, in a dumpling mixture, creamed and boiled. Among other vegetables, mushrooms, and in particular the wild woodland varieties, are especially delicious. Pasta, albeit in its southern German rather than Italian forms, is a surprisingly regular accompaniment to main courses.

Vegetarians will usually be able to find a few suitable dishes on most restaurant menus, or at least on those in former West Berlin. However, they should beware of the tendency to use animal fat in the preparation of many dishes that outwardly

Berlin itself, like most other German cities, has a number of small boutique breweries (*Hausbrauereien*) which have revived the medieval practice of making the beer on the premises; it is then served fresh to the customer in the adjoining bar. Most of the city's production, however, is concentrated in the two large conglomerates, *Kindl* and *Schultheiss*, plus the latter's subsidiary, *Engelhardt*. These produce their own version of *Pils*, but the city's own distinctive contribution to beer culture is the very different *Berliner Weisse*, a pale-coloured, fruity and acidic brew often dubbed 'the champagne of beers'. This epithet actually has French endorsement, Napoleon's occupying troops having referred to it as such. The most thirst-quenching beer, *Berliner Weisse* is primarily a summer refresher, though it is now available all year round. Its alcoholic content is very low, seldom rising above three per cent.

Because of the presence of a heavy yeast sediment, a bottle of *Berliner Weisse* must be poured slowly and carefully. In bars, it is almost invariably served in a large bowl-shaped glass which provides a further reminder of its champagne connotations. Taken neat, it has a sharp, tangy palate. However, very few people choose to drink it this way, preferring it *mit Schuss* (with syrup). This can be either *Rot* (red), a raspberry essence, or *Grün* (green), an extract from the herb woodruff. Different from the other and both transform the unadulterated version out of all recognition, converting it into a fruity beverage readily enjoyable even to those who usually shy away from alcohol. It is normal to imbibe through a curved straw, which can also be used for stirring up a frothy head whenever desired.

appear not to contain meat and will find their tastes best catered for in specialist establishments.

Desserts in restaurants seldom even begin to compare with the goodies available in a *Konditorei*. Following on from hefty main courses, they are almost inevitably cold and light, functioning more as a palate cleanser than any kind of climax to the meal. Many are fruit based, and those with berries, particularly when mixed together in a compote, are especially recommended.

Beer is the German national drink and is certainly the most appropriate accompaniment to a traditional Berlin meal (see above). The city is too far north for the effective cultivation of grapes, though there are, of course, plenty of wines available from elsewhere in Germany—the Mosel, Rhineland and Baden. Sparkling wines

prepared in the manner of champagne are a decent and economic substitute for the original, while hot mulled wine is a true German speciality, most effective in winter for warding off colds. Fruit-based liqueurs are a popular means of ending a meal, particularly for those who find schnapps too overpowering. Soft drinks are broadly similar to those in other European countries, though fruit juices, apple and grape especially, are often of a superior standard.

ON THE MENU

VERSCHIEDENE	VARIOUS
Brot	Bread
Brötchen	Bread roll
Butter	Butter
Ei	Egg
Essig	Vinegar
Hönig	Honey
Joghurt	Yoghurt
Käse	Cheese
Kloss, Knödel	Dumpling
Marmelade	Jam
Maultaschen	German form of ravioli
Öl	Oil
Pfeffer	Pepper
Reis	Rice
Salat	Salad
Salz	Salt
Senf	Mustard
Sosse	Sauce
Spätzle	Shredded noodles
Zucker	Sugar

SUPPEN	SOUP
Bohnensuppe	Bean soup
Erbsensuppe	Pea soup
Gulaschsuppe	Thick soup in imitation of goulash
Hühnerbrühe	Chicken broth
Kartoffelsuppe	Potato soup
Leberknödelsuppe	Clear soup with liver dumplings
Linsensuppe	Lentil soup
Ochsenschwanzsuppe	Oxtail soup

Organ-grinder and his monkey at the Brandenburg Gate

Soljanka	Spicy Ukrainian soup with sausages
Zwiebelsuppe	Onion soup

VORSPEISEN	HORS D'OEUVRES
Aufschnittsplatte	Plate of cold cuts
Lachsbrot	Smoked salmon on bread
Leberpastete	Liver pâté
Melone mit Schinken	Melon with ham
Sülze	Jellied meat loaf
Wurzfleisch	Supreme of pork

FLEISCH	MEAT
Eisbein	Boiled knuckle of pig
Hackfleish	Minced meat
Hammelfleisch	Mutton
Hase	Hare
Hirsch, Reh	Venison
Jägerschnitzel	Pork schnitzel with mushrooms
Kaninchen	Rabbit
Kasseler Rippen	Pickled pork chops
Kotelett	Pork cutlet
Lamm	Lamb
Leber	Liver
Rahmschnitzel	Pork schnitzel in a cream sauce
Rinderroulade	Beef olive
Rindfleisch	Beef
Sauerbraten	Braised pickled beef
Schinken	Ham
Schweinehaxe	Grilled knuckle of pig
Schweinesteak	Pork steak
Speck	Bacon
Wiener Schnitzel	Pork schnitzel in breadcrumbs
Wildschwein	Wild boar
Wurst	Sausage
Zigeunerschnitzel	Pork schnitzel in a paprika sauce
Zunge	Tongue

GEFLÜGEL	POULTRY
Broiler, Hähnchen, Huhn	Chicken

Ente	Duck
Fasan	Pheasant
Gans	Goose
Truthahn	Turkey
FISCH	FISH
Aal	Eel
Forelle	Trout
Hecht	Pike
Hering, Matjes	Herring
Kabeljau	Cod
Karpfen	Carp
Krabben	Prawns
Lachs	Salmon
Makrele	Mackerel
Muscheln	Mussels
Rotbarsch	Rosefish
Schellfisch	Haddock
Scholle	Place
Seezunge	Sole
Thunfisch	Tuna
Tintenfisch	Squid
Zander	Pike-perch
GEMÜSE	VEGETABLES
Blumenkohl	Cauliflower
Bohnen	Beans
Bratkartoffeln	Sautéed potatoes
Champignons	Button mushrooms
Erbsen	Peas
Gurken	Cucumbers
Kartoffelpuree	Creamed potatoes
Kartoffelsalat	Potato salad
Knoblauch	Garlic
Kopfsalat	Lettuce
Krautsalat	Cabbage salad
Möhren	Carrots
Pelzkartoffeln	Baked potatoes
Pilze	Mushrooms

Pommes frites	Chipped potatoes
Rosenkohl	Brussels sprouts
Rote Rübe	Beetroot
Rotkohl	Red cabbage
Rübe	Turnip
Salzkartoffeln	Boiled potatoes
Sauerkraut	Pickled green cabbage
Spargel	Asparagus
Tomaten	Tomatoes
Zwiebeln	Onions

OBST	FRUITS
Ananas	Pineapple
Apfel	Apple
Aprikose	Apricot
Banane	Banana
Birne	Pear
Brombeeren	Blackberries
Erdbeeren	Strawberries
Himbeeren	Raspberries
Johannisbeeren	Redcurrants
Kirschen	Cherries
Orange	Orange
Pampelmuse	Grapefruit
Pfirsich	Peach
Pflaumen	Plums
Schwarze Johannisbeeren	Blackcurrants
Trauben	Grapes
Zitrone	Lemon

NACHSPEISEN	DESSERTS
Apfelstrudel mit Sahne	Apple strudel with cream
Berliner	Jam doughnut
Eis	Ice cream
Gebäck	Pastries
Käsekuchen	Cheesecake
Keks	Biscuits
Pfannkuchen	Pancakes
Rote Grütze	Red berries compote with vanilla sauce

Schokolade	Chocolate
Schwarzwalder Kirschtorte	Black Forest gâteau
Torte	Cake

GETRÄNKE	DRINKS
Apfelsaft	Apple juice
Apfelwein	Cider
Bier	Beer
Glühwein	Hot mulled wine
Grog	Hot rum
Kaffee	Coffee
Kakao	Cocoa
Korn	Rye spirit
Kräutertee, Pflanzentee	Herbal tea
Likör	Liqueur
Milch	Milk
Orangensaft	Orange juice
Roséwein	Rosé wine
Rotwein	Red wine
Sekt	Sparkling wine
Selters, Sprudel	Sparkling mineral water
Tee	Tea
Traubensaft	Grape juice
Trinkschokolade	Drinking chocolate
Wasser	Brandy
Weisswein	White wine
Zitronenlimonade	Lemonade

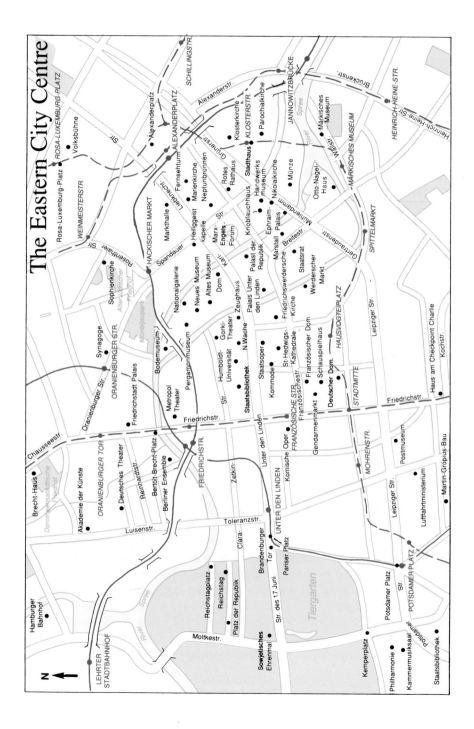

The Eastern City Centre

The Eastern Centre

Berlin's historic centre, the **Mitte** district, was allocated to the Soviets in the 1945 partition of the city, even though it protruded so far to the west that it was bordered on three sides by sectors held by the British and Americans. With its grand public buildings, it was perfectly suited to be the showpiece part of the capital city of East Berlin, but the militarist and imperialist connotations these structures boldly proclaimed inevitably created an uncomfortable incongruity. The attitude of the GDR authorities to this legacy was ambivalent and inconsistent: at first, some historic buildings were restored and redeployed; others, most notably the huge royal palace, the Stadtschloss, were razed; while a third group was left to crumble. As time went on, and as the psychological need to forge some kind of bond with the past became ever more apparent, there was a much greater readiness to spend money on restoration projects, though some buildings had to wait until reunification before the first proper steps towards repairing war damage were undertaken.

No such indecisiveness held back the desire to give the Mitte district a definite new 'Socialist' character. The result is the intrusion of bleak open precincts, hideous chicken-coop flats, show-off prestige public monuments and soulless offices to house the overweight state bureaucracy. If the eye is offended almost as often as it is charmed, the consolation is that Berlin's entire history is laid bare in a revelatory way. Though it will be many years before the true picture emerges, it will be fascinating to see how many of the imperial losses will be re-created, how much the Communist legacy will be obliterated, and what sort of attempt there will be to create a wholly new face in line with the district's role as the heart of what is likely to become Europe's most powerful and influential capital.

During the Cold War years, visitors from non-Communist countries tended to spend most of their time in West Berlin, seeing the Mitte district only on a day trip towards the end of their stay. This habit has become unnecessarily ingrained: it is now far more logical to begin a tour of the city in the time-honoured manner of visiting the most historical parts first. The broad boulevard of Unter den Linden, restored to its position as the city's main artery, is an obvious reference point. Flanking it to the north and south are the baroque extensions to the original city, while the western end terminates at the Pariser Platz and the celebrated Brandenburger Tor. At the opposite end, on the island site of the former town of Cölln, are many of the city's—and Europe's—greatest museums. Across the Spree lies the medieval core of Berlin, even if this is not immediately apparent from its predominantly modern appearance, in which the few remaining old buildings are dwarfed by their surroundings.

The Berlin Wall under construction at Checkpoint Charlie, 1961

YOU ARE LEAVING
THE AMERICAN SECTOR
ВЫ ВЫЕЗЖАЕТЕ ИЗ
АМЕРИКАНСКОГО СЕКТОРА
VOUS SORTEZ
DU SECTEUR AMERICAIN
SIE VERLASSEN DEN AMERIKANISCHEN SEKTOR

The Wall at Potsdamer Platz, 1976

The Berlin Wall

From 1961 until 1989, the entire character of Berlin was defined by its notorious Wall, a uniquely German phenomenon representing the ultimate in the ingrained national tendency to accept and obey authority and all its attendant rules and regulations, no matter how absurd. The only border construction in history designed to keep its citizens at home, rather than an invader out, it was a giant prison ordered and built by its own prisoners. Not only was it the most secure frontier ever devised, it was also the most bizarre: by remorselessly cutting right through the heart of a teeming 750-year-old metropolis, it divided it into two competing cities, each of which thereafter acted out its own fantasy role. East Berlin was the artificial capital of an artificial state whose very existence was irrevocably tied to that of the Wall itself; West Berlin was a supposed capitalist bulwark against Communism completely dependent on the sort of state subsidies fundamental to Communist ideology—and a place with an island mentality totally at odds with its status as the largest German city. The very illogicality of the Wall—the 'stablization of the impossible', as it was called—thus bred a perverse logic of its own.

Sixteen years after the division of the city in 1945, some 60,000 East Berlin residents still routinely crossed through any of the city's 80 border posts in order to get to their jobs in West Berlin. By the same means, anyone was free to emigrate, and the numbers choosing to do so steadily mounted as West Germany's economic boom showed no signs of abating, creating a demand for ever more labour; in August 1961, some 1,500 GDR citizens were leaving each day. Despite official denials that there were any plans to build a wall, GDR dictator Walter Ulbricht came to the conclusion that sealing off West Berlin was the only possible way to guarantee his state's continued existence. His apprehensions about its future viability were of far more than personal or local concern: the very *raison d'être* of the Soviet Union and all its satellites was at stake. As Marxist-Leninism insisted on the historical inevitability of its own triumph, the fall of a single Communist government would expose its entire philosophical system as a sham. Ulbricht accordingly had little difficulty in obtaining Soviet support for his scheme.

In the early hours of the 13th August, some 50,000 armed troops were deployed to block the streets at the border crossing points with barbed wire and other improvised barriers; at the same time, public transport links and telephone lines between the two parts of the city were cut. The next day, the area around the Brandenburger Tor was 'temporarily' sealed off, and the number of crossing points reduced to thirteen.

Three days later, work began on the construction of a wall of compressed rubble topped with barbed wire along the entire length of the frontier, a few metres inside GDR territory; its total length was 165 kilometres, of which 45 kilometres cut through the city itself, dividing some 150 streets in the process. An area of no-man's land was declared 100 metres behind the Wall. All the houses here had their west-facing doors and windows blocked off as a prelude to demolition, which would improve the sightlines of the border guards, who were ordered to shoot would-be escapers dead. East Berlin residents who had hitherto worked in the West were ordered to register with the authorities, who allocated them alternative employment. After a few days of apparent liberty, West Berliners were banned from entering the eastern part of the city.

The official justification for the building of the Berlin Wall was that it protected the GDR state against 'revanchists, militarists and imperialists'. The 'Anti-Fascist Protection Wall' was said to have forestalled a planned invasion of East Berlin by the Western Allies, an action which would have precipitated World War III. These preposterous myths were propagated throughout the remaining lifetime of the GDR, even in material for English-language consumption, such as state-sponsored guidebooks.

In the first year of the Wall, some 14,000 GDR citizens managed to overcome the enormous hazards involved in any escape attempt to reach the West safely. When security techniques were refined the following year, the number of escapees plummeted, and in 1963 the construction of the definitive Berlin Wall meant that only the most ingenious or the most foolhardy risked the crossing. Nonetheless, some 60,000 people were imprisoned for attempted flight; most served between one and two years, while life sentences were imposed on those found guilty of organized conspiracy. There were also many successful escapes each year using a host of ruses, from traditional tunnelling methods via the impersonation of Allied officers to the construction of home-made light aircraft. It is unknown how many people died in escape attempts: a figure around the 200 mark is the best estimate. If that seems a surprisingly low number, it is explained by the difficulty of the obstacles that had to be faced before a guard was in a position to shoot.

Most of the definitive Wall—around 111 kilometres of its length—was made of identikit reinforced concrete slabs. Each was 4.10 metres by 1.20 metres and bound together with steel rods; at the foot was a horizontal backing slab, while at the top was a pipe-shaped superstructure of asbestos. The type of concrete varied according to the location; it was hardest in the city centre, particularly around the Brandenburger Tor, where it was stronger even than that used in bridges and flyovers, being capable of withstanding a ramming from either side. The no-man's land (dubbed the *Todesstreife*, or Death Strip) was left as an area of wasteland, guarded on its eastern side by an electrically charged two-metre-high fence. In addition to 135 bunkers, 212 watchtowers and some 5,000 searchlights, there was a battery of other devices to catch fugitives, including trip wires, alarms, mines, automatic firing devices and packs of highly trained dogs. Where the international frontier was defined by a river, canal or lake, grilles and meshes were placed in the water, which was also patrolled by high-speed boats. A total of 13,000 guards were deployed around the Wall, of whom around a fifth would be on duty at any one time.

Quite apart from the initial planning and building costs, the upkeep of the Berlin Wall was a major item in the GDR's budget. To the regime, that was of little account, as the Wall was the guarantor of its existence, providing it with the captive labour market it required. Moreover, it became a means of obtaining desperately needed hard currency, as the West Berlin authorities were forced to pay for the U-Bahn lines which transited through East Berlin territory, as well as for the use of the S-Bahn, which was the property of the GDR rail network. As restrictions gradually relaxed on visits by Westerners, compulsory exchanges of money were introduced, with the unconvertible Ostmark deemed as having permanent parity with the mighty Deutschmark. Most lucrative of all for the GDR was the trade in human beings, whereby political prisoners and dissidents were transferred to West Germany, in the manner of star footballers, for huge sums of money.

In West Berlin, the Wall spawned a whole gamut of side-effects. For visiting politicians, it was a not-to-be-missed photo and sound-bite opportunity. For the local authorities, it was a readily marketable tourist attraction and viewing platforms were set up along the most visited stretches. It also became a do-it-yourself gallery for graffiti artists and scribblers of messages, both local and foreign. Most of the latter, which were often in English, were banal variations on the 'I was here' theme, but there were occasional snatches of caustic wit:

> *DDR=KZ (GDR=concentration camp)*
> Piss here
> Socialist Peep-Show, 10 Kopecks
> Last one over please turn off the lights
> Why not jump over and join the Party?

When the GDR finally opened its frontiers in November 1989, it was inevitable that the Wall, stripped of its function, would come down. Hoardes of bounty-hunters, readily seeing a golden marketing opportunity, immediately began hacking away at its fabric, offering chunks (or forgeries of the same) for sale as tourist souvenirs in improvised street stalls. Before its own demise, the state itself set up a company, *Limex-Bau*, to export substantial pieces of the structure as museum exhibits, earning sums of up to DM50,000 from the US and Japan. Throughout 1990, most of the Wall was demolished, though not without considerable difficulties, particularly regarding the part behind the Brandenburger Tor.

All that now remains are a few sections under preservation order as historic monuments: these include the Ostseitegalerie (East Side Gallery), the small sections at the Prinz-Albrecht-Gelande and Checkpoint Charlie, and the much longer stretch on Bernauer Strasse, where the Wall split one side of the street from the other. For anyone who knew the city during its years of division, the departure of the Wall has been a profoundly disorientating experience: the circuitous routes via official crossing points had become so familiar as to seem natural, while the previously curtailed streets took on an eerie dimension when stripped of the barrier that had subjected them to 28 years of separate lives. First-time visitors, on the other hand, are often disappointed at how little remains and how difficult it often is to work out where it used to be. Perhaps it is a pity that more of it was not preserved, though the local clamour for its total demolition was, to say the least, understandable. For, in neither function nor aesthetic appeal was the Berlin Wall remotely like the Great Wall of China, to which it was so often compared.

'Release me from this deadly embrace', Ostseitegalerie painted with a mural showing the former Soviet and GDR leaders Leonid Brezhnev and Erich Honecker in a passionate embrace

Makeshift cemetery for those shot while attempting escape over the Berlin Wall

Former watchtower

Making use of the new border crossing

Souvenir collectors near Checkpoint Charlie;
(opposite) *Volkspolizei patrolling the crumbling wall*

The Brandenburger Tor and Pariser Platz

The **Brandenburger Tor** (Brandenburg Gate) is the enduring symbol of Berlin. News-reels have made its appearance familiar the world over as the backdrop to the popular celebrations that attended the demise of the Berlin Wall—from the first euphoric chipping away at the hated frontier on 9th November 1989, via the party to end all parties on Hogmanay the same year, to the triumphal unification of the two German states on 3rd October 1990.

For all the momentousness of these events, they were only the latest in a long catalogue of epoch-making occasions enacted in the square. In 1815, Prussian troops held a victory parade at the gate on their return from Waterloo, where they had turned the tide in favour of the anti-Napoleonic alliance and thereby rid Europe of the French dictator. Following another victory over France in 1871, their successors celebrated the creation of the first ever united Germany. Hitler's appointment to the office of Chancellor of the German Reich in 1933 was marked by a parade of his Storm Troopers; twenty years later striking workers passed through the gate pro-testing about the injustices of Soviet rule. In 1961, the Brandenburger Tor was the first place to be sealed off on the night of 13th August as construction of the Berlin Wall began. Forming part of the restricted border area patrolled by armed guards, with the Wall, which ran immediately behind it, blocking it off from West Berlin, it was inaccessible to the general public for the next 28 years.

Cleansed of its familiar grime for the reunification celebrations, the Branden-burger Tor can be admired once more for the great monument it is. The only survi-vor of the city's 18 gateways, it was built between 1788 and 1791 to replace a far more modest structure; its name comes from the fact that it marked the start of the road to the city of Brandenburg, the original capital of the heartlands of the imperial Hohenzollern dynasty. Designed and built by the Silesian architect Carl Gotthard Langhans, it was modelled on the Propylaea on the Acropolis, thereby symbolizing Berlin's pretension to a latter-day Athens. The uncompromisingly neoclassical idiom marked a decisive break with the baroque and rococo styles then current. It was to serve as an inspiration for building activity in the city for several generations to come.

The classical theme is continued in the carved decoration by Johann Gottfried Schadow and Christian Bernard Rode: the roundels tell the story of Hercules, while the metopes illustrate the Battle of the Lapiths and Centaurs. Despite adopting the format of a triumphal arch, the Brandenburger Tor was originally known as the Friedenstor (Gate of Peace), signifying the Prussians' desire for an end to the con-tinual wars to which they had been subjected. When the city walls were demolished in 1867, the two side pavilions, which stretch forward like welcoming arms, were

Brandenburger Tor and Unter den Linden, 1936

remodelled as guardhouses. The southern of these regularly features contemporary art exhibitions.

Perched atop the gate is **The Quadriga**, a huge bronze group of the goddess Nike on her chariot by Schadow. Napoleon removed it to Paris as war booty following his victory in 1806, so gaining the nickname of 'The Horse Thief of Berlin'. On its return, Karl Friedrich Schinkel was commissioned to transform the sculpture: Nike was altered to a personification of Victory, bearing the newly created military decoration, the Iron Cross, and wearing a wreath with the Prussian eagle. When *The Quadriga* was recast from the original mould at West Berlin's expense in the 1950s, the Communists removed Schinkel's additions and turned the group round so that it faced east rather than west. Following damage caused during the 1989 celebrations, *The Quadriga*'s Iron Cross was reinstated, and it now looks westwards once again.

Nowadays, **Pariser Platz**, together with the wasteland to the south, sadly ranks among Berlin's worst eyesores, with no visible reminders of its prewar status as the most exclusive address in the city. Formerly, there stood the American, Dutch and French embassies; the luxury Hotel Adlon; the Arnim-Palais, home of the Prussian Academy of Arts; and the Dichterakademie (Poets' Academy), which was taken over by Albert Speer as the headquarters for his scheme to transform Berlin into Hitler's global capital, Germania. For the time being, the East German border guards have been replaced by a dwindling number of stallholders selling off alleged fragments of the Berlin Wall and the surplus uniforms of Warsaw Pact armies. Plans to re-create two sunken gardens in the square have been announced but the main decisions on redevelopment have yet to be taken.

Unter den Linden

Berlin's great central boulevard, the romantically named **Unter den Linden** (Under the Lime Trees), began life as a bridle path which linked the royal palace with the hunting grounds of the Tiergarten. At the end of the Thirty Years' War in 1648, Friedrich Wilhelm, the Great Elector, ordered its beautification and lime and walnut trees were planted. A century later, Frederick the Great made it the city's main axis and envisaged turning its eastern part into a complex of civic institutions on the model of a Roman forum, a dream only partially fulfilled due to his increasing disillusionment with Berlin and preference for nearby Potsdam.

Until the advent of the Third Reich, Unter den Linden's 1.4 kilometres were lined on both sides by grandiose buildings which served collectively as the hub of the city's cultural life. The first depredations came with the axing of the lime trees to allow room for Nazi processions; this was followed by extensive wartime damage. Although the Communists replanted the trees and restored most of the finest buildings, the street, then terminating to the west in a dead end, never recovered its former status. Even today there remains a jarring contrast between the partial redevelopment at the top of the street and the finely restored historic set pieces at the bottom.

During the GDR years some attempt was made to re-establish a diplomatic quarter at the eastern end of Unter den Linden. Inevitably, pride of place was given to the **Botschaft der UdSSR** (Soviet Embassy) on the first block of the southern side. Constructed in the early 1950s, it is a typical example of the Stalinist style, mixing the debased neoclassicism favoured by all 20th-century dictators with a few Cubist touches, most notably in the lantern tower. Although now taken over by the representatives of democratized Russia, a statue of Lenin continues to adorn the garden. Fronting the perpendicular Glinkastrasse immediately beyond are offices which postdate the embassy by a decade and were built to house other Soviet delegations: the news agency TASS, the airline Aeroflot and the travel agency Intourist.

As a refreshing change from the bloated monumentalism of these buildings, it is worth making a short detour down Schadowstrasse, the side street facing the embassy across Unter den Linden. Here, at No 10–11 is the **Schadowhaus** (Schadow House), built in 1805 as the home of the sculptor of *The Quadriga*. Its ground floor

The Quadriga *on the Brandenburger Tor*

doorways are topped off with delicate little stucco carvings by the master himself.

On Unter den Linden's next block is the **Komische Oper** (Comic Opera), the first of two opera houses on the street. Its exterior, a 1960s replacement for its war-damaged predecessor, presents yet another example of Communist Brutalism, but the auditorium was spared by the bombs and retains its opulent Viennese neobaroque aspect. The fare on offer is actually far more varied than the current name (the theatre's third) suggests, covering ballet in addition to everything but the grandest of grand operas. However, being a repertory company eschewing starry international names, it is very much the poor relation of the three opera houses the reunited city possesses, and hence the one most vulnerable to closure.

At the end of the same block stands the Japanese-designed **Grand Hotel**, built as the most luxurious hotel of the GDR's state-owned chain, with the purpose of extracting as much hard currency as possible from visiting foreign dignitaries, businessmen and journalists. As such, it was one of the most notorious surveillance hide-outs of the secret police, or Stasi, whose thirst for collecting information was so voracious that as many as a dozen highly trained spies were detailed to watch over any visitor deemed, however implausibly, to pose a potential security threat. Until World War II, this intersection of Unter den Linden and Friedrichstrasse was the location of several celebrated cafés, one of which, the Café Kranzler, took on a new lease of life by moving to the Ku'damm in West Berlin.

There are more insights into the legacy of the divided city on the next block to the east with the **Staatsbibliothek** (State Library), a ponderous edifice erected in the years before World War I in the stolid historicist style favoured during the Second Reich. Like so many institutions in this city, it has a counterpart across the former border: during the war many of its treasures were stored for safekeeping in what became the Western zones of occupation and were never returned. The two libraries united in 1990 but remain in their separate buildings. In the courtyard is a typical example of the socialist realist sculpture sponsored by the GDR: a worker is shown reading a Bertolt Brecht poem that chastises the tendency for history to remember the deeds of the rich and powerful rather that the honest labours of the masses.

Straddling the middle of Unter den Linden a bit further along is the bronze **Denkmal Friedrich II** (Monument to Friedrick the Great), which was unveiled in 1851, eleven years after its foundation stone had been laid. Sculpted by Christian Daniel Rauch, Schadow's most talented follower, it represents a modern interpretation of the great equestrian monuments of classical antiquity. The king is shown as if riding towards his own Forum Fridericianum, while the pyramid-shaped base is adorned with scenes from his life and portraits of members of his immediate entourage. Statesmen and soldiers receive pride of place, with writers and artists relegated to the short end below the horse's rear. Between 1962 and 1980, the monument was removed to the relative obscurity of Park Charlottenhof in Potsdam. Its reinstatement to a position only a few metres away from its original site was part of the GDR's reassessment of history. Estwhile hate-figures, such as Luther, Bismarck and Frederick himself, were reclassified as seminal influences on the inexorable march of history towards Communism and were therefore fit to be honoured as national heroes.

To the north of the monument is the main building of the **Humboldt-Universität** (Humboldt University), which began life as the town palace of Prince Heinrich, younger brother of Frederick the Great. Built in the classically inspired baroque style characteristic of Northern Germany, it was designed by the court architect Georg Wenzeslaus von Knobelsdorff and erected by the Dutchman Johann Boumann. In 1809, the building became part of the newly established Friedrich-Wilhelm-Universität, which was later renamed in honour of its founding father Wilhelm von Humboldt. The university was a key part of Humboldt's reform of the Prussian educational system along liberal lines, a response to the great military state's crisis of confidence following its defeats at the hands of Napoleon.

On either side of the entrance are marble statues of Humboldt and his even more influential younger brother, Alexander, a natural scientist who was a pioneering mountaineer, an indefatigable explorer of Latin America and a researcher into the mysteries of the cosmos. Two more statues in front of the façade commemorate distinguished later members of staff, the physicist Hermann von Helmholtz and the historian Theodor Mommsen, whose massively detailed researches into Ancient Rome (a sort of German counterpart to Edward Gibbon) were honoured by the award of the Nobel Prize for Literature in 1901. The university's most internationally famous teachers were Jakob and Wilhelm Grimm, who ended their careers there, preoccupied no longer with the folktale compilations that made them celebrities but with hefty intellectual projects such as the definitive German dictionary, the *Deutches Wörterbuch*, which was finally completed a century after their deaths. In 1949, the university's liberal reputation was dealt a severe blow by the foundation of the breakaway Freie Universität in West Berlin and by its own subsequent tailoring to Marxist-Leninist dogma. The readjustments that have had to be made since the fall of Communism have been painful, often hitting the national headlines.

Directly across from the university is a spacious square that the Communists renamed **August-Bebel-Platz** in honour of the man who jointly founded the Social Democratic Workers' Party in 1869. The old name of Opernplatz (Opera Square) has not been reinstated, partly because of its association with the night of 10th May 1933, when it was the setting for an event the like of which had not been seen in Western Europe since the Middle Ages. Under the direct supervision of Josef Goebbels, the Minister for Propaganda, thousands of Nazis gathered in the square to burn books written by authors deemed to have offended the Fatherland. This was not confined to

Hermann Göring's Birthday Party

The great ball in honor of the prime minister's forty-third birthday filled every corner of the Opera House. The elegant crowd surged through the labyrinth of foyers, corridors and anterooms. Champagne corks exploded from boxes whose balustrades were draped with rich fabrics. The seats had been removed and the great house was jammed with dancing couples. A huge orchestra completely filled the stage, giving the impression that it had been summoned to perform a symphonic poem by Richard Strauss . . . . In fact, all it was playing was a bold hodgepodge of military marches and jazz—forbidden in the Reich as a product of Negro immorality—which the great dignitary didn't want to deprive himself of on his birthday.

Here was gathered everyone who thought he counted for anything in this country, with the exception of the Führer himself, who had excused himself on grounds of a sore throat and nervous fatigue, and a few eminent party members somewhat too plebeian in origin to have been invited. However, several imperial and royal princes, a good many royal dukes and almost the entire nobility had put in an appearance; so had all members of the general staff of the Wehrmacht, a large collection of influential financiers and industrialists, a sprinkling of members of the diplomatic corps—most of them from embassies of small or distant lands—a number of ministers and well-known actors and even a poet, who looked very decorative and was, what is more, a personal friend of the Führer.

More than two thousand invitations had been sent out. Of these about half were complimentary tickets entitling their holders to the free enjoyment of the feast. Those who received one of the thousand remaining tickets had to pay a fifty-mark entrance fee. This meant that part of the enormous expense could be recouped; the rest of the burden was placed on the average taxpayer, who did not belong to the entourage of the prime minister and therefore was not a member of the elite in the new German society.

'Isn't this a marvelous party!' called the heavy wife of a Rhineland arms manufacturer to the wife of a South American diplomat. 'Oh, I'm having such a good time. I can't remember when I felt so good! I just wish everyone in Germany and all over the world could feel as good as I do now.'

The wife of the South American diplomat, who had trouble understand-

ing German and was bored, smiled sourly. Disappointed by this lack of enthusiasm, the wife of the arms manufacturer decided to move on.

'Forgive me, my dear,' she said graciously, lifting the glistening train of her dress. 'I must go over and have a word with an old friend of mine from Cologne, the mother of the director of our State Theater, you know, the great Hendrik Höfgen?'

At this point the South American woman opened her mouth for the first time and asked in English, 'Who is Henrik Hopfgen?' which provoked a cry of astonishment from the industrialist's wife.

'What? You don't know our Höfgen?' She pronounced the name with reproachful care—Herf-gen—rapping out the hard g. 'It's not Hopfgen, dear heart. And it's Hendrik, not Henrik—he's very particular about that little d.'

With that she sped forward to block the path of the distinguished lady in question, who was proceeding regally through the room on the arm of the poet who enjoyed the Führer's friendship.

'Dearest Frau Bella, it's been just ages since we last met. How are you, my dear? Do you ever get homesick for our Cologne? Of course, you've got such a splendid position here in Berlin! And how is Fräulein Josy, the dear child? Above all, what is Hendrik doing? Your famous son? Heavens, when you think of what he's become! He's really almost as important as a minister. I assure you, dearest Frau Bella, that we in Cologne all long to see you and your marvelous children again.'

If the truth be told, the millionairess had never given a thought to Frau Bella Höfgen when she lived in Cologne and her son had not yet made a great career for himself.

The two women had then had only a very passing acquaintance; Frau Bella had never been invited to the manufacturer's villa. Now, however, the jolly, soft-hearted millionairess clung to the hand of the woman whose son was counted among the closest friends of the prime minister as if she couldn't bear to let it go.

Frau Bella smiled graciously. She was dressed very simply, not without a certain touch of style. A white orchid shone against her black silk gown. Her gray hair contrasted interestingly with a face that had remained young and was made up discreetly. Her large gray-blue eyes looked with reserve and thoughtful friendliness upon the talkative woman whose glittering necklace, long earrings and Paris gown were the fruits of Germany's active preparations for war.

Klaus Mann, *Mephisto*, 1936

such obvious bogeymen as Karl Marx and Sigmund Freud. Nor did it stop at other German writers of world repute who had Jewish blood, such as the scientist Albert Einstein, the satirist Kurt Tucholsky, the novelists Alfred Döblin, Lion Feuchtwanger and Arnold Zweig, nor even at left-wing non-Jews like Heinrich Mann and Bertolt Brecht. The condemned included the living doyen of German letters, the apolitical Thomas Mann, the children's storyteller Erich Kästner, who himself witnessed the event, and a host of foreign luminaries including Jack London, Upton Sinclair, H G Wells, Emil Zola and Marcel Proust. Goebbels declared 'these flames not only illuminate the final end of an old era; they also light up the new'. In reality, they presaged a sickening collapse of cultural standards: libraries were almost immediately purged of the offending books and every single writer of standing was forced into exile.

The Nazi book-burning was an appalling misuse of a square that had been designed as a great cultural centre and was the only part of Frederick the Great's Forum Fridericianum to come to fruition. Work began in 1741 with the **Staatsoper** (State Opera) on the east side of the square, its porticoed façade facing Unter den Linden. Frederick boasted that it was the 'newest, longest and widest' theatre in the world; the fact that it was a freestanding building, rather than part of a complex, was a revolutionary idea that caused visitors to flock to see it under construction. The architect Knobelsdorff gave it four separate projections on the model of Palladio's classic Late-Renaissance Villa Rotonda near Vicenza; he also designed the auditorium so that the stalls could be raised and the open space used for balls and receptions. As such, the opera house features as the setting for Hermann Göring's birthday party in the prologue to Klaus Mann's *Mephisto*, a devastating *roman à clef* about artistic life in the Third Reich (see page 100). Although Knobelsdorff's original structure has been damaged by fire and bombs and subject to internal modifications, this remains one of the most delectable venues in the world in which to see opera and ballet. The distinguished performing tradition, with composers Giacomo Meyerbeer and Richard Strauss featuring among the list of past music directors, has been maintained to the present day. As a hangover from the years of heavy state subsidy, prices are very reasonable.

The second building erected on the square was **St-Hedwigs-Kathedrale** (St Hedwig's Cathedral) on the south side. It was one of only two church projects sponsored by Frederick the Great and was the first permanent place of worship of Berlin's Roman Catholic community, which then numbered some 10,000. Cynical political calculations were behind this ostensible show of religious tolerance by an agnostic king of the Protestant Hohenzollern line: the Silesian Wars had given Prussia its first province with a Catholic majority, which needed to be weened away from its natural preference for its erstwhile Austrian rulers. Frederick even provided the initial ideas for the church's shape, though it is uncertain whether he really did want it to be in the shape of an upturned teacup with handle, as legend has it. It may be that he intended an ironic twist by modelling the design on the pagan Pantheon in Rome; moreover, the centralized plan, much favoured in Protestant churches, is wholly unsuited to the requirements of the Catholic liturgy. Knobelsdorff drew up the plans, while Boumann was the executant architect.

The church, begun in 1747, was only completed, in a much simplified form, in 1773. It was inaugurated by Ignacy Krasicki, Bishop of Ermland (currently the Polish province of Warmia), nowadays honoured as one of Poland's greatest poets. Not until 1929 did St Hedwig's become a cathedral in its own right, half a century after its façade had been prettified with reliefs of the Passion and its dome plated with copper. Very badly damaged in World War II, the interior was refashioned in a modern form which nonetheless pays due respect to the destroyed original; curiously enough, this was carried out by the West German architect Hans Schwippert. The organ, which looks as spectacular as it sounds and serves as an essential complement to the church's great choral tradition, was likewise imported from across the barbed-wire frontier. In the spacious crypt can be seen the tomb of Provost Bernhard Lichtenberg, one of the most outspoken anti-Nazi churchmen, who died while being transported to the concentration camp of Dachau.

Two years after St Hedwig's inauguration, work began under Georg Christian Unger on the **Königliche Bibliothek** (Royal Library), which completes the square. For all its size, it took only five years to build. It was immediately dubbed the Kommode (Chest of Drawers), a nickname that remains in popular use, though it is unclear whether the striking curvaceous form was deliberately intended to resemble a giant piece of furniture. Certainly, it was another conscious effort to upstage the Austrians, in particular Frederick's perennial rival Empress Maria Theresa: the design is a plagiarization of plans drawn up in 1725 by Fischer von Erlach for an extension to the Hofburg in Vienna, which remained only partially built until the 1890s. When the Staatsbibliothek was constructed, the Kommode's contents were transferred there and the building, together with the adjoining neoclassical Altes Palais (Old Palace) on Unter den Linden, handed over to the university, in whose hands it remains.

On the eastern side of the Staatsoper stand Christian Daniel Rauch's monuments to the Prussian military heroes of the Napoleonic Wars: Gerhard von Scharnhorst is on Unter den Linden itself, while August Gneisenau, Gebhard von Blucher and Ludwig Yorck von Wartenburg are grouped on the lawn behind. Beyond is the **Operncafé**, an elegant café-cum-restaurant housed in an 18th-century baroque palace that was once the residence of the Hohenzollern princesses.

Next comes the **Palais Unter den Linden**, a structure of similar vintage enlarged in the 1850s for Crown Prince Friedrich, the future Kaiser. Used as a guesthouse for visiting VIPs in GDR days, it currently lacks a function. Outside stands a monument by Hermann Schievelbein to Baron Karl vom Stein, the statesman who played a key role in reforming Prussia after its repeated defeats in the first phase of the Napoleonic Wars. To the rear of the Palais is a pavilion incorporating a portal from Schinkel's celebrated **Bauakademie** (Architectural Academy). This strikingly angular structure, so anticipatory of the best of modern architecture, was the casualty of one of the Communists' worst acts of cultural vandalism. Damaged in the war, it was eminently repairable but instead was demolished to make way for the hideous black-and-white **Aussenministerium** (Foreign Ministry). Serious thought is now being given to extracting historical revenge by pulling down this redundant building in favour of a re-creation of the Bauakademie.

In the meantime, an extant example of Schinkel's work stands on the north side of Unter den Linden alongside the Humboldt-Universität. This is the **Neue Wache** (New Guard House), finished in 1818 for the use of the Palace Guards, with a secondary purpose as a memorial to the entire Prussian army and its recent victories. The architecture mirrors both functions: the plan is that of a Roman fort, with the Doric portico imparting the spiritual air of a temple. In the entablature are symbolic figures of the Victories by Schadow, while the pediment has an allegorical relief of the Napoleonic Wars, designed by Schinkel and carved by August Kiss. In 1931, the Neue Wache became a memorial to the dead of World War I; the Communists later changed this to commemorate victims of World War II and Nazism. The two slabs

inside cover the remains of an unknown soldier and resistance fighter, while the urns contain earth brought from a battlefield and a concentration camp.

Until 1990, the soldiers guarding the memorial goose-stepped in a bizarre visual demonstration of the affinity of the GDR had with its Prussian past. This ritual, described at the beginning of Christa Wolf's short story *Unter den Linden*, was so popular with tourists that there is talk of it being resumed on an occasional basis.

To the rear of the Neue Wache is the former **Sing-Akademie** (Song Academy); the initial designs for this provided by Schinkel were much altered in the construction supervised by his pupil Karl Theodor Ottmer. Originally, it served as the home of the eponymous choral society. In 1829, when the building was just two years old, the young Felix Mendelssohn-Bartholdy conducted the first performance of J S Bach's *St Matthew Passion* since the latter's death in 1750. This event spearheaded one of the biggest turnarounds in a man's posthumous reputation: within a few years, Bach, who had been famous during his lifetime primarily as a performing musician, had gained universal recognition as one of the supreme composers of all time.

The Sing-Akademie was also used for lectures, notably Alexander von Humboldt's famous series on the cosmos. There was a change in function in 1952, when the interior was remodelled to serve as the home of the Maxim-Gorki-Theatre, named in honour of the Russian founding father of literary socialist realism. The company has survived the political traumas of the past

Keystones of the Dying Warriors, *carved by Andreas Schlüter in the courtyard of the Zeughaus*

few years in surprisingly good shape, and its performances of modern classics are consistently well received.

Beside the theatre is the baroque **Palais am Festungsgraben**, once the residence of Prussian finance ministers. In the GDR period, it served as the Berlin Haus der Deutsch-Sowjetischen Freundschaft (House of German-Soviet Friendship), an unloved cultural institution with branches throughout the country. Following its demise, a complex of galleries, theatres, auction house and eateries has quickly filled the void.

At the far northeastern end of Unter den Linden is the **Zeughaus** (Arsenal), the oldest building on the street and arguably the finest in all Berlin. There is nothing to suggest its function as a mere arms depot: it is truly palatial in scale and magnificent in detail. It is the most potent visual symbol of the significance of militarism in the rise and development of Brandenburg Prussia, whose character was perfectly captured in the Comte de Mirabeau's dictum that it was 'not a state with an army, but an army with a state'. The national predilection for warfare goes some way to explaining why this baroque *tour de force* was largely created by foreign masons. Work began in 1695, under the Dutchman Johann Arnold Nering; he was succeeded three years later by the partnership of Jean de Bodt, a Huguenot refugee from France, and Andreas Schlüter, a native of Danzig, then an independent city-state under nominal Polish jurisdiction. The exterior was completed by 1706 but the building was not functional until 1730, when 604 Prussian cannon, plus a further 119 plundered from enemy forces, were moved into the ground floor, with smaller weapons stored upstairs.

Above the entrance doorway is a bust of Friedrich I, the first King of Prussia, and a large Latin inscription declaring the building to be dedicated to 'safeguarding the tools of war and the spoils and trophies of war'. The ground floor is adorned with 76 swaggering keystones of military trophies, carved in the workshop of de Bodt and Schlüter. A further 44 are found on the attic, together with colossal groups of Mars and Minerva and their entourages, all the work of another Huguenot sculptor, Guillaume Hulot.

The **Schlüterhof** (Schlüter Courtyard), a wonderfully harmonious central patio showing the classical form of baroque at its best, has the most spectacular sculptures of all, a series of keystones carved by Schlüter himself. They include the 22 *Dying Warriors*, a pictorial record of death unique in European art whose impact is such that, once seen, it can never be forgotten. A whole gamut of moods is depicted on the faces, from painful defiance to quiet resignation; the chiselling is dazzling, yet there is nothing glib about the message—in total contrast to the sculptures on the exterior, there is no glorification of the consequences of war. Plaster casts of another set of sculptures by Schlüter, the destroyed *Slaves* from the Stadtschloss, are displayed on the walls of the café on the waterfront side of the building.

For 150 years, the Zeughaus maintained its original function. It was then turned into a Hall of Fame for the army, which the Nazis developed into a military museum. The Communists dissolved this and created instead the **Deutsches Historisches Museum** (German Historical Museum), a turgidly didactic display interpreting Germany from the Marxist-Leninist standpoint. This was closed down soon after unification to be replaced by a changing series of exhibitions on historical themes. In due course, a nondoctrinaire historical museum will be established in line with a project that had been initiated in West Berlin just a year before the fall of the Wall. An architectural competition had already been held for a site in the Tiergarten, but this has been scrapped, thus saving on the duplication of yet another Berlin institution.

Unter den Linden ends at the **Schlossbrücke** (Palace Bridge), which carries traffic over the narrow arm of the Spree to the island opposite. The bridge was part of the redevelopment of central Berlin undertaken in the 1820s in the wake of victory in the Napoleonic Wars. Schinkel provided the designs, including characteristically detailed specifications for the decoration. The wrought-iron railings are fashioned into the shapes of dolphins and tritons, while the eight marble groups each depict a goddess of war accompanied by a mythological hero.

Friedrichswerder and Friedrichstadt

Friedrichswerder, the first baroque extension to medieval Berlin, lay southeast of Unter den Linden. Nothing survives of the original suburb, but its name lives on in Schinkel's **Friedrichswerdersche Kirche** (Friedrichswerder Church), which faced the market square Werderscher Markt. This is currently an area of wasteland, resulting in the loss of the church's architectonic purpose. Schinkel himself explained: 'In this somewhat enclosed quarter of the city, having an old-world quality because of the irregular street layout, a church in medieval style seemed appropriate. However, the building area is too confined to allow a great cathedral on the medieval model, therefore I deemed it appropriate to give the building more the character of an English chapel.' Certainly, there are clear echoes of Oxbridge colleges in the design, though the unusual twin towers, each of two identical superimposed cubes, inject a personal touch drawn from Schinkel's own neoclassical idiom.

The church was badly damaged in World War II but escaped the fate of the neighbouring Bauakademie, though it remained a ruin until the 1980s. Now deconsecrated and designated as the **Schinkel-Museum**, the interior is a single open space, featuring dressed and painted brickwork, stained-glass windows, two huge iron chandeliers and a wooden gallery running all the way round the interior. The gallery displays documents and plans from throughout the architect's career, placing particu-

lar emphasis on works no longer extant. Downstairs, there is a fine collection of neoclassical sculptures, including the terracotta reliefs from the Bauakademie, illustrating the art and practice of architecture, fashioned after Schinkel's own drawings. Other highlights include Schadow's original model for his charming double portrait of the Princesses Luise and Frederike; the second version of Rauch's sarcophagus of Queen Luise; Christian Friedrich Tieck's console figures from the Tea Salon in the Stadtschloss; and a roundel of Perseus and Andromeda by these Berlin sculptors' Danish contemporary Bertel Thorwaldsen.

Across Werderscher Markt is the bleak block of the **Finanzministerium** (Finance Ministry), built by the Nazis as an annexe for the main central bank, the Reichsbank. When the GDR was established in 1949, it served as the Finance Ministry but ten years later became the party headquarters of the ruling SED. It fulfilled this role until the fall of Communism when it reverted to its old function under yet another political master. On its eastern side, the Spree is crossed by two picturesque bridges. The first of these, the **Schleusenbrücke** (Canal Bridge), was erected during World War I and was later adorned with medallions showing Berlin scenes, some by Kurt Schumacher, a resistance activist murdered by the Nazis at Plötzensee. Further south is the **Jungfernbrücke** (Maidens' Bridge), a drawbridge dating back to the late 18th century and still preserving its original winding gear.

The larger and somewhat later baroque suburb of **Friedrichstadt** to the east is centred on the spacious **Gendarmenmarkt**. A decade ago, this square, traditionally regarded as the most beautiful in Berlin, was a sorry spectacle, its bomb-scarred buildings swathed in scaffolding or left as piles of rubble. Though it would be an exaggeration to claim that it has recovered all its splendour, the showpieces are gradually re-emerging in pristine shape. Originally, the square was known as Friedrichstädter Markt, it being the marketplace for the district. This was soon replaced in popular parlance because of the frequent presence of members of the Cuirassier Regiment, known by the French name of Gens d'Armes, whose stables were just off the square. In 1950, the Communists dropped this militaristic-sounding title in favour of Platz der Akademie in honour of the 250th anniversary of the foundation of the **Akademie der Wissenschaften** (Academy of Sciences), whose present headquarters are on the eastern side of the square. However, the old designation was restored in 1990.

The great Romantic master of the macabre, Ernst Theodor Amadeus Hoffmann, passed the final years of his life in an apartment overlooking the square at Charlottenstrasse 56. Having tried his hand at virtually all the arts and failed to make a successful mark with his desired vocation as a composer, he settled for secure salaried employment in Berlin as a legal official. Many of his leisure hours were spent carousing in the predecessor of the present Weinhaus Lutter und Wegner at Charlotten-

Neoclassical sculptural group on the Schlossbrücke

strasse 49. However, he also found time to indulge in the one artistic sphere where he showed undoubted genius, the writing of fantastical short stories. One of these tales, *My Cousin's Corner Window*, features an imaginative description of the markets held on the square (see page 112).

Dominating the Gendarmenmarkt are two churches, which at first glance seem identical but are actually quite different. On the north side is the **Französische Kirche** (French Church), built at the very beginning of the eighteenth century for the Huguenot community, whose descendants continue to worship there. The work of military engineer Jean Louis Cayart, it was modelled on their destroyed 'mother church' at Charenton in the outskirts of Paris. In accordance with Calvinist tenets, the architectural forms are of the utmost simplicity and feature a rustic exterior and a simple hall format for the interior.

In 1780, Frederick the Great decided to turn the Gendarmenmarkt into a magnificent public square on the model of the Piazza del Popolo in Rome. He commissioned Carl von Gontard to build an extension to the Französische Kirche known as the **Turmbau** (Tower Building). This resplendent domed edifice, crowned by a cupola and fronted by three great pedimented porticos, so dwarfs the original church that the latter seems a minor appendage. In reality, the Turmbau exists purely for show, with no liturgical function. The profuse sculptural programme was based on designs by Daniel Nikolaus Chodowiecki, an artist of Huguenot descent who is otherwise best known for his wonderful black-and-white vignettes and book illustrations, and by his predecessor as director of the Academy of Arts, Christian Bernard Rode. It includes reliefs of the life of Christ, statues of Old Testament figures, Evangelists and Prophets, allegories of the Christian Virtues, and, as a climax, the gilded cupola figure representing the Triumph of Religion.

Examples of Chodowiecki's graphic work can be seen in the **Huguenotten-Museum** (Huguenot Museum), a collection detailing the history of Berlin's French community, which is squeezed into the recesses of the ground floor (see page 325 for opening times). The hero's search for this little known attraction forms one of the many comic passages in what is probably the wittiest book about the GDR era, Ulrich Plenzdorf's novella *The New Sufferings of Young W*. There is free access via the stairway to the balcony, which offers a wonderful bird's-eye view over the square and central Berlin; on the way up is one of eastern Berlin's classiest wine restaurants. The carillon of 60 bronze bells rings out daily at noon, 3 pm and 5 pm in addition to fairly regular campanology concerts.

On the other side of the square, the **Deutsche Kirche** (German Church) was built for German and Swiss citizens of the quarter of both Lutheran and Calvinist persuasions. Restoration has lagged behind that of the Französische Kirche, partly because it no longer has a congregation: in future it will be used for exhibition purposes. The original church, a more elaborate and striking design than its neighbour, was built a few years later to designs by Martin Grünberg. Gontard's Turmbau, on the other hand, differs only in details from its counterpart across the square: the sculpture includes reliefs of the life of St Paul plus paired Old and New Testament scenes, while the gilded cupola statue represents the Triumph of Christian Virtue.

Between the two churches is the **Schauspielhaus** (Playhouse), built by Schinkel to replace Langhans' Nationaltheater, most of which had been destroyed in a fire. However, the stately Doric portico, approached by a broad flight of stairs, survived intact and was incorporated in the new building, even though it now has a purely decorative function, the actual entrances being at ground level. The pediment reliefs, also designed by Schinkel, show scenes from Greek mythology. On the roof are bronzes by Rauch: Apollo in a chariot pulled by a gryphon faces the centre of the square, while the winged horse Pegasus faces the rear. A month after the theatre opened in 1821, it hosted what has arguably been its most significant event, the premiere of Carl Maria von Weber's *Der Freischütz*. This is now generally regarded as marking the operatic debut of full-blown Romanticism; the other contender for this title is the slightly earlier but seldom performed *Undine*, written by E T A Hoffmann before he came to Berlin.

During the Third Reich, the Schauspielhaus was directed by the actor Gustav Gründgens, whose moral sellout to the Nazis inspired his erstwhile brother-in-law, Klaus Mann, to write *Mephisto*. Since reopening in 1984, the Schauspielhaus has served as a venue for concerts rather than theatre; its acoustics are not ideal but the splendour of the setting more than makes amends. The main hall, the Grosser Saal, has a coffered ceiling with representations of Orpheus and the animals, the Muses and St Cecilia, while dotted around the walls are busts of famous composers, poets and playwrights. Both the resident Berlin Symphony Orchestra and the Berlin Radio Symphony Orchestra feature regularly on the concert programme. Recitals by instrumentalists and chamber groups are held in the delectable little Kammermusiksaal, Schinkel's original concert hall, which is tucked away on the top floor of the southern wing.

Outside the Schauspielhaus is the **Schillerdenkmal** (Schiller Memorial), a fine commemorative marble monument in honour of the Enlightenment writer Friedrich Schiller, carved by Reinhold Begas and unveiled in 1871. The four female figures represent the Muses of Poetry, Drama, History and Philosophy, to each of which Schiller made a distinguished contribution. Best known abroad for the *Ode to Joy*, which Beethoven set in the finale of his Ninth Symphony, Schiller worked for most of his life as an academic historian, using his researches as the basis for weighty dramas, such as *Wallenstein*, *Maria Stuart* and *William Tell*. The liberal philosophy underpinning his work was the main reason the Nazis removed the monument from its promi-

A Room Overlooking the Gendarmenmarkt

It is necessary to mention that my cousin lives in a small room with a low ceiling, high above the street. That is the usual custom of writers and poets. What does the low ceiling matter? Imagination soars aloft and builds a high and cheerful dome that rises to the radiant blue sky. Thus the poet's cramped quarters are like the garden that consisted of ten square feet enclosed within four walls: neither broad nor long, but always at an agreeable height. Moreover, my cousin's lodgings are in the most attractive part of our capital city, overlooking the big market square* which is surrounded by magnificent buildings and has the colossal theatre, a work of genius, adorning its centre. The house where my cousin lives stands on a corner, and from the window of a tiny room he can overlook the entire panorama of the splendid square at a single glance.

It happened to be market-day when, forcing my way through the throng of people, I came down the street where my cousin's corner window can be seen from a considerable distance. I was not a little astonished to see in this window the well-known red cap which my cousin used to wear in happier times. Nor was that all! As I came closer, I noticed that my cousin had put on his fine Warsaw dressing-gown and was smoking tobacco in the Turkish pipe he used on Sundays. I waved to him and fluttered my handkerchief; this succeeded in attracting his attention, and he gave me a friendly nod. What hopes! I hurried upstairs with lightning speed. The ex-soldier opened the door; his face, which with its wrinkles and folds normally looked like a wet glove, had been smoothed out by some sunshine into a quite passable physiognomy. He said his master was sitting in the armchair and was available to visitors. The room had been cleaned, and on the screen separating the bed from the rest of the room had been pinned a sheet of paper on which the following words were written in big letters:

Et si male nunc, non olim sic erit.*

All this suggested the return of hope, the reawakening of vital energy.

---

* Though things are bad now, they will not always be so. (*Horace*, Odes, *ii,10*)

'Why,' called my cousin, as I entered the tiny room, 'here you are at last, cousin; do you know that I have really been longing for you? For although you don't care two pins about my immortal works, I still like you, because you're a cheery soul, and amusable if not exactly amusing.'

I felt the blood rising to my face at this compliment from my outspoken cousin.

'You probably think,' went on my cousin, ignoring my reaction, 'that my health is improving, or that I've made a complete recovery. That's anything but true. My legs are disloyal vassals who have refused obedience to the head of their ruler, and want nothing more to do with the rest of my worthy corpse. That's to say, I can't move from the spot, and cart myself to and fro in this wheelchair in the most charming fashion, while my old soldier whistles the most tuneful marches he remembers from his army years. But this window is my comfort; it is here that life in all its colour has been revealed to me anew, and I feel at home with its incessant activity. Come, cousin, look outside!'

I sat down opposite my cousin on a small stool for which there was just room in front of the window. The view was indeed strange and surprising. The entire market seemed like a single mass of people squeezed tightly together, so that one would have thought that an apple thrown into it would never reach the ground. Tiny specks of the most varied colours were gleaming in the sunshine; this gave me the impression of a large bed of tulips being blown hither and thither by the wind, and I had to confess that the view, while certainly very attractive, soon became tiring, and might give over-sensitive people a slight feeling of giddiness, like the not disagreeable delirium one feels at the onset of a dream. I assumed that this accounted for the pleasure that my cousin derived from his corner window and told him so quite frankly.

E T A Hoffmann, 'My Cousin's Corner Window', 1822

A man of varied artistic talents, Ernst Theodor Amadeus Hoffmann (1776–1822) first tried to establish himself as a painter. He switched to music, then turned to words. His short stories proved a fertile source of inspiration for subsequent composers and provide the basis for such great Romantic ballets as Delibes' Coppelia and Tchaikovsky's The Nutcracker, while Offenbach portrayed his bizarre personality in the opera The Tales of Hoffmann.

nent position and transferred it to Charlottenburg; it was only returned in 1988.

On Mohrenstrasse, just off the eastern side of Gendarmenmarkt, is Langhans' **Mohrenkolonnaden**, a decorative structure built as a replacement for the old city wall along the side of its moat. It is the only one of four such sets of colonnades to survive *in situ*, though a reconstruction of Gontard's slightly earlier **Spittelkolonnaden** can be seen on Leipziger Strasse just to the south, across the street from its original location. Leipziger Strasse itself is a sorry testimony to the urban blight of the GDR years. Despite a recent mini-revival in its fortunes, it is hard to believe that this boulevard of tasteless modern flats was Berlin's most fashionable shopping boulevard before the war, boasting the celebrated Tietz and Wertheim department stores, both Jewish owned and thus casualties of the Third Reich.

Towards the western end of the street, at the junction with Mauerstrasse, a typically pompous pile of Wilhelmine neobaroque serves as the custom-built premises of the **Postmuseum**, the first museum in the world dedicated to philately and the postal system. It is constructed around a quintessential Berlin architectural feature, a top-lit covered courtyard or Lichterhof. Visitors may peek through an aperture to view this, the shock being that the wartime bomb damage has yet to be restored. The museum has pull-out racks displaying a complete collection of German stamps from 1849 to the present: this serves as an entertaining history lesson, covering as it does the issues of formerly independent kingdoms such as Bavaria, Württemberg and Saxony, via those of now lost territories like Memel and Danzig, to the pictorial propaganda of the GDR era. On the upper floors are displays of equipment, ranging from a prototype of the telephone to historic postboxes and phone booths.

At the next junction to the west, Leipziger Strasse bisects Toleranzstrasse, the prewar Wilhelmstrasse and heart of the government quarter. Of this, the only surviving buildings are those in the block to the south, centred on Hermann Göring's **Luftfahrtministerium** (Air Ministry), one of the most significant surviving monuments of the Third Reich. Its size is indicative of the key role that Nazi ideology bestowed on aeroplanes, which were seen as symbols of the modern world they wished to create. This infatuation was to be part of their undoing: a conventional invasion might well have defeated Britain in 1940, whereas the delayed air strike mounted in its place gave the first clear evidence of the mastery of the RAF over the Luftwaffe. This aerial superiority was to have a devastating effect in the later stages of the war, when Göring's claim that he would change his name to the Jewish one of Meyer if a single bomb fell on Berlin became a very hollow boast as horrendous carnage and destruction were inflicted on virtually every city in Germany.

Ironically, the Luftfahrtministerium survived the bombardments and in the GDR period served a number of government departments as the Haus des Ministerium (Government House). Now the headquarters of the Treuhandanstalt, the trust estab-

Potsdamer Platz, 1914, photographed by Max Missmann who was one of the leading Berlin photographers in the early part of this century

lished to sell off the state-owned enterprises of the GDR, which in effect constitute the majority of the country's entire economy, it has been renamed Detlev-Rohwedder-Haus in honour of its first director, who was murdered by the Red Army Faction in 1991.

The building is sandwiched between two others, small only by comparison, erected around the turn of the century by Friedrich Schulze in neo-Palladian style. On Niederkirchner Strasse to the rear, right up against a preserved section of the Berlin Wall, is the **Preussisches Abgeordnetenhaus** (Lower House of the Prussian Parliament), now the seat of the Berlin House of Representatives; while facing Leipziger Strasse is the incongrously named **Herrenhaus** (Manor House), the former Upper House of the same legislature.

West of Toleranzstrasse and north of Leipziger Strasse is an area of wasteland where formerly stood Hitler's **Reichskanzlei** (Imperial Chancellory), built by Speer in 1938 and razed by the Soviet occupying forces just seven years later. A small hillock marks the site of the **Führerbunker**, the dictator's underground operations centre in the fatal closing months of the war and the scene of his joint suicide on 30th April 1945 with his long-time mistress and wife of one day's standing, Eva Braun.

Karl Friedrich Schinkel, Architect of Berlin

No architect has made such a profound impact on the appearance of Berlin and Potsdam as Karl Friedrich Schinkel. Despite the fact that his most visionary projects survive only on paper and that much of what he did build has been lost through war or civic vandalism, his distinctive imprint on both cities remains very evident. He was a man of diverse talents: a draughtsman of the highest class, an accomplished painter and designer, a pioneering conservator of historic monuments, and, in his capacity as a professional civil servant, a supervisor of the building work of others. However, it was as a practising architect, incorporating and blending the two main styles of the day, the Romantic and the classical, that he made his biggest mark.

Schinkel was born in 1781 in Neuruppin in the province of Brandenburg. His father was killed in the salvage operations following the conflagration that destroyed most of the town in 1787, and in 1794 his mother moved the family to Berlin. Three years later, a young architect named Friedrich Gilly exhibited a coloured drawing of a project for a spectacular Grecian-style mausoleum to Frederick the Great. It caused a public sensation and determined Schinkel's own choice of career. He went to live in the Gilly household and studied at the Bauakademie under Friedrich's father, David. While still a student, he designed and built his first work, the Pomona-Tempel in Potsdam; this singled him out as a worthy substitute for Friedrich Gilly, who died at the age of 28, before receiving any important commissions. On completing his formal studies, Schinkel travelled in Italy, where he became particularly fascinated by the embryonic relationship of architecture to its surroundings, making many topographical drawings as well as painting imaginary caprices.

Prussia's humiliating defeat by Napoleon in 1806 meant that the country offered few opportunities for architects, so Schinkel initially concentrated on painting and design. His large canvases are indebted to Caspar David Friedrich, who had created a new intensely spiritual approach to landscape painting. Whereas Friedrich specialized in depictions of raw nature, with or without human interest, Schinkel preferred meticulously detailed cityscapes that evoked the splendours of both Antiquity and the Middle Ages. He also produced metalwork and silverware designs for the sculptor Johann Gottfried Schadow and created dioramas and panoramas for the theatrical impresario Wilhelm Gropius, but the latter have sadly not survived.

In 1809, Queen Luise commissioned Schinkel to remodel a number of interiors at Schloss Charlottenburg and the Stadtschloss; she also secured him a salaried position in the Department of Public Works, which employed him until his death. When his patroness died the following year, he produced a gloriously ethereal design for a neogothic mausoleum in her memory. However, in accordance with the demand of King Friedrich Wilhelm III, it was a Doric temple that he actually built in the Charlottenburg grounds. From 1815, Schinkel designed stage scenery for the Staatsoper (State Opera), making over 100 sets in all with those for Mozart's *The Magic Flute* gaining cult status.

It was as a result of the eventual victory in the Napoleonic Wars that Schinkel was finally given a lead as an architect. He produced a watercolour design for a magnificent domed cathedral in honour of the dead, but the expense of building it proved beyond the state's resources. Instead, he created the spire-like memorial on the Kreuzberg and gave the existing Berliner Dom a new façade and interior. He then designed and built the Schlossbrücke at the end of Unter den Linden, along with three key public buildings—the Neue Wache, the Schauspielhaus and the Altes Museum—in a severe neoclassical idiom.

His first major private project, the conversion of the existing Schloss Tegel for his friend Wilhelm von Humboldt, was in 1820. This was followed by a number of commissions for the royal family, all of which are noticeably Italianate. The most ambitious, for Prince Karl at Klein-Glienicke, involved the creation of a series of whimsical garden structures in addition to the main Schloss. Others are the villa behind Schloss Charlottenburg, built for the king's second marriage, and the pairing of Schloss Charlottenhof and the Römische Bäder in Potsdam for the Crown Prince, the future Friedrich Wilhelm IV.

In 1826, Schinkel visited England and Scotland in connection with his work on the Altes Museum. He was unimpressed by the buildings of his peers but was bowled over by the sheer scale and dramatic appearance of the factories, warehouses, gasworks, dockyards and bridges thrown up by the Industrial Revolution. On his return home, he decided to make artistic use of some of the features he had seen; he also realized that brick had far greater possibilities as a material than he had hitherto realized, particularly as Prussian stone was generally of poor quality.

The Friedrichwerdersche Kirche, begun before his departure but not finished until 1831, is his most obvious homage to England and marries the picturesqueness of his beloved Tudor architecture to the functionalism of industrial brickwork. Unfortunately, his most original English-inspired buildings are no longer extant. The Fellnerhaus, built for a terracotta manufacturer, was destroyed in the war, while the town palaces of Prince Karl and Prince Albrecht, with their spectacular wrought-iron staircases, were demolished because of subsequent Nazi associations. The saddest and most unnecessary loss of all was the new Bauakademie, Schinkel's most forward-looking building and the one he himself regarded as his masterpiece (see page 104).

In 1830, Schinkel was appointed head of the Department of Public Works. His commitments meant that the construction of his last buildings often had to be entrusted to executive architects, though he continued to design as prolifically as ever. Four small churches—the Johanniskirche, the Elisabethkirche, the Nazarethkirche and the Paulskirche—brought his neoclassical style to the new suburbs of Berlin. Schloss Babelsberg on the outskirts of Potsdam, which bears a strong English imprint, is, of all Schinkel's built designs, the one with the greatest sense of fantasy. However, this pales before the detailed but unrealized plans for exotic dream palaces, including one for Otto von Wittelsbach, the first modern King of Greece, which was intended to stand alongside the Parthenon on the Acropolis in Athens. One late project that did come to fruition was the Nikolaikirche in the centre of Potsdam. This finally fulfilled Schinkel's lifelong dream of a great domed church, though he did not live to see the construction of the dome itself.

Schinkel died from overwork in 1841 and was honoured with a huge public funeral of a type normally reserved for political or military leaders. His biography had been prepared in his lifetime and was published the following year. All his surviving drawings, paintings and architectural models were purchased by the state and exhibited in the Bauakademie. Schinkel's shadow hung over architectural projects in Berlin and Potsdam for three decades after his death, particularly in the work of his two most prominent pupils, Ludwig Persius and August Stüler. It took German unification, which gave expression to a grandiose form of officially sponsored neobaroque, to put his style out of fashion.

As part of the same urban development that saw the laying-out of Pariser Platz and the Brandenburger Tor at the end of Unter den Linden, the elliptical Leipziger Platz and the Potsdamer Tor rounded off Leipziger Strasse. In time, the latter was replaced by a yet larger square, **Potsdamer Platz**, which developed into a major commercial area and an intersection so busy that in 1924 it became the first junction in Europe to be regulated by traffic lights. Flattened in the war and then partitioned between the two Berlins, the square became the backdrop for a spirited frontline propaganda campaign. In response to West Berlin's huge electronic newsboard, which beamed the latest headlines across the Wall, the GDR authorities reacted by erecting a sign urging all prudent Berliners to do their shopping in the East.

With unification, Potsdamer Platz and the wasteland to the north became a popular site for rock concerts and other open-air spectaculars. However, as the city's prime real estate, it was a ready target for developers and the car giant Daimler-Benz quickly snapped up 60,000 square metres at a knockdown price, despite widespread public protest at the hastiness of the decision. Several other multinational conglomerates each bought a share of the remaining land soon afterwards. The Italian Renzo Piano, best known for his collaboration with Richard Rogers on the Pompidou Centre in Paris, won the architectural competition for the redevelopment of the Daimler-Benz site, which, if all goes according to plan, will be transformed in the course of the next decade.

Fischerinsel

Cölln, the medieval fishing community that was Berlin's twin town, occupied the island in the Spree at the eastern end of Unter den Linden, the main part of which is now known as **Fischerinsel** (Fishermen's Island). Elector Friedrich II began to construct a castle on the island in 1443, so asserting his authority against stirrings towards municipal independence. This was later transformed into a grand Renaissance residence, thereafter known as the Stadtschloss (City Palace); it in turn was given a baroque facelift by Schlüter, and was further modified by Schinkel and his pupil August Stüler, who added a huge neoclassical dome. Badly damaged during World War II, but eminently restorable, the palace was razed by the Communists in 1950–1. The unwanted reminders it provided of the royal and imperialist past were sufficiently pressing to outweigh aesthetic considerations and fierce protests from the West.

The former Schlossplatz was renamed **Marx-Engels-Platz** in honour of the two founding fathers of Communism; oddly enough, this name is still in use. At first the square was left as a vast open space for parades but in the 1960s the **Staatsratsge-bäude** (Council of State Building) was built on the southern side in the ponderous officially sponsored architectural style of the time. This incorporates the only remaining part of the Stadtschloss' fabric, a portal designed by Schlüter and adorned with carvings by Balthasar Permoser, the great sculptor of baroque Dresden. However, the reasons for the portal's preservation had nothing to do with art and everything to do with ideology, as it was from its balcony that Karl Liebknecht issued his abortive proclamation of the establishment of a Socialist republic on 9th November 1918.

Overlooking the Spree on the east side of Marx-Engels-Platz is the **Palast der Republik** (Palace of the Republic), the GDR's belated replacement for the destroyed Schloss: it was begun in 1973 by order of the newly appointed General Secretary of the SED, Erich Honecker, and completed three years later. In addition to housing the Volkskammer, the rubber-stamp parliament, it served as a business, conference and cultural centre, complete with art gallery, theatre, restaurants, shops and the main post office. Constructed out of shiny white marble and reflective orange glass, with a plethora of chandeliers lighting up the interior, it had a certain originality but was always an unloved building and the recipient of a host of caustic nicknames—'Balast of the Republic' and 'Erich's Lamp Shop' being but two. In 1990, the building was found to be a health hazard because of the asbestos used in its construction and it was closed down indefinitely, the odds being that it will in fact be demolished as an embarrassment to the new democratic Germany. There is considerable popular pressure to replace it with a re-creation of the Stadtschloss, a temporary mock-up of which was erected alongside in 1993 to gauge public reaction, though whether there is sufficient will to embark on such a fiendishly expensive project is as yet unclear.

To the rear of the Palast der Republik is the chunky bulk of the **Neuer Marstall** (New Stables), built at the very end of last century as an appendage to the Schloss for the royal horses and carriages. Its architecture imitates, albeit none too successfully, the Berlin baroque style of two centuries before; nowadays, it is used for exhibitions. Breite Strasse, which separates it from the Staatsratgebäude, has several notable buildings. The gabled **Ribbeckhaus** at No 35 is the only significant Renaissance building left in Berlin; it was built in the 1620s for a royal official, whose coat-of-arms lies above the doorway. Next door, the **Alter Marstall** (Old Stables) of four decades later shows how quickly baroque had taken root in the city.

North of Marx-Engels-Platz is the **Lustgarten** (Pleasure Garden), whose history is nothing if not eventful. It began life in 1573 as the kitchen garden of the Schloss, but was made into an ornamental garden by the Great Elector in 1645. The Soldier King, Friedrich Wilhelm I, distasteful of such fancies, turned it into yet another parade ground for his troops, but it became a garden again in 1832 as part of Schinkel's redevelopment of the northern half of the island. During the Third Reich, it was

Berliner Dom, with a pleasure boat cruising on the Spree

paved once more and served as the site of two of Goebbels' most famous propaganda exercises: the announcement of the boycott of Jewish businesses in 1933, and the anti-Soviet propaganda exhibition of 1942. The latter was set on fire by a group led by the Jewish Communist Herbert Baum, an act of defiance for which the participants paid with their lives. A small memorial to them was placed among the trees replanted during the GDR epoch.

Between the Lustgarten and the eastern arm of the Spree stands the **Berliner Dom** (Berlin Cathedral), built by Julius Carl Raschdorff at the turn of the century as a replacement for its much smaller baroque predecessor, which had been remodelled by Schinkel as part of his plan for the area. Its pompously self-proclaiming Wilhelmine architecture, consciously symbolizing the intertwining of political and religious authority, has always met with critical derision: 'the height of decadence' was how one contemporary commentator described it.

Originally, there were three separate churches within the structure, but one was demolished when the overall silhouette was simplified in restoration work to repair war damage. The main **Fest- und Predigtkirche** (Feast Day and Preaching Church), which stands under the huge main dome, is built on the plan of a Greek cross. In the transepts are magnificent tombs of the Hohenzollerns, notably that of the Elector Johann Cicero, a Renaissance masterpiece cast in the Vischer workshop of Nuremberg, and those of King Friedrich I and Queen Sophie Charlotte by Schlüter. An aerial view of its vast central space can be enjoyed from the balcony at the head of the Kaiserliches Treppenhaus (Imperial Staircase), which has been laid out as a small museum with historical photographs and religious paraphernalia. Other services are held in the small **Tauf- und Traukirche** (Baptismal and Wedding Church) to the side.

Museumsinsel

The peninsula north of Lustgarten, once a swampy marsh, is popularly known as **Museumsinsel** in honour of the great public collections kept there in suitably grandiose custom-built homes. Berlin was a relatively late starter in the museum world, lagging well behind not only London and Paris, but also several German provincial capitals. Yet, within a century of King Friedrich Wilhelm III's establishment of the first museum, the island had become home to collections equal in range and quality to those of any rival city, offering dazzling displays drawn from all the great global civilizations.

With the division of Germany after World War II, however, objects that had been stored for safety in what became the Western zones were not returned to the Museuminsel, landing instead in new institutions in West Berlin. Since unification, the Stiftung Preussischer Kulturbesitz (Prussian Cultural Foundation), established in 1957 to administer the West Berlin museums, has taken over those on the Museuminsel and has mapped out a long-term programme for the rationalization of the collections. Some of these plans have already been implemented, though the situation will remain in flux for at least a decade. Further complicating matters is the mystery surrounding the fate of some of the greatest treasures of all—notably the bulk of Heinrich Schliemann's excavations from ancient Troy, and the larger Old Master paintings. The official line was that these were destroyed in a fire that broke out in the Flak tower where they were stored a few days after the end of the war. However, recent speculation, backed up by eye-witness reports from Russia, is that this was a Red Army ruse designed to provide a cover for the confiscation of the treasures as war booty, and that at least some of the works have been ensconced in an isolated Russian monastery ever since.

At the northern end of the Lustgarten, Schinkel built in his most extreme classicizing manner what subsequently became known as the **Altes Museum** (Old Museum). Originally, it stood in a carefully calculated relationship to the Dom and the Schloss, an effect now irreparably lost. The portico of 18 Ionic columns stretches the entire length of the building, giving the impression that it is of just one storey rather than two. In front stands the seven-metre-wide Granitschale (Granite Slab), fashioned in 1830 from a single Ice-Age block; formerly regarded as one of the wonders of Berlin, it is now vandalized and irreverently dubbed the 'soup bowl'. Guarding the top of the steps are two bombastic bronze sculptures: *Warring Amazon* by August Kiss and *Lion Fight* by Hubert Wolff.

Inside, the central rotunda, with its elaborate coffered vault, imitates the Pantheon in Rome far more closely than the earlier Berlin essay in this field, St-Hedwigs-Kathedrale. A truly magnificent space for exhibitions, it has been returned to its original function as a showcase for classical sculptures: between the pillars on the ground floor and in the niches upstairs are Roman copies of Hellenistic statues of deities. The upper rooms have been cleared of the collection of socialist realist art on display there until the demise of the GDR; at present they are used for hosting major loan exhibitions on special themes.

As Berlin's collections outgrew the Altes Museum, August Stüler was commissioned to build the **Neues Museum** (New Museum) immediately to the rear, linked by a covered bridgeway. Until World War II, when it was virtually destroyed by bombs, this housed the smaller pieces of Greek and Roman art plus finds from the celebrated Egyptian excavations started in the 1840s by Carl Richard Lepsius, whose success was crucial in launching German archaeology towards world supremacy. At the moment, the pick of both these collections are in Charlottenburg but they will return when the rebuilding of the museum, only recently started, is complete.

Immediately to the north is the **Pergamonmuseum**, inaugurated in 1930 to display the huge archaeological showpieces, several of which unquestionably rank among the most impressive exhibits to be seen in any museum anywhere in the world. At present, three separate museums are housed within. Centrepiece of the **Antikensammlung** (Collection of Antiquities) is the Pergamon Altar, which formerly stood on the acropolis of the eponymous town in Asia Minor, the present-day Bergama in Turkey. Despite being less than a century and a half old when it was destroyed in 156 BC,

Pergamon Altar, Pergamonmuseum

Pergamon spawned a brilliant civilization and the altar, which dates from the city's very last years, is the most outstanding surviving example of late Hellenistic art. A conjectural full-scale reconstruction of the altar occupies the entire length of the museum's central hall, while round the walls are the originals of its reliefs. The main frieze, 120 metres in length and with over 100 life-sized figures, is, after the Parthenon Marbles in the British Museum, the largest piece of monumental sculpture to have survived from Ancient Greece. It represents a frozen moment towards the end of the battle waged by the giants against the gods, whose victory was sealed only through the intervention of the mortal Hercules, father of Telephus, founder of the city of Pergamon. Despite the fragmentary nature of some of the scenes, the quality of the composition is always evident. Brimming with drama, movement and characterization, it shows the warrior gods and goddesses as unemotional and otherworldly, while the all-too-human giants writhe in pain and anguish. Telephus' life, distinguished by its lower level of relief, is told in a smaller frieze from the subsidiary altar for burnt offerings.

Original architectural fragments from a variety of archaeological sites are displayed in the halls to either side; the Greek examples to the north include the Temple of Athena from Pergamon, which predates the altar by a century. The Roman hall opposite is dominated by the colossal Market Gate of Miletus from the second century AD, together with the Orpheus Mosaic from the same city. Both floors of the north wing are devoted to small-scale antique art objects, beginning with works from the Archaic Period of the sixth and fifth centuries BC such as the so-called *Berlin Goddess* from Attica and the *Enthroned Goddess* from Taranto. Classical-period masterpieces range from the *Praying Boy* of the fourth century, a rare life-sized antique bronze, via the relief meteope of the sun-god Helios from Schliemann's Troy excavations, to a number of statues from Pergamon, including the figure of Athena from the Library and a bust of King Attalos I. From imperial Rome, the star pieces are a startlingly realistic yet posthumous bust of Julius Caesar, carved from green schist, and a mosaic of centaurs from Emperor Hadrian's fabled villa at Tivoli.

The **Vorderasiatisches Museum** (Near East Museum) occupies the ground floor of the south wing and is clustered around the spectacular reconstruction, based on original materials found during excavations, of the Processional Way and the Ishtar Gate of Babylon. These readily evoke the legendary luxury of the court of Nebuchadnezzar II, who ordered their construction out of specially durable baked and glazed bricks when his empire was at its peak around 600 BC. The sheer size of the original can be gauged from the fact that what seems in the context of the museum to be awesome in scale is very much a miniaturization: the Processional Way was three times broader and six times longer, while the gateway, itself built at a reduced height, was merely the prelude to a much taller construction behind. Babylon's protectress, the goddess Ishtar, is symbolized by the sleek parading lions of the Processional Way, which are moulded in high relief and set between geometric borders and friezes of rosettes. The bulls and dragons on the gateway personify the weather god and the city god respectively, while the façade of the throne room features lions alongside startlingly stylized palm trees and flowers. An adjoining room has a model showing the buildings in context, together with some fascinating fragments demonstrating two earlier phases of the gate's construction, firstly with plain bricks in relief, then with flat glazed ones.

Finds from German archaeological expeditions to other countries of the Near East fill more rooms. Among the oldest exhibits, the most striking are the brick façade of the Temple of Innin in the Sumerian city of Uruk, which dates back to the 15th century BC, and the tenth-century BC inner gate of the Sam'al citadel in northern Syria. The golden age of Assyrian art from the ninth to the seventh century BC is represented by carvings from the palaces of Nineveh and Nimrud, and by a water basin from Assur carved from a single block of basalt. No less striking is the glazed stone relief of a spear-bearer from the palace of King Darius I of Persia in Susa.

The upper floor of the south wing is given over to the **Museum für Islamische Kunst** (Museum of Islamic Art), which is mainly devoted to small-scale objects such as textiles, leatherwork, ceramics and miniature paintings. However, it too has a major set piece in the form of the façade of an eighth-century caliph's palace from Mschatta in present-day Jordan, whose exquisite filigree stonework features roses, animals and birds entwined in foliage. Also of note are the sumptuous prayer niches from two 13th-century mosques and a room from the early 17th-century house of a Christian merchant of Aleppo in Syria, in which biblical and literary depictions are bizarrely mixed with traditional Arab decoration.

On the other side of the elevated S-Bahn line, at the top end of Museumsinsel, is the triangular-shaped neobaroque pile of the **Bodemuseum**. Before the war, it was known as the Kaiser-Friedrich-Museum and housed what was arguably the finest collection of old master paintings in the world, many of which later found their way to the Dahlem Museum in West Berlin. Renamed by the Communists in honour of Wilhelm Bode, a former director of Berlin's museums, it serves as the home for several separate collections, which are grouped in courtyards off the central axis.

Dominating the entrance hall is a copy of Schlüter's equestrian statue of the Great Elector on its original base. Around it are four massive sandstone figures of gods by the same sculptor, which are among the few surviving decorations of the destroyed royal palace. The passageway beyond, in which are displayed Schlüter's sculptures from the vanished Villa Kamecke, leads to an imitation Florentine basilica, which is decked out with Italian Renaissance artworks, notably a set of inlaid walnut choir stalls. To the rear is a stairwell in the shape of a rotunda, which serves as a pantheon to Frederick the Great and his military commanders. The seven statues, which once stood in prominent public places, include two by Schadow—of Cavalry General Joachim von Zieten and Prince Leopold von Anhalt-Dessau, inventor of the goose-step. Also of special note is Jean-Pierre Antoine Tassaert's monument to Field Marshal James Keith, a Scottish Jacobite who had previously served both Spain and Russia.

Off the right-hand side of the basilica is the **Ägyptisches Museum und Papyrussammlung** (Egyptian Museum and Papyrus Collection). Despite being only a rump of the Neues Museum's dispersed displays, it presents a formidable survey of Egyptian art, ranging in date from the Baboon God of 3000 BC, the oldest monumental sculpture to have survived from Ancient Egypt, to the relief of the god Tutu from the third century AD, which is clearly influenced by Roman carvings. There is a fine group of sculptures from the Middle Kingdom's capital of Thebes in the 15th century BC, including two of the female 'King' Hatshepsut, one showing her as a sphynx, the other as a kneeling man. From slightly later is an unfinished quartz head thought to be of Queen Nefertiti, which makes for a fascinating comparison with its famous counterpart in Charlottenburg. The Papyrus Collection, exhibited on racks, comprises documents in Aramaic, Greek, Latin and Arabic as well as various Egyptian scripts; the highlight of the collection is the 13th-century BC *Guide to the Nether-world*, illustrated with illuminated vignettes.

On the other side of the basilica is the **Museum für Spätantike und Byzanti-nische Kunst** (Museum of Late Antique and Byzantine Art), which has the pick of the marvellous prewar collection. Its sculpture section begins with Roman sarcophagi and ends with exquisite carvings of birds from 12th-century Venice, while the most significant works are from Constantinople itself. These include the fifth-century reliefs of Christ and of Moses and the intriguing *Game of Marbles*, a block carved with scenes of the races at the Hippodrome, which was used, in conjunction with a set of coloured marbles, for determining the stadium's lane draws. The museum's most spectacular object, however, is one of only two monumental Byzantine mosaics to be found in northern Europe—the other being in Potsdam. Dating from the mid-sixth century and originally in the church of San Michele in Ravenna, it shows a youthful Christ between the archangels Gabriel and Michael, with doves and the Agnus Dei in the archway and a frieze of trumpet-blowing angels above.

The **Skulpturensammlung** (Sculpture Collection), housed in the rooms beyond, has a particularly strong German section. Medieval highlights include statues of prophets from the portal of the Liebfrauenkirche in Trier, fragments of the famous Schöne Brunnen (Beautiful Fountain) in Nuremberg, and the 15th-century high altar, with 13th-century predella, from the Dom (Cathedral) of Minden. From the inspired generation of German carvers who bridged the period between Late Gothic and the Renaissance are works by Anton Pilgram, Nicolaus Gerhaert, Sebastian Lo-schner and Tilman Riemenschneider. The Italian Renaissance and baroque are well represented in the paintings displayed upstairs, which include works by Giovanni Pisano, Donatello, Agostino di Duccio, Bernini and Algardi.

More sculptures by Schlüter stand at the top of the main stairway; their postal theme is explained by the fact that they came from the Alt-Post (Old Post Office). Most of the rooms beyond are given over to the **Gemäldegalerie** (Picture Gallery), now a very sorry reminder of its prewar self. Despite the general mediocrity, there are some outstanding pieces, particularly the free copy of Hieronymus Bosch's *Last Judg-ment* by Lucas Cranach the Elder, friend of Luther and court painter to the Electors of Saxony. The *Self-Portrait* by the great 17th-century French artist Nicolas Poussin is the only figurative work he painted, the two classical landscapes hanging alongside being far more typical examples of his style. Among the many Dutch paintings, the dazzlingly brilliant *Kitchen Scene with View of the Last Supper* by Joachim Wtewael represents Mannerism at its best, while the fine group of tenebrist works includes *Esau Selling his Birthright* by Hendrik Terbrigghen. Also on this floor is the **Münz-kabinett** (Mint Cabinet), a collection of coins and medals through the centuries.

North of the Neues Museum is the **Nationalgalerie** (National Gallery), built by Stüler in the most uncompromisingly neoclassical style imaginable. It houses paintings and sculptures of the last two centuries, with the emphasis firmly on German artists, many of whom deserve to be far better known abroad. On the ground floor, sculptures by Schadow (such as the original of the princesses Luise and Frederike) and Rauch (including the model of the monument to Frederick the Great) are juxtaposed with examples by their foreign counterparts, the Dane Thorwaldsen and the Italian Canova. There is also a notable group of canvases by the versatile Berlin artist Adolf von Menzel, which range from the unfinished historical blockbuster *Frederick the Great Addressing his Generals before the Battle of Lützen* to the sharp realism of *The Ironworks*, an enormously influential documentation of the Industrial Revolution.

The first floor is given over to displays of 20th-century German art. The exhibits generally include sculptures by Ernst Barlach, Wilhelm Lembrück and Käthe Kollwitz, plus paintings by the Impressionists Max Liebermann, Lovis Corinth and Max Slevogt; the Expressionists Ernst Ludwig Kirchner, Emil Nolde, Franz Marc and August Macke; the Dadaist George Grosz; the neorealist Otto Dix; and abstract luminaries such as Paul Klee and Wassily Kandinsky. Above the stairway is the huge canvas of *Plato's Symposium*, a ripely Romantic masterpiece by Anselm Feuerbach. The top floor is devoted to the Nazarene Brotherhood, a group comprising Friedrich Overbeck, Peter Cornelius, Philipp Veit and Wilhelm Schadow. These German forerunners of the English Pre-Raphaelites established a communal way of life in a disused monastery in Rome, where they worked at reproducing the form, style and colour of the early Renaissance masters. One of their main cooperative ventures was the cycle of *The Story of Joseph*, created for the residence of the German consul, the Casa Bartholdi, and reassembled here, in all its glorious freshness, completely intact.

The Medieval City Centre

Medieval Berlin lay on the eastern side of the Spree, facing Cölln. A handful of buildings remain as testimony to the city's origins, but although some are still prominent landmarks, they stand marooned in their predominantly modern surroundings. Indeed, the whole face of the quarter is mainly that of Communist-style planning, albeit one showing a shifting ideological perspective with the passage of time. An orthodox Marxist way of thinking is evident in the box-like structures along the north side of the axial Karl-Liebknecht-Strasse and in the **Marx-Engels-Forum** opposite, an open square with statues of the two founding fathers of Communism accompanied by other socialist realist sculptures. A welcome contrast to this is the **Heiliggeistkapelle**

(Chapel of the Holy Ghost) on Spandauer Strasse. The little chapel, built of red brick on a rough stone base, probably dates back to the 13th century and is the sole surviving part of Berlin's medieval hospital, the rest of which was demolished last century. A huge Wilhelmine university building was later added alongside and the chapel currently serves as its student refectory.

Berlin's most significant medieval survivor is the **Marienkirche** (St Mary's Church), which now stands in the open spaces of the Neuer Markt, the eastern continuation of Marx-Engels-Forum. A typical example of the red brick Gothic style characteristic of northern Germany, the church was begun in the mid-13th century, and extensively rebuilt following a fire in 1380. The tower belongs to the following century, with the exception of the upper storeys, built by Langhans in a pleasing fusion of neoclassical and neo-Gothic. Its porch is frescoed with a fascinating representation of a favourite medieval theme, the Dance of Death, painted by an unknown artist soon after the plague of 1484 to drive home the message that Death is no respecter of persons, power or wealth.

The main body of the building is in the archetypally German hall church style, with aisles the same height as the nave. Painted and carved epitaphs to local notables are crowded along the walls. One of the most artistic is that to Field Marshal Otto Christoph von Sparr on the left wall of the nave, executed by the Antwerp sculptor Artus Quellinus while the subject was still alive. There is a 15th-century bronze font resting on a base of fiery dragons, but the most notable furnishing is the pulpit by Schlüter, which is unusually florid by Protestant standards. Technically, it is a *tour de force*, taking the place of one of the pillars that support the main vault. It features figures of angels, reliefs of the Virtues, and, on the sounding board, a representation of the angelic host around the sun. Similar carvings can be seen atop the organ, the finest in Berlin, a baroque masterpiece by Joachim Wagner ideal for the performance of Bach's music.

Outside the Marienkirche is a stone cross, an act of atonement for the murder of the church's provost, Nikolaus von Bernau, by the Berlin mob in 1324. Nearby is the **Lutherdenkmal** (Luther Memorial), the only surviving part of a large Reformation monument. To the rear of the church is the **Neptunbrunnen** (Neptune Fountain), built in the 1890s by Reinhold Begas and moved here from its former position on Schlossplatz. Modelled on Bernini's great fountains in Rome, it shows the sea-god surrounded by creatures from his underwater realm. On the rim of the basin are female figures personifying the Rhine, Elbe, Oder and Weichsel. These serve as an inadvertent reminder of how Germany has shrunk in size: at the time the fountain was built, they were the country's four main rivers, but the last-named, now known as the Vistula, today lies entirely within Poland, while the Oder delineates the international border.

*Communist-era monument to
Karl Marx and Friedrich Engels*

Dominating the south side of Neuer Markt is the **Rotes Rathaus** (Red City Hall), an 1860s replacement for its medieval predecessor, which was carefully dismantled and re-erected in Schloss Babelsberg in Potsdam. The 'red' in its title refers to the bricks used in construction, and has nothing to do with the fact that it served as the seat of the Communist municipal authorities. They impart a distinctive northern German note to a building which, in accordance with the historicist tastes of the day, draws its inspiration from a variety of medieval sources, with Italian and Flemish influence clearly apparent in both the tower and the general outline. *The Berlin Chronicle*, a terracotta frieze above the ground-floor windows, illustrates the history of the city in 36 panels. Exhibitions are held in a neo-Gothic hall on the first floor; the rest of the building is now used by the Senate of the reunited city. Outside, two large sculptures pay tribute to the legions of ordinary citizens who worked so steadfastly to return the city to some semblance of normality following the devastations of World War II: the *Trümmerfrau* (Rubble Woman) symbolizes the women who cleared the bombed sites, while the *Aufbauhelfer* (Reconstruction Helper) honours the men who initiated the rebuilding process.

Towards the eastern end of Neuer Markt looms the 365-metre-high **Fernsehturm** (Television Tower), the most prominent landmark in Berlin and one visible from all over the city. Erected during the 1960s, when relations between the two German states were at their lowest point with each country effectively out-of-bounds to citizens of the other, it was intended as a highly visual symbol to the West that the East was in dynamic shape. However, in deciding on this propaganda weapon, the GDR authorities were hoisted by their own petard. Such television towers were actually very much a West German invention, having been pioneered in Stuttgart a decade earlier and copied in many other cities; moreover, this one utilized Swedish engineering skills in its construction. A further irony for the atheist GDR was that, when the sun shone, the tower cast a huge shadow in the shape of a cross, irreverently dubbed 'The Pope's Revenge' or, in a sarcastic reference to the then dictator Walter Ulbricht, 'Saint Walter'. With the passage of time, the tower has become a popular tourist attraction, thanks to the breathtaking views from its observation deck and its revolving restaurant, which rotates on its own axis once an hour.

To the east of the tower is the open space of **Alexanderplatz** (locally known as 'Alex'), the setting for most of the great popular uprisings in Berlin's history from the revolution of 1848 to the half-a-million-strong demonstration against Communist rule on 4th November 1989, which led to the opening of the Wall a few days later. Once a cattle and wool market, later a military parade ground, the square is named in honour of Czar Alexander I of Russia, who visited Berlin in 1805 to express solidarity with the Prussians against revolutionary France. Before World War II, Alexanderplatz was a major traffic intersection but its character was ruthlessly altered by the Communists. The only 'historic' buildings to survive are from the late 1920s and early 1930s: the labyrinthine S- and U-Bahn station and the angular **Berolinahaus**

and **Alexanderhaus**, No 1 and No 2 on the square. The last-named are late works by Peter Behrens, who began his career as a practitioner of *Jugendstil*, the German form of Art Nouveau, before concentrating on industrial and commercial designs.

Everything else bears a distinctive Communist imprint, though the general character of the square has altered beyond recognition through the influx of street traders, who have given the square back its original market function. The **Hotel Stadt Berlin** was an early example of a hotel built solely for Western guests, to bring in badly needed hard currency, and is complete with a 37th-floor

Fernsehturm, with the City Hall in the foreground

restaurant offering an excellent view over the city. Some attempt to maintain the square's tradition as a major shopping centre came with the construction of the Centrum-Warenhaus (now renamed the Kaufhof); this was the best-stocked department store in East Berlin, though a less-than-worthy successor to the classy Tietz and Wertheim emporia that stood there before the war. A lighter note was struck with the **Brunnen der Völkerfreundschaft** (Fountain of Peoples' Friendship), whose name took on a certain irony when it became an established pick-up point for local prostitutes. Only the **Weltzeituhr** (World Time Clock), which shows the current time in various cities around the globe, gained any place in local affections, becoming one of the city's most common rendezvous points.

The prewar square, together with the Scheunenviertel (Barn Quarter) to the north, holds an honoured position in German literature by courtesy of Alfred Döblin's epic novel *Berlin Alexanderplatz* (see page 134), published to instant acclaim in 1929 and later brought to a yet wider audience through the faithful 15-hour film adaptation directed by Rainer Werner Fassbinder. Of non-orthodox Jewish origin (he himself later converted to Catholicism), Döblin was a practising physician among the poor and a committed Socialist activist. Despite the other demands on his time, he specialized in enormous, densely crafted novels, at first utilizing vivid Expressionist prose before moving to a naturalist idiom as a result of the impact of James Joyce's *Ulysses*. In *Berlin Alexanderplatz*, his most famous book, Berlin is the main protagonist—though it is not the city of the rich and famous, nor even of the proletariat, but of the large sub-class made up of harlots and pimps, of impoverished Jewish refugees from Eastern Europe, of street traders on the breadline, and of armed gangs of robbers controlled by godfathers. In focusing on the disaffected groups on whom the Nazis fed, the novel ominously foreshadows the events of just a few years later.

South of Alexanderplatz is the broad boulevard of Grünerstrasse, with the **Gerichtsgebäude** (Courthouse) on the southern side. This eclectic complex was built at the end of last century by Paul Thoemer and Rudof Mönnich, a team who specialized in law courts, designing no fewer than five in Berlin itself. The main double stairwell, accessible from the entrance on Littenstrasse, is a fantastical concoction of Gothic, baroque and Art Nouveau. Opposite is the **Franziskaner Klosterkirche** (Franciscan Monastery Church), which was burnt out during World War II and left as a roofless shell in deliberate warning of the consequences of Nazism. Even in its present state it gives a good idea of the plain architectural forms favoured by the mendicant orders of friars. Built around 1300 in the Gothic brickwork style of the Brandenburg region, the monatery was secularized during the Reformation, becoming a prestigious grammar school whose alumni would include Schadow, Schinkel and Bismarck. The two large column capitals standing in the grounds are among the rare surviving fragments of the Stadtschloss.

Across from the church's west front is the northern entrance to the **Klosterstrasse U-Bahnhof**, the most imaginatively decorated underground station in the city. Its state of preservation has been helped by the fact that it lies on the underused U-2 line, which was split into curtailed east and west sections because of the Wall and has yet to be joined up again. The tilework includes reproductions of the Babylon exhibits in the Pergamonmuseum plus views of old Berlin and its public transport vehicles, while an old U-Bahn carriage from the days of the third-class transport system stands on the platform. Alongside the southern entrance to the station is the **Palais Podewils**, a handsome early 18th-century mansion by Jean de Bodt that has been restored to house a café and arts centre.

Across the street is the **Parochialkirche** (Parish Church), built around the same time by Johann Arnold Nering and Martin Grünberg in Dutch-influenced baroque style, with the tower added a few years later by Philipp Gerlach. On its eastern side is Waisenstrasse, on which stand a row of reconstructed 18th-century houses, including Berlin's oldest tavern, **Zur letzten Instanz** (At the Final Appeal), decked out in the traditional style with wooden tables and benches and a huge ceramic stove. To the rear is the only significant surviving fragment of the 13th–14th-century Stadtmauer (City Wall) that formerly surrounded medieval Berlin.

To the other side of the Parochialkirche is the massive bulk of the **Stadthaus** (City House). This imitates, notably in its domed tower, the late baroque architecture of Gendarmenmarkt, though it was in fact built by the municipal architect Ludwig Hoffmann in the first decade of the present century. Initially, it served as overspill accommodation for the Rotes Rathaus, the latter having become too small for its intended purpose as a result of the city's rapid growth in the previous decades. In the GDR era, the Council of Ministers took over the building; it is now used as the Berlin office of the Federal Chancellor. South of the Stadthaus is the old Molkenmarkt (Milk Market), with two more fine mansions which together used to house the GDR Ministry of Culture. The **Palais Schwerin** was built by Jean de Bodt for Otto von Schwerin, Minister of State to King Friedrich I; the reconstructed **Alte Münze** (Old Mint) alongside is adorned with a copy of a mock antique frieze by Schadow illustrating the techniques and processes of minting.

On the opposite side of Mühlendamm lies the **Nikolaiviertel**, a showpiece development carried out in the years leading up to Berlin's 750th anniversary celebrations of 1987, marking a sea change in the GDR's attitudes towards urban planning. Instead of the previous policy of razing old buildings and replacing them with brand new structures trumpeting the glories of the Communist way of life, it was decided not only to restore the key monuments of Berlin's oldest quarter, complete with its twisting street layout, but also to re-create there a number of vanished buildings from throughout the city. The district was quite shamelessly geared to tourism, and in

Alexanderplatz

Boom, boom, the steam pile-driver thumps in front of Aschinger's on the Alex. It's one storey high, and knocks the rails into the ground as if they were nothing at all.

Icy air, February. People walk in overcoats. Whoever has a fur piece wears it, whoever hasn't, doesn't wear it. The women have on thin stockings and are freezing, of course, but they look nice. The bums have disappeared with the cold. When it gets warmer, they'll stick their noses out out again. In the meantime they nip a double ration of brandy, but don't ask me what it's like, nobody would want to swim in it, not even a corpse.

Boom, boom, the steam pile-driver batters away on the Alex. . .

Everything is covered with planks. The Berolina statue once stood in front of Tietz's, one hand outstretched, a regular giantess, now they have dragged her away. Maybe they'll melt her and make medals out of her.

People hurry over the ground like bees. They hustle and bustle around here day and night, by the hundreds.

The street-cars roll past with a screech and a scrunch, yellow ones with trailers, away they go across the planked-over Alexanderplatz, it's dangerous to jump off. The station is laid out on a broad plan, Einbahnstrasse to Königstrasse past Wertheim's. If you want to go east, you have to pass police headquarters and turn down through Klosterstrasse. The trains rumble from the railroad station towards Jannowitz Brücke, the locomotive puffs out a plume of steam, just now it is standing above the Prälat, Schlossbräu entrance a block further down.

Across the street they are tearing down everything, all the houses along the city railroad, wonder where they get the money from, the city of Berlin is rich, and we pay the taxes.

They have torn down Loeser and Wolff with their mosaic sign, 20 yards further on they built it up again, and there's another branch over there in front of the station . . . .

There is a lot of wind on the Alex, at the Tietz corner there is a lousy draft. A wind that blows between the houses and through the building excavations. It makes you feel you would like to hide in the saloons, but who can do that, it blows through your trousers pockets, then you notice

Modern mural in Alexanderplatz

something's happening, no monkey business, a man has to be gay with this weather. Early in the morning the workers come tramping along from the Reinickendorf, Neukölln, Weissensee. Cold or no cold, wind or no wind, we've gotta get the coffee pot, pack up the sandwiches, we've gotta work and slave, the drones sit on top, they sleep in their feather-beds and exploit us.

Aschinger has a big café and restaurant. People who have no belly, can get one there, people who have one already, can make it as big as they please. You cannot cheat Nature! Whoever thinks he can improve bread and pastry made from denatured white flour by the addition of artificial ingredients, deceives himself and the consumer. Nature has her laws of life and avenges every abuse. The decadent state of health of almost all civilized peoples today is caused by the use of denatured and artificially refined food. Fine sausages delivered to your house, liverwurst and blood-pudding cheap . . . .

. . . From the east, Weissensee, Litchtenberg, Friedrichshain, Frankfurter Allee, the yellow street-cars plunge into the square through Landsberger Strasse. Line No. 65 comes from the Central Slaughter-House, the Grosse Ring, Weddingplatz, Luisenplatz; No. 76 from Hundekehle via Hubertusallee. At the corner of Landsberger Strasse they have sold out Friedrich Hahn, formerly a department store, they have emptied it and are gathering it to its forbears. The street-cars and Bus 19 stop on the Turmstrasse. Where Jürgens stationary store was, they have torn down the house and put up a building fence instead. An old man sits there with a medical scale: Try your weight, 5 pfennigs. Dear sisters and brethren, you who swarm across the Alex, give yourselves this treat, look through the *loophole next to the medical scale at this dump-heap where Jürgens once flourished and where Hahn's department store still stands, emptied, evacuated, and eviscerated, with nothing but red tatters hanging over the show-windows . . . .*

. . . The police tower over the square. Several specimens of them are standing about. Each specimen sends a connoisseur's glance to both sides, and knows the traffic rules by heart. It has putties around its legs, a rubber mace hangs from its right side, it swings its arms horizontally from east to west, and thus north and south, cannot advance any farther, west flows east, and west flows east. Then the specimen switches about automatically: north flows south, south flows north. The copper has a well-defined waist-line. As soon as he jerks around, there is a rush across the square in the direction of Königstrasse of about 30 private individuals, some of them stop on the traffic island, one part reaches the other side and continues walking on the planks. The same number have started east, they swim towards the others, the same thing has befallen them, but there was no mishap.

There are men, women, and children, the latter mostly holding women's hands. To enumerate them all and to describe their destinies is hardly possible, and only in a few cases would this succeed. The wind scatters chaff over all of them alike. The faces of the eastward wanderers are in no way different from those of the wanderers to the west, south, and north; moreover they exchange their rôles, those who are now crossing the square towards Aschinger's may be seen an hour later in front of the empty Hahn Department Store. Just as those who come from Brunnenstrasse on their way to Jannowitz Brücke mingle with those coming from the reverse direction . . . .

. . . Rrrr, rrr, the pile-driver thumps down, I beat everything, another rail. Something is buzzing across the square coming from police headquarters, they are riveting, a cement crane dumps its load. Herr Adolf Kraun, house-servant, looks on, the tipping over of the wagon fairly fascinates him, you beat everything, he beats everything. He watches excitedly how the sand truck is always tilting up on one side, there it is up in the air, boom, and now it tips over. A fellow wouldn't like to be kicked out of bed like that, legs up, down with the head, there you lie, something might happen to him, but they do their job well, all the same.

Alfred Döblin, Berlin Alexanderplatz, *1929*

particular towards Westerners with expensive taste, through the provision of a whole range of restaurants, bars, cafés, souvenir shops and luxury boutiques. These Disneyland touches readily provoked the caustic Berlin wit, earning the Nikolaiviertel—the brainchild and artistic testament of the GDR dictator—the nickname 'Honeckerland'. With the downfall of Communism, the quarter has lost much of its incongruity, though the theme-park overtones are still much in evidence.

Its centrepiece is the **Nikolaikirche** (St Nicholas' Church), which was restored from a condition akin to that of Franziskaner Klosterkirche. The oldest church in Berlin, it was first constructed around 1230 as a rough-hewn fieldstone basilica, some of whose masonry can be seen on the lower parts of the walls. Gradually, most of this was converted into a brick Gothic hall church similar to the Marienkirche, but the upper part of the façade, with its composite tower and sharply pointed twin steeples, only dates from the 1870s. In 1539, the Reformation was introduced to the province of Brandenburg here. The church's pastors included the 17th-century religious poet Paul Gerhardt, author of several much loved hymns, including the great Passion chorale *O Sacred Head Sore Wounded*. On 2nd December 1990, the newly elected constituent assembly of the reunited Berlin revived an old tradition by convening in the Nikolaikirche, which continues to be used for the odd special occasion but is otherwise a branch of the nearby Märkisches Museum.

Among the many epitaphs and memorials lining the interior is Schlüter's monument to the court goldsmith Daniel Mannlich on the west wall. A gilded relief portrait of the deceased and his wife hangs above a mock doorway. Other furnishings include a late 15th-century polychrome triumphal cross, suspended from the vault above the entrance to the chancel, and the early 16th-century high altar. In the sacristy is the Spandau Madonna, a masterpiece of late 13th-century carving named after its former home in the Nikolaikirche in the suburb of Spandau. Of a similar vintage is the Lenten altar covering displayed alongside, woven by the nuns of the Heiligkreuz convent. Back in the church itself, the display cabinets feature a range of local artefacts which illustrate the history of the city up to the end of the Thirty Years' War; the most interesting item is a bear-shaped drinking vessel, the only surviving original piece of Berlin's municipal silverware.

Across the square from the church, at the corner with Poststrasse, is the **Knoblauchhaus**, one of only four houses on the prewar Nikolaiviertel to have survived. Its rococo core was finished in 1761 for the master tailor Johann Heinrich Knoblauch, the grandson of Czech Protestant refugees from Kaschau (now the Slovak town of Kosice), who came to Berlin to escape the persecutions of the Counter-Reformation. The Biedermeier interiors provide an excellent insight into upper middle-class Berlin home life of the early 19th century. In addition, there are displays on the achievements of the many prominent members of the family, who include Eduard, architect of the Neue Synagoge, and Arnaud, founder of the Böhmische Brauerei (Bohemian Brewery), which introduced to Berlin the new technique of fermenting beer from the bottom rather than from the top, thus enabling year-round production. On the ground floor, there is a re-creation of a wine restaurant patronized by Berlin's late 19th-century theatrical avant-garde, including the playwrights Henrik Ibsen, August Strindberg and Gerhart Hauptmann.

At the end of Poststrasse, facing the busy Mühlendamm, is a far more ornate rococo mansion, the **Ephraim-Palais**, built for Frederick the Great's court jeweller and mint master, Nathan Veitel Heine Ephraim. Its original location was actually a few metres away from where it currently stands: it was demolished by the Nazis, more because they wanted to widen Mühlendamm than for its Jewish associations. The stones of the façade were spared and stored in what became West Berlin, to be returned in 1981 in order to make as faithful a reconstruction as possible. There is a genteel café on the ground floor, while the upstairs rooms serve as another branch of the Märkisches Museum, with changing exhibitions of contemporary art along with a permanent rococo collection, which includes paintings by Antoine Pesne, Nikolaus Daniel Chodowiecki and Christian Bernard Rode. The last-named's *Memorial to Frederick the Great* portrays the king in the manner of a Roman emperor, with a medallion-shaped bust profile.

Also on Mühlendamm, a block to the east, is the **Handwerkmuseum** (Handcrafts Museum), featuring mock-up workshops of old trades practised in Berlin. On Probststrasse, on the northern side of the Nikolaikirche, is a reproduction of one of Berlin's most famous taverns, **Zum Nussbaum** (The Nut Tree). The original, one-time haunt of the artists Heinrich Zille and Otto Nagel, stood on the nearby Fischerinsel; this is a faithful copy, down to the walnut tree in the garden. Aesthetically more dubious is the **Gerichtslaube** (Law Court) on the upper section of Poststrasse, which reproduces the general outline of the Rotes Rathaus' medieval predecessor. This houses restaurants on each of its floors but seems needlessly gimmicky and incongruous, given that the rebuilt original is on view in Potsdam. A more effective adornment to the district is the monumental bronze group of St George and the Dragon on Spreeufer, which formerly stood in one of the courtyards of the royal palace and was a personal gift of the sculptor August Kiss to Kaiser Wilhelm I.

South of the Spree is the former suburb of Neukölln am Wasser, now usually known as Am Köllnischen Park, which was first settled around 1670. Its skyline is dominated by the **Märkisches Museum** (Museum of the March), which, at least from a distance, resembles a huge medieval monastery. The architecture is in fact a clever foretaste of the collections inside, being an early 20th-century pastiche of several major buildings in the March of Brandenburg. In the entrance hall is the horse's head from Schadow's casting of *The Quadriga* on the Brandenburger Tor, the only important surviving fragment of the original sculpture. Several carved memorials by the same artist can be seen in the hall beyond, which leads to a department illustrating the city's distinguished theatre tradition. Downstairs, the archaeology section displays begin with arrowheads from the tenth century BC and part of a hunter's mask from the seventh century BC; on the same floor, the history of Berlin since the Thirty Years' War is documented with the help of plans and models. On the top floor are examples of applied arts, a special collection of mechanical musical instruments, and a gallery of paintings by local artists, including the 19th-century topographic specialists Eduard Gaertner and Carl Graeb, the Impressionist Max Liebermann and the Expressionist Max Pechstein. The museum holds the finest archive of historic photos of Berlin as well as many works by the satirical illustrator Heinrich Zille, whose statue stands outside, but neither of these is permanently on display.

To the rear of the museum is a shady park whose bearpit comes complete with live brown bears. On Inselstrasse, just to the west, is the **Dokumenta-artistica**, a branch of the Märkisches Museum devoted to the history of circus, cabaret and variety theatre in Berlin. Round the corner on the quayside known as Märkisches Ufer stands the rococo **Ermeler-Haus**, another example of a building reassembled in a new location with the help of some surviving masonry; it now houses two restaurants.

A few doors along is the **Otto-Nagel-Haus**, consisting of two baroque burghers' houses knocked into one. It is named after the painter Otto Nagel, chronicler of Berlin working-class life, and was given to the GDR state by his widow in 1973. After a period as a showpiece for 'proletarian-revolutionary and anti-Fascist art', it has reverted to its intended function as an annexe for the Nationalgalerie's collections of interwar German art. On the ground floor, Nagel himself is represented by a number of canvases, including the seminal *Park Bench in Wedding*; there are also fine sculptures by Barlach and Käthe Kollwitz. Upstairs, the works range from Otto Dix's *View of the Elbesandsteingebirge* via Ludwig Meidner's *Portrait of Johannes R Becher* (the poet and GDR Minister of Culture) to the surrealist fantasies of Edgar Ende, the abstract compositions of Willi Baumeister and the frenzied visions of Hans Grundig.

North of Unter den Linden

Between the laying-out of Friedrichwerder and Friedrichstadt, Berlin was extended north of Unter den Linden by the baroque quarter of **Dorotheenstadt**, which was later joined by several other inner suburbs. These are full of fascinating corners that are, for the most part, well off the beaten tourist track. The normal approach is via what should be one of Berlin's main thoroughfares, the 3.5-kilometre-long **Friedrich-**

strasse, which stretches from Mehringplatz in Kreuzberg up to Oranienburger Tor north of the Spree. During the Second Reich, it was the hub of the business and entertainment quarter, but after 1918 it acquired a seedy reputation as a favoured haunt of prostitutes. Almost all its buildings were destroyed in World War II, after which the street was partitioned between the two halves of the city. Those parts closest to the border were abandoned and left to decay, and, although there has been a modest revival in its fortunes since the fall of the Wall, it still has a long way to go before it reclaims its rightful role.

In the meantime, the street's name is indelibly associated with its station, **Bahnhof Friedrichstrasse**, a typically cavernous Berlin terminal of the 1920s whose mass of elevated and underground lines play a pivotal role in the city's public transport network. Throughout Berlin's years of partition, there was little doubt of its status as the most fascinating railway station in the world, one guaranteed to confuse and baffle any visitor, who could have been forgiven for thinking (quite wrongly) that it represented a chink in the Wall. As it straddled both halves of the divided city, the platforms for westbound trains were discreetly fenced off from the bulk of the station by customs and passport controls, thus making it impossible for GDR citizens to board the international trains to Bahnhof Zoo or the tubes plying U-Bahn line 6, which started and finished in West Berlin suburbs. S-Bahn trains from both east and west were forced to terminate at heavily guarded dead ends, before returning in the same direction from whence they had come.

Those crossing eastwards had to queue up, often for hours, in the suffocatingly claustrophobic atmosphere of the station's enclosed corridors. The point of departure for those going in the opposite direction was the concrete and glass extension beside the Spree, known as the **Tränenpalast** (Palace of Tears) due to the emotional exchanges enacted outside. Here the cruelty of the artificial division of the city could be seen at its most elemental, as West Berliners visiting on their standard day permits took leave of friends or relatives forced to live on the other side of the Wall and forbidden by their government from making a reciprocal call. To anyone who knew it during the Cold War years, Bahnhof Friedrichstrasse remains irrevocably haunted by the ghosts of the past. Yet, to the first-time visitor it seems disappointingly like just another busy city-centre station, with the previously curtailed services reinstated and all traces of the hated border erased.

While much of Bahnhof Friedrichstrasse retains the scruffy and forbidding appearance of times past, the arches on the eastern side have been converted into a series of smart boutiques. Among them is the **Heinrich-Zille-Museum**, which offers the best permanent display of the lithographer, book illustrator, caricaturist and photographer who ranks among Berlin's best-loved artistic personalities. Although his sense of humour verges on the saucy, often reminiscent of that of English seaside postcards, Zille was a serious social commentator whose work was instrumental in focusing public attention on the plight of the city's underprivileged.

Towering above the south side of the station is the **Internationales Handels-zentrum** (International Trade Centre), a 93-metre-high skyscraper built by Japanese contractors in 1978. One of Berlin's most prominent landmarks and the first sight greeting Western visitors emerging from border controls, it was intended as a blatantly self-conscious symbol of the confidence of the GDR regime and its commitment to rival the West.

On the opposite side of the station is the **Admiralspalast**, built in 1910 as a swimming pool and ice rink in the luxuriant German form of Art Nouveau known as *Jugendstil*. In April 1946, it was the scene for the merger of the two left-wing parties in the Soviet sector of Germany, the Social Democrats (SPD) and Communists (KPD), into the Socialist Unity Party (SED), which was thereafter moulded, on the Soviet ideal, into the permanent governing party. The part of the complex facing the street houses **Die Distel**, which gamely tries to keep alive Berlin's famous satirical cabaret tradition. It really came into its own during the downfall of Communism but has been on the slide ever since. Across the courtyard is the **Metropol-Theater**, which presents Broadway-style musicals, operettas and other lowbrow entertainment.

Friedrichstrasse is carried over the Spree by the wrought-iron Weidendammer Brücke to the Schiffbauerdamm, named after the shipbuilders who set up their workshops there in 1738. The quayside in turn gave its name to the Theater am Schiffbauerdamm, which was renamed the **Berliner Ensemble** in 1954 when it became the permanent home of the company established and run by the GDR's biggest international celebrity, Bertolt Brecht (see page 143). This renewed the prewar association of the playwright with the theatre: *The Threepenny Opera*, his most successful collaboration with the composer Kurt Weill, had been premiered there in 1928. Although Brecht died in 1956, the company continued to flourish under his widow, the actress Helene Weigel, who was in turn succeeded by their son-in-law, Ekkehart Schall. With Brecht's plays the mainstay of the repertoire, the Berliner Ensemble occupied a privileged position in GDR society and toured widely in the West. Already on the slide in the 1980s, the fall of Communism has dealt it a severe blow, placing a question mark against its very existence. Now that Brecht's own reputation is in eclipse—ironically at a time when Weill's is very much on the ascendancy—it is not unusual for the company to do the previously unthinkable and go for months on end without performing any of his plays. However, the theatre itself seems sure to survive: it is a plush example of 1890s neobaroque, to which a then revolutionary revolving stage was added a decade later.

Further up Friedrichstrasse is the **Friedrichstadtpalast**, which maintains the Berlin tradition of salacious high-kicking song-and-dance revues. The present build-

*Once the most prestigious department store of the GDR (now renamed the Kaufhof).
In the background is the Hotel Stadt Berlin.*

ing is a 1980s replacement for its celebrated predecessor, which had been specially remodelled for Max Reinhardt, the guru of Berlin's theatrical life for three decades before his emigration the year before the Nazi takeover. Reinhardt also directed the **Deutsches Theater** on Schumannstrasse just to the west, and founded the intimate **Kammerspiele** in the building alongside. The main theatre boasts a particularly beautiful auditorium, which was successfully restored for its centenary in 1983. It is arguably the best place in Germany to see performances of the classics.

To the rear of the Deutsches Theater, entered from Luisenstrasse, is the campus of the veterinary school. Hidden among a mass of later buildings is the graceful **Tierärztliche Anatomie** (Veterinary Anatomy Building). Constructed by Carl Gotthard Langhans in tandem with the Brandenburger Tor, it features a central domed lecture hall modelled on a Greek amphitheatre. Across the street is the enormous complex of **Charité**, Berlin's leading hospital. This was established in 1710 as a safety measure against a plague epidemic that never reached the city. A century later, it became the medical school of the newly established Humboldt-Universität, a position it retains to this day. The square at the top end of Luisenstrasse, named after the bacteriologist Robert Koch, pioneer of cures for tuberculosis, has a statue of the famous scientist.

Also on Luisenstrasse is the **Akademie der Künste** (Academy of Arts), one of two schools to succeed the one founded in 1696 to promote the fine arts and numbering Schlüter, Rode, Chodowiecki and Schadow among its directors. Its most important holding is the often exhibited archive of the Dadaist John Heartfield, who adopted

Man of the People

Bertolt Brecht has often been hailed as one of the great artistic innovators of the twentieth century, a man who moulded the future course of literature, and in particular drama, in much the same way as Stravinsky did of music, and Picasso the visual arts. Yet his true worth is a matter of controversy and has been subject to major shifts in critical opinion. In his lifetime, he was known primarily as a playwright and channelled most of his energies in this direction, publishing only 170 of the 1,000 poems he wrote with remarkable facility throughout his career and which now seem his most lasting achievement. While Brecht's posthumous reputation was enhanced by the discovery of the full extent of his poetic output, it has subsequently been tarnished by the failures and eventual collapse of Communism, whose cause he directly championed in most of his work.

Brecht was born in Augsburg in southern Germany in 1898, the son of a paper-mill manager. He studied medicine at Munich University and served as a medical orderly during World War I, in the process becoming a bitter opponent of militarism. Already a fairly accomplished poet, he abandoned his studies in favour of the lure of the stage and was drawn inexorably to Berlin, where he settled in 1924. *Baal*, his first major play, is Expressionistic in tone and content but foreshadows his later work in incorporating a number of songs. The music is by Brecht himself, who possessed a highly distinctive if somewhat gritty singing voice and loved to perform in public to his own guitar accompaniments.

As a result of his studies of Erwin Piscator's proletarian theatre and Marx's theories of dialectical materialism, Brecht formulated his own dramatic concepts and made a clean break with established theatrical styles. These became known, not entirely appropriately, as epic theatre and epic opera and are primarily narrative in approach, conveying a direct political message. Brecht's intention was to stimulate the audience to a critical analysis of reality and a variety of 'distancing' effects, such as exotic or historical settings, monotone lighting and unrealistic stage scenery, were employed to prevent the audience from becoming too emotionally involved in the action. In his 'operas', Brecht stood in polar opposition to the *Gesamtkunstwerk* ('complete work of art') approach of Wagner. He used music for the didactic role of providing a commentary on the text, not to support the words nor far less harness them for the creation of an essentially sonic sound. To this end, he favoured syncopated or irregular rhythms, woodwind instruments rather than strings, and lean, lithe orchestration through which every word could be heard.

These concepts proved a challenge, and a potential irritant, to the composers with whom Brecht worked; yet he struck up three remarkable partnerships. The first and most celebrated of these was with Kurt Weill, with whom he collaborated in 1927 on a musical, *The Little Mahoganny*. A year later this was followed by the spectacularly successful *The Threepenny Opera*, which updated John Gay's *The Beggar's Opera* to Victorian times, thus placing the blame for the plight of the London underworld squarely on the shoulders of bourgeois society. Subsequently, the pair reworked their first venture into full-scale opera on the follies of materialism, *The Rise and Fall of the City of Mahoganny*, and wrote another musical, *Happy End*. However, the partnership broke up after only three years: Weill was unhappy at the condescending way Brecht treated him as well as being unconvinced by the latter's doctrinaire politics. In the event, both were forced into exile by the Nazis in 1933—Weill for his Jewishness, Brecht for his Communism—and they worked together on a 'sung ballet', *The Seven Deadly Sins*. Although they spent most of the war years in the United States, where Weill finally settled, attempts at reviving the old partnership came to nothing. Critical judgement now vindicates the composer, who is increasingly regarded as one of the most original voices in 20th-century music, and few would dispute that the continued popularity of their joint scores is due far less to Brecht's texts than to Weill's marvellously pungent melodies.

Before his fallout with Weill, Brecht had found a more congenial musical partner in Hanns Eisler, with whom he shared political beliefs and wrote unashamedly propagandist pro-Communist and anti-Nazi songs as well as theatre music. According to his own writings, Eisler setting one of Brecht's poems to music was the equivalent of putting a Brecht play into production—the ultimate test. Brecht's best dramatic works all date from his years of exile, in which he moved successively from Switzerland to Denmark, Russia and California. Their success is largely due to the existence of other layers of meaning in addition to the didactic purpose, though these were often unwitting. Brecht never concealed his dismay that audiences identified with the eponymous central character of his drama about the Thirty Years' War, *Mother Courage and her Children*: to him she was a symbol of the misery and futility of warfare, yet she comes over as an enormously humane, tragic figure. Similarly, in *The Life of Galileo*, the universal themes of integrity and weakness rise above the intended political message, while the two 'parables' with Chinese settings—*The Good Person of Setzuan* and *The Caucasian Chalk Circle*—are each imbued with a lyricism and sensitivity that overshadow the underlying ironies.

In the United States, Brecht had only limited success with his attempts to become a Hollywood scriptwriter, but found a kindred spirit in another exiled composer, Paul Dessau, who provided the musical score for *The Caucasian Chalk Circle*, and subsequently set many of Brecht's poems. Brecht was hauled before the Committee for Un-American Activities in 1947 but acquitted himself well, avoiding implication of his artistic circle. This experience, however, prompted his immediate return to Europe, where he threw his lot in with the fledgling GDR state by settling in East Berlin in 1949—but not before taking the precautions of acquiring Austrian citizenship and lodging copyright for his works with a West German publisher, thus ensuring himself a hard currency income.

Although only one of the many prominent intellectuals who had voluntarily chosen to live in the new Communist state, Brecht was nevertheless its biggest celebrity and was accorded a suitably pampered and privileged lifestyle. He founded his own theatrical troupe, the Berliner Ensemble, which was primarily dedicated to revivals of his own works. It soon became one of the lynchpins of the state's cultural policy: in addition to generous subsidies, it was allocated the Theater am Schiffbauerdamm as its permanent home and permitted extensive tours abroad. Brecht's relationship with the regime was not entirely cozy: he had long been aware of the realities of Soviet 'justice', and the use of tanks to crush the workers' rebellion of 1953 led to his acerbic retort that the government should 'dissolve the people and elect another'. However, he was never tempted into outright opposition and willingly accepted the awards and privileges showered on him.

A Painter Writes about a Writer

Another of my friends was Bert Brecht, known at home and abroad for his chansons and ballads, all written faithfully in the old style. They were real works of art in miniature, albeit not nearly such great hits as his Threepenny Opera, a work inspired by Villon and by Gay's Beggars' Opera and with music by Kurt Weill. For a time there was nowhere you could go at night without hearing 'Mack the Knife', 'A Ship with Eight Sails' or the 'Beggars' Song'.

Brecht was a strange man. He came from a moneyed background and started his literary career as an expressionist playwright, whose Baal and Drums in the Night were highly praised by the younger critics. Meanwhile, he wrote his ballads and sang them to friends, accompanying himself in a rather curious fashion on the guitar. Later, he turned his back on expressionism and became involved with education, statistics and socialism, displaying his new-found knowledge in a series of didactic plays. Because he admired Pestalozzi, he had all of them printed to look like school books. 'I write educational texts,' he told me one day, 'for that is what matters today.' His poems, too, became increasingly didactic, perhaps to thwart the then fashionable search for hidden meanings. ('Before you take your medicine,' people would say, 'make sure you know what its social ingredients are . . .)

Brecht was interested in English writers and Chinese philosophers. He read Swift, Butler and Wells, and also Kipling. Whatever he wrote betrayed some influence. He openly declared that the writer must take his material from whatever sources he can find, just as Shakespeare had done. Many critics and more sentimental colleagues took him to task for this eclecticism but in vain, for Brecht was an intelligent man who knew what he was doing. For the rest, he liked to mix with people who did not share his literary pursuits, for instance the boxer Samson-Körner – such contacts refreshed him and often lent his writings an unliterary originality.

On his wall Brecht kept a large map of the world, for his thoughts and contacts transcended the streets of Berlin. He loved the Moscow Underground, *and was proud that* Pravda *had printed one of his long poems on its front page. He was not melancholic like many poets, nor was he quiescent. What he said was always original and often better than what he wrote, and although he was anything but colourless, he loved greyness, not the opaque but the sober unromantic grey of the theorist, expounder and schoolmaster. He would have preferred a good electric calculator where his heart was, and the spokes of a car wheel in the place of his legs.*

He dressed like nobody else in our circle, and looked like some kind of engineer or car mechanic, always wearing a thin leather tie—without oil stains, of course. Instead of the usual sort of waistcoat, he wore one with long sleeves; the cut of all his suits was baggy and somewhat American, with padded shoulders and wedge-shaped trousers. (Real Americans had, of course, stopped wearing such suits long before, but in Germany they still looked 'American'.) He never wore a hat, generally donning a leather cap, and in cold weather he wore a leather shooting jacket. Without his monkish face and the hair combed down on to his forehead he might have been mistaken for a cross between a German chauffeur and a Russian commissar.

Brecht was an excellent driver, one of the fastest and most daredevil I knew. In Langeland, Denmark, where I visited him in the thirties, he owned an ancient Ford that had to be cranked and that rattled and shook when it was finally persuaded to go. But it obeyed Brecht with slavish devotion, its age notwithstanding. When I saw him standing beside that shaky old Ford, in overalls and leather cap, I had to laugh: it was like a scene from a Brecht farce: 'Bert and his Comical Automobile', with crank accompaniment.

I like to think back on those far-off days and our never to be forgotten 'Conversations in the Langeland Woods'. All was peaceful still, although sheet lightning could now be seen on the horizon. I returned to America soon afterwards. Brecht followed later—as a refugee, after a Russian detour. He settled in Hollywood but failed to obtain a job as a cutter in that giant bespoke tailor's shop, which is surprising since he had always been in favour of ready-made suits and the remodelling of man . . . After the war he returned to Germany, an American literary prize in his pocket and with the thanks of the authorities for the readiness with which he had sworn that he had never been a Communist.

George Grosz, A Small Yes and a Big No, *1955*

this anglicized name as a protest against German xenophobia in World War I. He is best known as the inventor of the photomontage, which he used to devastating effect in ridiculing the Nazis and all they stood for. Sadly, the haunting images he created were dependent on adversity: along with many other artists and writers, he opted to return from exile to live in the GDR, but found his stimulus curtailed by the need to conform to the state's official requirements.

The Humboldthafen and the Schiffahrtskanal on the western side of Charité marked the boundary between East and West Berlin. One of the most bizarre consequences of this division was suffered by the **Invalidenfriedhof** (War Veterans' Cemetery) on Scharnhorststrasse. Part of this was razed in order to improve the sight lines of the border guards—among the tombs destroyed was that to Manfred von Richthofen, the 'Red Baron' dogfight ace of World War I—and access was forbidden to all foreigners, and to GDR citizens unless armed with a special pass. The graveyard has a wonderful range of neoclassical, *Jugendstil* and *Neue Sachlichkeit* tombstones. Pride of place is taken by that of Gerhard von Scharnhorst, on which three of the finest Berlin artists collaborated: the overall design is by Schinkel, the reliefs narrating his life are by Tieck, while the monumental lion was cast by Rauch.

South of here is Invalidenstrasse, on which stand a number of monumental university-owned buildings from the Second Reich, among them the **Museum für Naturkunde** (Natural History Museum). Notwithstanding its lofty academic purpose, this museum is much loved by children and the old-fashioned style of the displays only adds to its charm. The central *Lichterhalle* is dominated by the fruits of the palaeontological expedition of 1909–13 to German East Africa (present-day Tanzania). This yielded five reasonably complete dinosaur skeletons, each thought to be around 150 million

Dinosaur exhibit at the Museum für Naturkunde

years old; among them is the *Brachiosaurus brancai*, the largest and most spectacular yet discovered anywhere in the world. Equally precious is the fossil of the earliest known bird, the *Archaeopteryx lithographica*; this coincidentally dates from the same Jurassic period as the dinosaurs and was found in the Altmühl valley in Bavaria; unfortunately, the original is so delicate that only a facsimile can be kept on permanent display.

The room to the right contains more remarkable fossils, notably that of the marine lily *Seirocrinus*, and the skeleton of a *Glyptodon*, a giant armadillo of the Tertiary period. Its counterpart to the left has a kaleidoscopic display of minerals, including an extensive range of meteorites. Most of the rest of the museum is devoted to stuffed animals, among them a number of erstwhile favourites from Berlin Zoo such as the zebra-like quagga and Bobby, the first gorilla in Europe to develop from cub to adult in captivity. There are also a number of beautifully made dioramas: the trio of Island Rocks, Bavarian Alps and Tyrolean Alps dates back to the 1920s—they were the first to be made outside the United States.

The building immediately east of the museum, the **Landwirtschaft Facultät** (Agricultural Faculty) has another fine *Lichterhalle* in which stands Rauch's last work, the monument to Albrecht David Thaer, a pioneer of the scientific study of farming. Further along Invalidenstrasse, at the junction with Bergstrasse, is the **Sophienkirche Friedhof** (Cemetery of St Sophia's Church), a traditional burial place for musicians, among them the Romantic composer Albert Lortzing whose operas and operettas, though neglected abroad, remain staples of the Berlin stage, and Carl Bechstein, founder of the celebrated piano factory.

Bergstrasse leads north to Bernauer Strasse and the **Gedenkstätte Berliner Mauer** (Memorial of the Berlin Wall), a large preserved section of the hated frontier which conveys some idea of its scale, as well as the arbitrary nature of the division it caused. At the far end of Invalidenstrasse is the **Elisabethkirche** (St Elizabeth's Church), one of four small churches built by Schinkel in the inner suburbs to cater for Berlin's rapidly expanding population. Its design, based on a porticoed Greek temple, illustrates his neoclassicism at its most expansive. Sadly, it was burnt out in World War II and is still a propped-up, roofless shell, albeit one that at last has reasonable prospects of being restored in the foreseeable future.

Back towards the Museum für Naturkunde, a left turn down Chausseestrasse leads back towards the Oranienburger Tor. At No 125 on this street stands the **Bertolt-Brecht-Haus**, home and workplace of Brecht and Helene Weigel from 1953. There are regular guided tours through the rooms of the modest two-storey tenement flat, whose furnishings give many insights into Brecht's private tastes. The large collection of English-language crime novels, which he read in the original, show an unexpected literary preference. In the cellar restaurant at the entrance to the courtyard, the dishes served are prepared according to Helene Weigel's own recipes.

The Brechts are buried beside each other, in a plain plot with uncut headstones, in the **Dorotheenstädtischer Friedhof** (Dorotheenstadt Cemetery) immediately to the south. This cemetery contains the tombs of many of the brightest stars of Berlin's artistic galaxy; among them the architect Schinkel and the sculptors Schadow and Rauch; the artist John Heartfield; the philosophers Hegel and Fichte; the novelists Heinrich Mann, Arnold Zweig and Anna Seghers; and the composers Hanns Eisler and Paul Dessau, the more ideologically influenced successors to Weill as Brecht's musical collaborators. Adjoining is the much smaller **Huguenotten Friedhof** (Huguenot Cemetery), with the grave of the artist Nikolaus Daniel Chodowiecki. A much larger cemetery for descendants of French settlers lies about ten minutes' walk to the north on Wöhlerstrasse, close to Schwartzkopffstrasse U-Bahn station; this is the resting place of the supreme novelist of 19th-century Berlin life, Theodor Fontane.

Oranienburger Strasse, which runs east from Oranienburger Tor, was the heart of Berlin's prewar Jewish quarter. Following the depredations of the Nazis, it was left as one of the most neglected and rundown parts of the Mitte district throughout the GDR period, but has enjoyed an extraordinary comeback in the past few years. For the most part, this is due to an influx of West Berliners who have set up trendy bars, cafés and art galleries, but there has also been an unexpected mini-revival of Jewish life which may yet take on greater significance: in a truly ironic twist of history, thousands of Jews from the Soviet Union have applied to settle in the very city where their attempted mass genocide was planned just half a century before.

At the junction of Oranienburger Strasse and Tucholskystrasse is the **Postführamt** (Postal Office), a large domed structure erected in the 1870s in the then fashionable mock Moorish style, its main function being as stables for 200 horses used in the mail delivery service. On Tucholskystrasse itself are several buildings whose Jewish emblems and inscriptions give notice of their former role. The street is named in honour of Kurt Tucholsky, the most effective satirist of the Weimar Republic years (see page 30). Although born a Jew, Tucholsky renounced Judaism and reserved some of his strongest bile for German Jews who failed to anticipate the Nazi menace until it was too late: his most enduring creation is the series of monologues of the complacent and politically naïve Jewish businessman Herr Wendriner, which now resound with a chillingly prophetic ring.

A little further along Oranienburger Strasse is the **Neue Synagoge** (New Synagogue), begun in 1859 at a time when Berlin's Jewish community was at the peak of its influence and was seemingly the most assimilated of that of any city in Europe. This is reflected in the synagogue's prominent position, facing directly onto a main street instead of the traditional placing in a secluded courtyard. It is also highly significant that two of Berlin's most eminent architects, Eduard Knoblauch and August

Stüler, neither of whom were Jews, were chosen to design and build it, opting for a blend of Byzantine and Moorish elements. Furthermore, the inauguration ceremony in 1866 took place in the presence of King Wilhelm I of Prussia, the future Kaiser.

Although damaged in the Nazi's notorious *Kristallnacht* of 9th November 1938 (see page 36), the Neue Synagoge's special historic status saved it from the total destruction that befell most monuments of Jewish culture throughout Germany. It was, however, reduced to rubble in an Allied air raid in 1943; most of this was cleared away after the war, with only the façade left standing. Just before the demise of the GDR, work began on restoring the façade, which has now been returned to its full gilded magnificence, the glittering dome providing one of Berlin's most noticeable landmarks. It is hoped to rebuild the rest of the structure over the next few years, to serve both as a place of worship and as a Jewish archive and cultural centre.

Diagonally across Oranienburger Strasse is the **Park Monbijou**. Until the war, this was the site of one of the former royal palaces. It suffered exactly the same fate as the main Stadtschloss: Allied bomb damage followed by Communist levelling of the ruins. Now, it serves as a play area and seems unlikely to rise again. A statue in the grounds commemorates the French-born Adalbert von Chamisso, one of the great personalities of early 19th-century Berlin. His literary output, though slender, includes the poems that served as the text for Schumann's song cycle *Frauenliebe und Leben* (A Woman's Love and Life), and the classic children's novel *Peter Schlemihl*, the story of a man who sold his shadow to the devil. Chamisso was also active as a scientist, participating in a three-year-long voyage round the world sponsored by the Russian government, before returning to Berlin as director of the Botanical Gardens.

A little further along Oranienburger Strasse is the junction with Grosse Hamburger Strasse, site of the **Alter Jüdischer Friedhof** (Old Jewish Cemetery). Its tombstones were smashed by the Nazis on *Kristallnacht* and the space has since been grassed over; one of the few to be re-erected is that of Moses Mendelssohn, the Enlightenment philosopher, confidant of Frederick the Great and grandfather of composer Felix. Nearby, a memorial tablet stands in place of the Jewish old people's home that was the rounding-up point for the 55,000 Berlin Jews transported to almost certain death in the concentration camps.

Further up the same street is the front entrance to the **Sophienkirche** (St Sophia's Church), which is set in its own quiet close with a cemetery to the rear. It is the sole early baroque church in Berlin and the only historic church in the city centre to survive World War II unscathed. Endowed by Queen Sophie Luise and built by Johann Friedrich Gael at the beginning of the 18th century, it is strikingly reminiscent of Wren's churches in London. The majestic tower is an adaptation of Schlüter's design for the Stadtschloss' Münzturm (Mint Tower), which collapsed due to weak foundations. Concerts are frequently held in the galleried interior, whose decoration

looks convincingly authentic despite being a late 19th-century pastiche. Behind the church, at No 18 on Sophienstrasse, is the **Handwerkervereinshaus** (Craft Workers' Association Headquarters), a noted bastion of left-wing political activity, where the Spartakus League, the embryonic Communist party, was founded in 1917.

The remaining places of interest in the Mitte district lie at its far corners. To the northeast, beyond the end of Invalidenstrasse, is the **Volkspark am Weinberg**, a vineyard converted into a public park. On Veteranenstrasse on its northern side is a monument erected in GDR times to Tucholsky's great literary forefather, Heinrich Heine, another German Jew who repudiated Judaism while remaining something of an outsider. The favourite poet of the principal 19th-century lieder composers—Schubert, Schumann, Brahms and Wolf all composed many settings of his verses—Heine possessed a biting wit and a deceptively mellifluous tone. His appropriation by the Communists was, to say the least, dubious: although he was an acquaintance of Marx, he kept faith with the bourgeois liberal tradition.

At the end of the street is the **Zionskirche** (Zion Church), a heavy 19th-century historicist building that was one of the key places in the downfall of Communism. Its courtyard served as a venue for rock concerts, often by bands barred from normal venues. For a while these passed off without incident until, in October 1987, one was broken up by skinheads, which provoked the intervention of the police, who, it was widely rumoured, had stage-managed the whole affair. A few weeks later, the police invaded the parish house at No 16 on nearby Griebenowstrasse. This was the original site of the now celebrated **Unweltbibliothek** (Environmental Library), which kept records on the officially denied yet all too real ecological disasters occurring through-out the GDR as a result of the regime's commitment to outdated technologies. The raid and subsequent detention of several church members was followed by candle-lit vigils and protest marches—the first public opposition to the regime for over two decades.

Finally, at the eastern extremity of the Mitte district, beyond the Scheunenviertel of Döblin's *Berlin Alexanderplatz*, is Rosa-Luxemburg-Platz. At its heart is the **Volks-bühne** (People's Theatre), built just before World War I with money raised from the public by a trust fund. Inevitably, its first director was Max Reinhardt and the empha-sis lay on experimental productions, a tradition maintained to this day. The strikingly Expressionist tenement buildings around the square were put up in the late 1920s by Hans Poelzig, a leading light in the German Arts and Crafts movement, the *Deutscher Werkbund*. Incorporated within them is the **Kino Babylon**, which even in GDR times had the reputation of being Berlin's most innovative cinema.

Neue Synagogue, destroyed by the Nazis on Kristallnacht, *now under a long-term restoration programme*

Different Perspectives from East and West

The next day we're sitting in front of the evening news. The strikes in Poland: the eastern anchor man reports what Pravda *and the Polish Party organ,* Tribuna Ludu, *have to say. Anti-socialist elements incited by the West European powers are sowing chaos and anarchy. On the same subject, the Western anchor man quotes exclusively from statements by the Polish Solidarity Union. He adds that the Party organ's campaign against anti-socialist elements is picking up. Network executives on both sides are laughably alike: in their own camp, they let only the rulers speak; in the enemy camp, only the oppressed.*

Afterwards we watch a program on West German TV about the history of the German partition. They have added color to the documentary footage of bombed-out Berlin, as if only the fullest technical exploitation of the medium could bring out the horror. It becomes obvious that there is no life behind the house fronts left standing when a woman's form appears at the edge of the screen, searching through the ruins.

'At the time,'. the commentator says, 'experts calculated that it would take ten freight trains a day for sixteen years to haul away the rubble of Berlin. But they were wrong; Berlin was rebuilt in just eight years.'

'In the West, you asshole,' says Pommerer. 'We had to work and rebuild ten times longer than you. You got whatever they could give, we lost whatever they could take.'

'Directly after the surrender,' the voiceover continues, 'the Soviets set busily to work filling all the important posts in the Eastern part of the ex-capital with Communists.'

'What does he mean, Communists!' Pommerer breaks in. 'They were looking for people with clean records. And most of the anti-fascists happened to be Communists.'

I point out that Social Democrats and Christians also fought against Fascism.

'Precisely—and the Soviets offered them jobs in the bureaucracy, the schools, management; they begged them to participate. But there's one thing he didn't mention: in the 1946 Berlin elections, the Communists got twenty percent of the vote.'

'Twenty percent isn't a majority.'

'What do you mean, majority!'

'I mean you didn't choose communism.'

'Just as much as you did your American democracy.'

'But that only proves that neither system is home-grown German.'

'True,' says Pommerer. 'But what was better for a people who elected Hitler in a landslide: imposed capitalism or imposed communism?'

It will take us longer to tear down the Wall in our heads than any wrecking company will need for the Wall we can see. Pommerer and I can dissociate ourselves from our states as much as we like, but we can't speak to each other without having our states speak for us. If I insist on majorities as instinctively as Pommerer distrusts them, it is because we have been equally receptive sons of the system that has brought us up. The possessive 'yours' and 'ours', 'on our side' and 'on your side' that creep into every German-German family reunion are not just a simple shorthand for the two states. They indicate a kind of belonging that transcends political options. The shorthand conceals a lesson preliminary to any exchange: only when both speakers have recited it can they begin to discuss the life that each still lives behind the Wall.

Peter Schneider, The Wall Jumper, 1984

Resident in Berlin since 1961, Peter Schneider (b. 1940) was active in the radical student movement of the late 1960s, a period he commemorated in his novel Lenz (no English translation). He gained international recognition with The Wall Jumper, whose cameos brilliantly encapsulate the comedies and tragedies of the Berlin Wall. His major work of political comment, a reflection on the problems thrown up by the unification of the two German states, is available in English under the title The German Comedy.

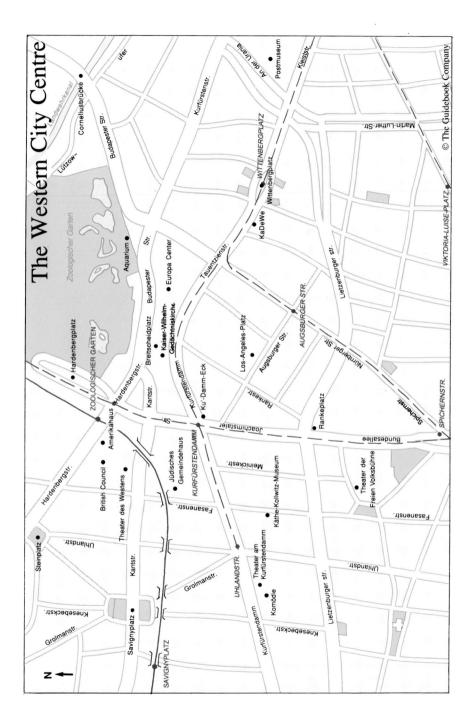

The Western City Centre

N

© The Guidebook Company

The Western Centre

Kurfürstendamm, Zoo and the Shopping Area

Christopher Isherwood described Berlin's western centre as 'a sparkling nucleus of light, like a shady diamond, in the shabby twilight of the town', and this remains an apt enough summary today. The area is seen at its best by night, when it buzzes with crowds and glows with neon signs: in Cold War days, the contrast between this and what lay on the other side of the Wall could not have been more palpable. The seedy and the chic coexist side by side, with prostitutes and impoverished immigrant hawkers alike selling their wares against a backdrop of the city's classiest shops and cafés.

Just as the Brandenburger Tor has become the symbol of a united Berlin, so the **Kaiser-Wilhelm-Gedächtniskirche** (Kaiser Wilhelm Memorial Church), a pristine, highly distinctive new church rising out of the ruins of its predecessor, symbolized the half-city of West Berlin. Only 'the hollow tooth' or shattered tower survives from the original church, which was devastated by bombs in 1943 and again in 1945. It was consecrated in 1895 on the 25th anniversary of the Prussian victory over the French at the Battle of Sedan, an event that paved the way towards the first unification of Germany. Intended both as a parish church and as a memorial to Kaiser Wilhelm I, Franz Schwechten's design imitated the grand, aggressively picturesque Late Romanesque basilicas of the Rhineland, thus evoking an earlier golden age of German imperial power, a period when Church and State were closely linked. In the entrance hall the remains of the church's rich carved and mosaic decoration can be seen. This includes a procession of Hohenzollern rulers from Elector Friedrich I to Crown Prince Wilhelm, son of the last Kaiser, but significantly omits the dynasty's most famous member, the agnostic Frederick the Great.

At the beginning of the 1960s, the town planner Egon Eiermann skilfully incorporated the old tower into a spare avant-garde concrete and glass ensemble in a scheme strikingly reminiscent of that pioneered at Coventry Cathedral in England. The walls of the octagonal church are filled with brilliantly luminous stained glass produced in the French city of Chartres, home of the greatest medieval examples of this art. Above the altar is a 4.6-metre-high brass statue of the risen Christ. Alongside is the *Stalingrad Madonna*, a charcoal drawing by a surgeon who tended the wounded at the Russian battlefield where Nazi Germany's fortunes first went into reverse. The huge organ can normally be heard on Saturday evenings, when free concerts of sacred music are given as part of the church's mission to the inner city. Alongside, the detached hexagonal tower, nicknamed 'the lipstick tube', houses a shop selling Third World goods.

Rudolf-Breitscheid-Platz, the square on which the church stands, was formerly known as Viktoria-Luise-Platz after a Hohenzollern princess, but was renamed in memory of a Social Democrat politician who died in Buchenwald concentration camp. It was turned into a pedestrian precinct in 1983, when it acquired the **Weltkugelbrunnen** (Globe Fountain), which Berliners call 'the water dumpling'. At the eastern end of the square, occupying the entire space between Budapester Strasse and Tauentzienstrasse, is the colossal **Europa-Center**, a typical piece of the 1960s 'big is beautiful' school of planning crowned by that omnipresent symbol of modern German commercial success, the three-pointed star of Mercedes-Benz. The centre contains shops, the main tourist office, a casino, an audiovisual presentation on the city called *Multivision*, and an observation platform commanding an excellent view.

On Hardenbergstrasse to the north of the square is the **Zoo-Palast**, a normal commercial cinema that every second February becomes the main home of the Berlinale, Europe's second largest film festival. Round the corner on Hardenbergplatz is the famous **Bahnhof Zoo** (Zoo Station), a combined mainline, S-Bahn and U-Bahn terminal that in Cold War days was the arrival point for virtually every Western visitor who travelled overland to the city. Its elevated covered platforms, built for the 1936 Olympic Games, make a suitably imposing entrance to the city. However, despite the expenditure of considerable sums of money on the station in 1987 for Berlin's 750th anniversary celebrations, it remains a forbidding place, one of the least secure spots in what is, generally speaking, one of the safest cities in the world.

Berlin's most famous shopping street, **Kurfürstendamm**, universally known as Ku'damm, stretches across the entire length of Charlottenburg and most of neighbouring Wilmersdorf. It was the brainchild of Chancellor Otto von Bismarck, whose masterly manipulations of the international situation were primarily responsible for the belated achievement of German unity in 1871. He wanted the new national capital to have a grand boulevard equal to Paris' Champs Elysées. This was laid out along the old bridle path to the Jagdschloss Grunewald, hunting lodge of the Brandenburg Electors, hence the street's name, which literally means 'Electors' Embankment'.

Unlike Unter den Linden, Ku'damm has no outstanding buildings: a few pompous Wilhelmine structures survive from its early development, but most have modern replacements. Many of these are downright ugly, notably the large shopping centre **Ku'damm-Eck**, which also contains the **Berliner Panoptikum** (Berlin Waxworks), featuring effigies of some 400 celebrities. A further diminution of the street's character has occurred with the arrival of porn shops and fast-food joints.

Nonetheless, Ku'damm retains a certain style, justifying its position as the city's most expensive real estate. In large part this is due to its imposing length (3.8 kilometres) and breadth (53 metres), though there are many other factors. Echoes of Berlin's prewar coffee house tradition, for example, can be found in the **Café Kran-**

zler and the two branches of the **Café Möhring**, even if tourists rather than local intellectuals now make up most of the clientele. The **Hotel Bristol Kempinski**, which features in Günter Grass' satire *Local Anaesthetic* (see page 69), stands as the nearest modern equivalent to the palatial grand hotels—all of them casualties of wartime bombs—which once filled the city. Similarly, the **Wertheim** department store, flagship of Germany's most upmarket retail chain, maintains the boulevard's reputation for grand emporia and is but one of a host of smart shops clustered at its eastern end.

Some idea of how Ku'damm must once have looked can be gained from the southern half of the perpendicular Fasanenstrasse, where three fine late 19th-century houses form a mini cultural enclave. The first of these, No 23, is highly untypical of central Berlin, as it is a detached villa set in its own garden. Now designated the **Literaturhaus** (House of Literature), it contains memorabilia of numerous writers, notably Kurt Tucholsky, while contemporary literati frequently give readings in its café. Next door is the **Käthe-Kollwitz-Museum**, which displays its extensive collection of the artist's sculptures and graphics in a series of changing exhibitions. This is an offshoot of the neighbouring commercial gallery housed in the **Villa Grisebach**. Although joined together in the same terrace, the two have the character of detached houses, the classicism of the museum building offset by the fanciful Romantic medievalism of the villa.

The **Jüdisches Gemeindehaus** (Jewish Community Centre), a key location in the recent modest revival of Berlin Jewry, stands on the section of Fasanenstrasse north of Ku'damm. It was built in the late 1950s to replace a large pseudo-Moorish-Byzantine synagogue, which was left as a charred ruin on *Kristallnacht* and whose portal has been incorporated into the present façade. The lobby contains a display of liturgical treasures, while upstairs is a kosher restaurant. The rear courtyard is laid out as a touchingly undemonstrative memorial to the Berlin Jews massacred by the Nazis.

Just to the north is Kantstrasse, on which stands the **Theater des Westens** (Theatre of the West), a leading venue for musicals and operettas. Its architecture brims with *fin de siècle* self-confidence, mixing a variety of styles, neo-Renaissance, historicism and *Jugendstil* (Art Nouveau), into one exuberant cocktail. Further west is **Savignyplatz**, heart of what might loosely be described as Berlin's Latin Quarter. In the neighbouring streets are some of the city's best bookshops, along with many places to eat and drink.

To the north lies the huge circular traffic intersection of **Ernst-Reuter-Platz**, named after the first mayor of West Berlin. On the eastern side of the square, straddling the Strasse des 17 Juni, is the campus of the **Technische Universität** (Technical University), with the original neo-Renaissance main building now dwarfed by a host of futuristic accretions. A little further down the street is the site of a weekend flea market, the city's largest.

KÄTHE KOLLWITZ

The cause of Käthe Kollwitz, one of the greatest female artists of all time, requires no special pleading from feminist art historians. One of the major figures of 20th-century German art, she stood firmly in the tradition of the nation's most esteemed old masters, such as Albrecht Dürer, above all in her preference for the black-and-white media, which encourage the strong expressive contrasts in which German artists have always excelled. She was thus able to obtain the maximum dramatic effect for the social and political messages which formed the inspiration for her art: her aim was 'to express the suffering of Man which never ends and now is immeasurably great'. A meticulous technician, she often made dozens of preparatory drawings for each composition; these offer a fascinating documentary record of her working methods.

Born in Königsberg in 1867, the then Käthe Schmidt studied art in Berlin, making her first professional engraving in 1890. The following year, she married the doctor Karl Kollwitz and settled in the suburb of Prenzlauer Berg, where her husband practised among the poorer strata of the working class. Her first major cycle of etchings, *Ein Weberaufstand* (A Weavers' Revolt), was inspired by Gerhart Hauptmann's *The Weavers*, which had taken the Berlin stage by storm when it was premiered in 1893. Executed over the following five years, the engravings provide a vivid illustrative counterpart to the play, depicting the harshness and misery brought to the old communities of Silesia by the advent of mechanized industrialization.

Pietà *by Käthe Kollwitz*

While teaching at a school for female artists, Käthe Kollwitz began her second important cycle, *Bauernkrieg* (Peasants' War), depicting the rebellion of 1524–25, which foundered when Luther opted to restrict his Reformation to the spiritual level and opposed this attempt to furnish it with a radical political character. For this work, which experimented with a variety of different graphic techniques, she was rewarded with the Villa Romana prize, enabling her to spend a year in Florence. In 1910, she began producing sculptures under the influence of Ernst Barlach, the greatest Expressionist master of the art; thereafter, this formed an important part of her *œuvre*.

The death of her younger son on a Flanders battlefield at the beginning of World War I was primarily responsible for her long preoccupation with the mother and child theme. Particularly heart-rending are her reinterpretations of the traditional Italian subject of the Pietà, which are portrayed with a spiritual intensity reminiscent of those by Michelangelo. Another recurrent image in her work is the self-portrait: here she showed herself the heir to Rembrandt in her lifelong quest for inner knowledge, never shirking from betraying her deepest and most personal emotions.

In 1919, Käthe Kollwitz became the first female member of the Prussian Academy of Arts when she gained the courtesy title of professor. Soon after, she made a propaganda woodcut in memory of the murdered Karl Liebknecht. This was followed by two cycles in the same medium: *Krieg* (War) and *Proletariat*, the first of which was intended as a direct statement of the viewpoint of a wife and mother. She travelled to the Soviet Union in 1927 to attend exhibitions of her work in Moscow and Kazan but was disillusioned at seeing the effects of the Communist system in practice. A year later, she took charge of the graphics course of the Academy, but was dismissed when the Nazis came to power in 1933, shortly after she had completed a large memorial for the cemetery where her son was buried. Her last major cycle, a set of lithographs entitled *Tod* (Death), was made during the following two years. In 1936, she was banned from exhibiting publicly, being classed as a 'degenerate' artist.

The war years were ones of intense sadness for Käthe Kollwitz: her husband died, her grandson was killed in action, and her house was flattened in an air raid. In 1943, she moved to Schloss Moritzburg near Dresden as the guest of Prince Ernst Heinrich of Saxony, where she died two weeks before the end of hostilities.

The Tiergarten

The **Tiergarten** district, which lies immediately west of the historic centre, is named after the large park which forms its core. An abnormally large oasis of greenery in the very heart of the modern metropolis, its literal meaning of 'animal garden' is explained by the fact that it formerly served as the hunting ground of the Brandenburg Electors and their successors, the Prussian kings, who profited from its location midway between their palaces in Berlin and Charlottenburg. Nowadays, the zoo at the far end of the park provides a modern update of the traditional role. The administrative district also includes several built-up quarters, among which can be found many of Berlin's most distinguished modern buildings, as well as an exceptional grouping of museums and other cultural institutes.

THE GOVERNMENT QUARTER

At the extreme eastern end of the Tiergarten district, just a few paces from the Brandenburger Tor, which formerly lay on the opposite side of the Wall, is the **Reichstag** (Imperial Parliament), built between 1884 and 1894 by Paul Wallot in an extravagant historicist style inspired by the Italian High Renaissance. The inscription *Dem Deutschen Volk* (To the German People), though part of the original design, was only added in 1916: Kaiser Wilhelm II disliked its democratic overtones and only consented to its inclusion as a wartime sop to public opinion. Two years later, the Social Democrat deputy Philipp Scheidemann proclaimed the establishment of a democratic republic from one of the balconies.

On 28th February 1933, a month after Adolf Hitler had been appointed chancellor of a coalition government, the building was set on fire. Opinion among historians remains divided as to whether this was the work of a simple-minded Dutch Communist, Marinu van der Lubbe, who was arrested, tried and executed for the offence, or whether it was a ruse carried out by the Nazis, who used the event as an excuse to impose emergency powers, gag opposition politicians and win the subsequent elections. With the proclamation of the Third Reich, the Reichstag in any event became redundant, a situation which persisted after World War II with the removal of the West German parliament to Bonn.

In 1957, work began on a fifteen-year-long restoration programme, with a view to using the Reichstag for occasional plenary sessions of parliament. In the process, the building's outline was simplified, notably by the omission of its dome. A large pedagogical exhibition, entitled *Fragen an die deutsche Geschichte* (Questions on German History), was set up in some of the surplus space. This is worth a look for the sake of the archive photographs and other illustrated material, but the German-only accom-

View towards the Kaiser-Wilhelm-Gedächtniskirche, the part-ruined, part-modern church that used to be the symbol of West Berlin

panying text betrays the all-too-prevalent national tendency to gloss over the more uncomfortable events in the country's past.

On 4th October 1990, in a highly significant symbolic gesture, the new all-German parliament held its first session in the Reichstag. When Berlin was later confirmed as the national capital and seat of government, the building was earmarked for a return to its old role. However, as it is no longer large enough to house all the offices and services required by a modern parliament, two architectural competitions were announced: one for the redevelopment of the surrounding area, the Spreebogen (Spree bend), as a government quarter, the other for the redesign of the Reichstag itself. The first of these, won by the local architect Axel Schultes, adopts a linear layout on an east–west axis, surprisingly making no use of the dramatic possibilities afforded by the river's sharp curve. An even bigger surprise was that the jury shared the prize for the Reichstag among three entrants, none of them German, and asked them to come up with further plans. The most controversial of these, by the

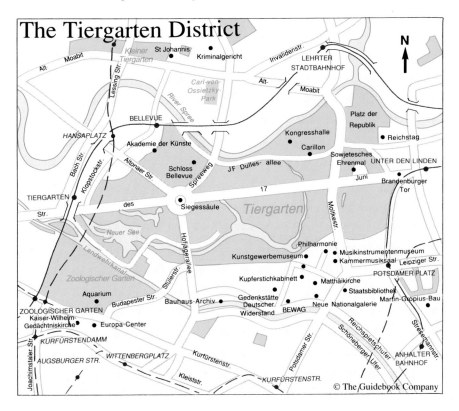

© The Guidebook Company

Englishman Norman Foster, places the building under a huge translucent canopy, thereby providing it with a semi-open forum outside. One of the alternatives envisages a return to the prewar shape, complete with dome; the other adds a modern wing to the northern side.

No matter what is actually built, the area around the Reichstag will clearly be subject to striking visual change in the coming years. In the meantime, there are only a couple of interesting parts. By the riverside at the northeastern corner of the building is one of several small improvised cemeteries close to the former Berlin Wall, with crosses—many marked *Unbekannt* (Unknown)—commemorating those who lost their lives trying to escape. Southwest of the Reichstag is the **Sowjetisches Ehrenmal** (Soviet Memorial). In Cold War days, this was the scene of one of the divided city's biggest ironies: it was guarded by Russian soldiers who in turn were watched over by Allied troops. Constructed out of rubble from Hitler's Reichskanzlei, it is a much simpler affair than its counterpart in East Berlin. Beside it stand two tanks, allegedly those which first penetrated the city in 1945.

The **Kongresshalle** (Congress Hall), which lies close to the Spree a few minutes' walk west of the Reichstag, was built in 1957 as a conference centre for scientific and cultural societies. Intended as an expression of friendship between Germany and the United States, it was designed by the American Hugh A Stubbins, former associate of Bauhaus guru Walter Gropius. The building technology of the day was taken to its very limit in the construction of the auditorium roof, whose two bold curves are supported only by the outer abutment piers. Although hailed as a modern masterpiece among cognoscenti, this bravura creation was greeted with typical Berlin scorn, gaining the apt nickname of 'the pregnant oyster'. In 1980, rusting of the steel supports caused a partial collapse and the building remained closed until it was restored for Berlin's 750th anniversary celebrations seven years later. Now renamed *Haus der Kulturen der Welt* (House of World Culture) it features regular temporary exhibitions, mostly on Asian or Third World themes, along with concerts of ethnic music.

Outside the Kongresshalle is a typical Henry Moore sculpture, *Two Forms*. Further east is Daimler-Benz' birthday gift to the city, the **Karillon**, a concrete bell-tower without the slightest pretension to artistic merit. Its chimes can be heard daily at noon and 6pm. The nearby street of In den Zelten (literally 'In the Tents') is a reminder of the once famous amusement park that long occupied the site. Its tradition lives on, at least to a certain extent, in the Tempodrom nightclub, which is partly constructed out of canvas.

TIERGARTEN PARK
The **Tiergarten** proper was landscaped into an English-style park by Peter Joseph Lenné in the 1830s. It was heavily bombed in World War II, then chopped down for

(following pages) *The 35-ton statue of the goddess Victory on the top of the Siegessäule*

firewood and replaced by market gardens, but was subsequently replanted. Now restored to something like its prewar appearance, it is a popular area for undemanding activities such as walking, boating and sunbathing on which so many Berliners spend their weekends. There are some 30 kilometres of zigzagging paths, along with numerous monuments to literary and artistic figures such as Goethe, Lessing, Fontane, Haydn, Mozart, Beethoven and Wagner.

Cutting a dead-straight central axis through the park is the **Strasse des 17 Juni**, the western continuation of Unter den Linden. Formerly called the Charlottenburger Chaussee, it received its present name in honour of the abortive East Berlin uprising of 17th June 1953. Its primary interest is the tantalizing glimpse it offers of Hitler's vision of Berlin transformed into his world capital city, Germania. Much impressed by the street's length and breadth, he chose it as the setting for some of the most spectacular parades, heightening its dramatic impact by arranging for a number of monuments to be moved from outside the Reichstag to the street's circular central intersection, the Grosser Stern.

The most prominent of these is the **Siegessäule** (Victory Column), built by Johann Heinrich Strack in 1873 to commemorate Prussia's defeats of Denmark, Austria and France in the years 1864–71, events that presaged the achievement of German unity for the first time. On the base are reliefs depicting these triumphs, while the colonnaded hall bears a mosaic illustrating the aftermath. The column shaft is adorned with weapons captured in battle, all gilded in order to enhance their decorative effect. A spiral stairway leads to a viewing platform which affords a good view over the city, albeit one in which trees form most of the foreground. There is also a close-up view of the 35-ton statue of the goddess Victory by the sculptor Friedrich Darke, which towers above, pointing towards vanquished France.

To the north of the Siegessäule are monuments to two of the men who played a crucial role in the Prussian campaigns: Field Marshal Hermann von Moltke and War Minister Albrecht von Roon. Between them, set within the park itself, is the appropriately grander **Bismarckdenkmal** (Bismarck Memorial), honouring the political titan who masterminded the whole process. Designed in 1901 by Reinhold Begas, it features four allegorical sculptural groups: Atlas bearing the world on his shoulders, the German mythological hero Siegfried forging his sword, the Egyptian sphinx as a personification of knowledge, and the subjugated panther as a symbol of defeated foes.

A short distance further north is **Schloss Bellevue**, a French-style rococo palace built by Philip Boumann for Prince Ferdinand, the younger brother of Frederick the Great. Used by the Nazis as a guesthouse for visiting dignitaries, it is currently the Berlin residence of the Federal President, who hosts official banquets in the opulent setting of Carl Gotthard Langhans's Oval Dining Room, the only surviving part of the original interior. The palace itself is not open to the public, though the **Englischer Garten** (English Garden) to the rear can be visited.

At the southwestern corner of the Tiergarten is the **Neuer See**, an artificial lake where boats are offered for hire. It has a mordant place in history as the dumping-ground of the body of the Communist leader Karl Liebknecht following his execution, allegedly for attempted escape, by members of the militia who captured him during the abortive coup of January 1919. His colleague Rosa Luxemburg was beaten and thrown into the nearby **Landwehrkanal**, near one of whose bridges, the Lichten-steinbrücke, is a small memorial to the martyred pair. Its discreet placing reflects the ongoing controversy surrounding their rightful place in history: it was certainly no help to their long-term cause that they occupied two of the highest places in the GDR's pantheon of heroes.

The same bridge divides the main track of the **Zoologischer Garten** (Zoological Gardens) from a recent extension to the north, though visitors can only enter via either the Löwentor (Lion Gate) on Hardenbergplatz or the Elephantentor (Elephants' Gate) on Budapester Strasse, beside the **Aquarium**, which can be visited separately if desired. Berliners are rightly proud of their zoo, which was founded in 1844 with Alexander von Humboldt and Peter Joseph Lenné among the commissioners who administered it. Subsequently, a series of whimsical 'exotic' buildings were added and these remain among the zoo's most charming features: the Elephant House is in the shape of a Burmese pagoda, the Antelope House is an imitation mosque, while the Zebra House adopts the form of an Arab fort.

The stock of animals was almost entirely wiped out in World War II, but the zoo has been painstakingly built up again and currently has around 14,000 creatures, representing almost 1,500 different species. It has been beautifully landscaped with trees and flowers and there are many fine views through the former to the landmarks of the city centre. As far as possible, the animals are kept out of cages, being allowed to roam freely in skilful re-creations of their natural habitats. A particularly innovative feature is the Nocturnal Animal Enclosure, a series of underground chambers with simulated moonlight conditions, which enables the display of a host of species it is seldom possible for zoos to put on public view.

THE KULTURFORUM

East of the Lichtensteinbrücke, a built-up area fans out between the park and the Landwehrkanal. It was the first part of the Tiergarten district to be populated, settled in the main by the well-to-do, some of whose villas were later taken over by foreign missions, thereby forming the heart of Berlin's diplomatic quarter. Partially cleared by the Nazis and badly bombed in World War II, it has gained a wealth of impressive modern buildings in compensation. Many of these are associated with a series of

The Bauhaus

There can be no doubt of the status of the Bauhaus (the name literally means Building House) as the most influential artistic movement of the 20th century—for both good and ill. Not only did it revolutionize the teaching of arts and crafts, it has also been instrumental in determining the whole trend of modern design by shaping the general appearance of mass modern architecture, as well as a host of everyday utilitarian objects. This achievement is all the more remarkable given that its history coincided almost exactly with that of the Weimar Republic, the failed interwar German experiment in democracy, whose demise at the hands of the Nazis it shared. Moreover, in comparison with other artistic institutes, it had a modest number of students—some 1,250 in total, with an average of about 100 at any one time.

Like the Republic, the Bauhaus was founded in the small provincial town of Weimar in 1919. It was formed out of a merger between the traditionalist Academy of Art and the practically orientated School of Arts and Crafts established by the Belgian Henry van de Velde. Walter Gropius, who had made his reputation as a modernistic industrial architect, was its main motivating force and the first director. His initial aims, articulated in a manifesto, owed much to the 19th-century theorist William Morris. Instead of artistic specialization, there would be collaboration and multi-disciplinary versatility, such as had existed in the Middle Ages. The snobbish distinction that placed the fine arts on a higher plane than crafts would be abolished. Eventually, it was hoped that the school would forge links with key sectors of industry, thus eliminating its dependence on the state government of Thuringia, the main source of its funds.

The Bauhaus revived many of the practices of the medieval guilds. Most activity was centred on workshops, which were arranged thematically, with mural painting, woodcarving, pottery, cabinet-making, theatre design, printing, book-binding, metalwork, tile production and stained glass among the subjects on offer. Students were classed as apprentices when they arrived, later becoming journeymen. Members of staff were designated either as Workshop Masters, who were skilled craftsmen, or Masters of Form, who were artists. Most of the latter already had established reputations: they included the eccentric theorist Johannes Itten (who planned and taught the Bauhaus's much imitated compulsory foundation course on form, colour and materials), the sculptor Gerhard Marcks and the painters Lyonel Feininger, Georg Muche, Paul Klee, Wassily Kandinsky and Oskar Schlemmer. For the first four years of its existence, the

The Bauhaus-Archiv, erected after the death of Walter Gropius, the Bauhaus movement's founder

Bauhaus was strongly idealistic and orientated towards Expressionism, the artistic tendency then dominant in Germany.

A sharp change in policy occurred in 1923, partly through political pressure—the school was seen by many as a utopian institution making wasteful demands on public funds—and partly as a result of the appointment to the staff of the Hungarian László Moholy-Nagy, who was besotted with machinery and keen to train a new generation of designers who would make artefacts which could be mass produced. He took over the prestigious foundation course from the unworldly Itten, teaching it with the assistance of Josef Albers, the first student to be recruited as staff. As Moholy-Nagy's ideas dovetailed with Gropius's goal of establishing a certain degree of financial independence for the school, the director decided to mount a large exhibition of Bauhaus work. This succeeded in making many industrial contacts but antagonized local craftsmen, who saw their livelihood threatened. When a right-wing government took control of Thuringia the following year, it cut off the school's funds, thus forcing it to seek a new home.

An offer was accepted from the town council of Dessau, capital of the tiny state of Anhalt, and the Bauhaus was re-established there in 1925. Gropius designed custom-built premises for the school, along with houses for the senior members of staff. Several graduates were given permanent teaching positions. These included Herbert Bayer, who invented the distinctive Bauhaus typography, without capital letters and serifs; Marcel Breuer, who had created a sensation with his varied chair designs; and Gunta Stölzl, the first female member of staff, who was equally adept at making handwoven and machine-produced weaving patterns. A depart-

Teapot by Marianne Brandt, 1924

ment of architecture was established for the first time, headed by Hannes Meyer, a Swiss who believed that the architect's only worthwhile role was the utilitarian one of striving to improve the lifestyle of the common man. His pet project was the partially realized scheme for blocks of cheap flats in the suburb of Törten at the southern edge of the town.

In 1928, Gropius resigned the directorship in order to return to his private practice, nominating Meyer as his successor. This choice was a fateful one: Meyer's prickly personality and blatantly anti-artistic stance antagonized most of his colleagues and students, while his hardline Marxist views made him a major political liability—a potentially serious problem given the dependence on council support. His somewhat paradoxical response to this was to forge ever closer ties with capitalist industry, concentrating the school's activities on the design of objects for mass-market production. To balance this, he introduced social sciences to the curriculum and encouraged political activism amongst the students.

In 1930, Meyer was ousted in a staff coup that had the full backing of the local council. He was replaced by Ludwig Mies van der Rohe, an architect whose background and outlook were very different, his main commissions having been for wealthy private clients. Mies attempted to reorganize the school along traditional lines in order to ensure its survival: Meyer's student supporters were expelled, and several workshops were merged to form a deparment of interior design, in effect transforming the Bauhaus into an academy of architecture. However, the school still attracted the virulent opposition of the emergent Nazi Party, who detested its internationalistic philosophy, which they deemed anti-German: the flat roofs favoured by the Bauhaus were a particular source of anathema, being seen as a Mediterranean, and hence Jewish, import. When the Nazis gained control of Dessau town council in 1932, they closed the school down, vandalized the building and left it as a boarded-up ruin.

As a last fling, Mies attempted to re-establish the Bauhaus as a private enterprise venture in Berlin, operating from a disused telephone factory in Steglitz. However, Hitler's appointment to the office of Federal Chancellor in January 1933 sealed the fate of the school, which was compulsorily closed on 11th April 1933 in the first clear manifestation of the Third Reich's cultural policy. Mies was informed that he would be allowed to reopen in the autumn subject to certain conditions, including the dismissal of politically unreliable staff, but he refused to bow to these demands and formally wound the institution up.

Without the Nazis' hostility, it is doubtful if the Bauhaus would ever have become as influential internationally as it did. Many of its leading figures emigrated to the United States, often landing up in key academic positions: Gropius in Harvard, Albers in both Black Mountain College and Yale, and Mies in Chicago, where Moholy-Nagy established the New Bauhaus in 1937, the nearest anyone came to reviving the school.

In Germany, postwar reactions were mixed. Both Weimar and Dessau lay in the GDR, whose regime was reluctant to acknowledge the undoubted influence on its own architecture and design of an institution with ties to capitalist industry, but this stance was modified in later years when considerable sums were lavished on restoring the Bauhaus buildings in Dessau. However, it was West Germany which took the lead in recognizing the full significance of the school, which was seen as demonstrating the key role the nation had played in the modernist movement before sinking into the depravities of the Third Reich. In 1950, an Institute of Design was founded in Ulm to continue the Bauhaus ideals under the direction of one of its former students, Max Bill. Ten years later, the Bauhaus-Archiv, a centre for research and documentation, was established in Darmstadt, gaining its present permanent home in West Berlin in 1971.

Classic 20th-century style chair,
Marcel Breuer, 1927

cultural institutions and the quarter is often referred to as the **Kulturforum**, though strictly speaking this term applies only to the assemblage at its eastern end.

The **Bauhaus-Archiv** (Bauhaus Archive), occupying a quayside setting at the junction of Klingelhoferstrasse and Von-der-Heydt-Strasse, is one of Berlin's most distinguished modern buildings. It was designed in 1964 by Walter Gropius, the first director of the Bauhaus, who intended to build it on a hillside setting in Darmstadt, the original home of the archive. This project fell through and another opportunity to use the design did not arise until 1979, a decade after Gropius's death. Modifications had to be made in order to adapt it to this flat location, hence the presence of so many paths and ramps leading to the gleaming white concrete façade, which is made up of blocks of identical north-facing skylights.

Unless displaced by a special thematic retrospective, the exhibition halls display some of the classics of Bauhaus design. Of these, Marcel Breuer's tubular steel chair, which superceded his earlier African and De Stijl models, is particularly renowned. 'They get better and better with every year that passes; in the end you'll be sitting on an elastic column of air', the artist commented, though in fact the chair remains in production to this day with only minor alterations. The tea and coffee set by Marianne Brant, who, like Breuer, was a student at the Bauhaus, has been similarly influential. László Moholy-Nagy's *Light-Space Modulator*, an early example of the now common tendency to add a mechanical component to sculpture, is also on show together with a selection of paintings on canvas and paper by leading Bauhaus teachers such as Paul Klee, Wassily Kandinsky, Lyonel Feininger and Oskar Schlemmer.

Beyond the neoclassical **Villa Von-der-Heydt**, now the headquarters of the Prussian Cultural Foundation, the name of the quayside changes to Reichspietschufer. Rearing up a little way further along is the vast bulk of the **Reichsmarineamt** (Imperial Navy Office), built between 1911 and 1914 as the culmination of the long-term strategy of Kaiser Wilhelm II and his naval supremo, Admiral von Turpitz, to create a fleet strong enough to challenge British domination of the high seas. When wartime defeat led to an enforced curtailment of the size of the German navy, the building became far too bloated for its purpose and was thereafter shared with the army. Four days after being appointed chancellor, Hitler delivered a speech there to military chiefs on one of his favourite themes—that of *Lebensraum* (living space), through which he intended to expand Germany by annexing territory held by Poland and Czechoslovakia.

Hitler eventually aimed to extend his war machine's headquarters all the way to Potsdamer Platz. The only part to be built, however, was an eastern extension to the Reichsmarineamt, known as the **Bendlerblock** after the street on which it stands, which has since been renamed Stauffenbergstrasse in honour of Claus Schenk, Count of Stauffenberg, the one-eyed, one-armed colonel who was the central figure in the

Bomb Plot of 20th July 1944. This conspiracy of senior army officers was the only serious attempt to assassinate Hitler, but was foiled by the cruelest of luck. Stauffenberg had visited Hitler's campaign headquarters, the Wolf's Lair at Rastenberg in East Prussia, armed with a briefcase containing a bomb. Having slipped this under the table close to the Führer and set off the detonator, he left the room, waited for the resultant blast, then flew back to Berlin, where the conspirators planned to install a democratic government and sue for peace. Yet Hitler suffered only slight injuries as a result of another officer having stumbled on the case, moving it away from its target. On his return to Berlin, Stauffenberg was arrested along with his co-conspirators. The most senior officer involved, General Ludwig Beck, was given leave to shoot himself; the others were executed in the courtyard of the Bendlerblock, where there is a simple monument in their memory.

The rooms on the second floor, where the plot was hatched, have been designated the **Gedenkstätte Deutscher Widerstand** (Memorial to the German Resistance). The memorial provides an impressive documentary record, complete with some 5,000 archive photographs, of the wide variety of groups and individuals who actively opposed the Third Reich, despite the risk of imprisonment or death this automatically entailed. As such, it serves as a useful corrective to the wartime propaganda view, still believed in many circles today, that virtually all Germans were Nazis. It does, however, leave unanswered the puzzle as to why the opposition was so ineffective and why so many of its leading lights, including Stauffenberg and his fellow-conspirators, served Hitler for years before tumbling to his true nature.

At the corner of Stauffenbergstrasse and Reichpietschufer is the **BEWAG-Zentrale** (Headquarters of the Berlin Light and Power Corporation), occupying the extended premises of the city's most striking Expressionist structure, Emil Fahrenkamp's *Shell-Haus* of 1930–2. This was the first building in Germany constructed round a steel frame; the wavy recessions and gradual reductions in height of the component blocks of the audacious façade mirror the curvature of the canal-side road. A little further along is the equally attention seeking **Wissenschaftzentrum** (Science Centre), erected by the British architect James Stirling between 1984 and 1988. Tacked on to a contrastingly stolid Prussian office building from the end of last century, this complex imitates a whole gamut of European architectural styles, all highlighted in a startling pink and blue colour scheme.

The **Neue Nationalgalerie** (New National Gallery) at the junction with Potsdamer Strasse has long been recognized as a masterpiece of modern architecture. Built between 1965 and 1968, it was one of the last commissions of Ludwig Mies van der Rohe, who had long been a resident of the United States, though he had directed the Bauhaus in its last years, including its short sojourn in Berlin. This glass palace, set under a cantilevered roof resting on steel supports, appears as the very epitome of

The Neue Nationalgalerie by Mies van der Rohe, with a sculpture by Alexander Calder in the foreground and the Matthäikirche in the background

simplicity, with architecture reduced to its basics. The design, however, is far more complex than it seems at first, as the display section visible at street level, used for special exhibitions, is only about a third of the total area.

Downstairs, windowless galleries house the permanent collection of painting and sculpture from the mid-19th century onwards, though this is likely to be in a state of flux for some time, given that it is now interchangeable with its counterpart on Museumsinsel. There is a particularly fine group of canvases by Adolf von Menzel, ranging from historical re-creations of the life of Frederick the Great's court at Potsdam, via documentary records such as *The Departure of Kaiser Wilhelm I to Inspect the Troops at Sedan*, to the realist depictions of Berlin tenement life. Two other distinguished German painters of the late 19th century, Anselm Feuerbach and Hans von Marées, are well represented as is their Swiss counterpart Arnold Böcklin, creator of some of the most potent images of late Romanticism. Ernst Ludwig Kirchner's *Potsdamer Platz* is a seminal example of Expressionism, even if it has little in the way of recognizable local colour. Another key painting with a definite Berlin connection is George Grosz's *The Pillars of Society*, a searing indictment of Weimar Republic hypocrisy. Otto Dix, Max Beckmann and Max Ernst are other modern German masters who feature strongly; the foreign section is less impressive but includes notable examples of Manet, Monet, Renoir, Munch and Dalí.

To the north of the Neue Nationalgalerie is August Stüler's **Matthäikirche**. Dating back to the 1840s, it is by far the oldest building in the Kulturforum, its incongruity in this otherwise uncompromisingly modern location heightened by its Romantic evocation of the Italian Romanesque style. The church has a distinguished musical tradition and concerts are often held in its interior, which was modernized after war damage. Its tower, though not on any tourist trail, offers one of the best general views of Berlin, with the added bonus of a grandstand perspective over the extensive building works going on in the immediate vicinity.

Prominent among these is the **Museum der europäischen Kunst** (Museum of European Art) rising up immediately alongside. This was planned a few years back as a custom-built home for the magnificent collections of old master paintings, sculptures and graphics which have been kept for so long in unsuitable temporary accommodation in Dahlem. The fall of the Wall has presented the opportunity to reunite material artificially divided between the two parts of the city and necessitated something of a rethink, with the result that work on the project has been held up.

Pending further developments, only the **Kupferstichkabinett** (Cabinet of Engravings) is open, displaying its holdings, which include drawings and watercolours as well as all types of graphic art, in a series of rotating exhibitions. The recent reunion of its two parts has been of particular significance with regard to its most celebrated possession, Botticelli's illustrated version of Dante's *Divine Comedy*, whose fate during the years of partition was a microcosm of that of the city itself, with 27 of its drawings held in Dahlem and 57 kept on Museumsinsel. When the former were last put on public display, a year before the Wall came down, the poli-tical considerations of the time dictated that only facsimiles of their East Berlin counterparts could be shown alongside.

Immediately to the north, the completed **Kunstgewerbemuseum** (Museum of Applied Art) faces a problem of its own as a result of reunification: as it was specially built for the West Berlin collection, it is not large enough to accommodate its Eastern counterpart. That drawback apart, it is a marvellous museum benefiting from ultramodern display techniques that deserves far more visitors than it gets. On the ground floor is a dazzling array of medieval artefacts, beginning with items from the Dionysian treasures of the Westphalian town of Enger, notably the eighth-century purse-shaped reliquary which belonged to Duke Widukind, leader of the Saxon resistance to Charlemagne, founder of the Holy Roman Empire. The stupendous treasures of the Welf family, ancestors of Britain's Hanoverian dynasty, were formerly kept in the Dom (Cathedral) of Brunswick: these include a highly elaborate 11th-century crucifix, studded with gems, diamonds and other precious stones; a 12th-century reliquary in the form of a domed church, adorned with beautiful ivory carvings; and a 14th-century book cover of jasper, rock crystal and parchment miniatures of courtly and mythological scenes. No less exceptional are the items from the Münster (Minster) of the Swiss city of Basel, notably the 11th-century Golden Crucifix donated by Emperor Heinrich II and the 15th-century Agnus Dei monstrance.

In the adjoining rooms, a series of Brussels tapestries illustrating Petrarch's *Trionfo* line the walls, while the glass cases display the finest array of Renaissance silverware in existence. This includes the complete set of municipal silverware of the Hanseatic city of Lüneburg in northern Germany: 32 pieces in all, each elaborately gilded. Even more imaginative are the fantastical creations by the craftsmen of Nuremberg and Augsburg, notably the Imperial Goblet by Wenzel Jamnitzer and the Elephant Hunt by his nephew, Christoph. Further outstanding Renaissance objects can be seen at the entrance to the top floor, where the surviving parts of the Pommersche Kunstschrank, an ebony cabinet of curios formerly in the Stadtschloss, are on show. The succeeding galleries trace the history of applied art from rococo via historicism to Art Nouveau and Art Deco, while the basement has a small permanent Bauhaus display plus a suite of rooms used for temporary modern design exhibitions.

To the right of the Kunstgewerbemuseum is the gold-plated **Philharmonie** (Philharmonic Hall), home of the Berlin Philharmonic Orchestra, which is recognized by all but the most curmudgeonly as the world's leading symphony orchestra, one capable of a richness of tone, precision of intonation and unanimity of attack no rival can match. The earliest building of the Kulturforum development, it was built between 1960 and 1963 to replace the former hall on nearby Bernburger Strasse, which had been damaged beyond repair by wartime bombs. Hans Scharoun, who designed it, was also responsible for drawing up the general plan for the Kulturforum. He had been a fashionable young architect during the Weimar Republic but fell out of favour for thirty years, before enjoying this spectacular Indian summer to his career.

The Philharmonie's basic shape is an irregular pentagon below a tent-like roof. Its interior arrangement is startling: in defiance of tradition, the terraced seating is placed around a central orchestral podium affording each spectator a clear view as well as excellent acoustics, the latter owing much to the surrealistic sail-like structures suspended from the ceiling. Herbert von Karajan declared, 'I know of no other existing concert hall in which the problem of seating has been given such an ideal solution'. Irreverent Berliners, however, dubbed the building 'Karajan's Circus', in reference to the conductor's notorious machinations as much as to the exterior's more than passing resemblance to a big top.

On the south side of the Philharmonie complex is the **Kammermusiksaal** (Chamber Music Room), built to Scharoun's plans between 1984 and 1987 by his pupil Edgar Wisniewski. This has about half the capacity of the larger hall and is versatile enough for anything from solo recitals to concerts by Mozartean sized orchestras. The principle of 'music in the round' pioneered in the older hall is further developed by the inclusion of an aisle enabling performers to promenade round the audience, and by galleries which are often used by experimental groups requiring echo effects.

Immediately before beginning work on the Kammermusiksaal, Wisniewski had implemented Scharoun's plan for the **Musikinstrumentenmuseum** (Museum of Musical Instruments) on the Philharmonie's northern side. Among the impressive array of musical instruments past and present are several ornate rococo musical clocks for which petty 18th-century princes commissioned composers as great as Haydn, Mozart and Beethoven to write frivolous jingles, often inadvertently gaining profound miniature masterpieces as a result. In appropriate contrast are two full-sized organs: a fine early 19th-century English example by John Gray, and a 'Mighty

The gold-plated Kammermusiksaal of the Philharmonie

Wurlitzer' that is occasionally put through its paces in public airings. Recordings of appropriate short pieces of music have been made on many of the instruments; these have been arranged in batches of six on tapes that can be heard via the headphones placed throughout the museum.

On the opposite side of Potsdamer Strasse is the **Staatsbibliothek** (State Library), another complex begun by Scharoun and finished by Wisniewski. It offers a variation on the Philharmonie's theme of a mass of continuous space, with visual interest concentrated on the windowless, stack-like central block. Now united with its counterpart on Unter den Linden, the library will in future contain the combined post-1945 holdings only. In the meantime, special exhibitions of historic books are held in a ground-floor room.

East of here, a magnetic overhead railway, known as the M-Bahn, was built between 1983 and 1989, with its terminus at Kemperplatz alongside the Philharmonie; it was intended both as a serious (and extremely costly) experiment in transport technology and as a tourist attraction. By utilizing the disused tracks of the U-2 line, which had been split into eastern and western parts, it offered conclusive if unwitting proof that the authorities then accepted that the Berlin Wall, of which the railway offered a grandstand view, was an established and permanent international border.

THE BERLIN PHILHARMONIC ORCHESTRA

Until the advent of the Second Reich, Berlin's musical reputation lagged well behind that of other major German cities such as Leipzig, Dresden, Munich and Hamburg. As the city's population grew, a number of privately owned orchestras were established to fulfil the demand for concerts. One of these was the Bilsesche Kapelle, which took its name from its autocratic owner-director, Benjamin Bilse. In 1882, 54 of the 70 members of the orchestra, incensed at having been issued with fourth-class tickets for a rail journey to Warsaw, set up as an independent body under the patronage of the impresario Hermann Wolff. This group took the name of the Berlin Philharmonic Orchestra (Berliner Philharmonisches Orchester) and set itself up along democratic lines, with elections for both board members and new recruits.

From 1884, the orchestra was conducted by the great violinist Joseph Joachim, a close friend of Brahms. The latter was among the famous composers who made appearances as guest conductors: others included Grieg, Tchaikovsky and Richard Strauss, who condemned the woodwind and brass sections as 'wretched' while admiring the quality of the strings. In 1887, Hans von Bülow took over as a permanent musical director. Having initially made his reputation as a pianist, he became one of the first of a new breed of baton-waving virtuoso conductors. A flamboyant showman, he was wont to make political speeches at his concerts, promoting himself as a populist opposed to the Kaiser and his government. As a corollary to this, he instilled in the orchestra a collective ethos and a sense of self-confidence that it has maintained ever since. His musical tastes were broad-ranging: he was the leading interpreter of both Brahms and Wagner, who had divided German music lovers into two hostile camps. In the case of the latter, Bülow showed extraordinary magnanimity, as the composer had stolen his wife Cosima, the daughter of Liszt.

A year after Bülow's death in 1894, he was succeeded by the Hungarian Arthur Nikitsch, one of the first conductors to dispense with a parallel career as an instrumental soloist. This left him time for other conducting commitments both at home and abroad: in addition to appointments in Leipzig and Hamburg, he had stints in charge of both the London Symphony Orchestra and the Boston Symphony Orchestra. Nikitsch pioneered the ideal of musical interpretation as a creative act in its own right, one giving living expression to the bare notes of the manuscript. His performances were passionate in spirit yet controlled in effect, utilizing broad, flexible tempi and emphasizing beauty of tone.

In 1922, the musical directorship passed to Wilhelm Furtwängler, who had been a prolific composer while still a teenager, turning to conducting in part because he wished to direct his own compositions. He developed Nikitsch's views on the interpretative act, insisting that each performance was a unique, unrepeatable event. To that end, he was flexible in his attitude to composers' markings in the printed score and allowed great freedom of expression to individual players within the orchestra. A spiritual, unworldly man, he had an almost hypnotic effect on his charges, and his recorded legacy gives proof of his legendary mastery of structure, with each phrase moulded seemlessly into the overall design. Under his direction, the Berlin Philharmonic became established as the supreme performers not only of the core repertoire of German music from Bach to Hindemith, but also of the nationalist schools of the 19th century and of most internationally recognized contemporary composers. Alongside the novelist Thomas Mann, he was regarded as Germany's greatest cultural ambassador.

Furtwängler's association with the Third Reich remains a matter of controversy to this day, though his postwar vilification as a Nazi stooge is increasingly being replaced by one of respect for the stance he took. The Nazis were particularly keen to appropriate music for their own ends, this being the one area of artistic activity where Germany could legitimately claim world supremacy. Because it was also the one least susceptible to direct political manipulation, musicians were far less likely than writers or painters to feel the need to emigrate. By remaining in Germany and continuing to give concerts, Furtwängler permitted a degree of identification between himself and the regime that was ruthlessly exploited by the Nazis for propaganda purposes. Although compromised, he felt this was necessary in order to uphold the nation's finest traditions and to give succour to the population at a time of appalling trauma. His political opposition was symbolized by his refusal to give the obligatory Nazi salute at concerts, even when Hitler was present; he also tried to avoid performing in occupied countries. Most significantly of all, he repeatedly intervened on behalf of persecuted Jewish musicians, both famous and obscure.

After the war, Furtwängler was required to undergo an extensive de-Nazification process. The flamboyant Romanian Segiu Celibadache, who had only recently completed his musical studies, was catapulted to the position of temporary conductor of the Berlin Philharmonic, gaining a certain mystique as a result of his stubborn refusal to make records. Furtwängler returned to the orchestra in 1947, having resisted Soviet attempts to lure him to East Berlin. He remained until his death in 1954, though these years were marked by an intense and bitter rivalry with the man who succeeded him, Herbert von Karajan.

An Austrian of Greek and Slovak ancestry, Karajan had been a far from reluctant Nazi, who, throughout his life, was besotted with the Nietzschean idea of the artist as superman. He was a ruthless manipulator who exploited the communications of the jet age to the full, obtaining a series of influential appointments throughout Europe. In total contrast to Celibadache, he was mesmerized by the recording process. By maintaining key contracts within several companies, and by taking a close interest in each stage of the record industry's technological development, he was able to commit his favourite music to disc virtually as and when he pleased. He made nearly a thousand recordings, including many repeat performances showing only the most marginal differences of interpretation. In the process, he became fabulously wealthy, owning several homes (though not in Berlin, where he stayed in a penthouse suite at the Hotel Bristol Kempinski), as well as fast cars, yachts and a private plane which he piloted himself. When he died, his fortune was conservatively estimated at DM500 million—a sum comparable with that of the richest pop stars and many times more than any serious musician had ever previously earned.

Karajan's stated aim was to unite Furtwängler's sense of fantasy with the precision favoured by the latter's Italian rival, Arturo Toscanini. However, it increasingly seemed that he was bent on subordinating the work of every composer to the supremacy of his own interpretative vision. A distinctive 'Karajan sound' was cultivated, characterized by a highly polished sheen, an extreme refinement of tone, transparency of texture, beauty of phrasing, sensuousness of colouring, and by a flowing, rounded legato line. These features became ever more noticeable as time went on, sharply dividing opinion among music-lovers, who tended to be either adulatory or hostile. For the colourful showpieces of the orchestral repertoire, and for the most ripely Romantic composers such as Wagner and Strauss, Karajan's approach was perfection itself. However, his Bach and Mozart, paying no heed to musicological research, came over as bloated; his Tchaikovsky, Mahler and Sibelius sounded unidiomatic, while even his renowned Beethoven interpretations suffered from a smoothing over of the struggle and tension so endemic to the music.

Not content with his title of 'conductor for life', Karajan began interfering in the orchestra's cherished democratic procedures. The first major crisis came in 1982, when he launched an opportunistic assault on its all-male traditions by attempting to appoint a female clarinettist to its ranks. Relations between himself and the orchestra deteriorated thereafter, never to recover. A few months before his death in 1989, Karajan resigned in a botched attempt to secure the succession for his American protégé James Levine. The orchestra responded by immediately electing the Italian Claudio Abbado, a personality as diametrically opposed to Karajan as it was possible to imagine. An outspoken champion of left-wing causes, Abbado enjoyed almost unanimous respect with players, audiences and critics for the profundity of his musicianship. As expected, his first seasons in charge have offered a widening of the repertoire, with a strong emphasis on contemporary music, a field Karajan had almost entirely eschewed.

This miscalculation condemned the M-Bahn to oblivion when the Wall came down only a few months after it opened, necessitating the reinstatement of all curtailed lines; although still touted in some tourist brochures as a brand new attraction, all traces of its existence have already been removed.

THE HANSA-VIERTEL

At the northwestern end of the Tiergarten park, in the small area separating it from the elevated S-Bahn, is the **Hansa-Viertel** (Hansa Quarter), a showpiece garden city developed in 1957 and intended as a direct ideological response to East Berlin's Stalinallee, begun five years earlier. Originally the centrepiece of the International Building Exhibition of that year, it features the work of 53 architects from 14 different countries. Among the Germans who took part were Walter Gropius (whose contribution can be seen at Handelallee 3–9), Bruno Taut, Paul Baumgarten and Hans Schwippert; the best known of the international contingent were the Finn Alvar Aalto, the Dane Arne Jacobsen and the Brazilian Oskar Niemeyer, whose apartment block at Altonaer Strasse 4–14 is arguably the most striking design of the lot.

In addition to flats, the Hansa-Viertel includes a kindergarten, Protestant and Catholic churches, a shopping centre, library, cinema and theatre. The last of these, the **Grips-Theater** at Altonaer Strasse 22, has gained an international reputation for its performances for children, its main speciality. At the eastern fringe of the quarter is the **Akademie der Künste** (Academy of Arts), which has now been reunited with its counterpart in the Mitte district. It usually has several exhibitions of contemporary art on show at any one time and is also a regular concert venue, particularly for avant-garde music. The other public institution in Hansa-Viertel is the **Berlin-Pavillon** beside the Tiergarten S-Bahn station, which has documentary displays pertaining to current planning projects in the city.

MOABIT

Across the Spree is **Moabit**, one of the original early 19th-century working-class districts of Berlin, settled by Huguenot descendants who named it after the biblical land of Moab. It features as the main backdrop to one of the finest novels ever written about Berlin, Hans Fallada's *Little Man, What Now?*, a telling picture of working-class life on the eve of the Nazi takeover (see page 186).

Moabit's historical sights are few and far between. The most interesting is the **Johanniskirche** (St John's Church) on the main thoroughfare, Alt-Moabit. It was one of four churches built in the early 1830s by Schinkel in the rapidly expanding northern suburbs, though he would hardly recognize the present inflated construction as his own creation: August Stüler added a belfry and portico two decades later, while the ground plan was subsequently increased to three times its former size. At the end of Turmstrasse, just to the rear of the church, is the **Kriminalgericht** (Criminal Court), a typically elaborate turn-of-the-century complex in a mishmash of derivative styles by the court building team of Paul Thoemer and Rudolf Mönnich. Behind it stands Berlin's best known prison.

At the junction of Huttenstrasse and Berlichingenstrasse towards the western end of Moabit is a classic of industrial architecture, the former **AEG-Turbinenfabrik** (Turbine Factory of the German General Electric Corporation), which was built by Peter Behrens in 1908, shortly after his appointment as the company's house architect. Its most striking feature is the long glass façade punctuated by steel supports, which anticipates the Neue Nationalgalerie of over half a century later.

The **Westhafen** (West Harbour) at the northern end of Moabit is the second largest inland harbour in Germany. Set at the intersection of three canals, it forms the focus of the waterway system linking the Spree, Havel and Oder rivers. The grandiose red brick constructions, which mimic the style of harbour buildings of bygone days, belong to the original development, which was built immediately after World War I.

Moabit's final monument of note is the former **Hamburger Bahnhof** (Hamburg Station), located across the Schiffahrtskanal from the Charité hospital, which lay on the other side of the Wall. It is the only remaining example of the first generation of Berlin railway terminals, built in the 1840s in a grand neo-Renaissance manner for services to the North Sea coast. The two arcades, which now serve as doorways, allowed trains to pass into the forecourt, where they were turned in order to face back in the direction of travel. That the station has survived is all the more remarkable since passenger trains ceased using it in 1884; thereafter, it was used for goods only, before being converted into a transport museum in 1905. More recently, it has been given a further lease of life as an outhouse of the Neue Nationalgalerie, though it is only open when an exhibition is being staged.

What Pinneberg Thought About Nudism

They were now beside the pool itself. Not many people, thought Pinneberg at first. But quite a crowd soon collected. A large group were standing on the spring-board, all incredibly naked, and one after another they walked along the plank and dived into the water. 'I think,' said Heilbutt, 'you had better stay here. And if you want anything just wave.'

With that the pair departed, and Pinneberg was left in his corner, secure and undisturbed. He watched what was happening on the spring-board. Heilbutt seemed to be a personage of some importance, they all hailed him with laughter and applause, and shouts of 'Joachim' reached Pinneberg's ears.

Yes, among them were well-grown young men and girls, youthful creatures with straight lissom bodies; but they were greatly in the minority. The main contingent consisted of respectable elderly gentlemen and stout ladies. Pinneberg could well imagine them listening to a military band and drinking coffee; in this place they looked utterly improbable.

'I beg your pardon, sir,' whispered a very polite voice behind him. 'Are you a guest too?'

Pinneberg started and looked round. A sturdy, rather thick-set woman stood behind him (thank heaven fully clothed), wearing a pair of horn-rimmed spectacles on her rather prominent nose.

'Yes, I am a guest.'

'So am I,' said the lady, introducing herself; 'Nothnagel is my name.'

'Mine is Pinneberg.'

'Very interesting here, isn't it?' she asked. 'So unusual.'

'Yes, very interesting,' agreed Pinneberg.

'You were brought here by—' she paused and went on with almost portentous discretion—'a lady?'

'No, by a man friend.'

'Ah, so was I. And may I ask whether you have decided yet?' pursued the lady.

'What about?'

'About joining. Have you decided to become a member?'

'No, not yet.'

'Neither have I. This is the third time I've been here, but I haven't yet been able to make up my mind. It isn't so easy at my age.'

She surveyed him cautiously. Pinneberg said: 'No, it isn't at all easy.'

She was delighted: 'Well now, that's exactly what I always say to Max. Max is my friend. There—no, you can't see him just at the moment.'

But Max was visible in a minute or two, a man of forty, good-looking, tanned, upstanding, dark, the pattern of an energetic business man.

'I always say to Max that it isn't so easy as he thinks, it isn't easy at all, especially for a woman.' She again looked appealingly at Pinneberg, and there was nothing for it but to agree: 'Yes, it's terribly difficult.'

'There now! Max always says I must think of the business side of it— it's good for business, if I join. He's quite right, and he's done himself a lot of good by joining.'

'Yes?' said Pinneberg politely. He was curious.

'Well, I can't see any reason why I shouldn't talk to you about it. Max has a carpet and curtain agency. Business got worse and worse, and Max joined this society. When he can, he always joins an association of any size, and does business with his fellow-members. Naturally he gives them a good discount, but still he makes a decent profit, so he says. Yes, for Max, who's so good-looking and amusing and is so popular wherever he goes, it's quite easy. For me it's much more difficult.'

She sighed deeply.

'Are you also in business?' asked Pinneberg.

'Yes,' she said, looking up at him confidentially. 'I'm also in business. But I don't do very well. I had a chocolate shop; it was quite a good business in a good position, but I haven't the talent for it. I've always had bad luck. Once I thought I would try and do better; I got a window-dresser, and paid him fifteen marks to dress my shop window; there was two hundred marks worth of stuff in it. And I was so pleased and excited that I forgot to let down the blinds, and the sun—it was summer time—shone into the window, and the chocolates were all melted when I noticed it at last. They were all ruined. I sold them to children for ten pfennigs a pound; just think, the most expensive chocolate creams for ten pfennigs a pound. Wasn't it dreadful?'

She looked at Pinneberg gloomily, and he felt quite gloomy too—both gloomy and amused; he had long since forgotten about the bathing.

'Didn't you have anyone who could have helped you a bit?'

'No, no one. Max didn't come along till later. I had then given up the business. And Max got me an agency in hygienic belts, hip-supports, and bust-bodices. It ought to have been a very good agency, but I don't sell anything. Or hardly anything.'

'Yes, it's difficult these days,' said Pinneberg.

'Isn't it?' she said gratefully. 'It is difficult. I run around all day long, upstairs and downstairs, and often I don't sell five marks worth of stuff the whole day. Well,' she went on, and tried to smile, 'that isn't the worst— people haven't got much money. But if only they weren't so beastly to me. Do you know,' she said cautiously, 'I'm Jewish—perhaps you noticed it?'

'No . . . not particularly,' said Pinneberg awkwardly.

'You see, people do notice it. I always say to Max that people notice it. I think people who are anti-Jew should put up a placard on their doors, and then they wouldn't be bothered. As it is, I never know what to expect. 'Take your stuff away, you old Jewish sow,' someone said to me, yesterday.'

'Brute!' said Pinneberg savagely.

'I have often thought of leaving the Jewish church, I'm not a very believing Jew; I eat pork and everything. But I feel I can't do that now when everyone is so down on the Jews.'

'Quite right,' said Pinneberg heartily. 'I shouldn't do that.'

'Yes, and now Max thinks I ought to join this place, and he's right; most *of the women—I don't mean the girls—do need supports for their hips and breasts. I know what every woman here needs, and this is the third evening I've come. Max keeps on saying: 'Make up your mind, Elsa; it's money for jam.' And I can't make up my mind. Do you understand why that is?'*

'Yes, I quite understand. I wouldn't be able to make up my mind either.'

'Then you think I had better not join in spite of the business?'

'It is very hard to advise,' said Pinneberg, looking at her reflectively. 'You must know whether you think it absolutely necessary, and whether it will really be of service to you.'

'Max would be angry if I said I wouldn't join. Anyhow, he has been so impatient with me lately that I'm afraid—'

But Pinneberg had a sudden fear that he might have to listen to this chapter of her life as well. She was a poor little gray creature, certainly, and as she talked he found himself hoping that he might not die soon, so that Bunny should be spared all this torment; he really could not conceive of any future for Frau Nothnagel. But he was already depressed enough that night, and he suddenly cut short what she was saying: 'I must go and telephone. Excuse me.'

And she said, very politely: 'Of course; don't let me keep you.'

And Pinneberg fled.

Hans Fallada, Little Man What Now?, 1933

Hans Fallada was the pseudonym of Rudolf Ditzen (1893–1947), whose early life was spent in a succession of low-paid agricultural and office jobs. These gave him an innate sympathy for the poor and downtrodden, whose cause he championed in a series of social realist novels, among them Little Man, What Now?, which quickly gained an international readership. Fallada himself eschewed a direct commitment to any political movement; that the Nazis mistakenly regarded his novels as being sympathetic to their cause has been to the unfortunate detriment of his long-term reputation.

The Western Suburbs

Charlottenburg

The district of **Charlottenburg** formed the heart of West Berlin—the shopping district at its eastern end is certain to maintain its role as the main commercial centre of the reunited city, while political and administrative life becomes concentrated around Unter den Linden. This particular duality is not, as is often imagined, simply a hangover from the long period of political division: in *Goodbye to Berlin*, written in 1933, Christopher Isherwood specifically characterized the city as possessing two distinct centres. The main reason for this was that Charlottenburg was a separate town until 1920 when, together with a string of other communities, it was absorbed into Greater Berlin.

Originally the village of Lietzow, a satellite of the royal palace of Lietzenburg, Charlottenburg received its name in 1705 in honour of the recently deceased Queen Sophie Charlotte, consort of Friedrich I, the first King of Prussia. It remained a sleepy backwater until the foundation of the Second Reich in 1871, when it was developed as a mercantile and residential area favoured by the prosperous sections of the middle class.

Nowadays, it presents a mixed bag of attractions. The most obvious tourist sights are grouped around the palace some distance away from the shopping streets, which, although an essential component of any visit to Berlin, are not notable for any great visual appeal. (See Ku'damm and the Shopping Area, page 157.)

THE SCHLOSS

Schloss Charlottenburg (Charlottenburg Palace), its park and outlying buildings make up the most attractive and historic complex in former West Berlin, offering a taste of all the best features of the royal Prussian heritage and a welcome oasis of calm in the midst of the swirling bustle of city-life. Intended as a quiet summer retreat for the Electress Sophie Charlotte, the Schloss was gradually expanded over the years in a direct reflection of Prussia's increasing international standing. Most of the leading artists and architects associated with Berlin were involved at one time or another, and the result is comparable in grandeur with Sanssouci in Potsdam.

The oldest part of the main Schloss is now known as the **Nering-Eosanderbau** (Nering and Eosander Building) in honour of the two architects who built it. Johann Arnold Nering's original palace, begun shortly before his death in 1695 and completed three years later, was a modest building, comprising the two lower storeys of the central tract in the main block. With Prussia's promotion to the rank of a king-

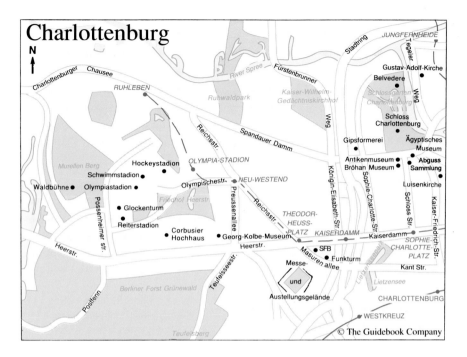

Charlottenburg

N ↑

JUNGFERNHEIDE

Charlottenburger Chausee

RUHLEBEN

River Spree — Fürstenbrunner

Kaiser-Wilhelm-
Gedächtniskirchhof

Ruhwaldpark

Stadtring

Tegeler Weg

Gustav-Adolf-Kirche

Belvedere

Schlossgarten
Charlottenburg

Schloss
Charlottenburg

Reichsstr.

Spandauer Damm

Weg

Gipsformerei

Ägyptisches
Museum

Mürellen Berg

Hockeystadion

OLYMPIA-STADION

Antikenmuseum

Abguss

Schwimmstadion

Olympischestr.

NEU-WESTEND

Bröhan Museum

Sammlung

Waldbühne

Olympiastadion

Friedhof Heerstr.

Reichsstr.

Königin-Elisabeth-Str.

Sophie-Charlotte-Str.

Luisenkirche

Schloss Str.

Kaiser-Friedrich-Str.

Pössenheimer str.

Glockenturm

Preussenallee

THEODOR-
HEUSS-
PLATZ KAISERDAMM

Kaiserdamm

SOPHIE-
CHARLOTTE-
PLATZ

Heerstr.

Reiterstadion

Corbusier
Hochhaus

Georg-Kolbe-Museum

Heerstr.

Masurenallee

SFB

Funkturm

Kant Str.

Teufelsseestr.

Messe-

Lietzensee

Berliner Forst Grünewald

Postfenn

und

Austellungsgelände

CHARLOTTENBURG

WESTKREUZ

Teufelsberg

© The Guidebook Company

dom in 1701 something considerably more ostentatious was required, and the Swede Johann Eosander von Göthe was commissioned to carry out an expansion modelled on the royal palaces of France. He tripled the length of the façade, added a main courtyard in front and an orangery to the west, and crowned Nering's structure with a magnificent towering dome, which still ranks among the city's most prominent landmarks.

The gilded statue of Fortuna on the dome's cupola, which doubles as a weather vane, is a replacement for one destroyed in World War II. As can be seen from photographs displayed inside, the whole palace was badly damaged, and restoration has been a long and painstaking process. One bonus has been the acquisition of the **Denkmal des Grossen Kurfürsten** (Memorial to the Great Elector), which stands in the courtyard. This swaggering baroque masterpiece by Andreas Schlüter was commissioned by Elector Friedrich III in honour of his father, and was modelled on the great equestrian monuments of ancient Rome. It formerly stood facing the Stadt-schloss on Lange Brücke (the present Rathausbrücke), but was removed during the war for safekeeping. The barge that transported it sank in the Tegeler See and the memorial was not salvaged until several years later. As it had been found in what was West Berlin territory, it was not returned to its former location but placed instead in the most suitable alternative. For the time being at least, the statue remains separated from its original base, which is in the Bodemuseum.

The historic apartments of the Nering-Eosanderbau can only be visited on German-language guided tours. For the most part, they are intimate in character with nothing to rival the majestic outlines of the exterior. The most distinctive room is the sumptuous Porcelain Chamber overlooking the gardens, which has been re-created virtually from scratch after the original pieces were smashed in the war. A similar labour of love has been necessary to restore the adjoining chapel, which is still not open to the public. Also of special note is the panelled Oak Gallery, used for fairly frequent chamber music concerts.

Under Friedrich Wilhelm I, the Soldier King, there were no additions to the palace but his successor, Frederick the Great, ordered an eastern extension soon after his accession in 1740, now called the **Knobelsdorff-Flügel** (Knobelsdorff Wing), again in honour of its architect. It is fronted by a copy of Schlüter's statue of King Friedrich I: the original was removed to Königsberg in 1801 for the centenary celebrations of his coronation there, but vanished in 1945 and is now either lost or stowed away in a secret Russian location.

The main reception rooms on the first floor of the Knobelsdorff-Flügel can be visited independently. Unfortunately, the White Hall was damaged beyond meaningful repair in the war and its original ceiling paintings were given a free modern reinterpretation. The stately Golden Gallery is one of Knobelsdorff's finest achievements, albeit one little used by its patron, who virtually abandoned Charlottenburg in favour of Sanssouci. The small rooms beyond the gallery contain Frederick's personal collection of French rococo paintings, many of which formerly hung in one or other of the Potsdam palaces. Chardin, Lancret, Pater and the court painter Pesne are among the artists represented, though all their works pale beside the eight creations of Watteau, the finest group of his work anywhere in the world. They range across his career, from the early *Actors at a Fair* and *The Village Bride* to the valedictory *Shop Sign of the Art Dealer Gersaint*. This, a continuous composition along two canvases, was painted by the dying artist in just eight mornings as a present for a friend who owned a shop on the Pont Notre Dame, and mixes reality and illusion in a startlingly novel way. More typical of his art is the celebrated *Embarkation for the Isle of Cythera*, an effervescent idyll evoking the impossibly carefree, dream-like existence of the rococo imagination.

The ground floor of the Knobelsdorff-Flügel is currently occupied by the **Galerie der Romantik** (Gallery of Romantic Art), which will be moved to the Kulturforum in the Tiergarten at a later date. Its highlight is a collection of some two dozen works by Caspar David Friedrich, one of the greatest artists Germany ever produced. He revolutionized landscape painting, imbuing it with a spiritual quality which often incorporates a direct religious message. In works such as *Mount Watzmann* (in the Bavarian Alps) or *The Riesen-gebirge* (now part of the Czech-Polish frontier) which show some of the country's most spectacular scenery, he depicted Nature as awesome, immense and unconquerable; when figures are present, as in *Monk by the Sea*, they are typically shown from behind, thus drawing the viewer into the picture, and as wholly insignificant in the context of their surroundings. A similar message is present in the best known work on display *Monastery among the Oak Trees*; here the crumbling ruin symbolizes the transitoriness of human existence.

One of Friedrich's few contemporaries capable of comparably memorable images was Karl Friedrich Schinkel, who overcame the disadvantage of being no more than an occasional painter to produce visionary compositions characterized by a meticulous rendering of architectural detail. On canvas he was even more effective at evoking the Middle Ages than the Antique World which inspired most of his buildings. *Medieval City by a River* and *Gothic Cathedral on a Rock by the Sea*, both painted in 1815 as allegories of the defeat of Napoleon, give a clear impression of the sort of monument Schinkel hoped in vain to build in celebration of Prussia's victory. Carl Blechen, whose career marks the transition from Romanticism to realism, is represented by a large group of paintings, of which the most interesting are *Park Sanssouci*, complete with the huge spouting fountain which was not yet operational at the time the painting was made, and *The Rolling Mill at Neustadt-Eberswalde*, an early unidealized portrayal of an industrial landscape.

The suite of rooms to the left of the entrance contains a number of topographical views of Berlin by Eduard Gaertner, which make for fascinating comparisons with the present day: *Unter den Linden* shows the great boulevard in pristine shape, while *The Bauakademie* provides a worthy record of the greatest of Schinkel's buildings, now destroyed. Alongside are a number of small canvases by the Biedermeier artist Carl Spitzweg, a subtle humorist whose satire never degenerates into cruelty: *English Tourists in the Campagna* is a typical example of his style. At the far end of this wing, though not always on view, is one of Jacques-Louis David's most famous works, *Napoleon Crossing the Alps*.

The final addition to the main structure of Schloss Charlottenburg was the **Theaterbau** (Theatre Building), built at the extreme western end by Carl Gotthard Langhans at the behest of King Friedrich Wilhelm II. The severe neoclassical style, although masterly in its own way, is rather at odds with the rest of the palace. Nothing remains of the original interior; instead, a series of modernized rooms house the **Museum für Vor- und Frühgeschichte** (Museum of Pre- and Early History). This miscellaneous collection ranges from animal bones reckoned to be 150,000 years old, which were found in the suburb of Neukölln, to an extensive array of ceramics, jewellery and tools from Iran and Mesopotamia. The most eye-catching items, the Bronze-Age hoard of gold found in nearby Eberswalde, and the fabulous treasures unearthed by Heinrich Schliemann in Troy, vanished during the war. For the time

being they are represented only by copies, though hopes are high that at least the latter, which were probably taken to Russia as war booty, will eventually be returned.

A few metres away from the northeastern corner of the Schloss, the freestanding **Schinkel-Pavillon** (Schinkel Pavilion) provides a more satisfactory architectonic solution for a neolassical addition, as its modest dimensions contrast dramatically with those of its neighbour. Built in 1824–5 as a retreat for King Friedrich Wilhelm III and his second wife, Auguste, Princess of Liegnitz, the pavilion is closely modelled on the Villa Reale Chiatomone in Naples, which the king had visited shortly before. Almost all the details of the interiors, which are arranged around a central stairwell, were designed by Schinkel himself; a number of his drawings and paintings have since been added to help create an even more integrated effect. Another highlight is Gaertner's most spectacular work, the hexagonal *Panorama from the Friedrichswerdersche Kirche*, which offers a faithful representation of central Berlin at its most salubrious. By the same artist are topographic views of Paris and Moscow, the latter in the form of a triptych. There are a number of fine portrait busts by Christian Daniel Rauch, who was also responsible for the two huge **Viktoriasäulen** (Victory Columns) flanking the pathway outside.

(above) *Statue of Friedrich I at Charlotten Tor;* (below) *Denkmal des Grossen Kurfürsten (Memorial to the Great Elector) in the courtyard of Schloss Charlottenburg*

The Schlossgarten

The **Schlossgarten** (Palace Garden) is a
mixture of different elements of landscaping styles. Nearest to the Schloss, a
formal baroque garden has been re-
created, laid out in regular geometric
patterns with clipped hedges. Elsewhere,
the park bears the clear imprint of Peter
Joseph Lenné, who arranged it according
to the Romantic preference for simulated
Nature. Water plays a key role in the
layout. The Spree, which forms the park's
eastern and northern boundaries, is
complemented by a series of ponds and
canals spanned by many graceful little
bridges. Unexpected vistas constantly
reveal themselves, providing ample reward for anyone who takes the time, as
the original gardeners intended, to stroll
around at leisure.

Overlooking the Spree towards the
northeastern corner of the park is the
domed oval **Belvedere**, built by Langhans
as an outlook tower, teahouse and chamber music venue for the court. In contrast to most of his buildings, which tend
to be uncompromisingly neoclassical,
this is still marked with the sense of
playful fantasy of the superceded rococo
style. The three floors of the interior are
now devoted to a historical display of
Berlin-made porcelain. On the top floor
are the rococo creations of the first two
local manufacturers, Wilhelm Caspar
Wegely and Johann Ernst Gotzkowsky,
who began production in 1751 and 1761
respectively. In 1763, the Königliche
Porzellan-Manufactur (Royal Porcelain
Factory) was established by Frederick the

(above) *Statue of Sophie Charlotte at Charlotten Tor;*
(below) *Dome of the Nering-Eosanderbau*

Schlossgarten Charlottenburg

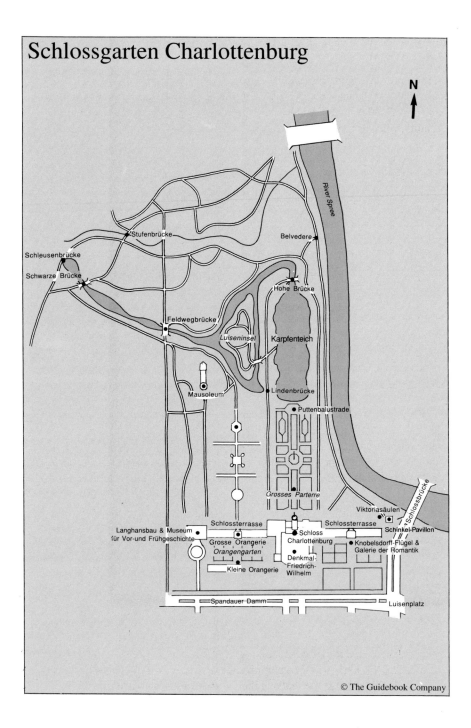

N

River Spree

Stufenbrücke

Belvedere

Schleusenbrücke

Schwarze Brücke

Hohe Brücke

Feldwegbrücke

Luiseninsel

Karpfenteich

Mausoleum

Lindenbrücke

Puttenbalustrade

Schlossbrücke

Grosses Parterre

Viktoriasäulen

Schlosserrasse

Schlosserrasse

Schinkel-Pavillon

Langhansbau & Museum
für Vor-und Frühgeschichte

Grosse Orangerie

Orangengarten

Schloss
Charlottenburg

Knobelsdorff-Flügel &
Galerie der Romantik

Kleine Orangerie

Denkmal-
Friedrich-
Wilhelm

Spandauer Damm

Luisenplatz

© The Guidebook Company

Great, and is still going strong today, with the blue sceptre of Brandenburg forming its trademark. Exhibits from its early years include pieces made for Frederick himself and for Catherine the Great of Russia. However, its heyday came in the early 19th century, when its productions included the Empire-style service with botanical illustrations, which was commissioned by Empress Josephine of France, and the later neoclassical set made for the Russian court, adorned with depictions of antique scenes, famous paintings and views, including one of the Belvedere.

At the end of a shady alley of pine trees at the western side of the park is the **Mausoleum** built in memory of Queen Luise, first wife of Friedrich Wilhelm III (1770–1840), who died in 1810. The young Schinkel produced a watercolour drawing for a gloriously ethereal neo-Gothic shrine, but this was vetoed by the king, who preferred a conventionally solemn neoclassical temple. Though Schinkel had a hand in the design, its construction was entrusted to the court building director, Heinrich Gentz. Christian Daniel Rauch carved the tomb of the queen, whom he depicted in peaceful repose. In collaboration with Friedrich Tieck, he also created the two tall, tapering candelabra, which bear statues of the Four Seasons and the Three Fates respectively; three decades later, he conceived the companion monument to the king. Various other members of the Hohenzollern family were subsequently buried in the mausoleum, among them Kaiser Wilhelm I and the Empress Augusta, who are honoured with grand sarcophagi carved by Erdmann Encke.

The Museums

Facing the Schloss across the busy Spandauer Damm are the twin **Kaserne** (Barracks), built by August Stüler in the 1850s to house the attachment of the royal guard. Their general appearance mirrors the baroque aspect of the Schloss, with each building culminating in an elegant dome. Although basically functional, the barracks were also intended to form a fitting climax to the straight axis of Schloss Strasse, the main ceremonial approach to the palace.

The eastern wing of the Kaserne contains the renowned **Ägyptisches Museum** (Egyptian Museum), though this will return to the Museumsinsel when the Neues Museum is rebuilt. By far the most famous exhibit is the remarkably well-preserved polychrome limestone bust of Queen Nefertiti which occupies centre-stage on the first floor. Nowadays something of a cultural symbol of Berlin, it presents a distinctive idealization of femininity, characterized by flawlessly symmetrical features, a consciously beautiful face and a long, graceful neck. The queen wears an ornamental necklace-collar and a flat-topped blue crown bearing a band of gold and semi-precious stones and the coiled uraeus, symbol of Egyptian royalty. As only one eye is coloured in, it is likely that the statue served as a master copy from which others were made. It was left in the studio of the sculptor Thutmosis when the city of

Amarna was abandoned in 1335 BC on the death of King Akhenaten, Nefertiti's husband, remaining undisturbed until its discovery by German archaeologists in 1912. Among many other outstanding finds from the same site are a stucco bust of Akhenaten himself, a wooden head of his mother Queen Tiyi, and a relief of a young couple, probably his daughter and son-in-law, strolling in a garden.

Other highlights of the collection are the statue of the pig-goddess from around 3500 BC; blue faience funerary objects, including a hedgehog and a hippopotamus, from about 1800 BC; and the startlingly modernistic Green Man, a bust of a priest made around 300 BC, which shows an absolute mastery of anatomical modelling and facial characterization. On the ground floor, at the entrance to the hall which formerly served as the royal stables, is the largest exhibit, the Kalabsha Temple Gate dating from 20 BC; this was salvaged by Germans during the frantic excavations that preceded the construction of the Aswan Dam in the 1960s and was presented to the museum by the Egyptian government. Its sandstone reliefs show the Roman Emperor Augustus in the guise of a Pharaoh paying homage to various Egyptian gods.

Across the street, the **Antikensammlung** (Collection of Antiquities) is an equally distinguished museum, albeit one frequently overlooked. Its collection of Greek sculpture begins with abstract Cycladic figures of 2200 BC; it continues via a fine group of eighth-century BC votive figures from Olympia and the outstanding seventh-century BC Ram Carrier from Crete to the first-century BC clay statuettes found in the German excavations of Priene in Asia Minor. Among the Roman sculptures, the most outstanding pieces are a marble bust of Cleopatra, one of only two known surviving likenesses made during her lifetime, and a superb bronze statuette of the goddess Luna.

On the first floor, helpfully arranged by subject matter, is the finest array of Attic vessels in the world. The star piece is the so-called Berlin Amphora from Vulci in Etruria, made in around 490 BC in a consummate design showing the god Hermes, a lyre-playing satyr and a deer. Also of special note is the Duris drinking bowl from the following decade, which gives a comprehensive illustration of Greek schooling methods.

The treasury in the basement includes a sixth-century BC Scythian horde, centred on a gold fish, found in Vettersfelde in the southeast of the province of Brandenburg. Other masterly pieces of jewellery are the fibula in the form of a hawk from eighth-century BC Ephesus, the silver ibex from sixth-century BC Persia, and a host of gems and cameos from Roman times. Finest of all is the Hildesheim Silver, a trove of some seventy pieces of silverware from the first century BC and the first century AD named after the Lower Saxon city where it was found, though it was probably taken there as war booty from the eastern part of the Roman Empire. The ornamental Athena Dish, bearing a graceful relief of the eponymous goddess, is deservedly the most admired piece, but the boisterous pair of drinking vessels, festooned with deities, masks, trees, animals and musical instruments, are almost equally as attractive.

Next door to the Antikensammlung is the **Bröhan Museum**, a refreshingly unorthodox museum dedicated to the two artistic movements of Art Nouveau (*Jugendstil*, or 'young style' as it is known in German) and Art Deco; German artists predominate, though there is also a wide selection of French work. Many of the *objets d'art*, which include furniture, glass, ceramics, gold, silver, ivories and tapestries, are grouped together as simulated interiors of the period 1890–1935. The walls are hung with paintings of the Berlin Secession, among which the luxuriant landscapes of Karl Hagenmeister are particularly delightful.

Back across the road, the **Abguss Sammlung Antiker Plastik** (Cast Collection of Antique Sculpture) occupies new premises at the rear of the Ägyptisches Museum, though it is actually one of Berlin's oldest collections, dating back to the time of the foundation of the Academy of Arts in 1696. The casts, all relentlessly white, reproduce the most famous sculptures of the Ancient World and were made for the benefit of students in the modelling classes.

Just east of here, on Gierkeplatz, is the original parish church of Charlottenburg, the **Luisenkirche** (Luise Church), built in the early 18th century by Martin Böhme in an unadorned baroque style. After being renamed in honour of Queen Luise, it was modified by Schinkel, who added the tower. To the north, almost directly across the Spree from the Belvedere, is the **Gustav-Adolf-Kirche** (Gustav Adolph Church), a seminal piece of modern religious architecture. Fashioned from reinforced concrete and steel, it was built between 1932 and 1934 by Otto Bartning, a member of the *Neue Sachlichkeit* (New Objectivity) movement which also included the painter Otto Dix. The needle-like tower makes the most of the corner site and serves as linchpin for the sharply angular segments of the centrally planned design.

WESTEND

Southwest of Schloss Charlottenburg is the quarter known as **Westend**. Its most prominent landmark is the 150-metre-high **Funkturm** (Radio Tower), built in the 1920s as a slender cut-price variant of the Eiffel Tower. At the base, the **Deutsches Rundfunk-Museum** (German Radio Museum) illustrates the history of broadcasting equipment, including a mock-up of the site's original studio. An elevator whisks visitors up to the restaurant, located at 55 metres, and to the observation platform, at 126 metres.

The Funkturm now stands in the grounds of the **Internationales Congress Centrum** (International Congress Centre), built in the 1970s as one of the most extensive complexes of its kind in the world with no fewer than 80 halls and a main auditorium that can seat 5,000 people. Important annual events are the Green Week in January, a massive agricultural, gardening and nutritional show, and the International Tourism Trade Fair in March; the equally comprehensive International Electronics Exhibition is held in August but only in odd-numbered years. Despite its very different function, the ICC has often been compared to the contemporary Centre Pompidou in Paris and there are certainly elements of similarity in the architectural language used, though the silvery aluminium plating employed throughout makes for a very different surface effect.

On Masurienstrasse, just east of the Funkturm, is the **Haus des Rundfunks** (Broadcasting House), built in the last years of the Weimar Republic by Hans Poelzig to a striking heart-shaped design. It is now linked to the futuristic **Fernsehzentrum SFB** (Television Centre) in front. The latter dominates the capacious square, which once bore the name of Adolf-Hitler-Platz and is now called Theodor-Heuss-Platz after the first federal president of West Germany.

OLYMPIA-STADION AND ENVIRONS

Towards the western end of Charlottenburg is Berlin's largest surviving Nazi monument, the **Olympia-Stadion** (Olympic Stadium), which was constructed by Werner March for the 1936 Olympiad to replace the much smaller stadium the architect's father had built for the aborted 1916 Games. The pillared stone exterior in the neo-classical style favoured by Hitler is a clever illusion. Reaching to a height of only 16.5 metres, it disguises the actual size of the reinforced concrete arena, which is sunk 12 metres below ground level, thus making for a thrilling first-sight impression. There is seating for some 90,000 spectators, about a third of them under cover in the grandstand areas.

The stadium forms the centrepiece of the **Reichsportfeld** (Imperial Sports Ground), which also includes separate stadia for swimming, hockey and equestrian events, as well as a multipurpose sports hall and additional facilities, several of which were taken over by the British army after the war. Dotted around are a number of larger-than-life Nazi sculptures intended as expressions of heroic values but which now seem embarrassingly vapid.

Most of the western part of the ground is taken up by the **Maifeld** (May Field), which provided a venue for the big set-piece Nazi parades that Berlin had been unable to stage prior to 1936 for want of suitable facilities. At the far end of this, though accessible to the public only from Possenheimstrasse to the rear, is the **Glockenturm** (Bell Tower), one of the best vantage points in Berlin with a bird's eye perspective of the Reichsportfeld, an extensive view over the nearby forests, and a skyline panorama of the distant city centre. The tower was blown up by the British after the war but was carefully reconstructed in the early 1960s from the old plans, though without the original Olympic Bell, which has been moved, in its shattered state, to the stadium's

THE NAZI OLYMPICS

No sporting event has ever made such a startling impact on the world as the Olympic Games of 1936, a carefully stage-managed propaganda exercise of awesome proportions which had numerous long-term ramifications—some tragic, some sinister, others unexpectedly beneficial. By integrating sport and politics, it created a bond between the two that has remained ever since. While the integrity of sport has suffered as a consequence, it is doubtful it would otherwise have attained the lofty role it now holds in modern popular culture.

Berlin had already been awarded the 1936 Games before the Nazis came to power. Although Hitler paid considerable lip-service to the notion of sporting activity as a symbol of health, a theme that the 18th- and 19th-century Prussian educational theorists had helped to elevate to the status of a cornerstone of military training, he himself was completely unathletic and had little interest in sport as a spectacle. As a xenophobe, the whole concept of the Olympic movement was anathema to him and he was mindful to issue a unilateral decree cancelling the Games he had inherited.

He was persuaded to take a totally contrary view, however, when, as a result of the pleas of the Propaganda Minister Josef Goebbels and the apolitical German Olympic Committee, he came to realize that he had been presented with a golden opportunity to present Nazi Germany to the rest of the world in the best possible light. His perverted artistic imagination was also stirred to the full: here was a chance to build on a grand scale, upstaging every other sports ground in the world, so bestowing on Berlin facilities commensurate with its intended future status as the world's premier city. Moreover, the Games made sound commercial sense: the huge influx of visitors would not only bring in enough hard currency to pay for all the prestige projects, which in turn would relieve the still serious unemployment problem, but would also lead to a large surplus. Thus, although the cost of building the main stadium rose during the construction period from an estimate of 28 million marks to 77 million marks, its spin-off was around seven times the latter figure.

For the duration of the Games, the most evil features of Nazism were suspended. The normally all-prevalent anti-Semitic signs, such as 'Jews not welcome here' or 'Jews enter at their own risk' were removed; the most notorious racist paper, *Die Stürmer*, was withdrawn from newsstands; and two athletes of Jewish blood were included in the German team. Persecution of Christian churches was eased up, with freedom of worship openly allowed. Thousands of political prisoners were released from concentration camps.

A carnival atmosphere was encouraged throughout the city. The police rounded up known petty criminals and were able to create the illusion of a peaceful,

Olympia-Stadion, the setting for the notorious Nazi Olympics of 1936

trouble-free environment. Nazi leaders hosted glittering society events which trumped the Hollywood glitz of the previous Olympiad at Los Angeles just as surely as the Berlin stadium upstaged its predecessor. Goebbels took over the Pfaueninsel to throw a party for 2,000 guests, for which he linked the island to the mainland by a temporary pontoon bridge and arranged for the fountains to flow with champagne. His great rival, Herman Göring, responded to this by installing a complete mock-18th century village in the garden of his villa to serve as the backdrop to his reception.

At the stadium itself, the spectacular opening ceremony was planned and executed with minute precision. For the first time, this featured the arrival of the flaming Olympic torch, which had been transported by a relay of athletes on its twelve-day journey from Greece. The Berlin Philharmonic was augmented by dozens of musicians to form a huge super-orchestra under the direction of Germany's most famous living composer, Richard Strauss, who wrote and performed an Olympic Hymn for the occasion. Mindful that pampered journalists were likely to produce flattering copy, members of the foreign press were allocated the best seats and given free access to a battery of telephones, typewriters and writing booths.

Hitler's favourite film director, Leni Riefenstahl, was commissioned to make a no-expenses-spared documentary of the Games as a sequel to her earlier *Triumph of the Will*, a eulogy to the annual Nuremberg Rallies. Drawing on the services of 43 cameramen, one of whom was based in a brand-new Zeppelin airship which floated high above the stadium, she effectively invented the art of sports cinematography: until then, films of sporting occasions had been one-dimensional views from the stand. The resultant *Olympia*, a two-part epic, each of three hours, utilized the entire gamut of possible camera angles, drawing on both the individual human drama, with telling close-up shots of the athletes, as well as the sweepingly grand pageantry of the occasion. Put together from 400,000 metres of original spool after 18 months in the editing room, the film is an object of controversy today, with many critics arguing that its visionary qualities heighten it to the status of artistic masterpiece, regardless of its propaganda connotations.

When it came to the competition itself, past experience and current form both suggested that the Germans would flounder against the might of the United States, and that Hitler would receive a sharp rebuttal of his belief that the supposed moral superiority of his regime over the decadent democracies would be mirrored in the results. However, on the very first day of the track and field programme, the mainstay of the Games, events went as if Hitler had written the script himself. German athletes won both the men's shot and the women's javelin, whereupon the victors received the personal congratulations of the Führer in full public view.

Hitler thereafter attended the Games as often as affairs of state permitted, and was delighted by the final medal tally, in which the Germans won 33 golds, 26 silvers and 30 bronzes—the highest in each category. The United States, with 24, 20 and 12 respectively, was the only nation to mount any kind of serious rivalry to this supremacy, and it seems undeniable that German athletes performed well above themselves as a result of the frenzied atmosphere of expectation that surrounded them. Moreover, it was noticeable that other authoritarian regimes, such as Hungary, Italy and Japan, achieved sizeable medal hauls. This lesson was not lost on future dictators, and the way was accordingly set for the scientific production of athletes in the postwar period by the Soviet Union (a non-participator in 1936) and

The Olympic Bell, now removed from its belfry and placed outside the Oympia-Stadion

its many satellites—most notably the GDR, heir to so many features of the Nazi tradition, which became an improbable third superpower in the Olympiads of the 1980s.

The one place where Hitler's intended script went badly awry was in the performance of the black American athletes, who were included in strength in the US team for the first time. There could be no doubt that the hero of the Games was James Cleveland (J C hence 'Jesse') Owens, who won gold medals in the 100 metres, 200 metres, broad (long) jump and 4 x 100 metres relay—a feat that has since been matched only once, and never surpassed. Owens also equalled or broke the Olympic record in each event, becoming a huge international celebrity in the process. His black teammates scooped the 400 metres, 800 metres and high jump, convincingly disproving the Nazi theory that blacks were 'subhuman'. From then on, their high profile in American sport, previously confined to boxing, was assured: changes in their general social status were also set in train as a consequence.

Curiously, Owens himself was unfazed by Hitler's racism; indeed, he went so far as to claim that American journalists 'showed bad taste in criticizing the man of the hour in Germany'. To be fair, the oft-quoted story that Hitler refused to shake Owens' hand is apocryphal: the truth of the matter is that, during the first day, he was told by the Olympic Committee that he had exceeded his benefactor's role of congratulating the medallists in public. Thereafter, his handshakes took place in private only, and were confined to German winners: thus Owens was no more snubbed than anyone else.

The brilliant stage-management of the Games duped not only Owens, but most foreign visitors, as to the true nature of the Third Reich, whose praises were sung by many influential people on their return home. Outwardly, Germany seemed to have come a long way since the Nazis had displaced the chaotic Weimar Republic, whose unstable governments had been unable to forestall economic collapse, to impose law and order, or to gain much international respect. In a few short years, it seemed that Germany had become a peaceful, prosperous and orderly society ready to resume its rightful place as a leading member of the international community. In reality, this was a gigantic con trick—albeit one that readily fooled the rest of the world.

southern entrance. Across the road from the Glockenturm, is the **Waldbühne** (Forest Theatre), also by Werner March, an amphitheatre built for Nazi spectaculars and now used for open-air classical music and rock concerts in the summer months.

Reichsportfeldstrasse leads south from the stadium to the gigantic **Corbusier-Hochhaus**, which, like the Hansa-Viertel, formed part of the International Building Exhibition of 1957. In common with its numerous counterparts in France, this represents a variant on Le Corbusier's theme of a unified community within a tower block structure, first put forward in his Ville Contemporaine plan of 1922. There are 557 apartments in all, many of them two-storey maisonettes with their own internal stairway, plus an independent generating plant, shopping mall and post office. While not entirely unattractive—Le Corbusier's characteristically precise articulation and liberal use of bright primary colours help to differentiate it from a standard issue block of flats—the entire underlying concept of the project is now irredeemably dated.

The **Georg-Kolbe-Museum** on nearby Sensburger Allee occupies the house-cum-studio of the eponymous sculptor, whose work is displayed in rotation in a changing series of displays, with a few of the more heroic pieces permanently on view in the garden. Kolbe was a fashionable portraitist but is best known for his large-scale nudes, which were influenced variously by Egyptian, West African and Gothic sculpture and are alternatively Expressionistic and naturalistic in style. The nudes gained the approval and patronage of the Nazis—which in turn has meant that the sculptor's posthumous reputation remains inevitably tarnished.

Spandau

Of all Berlin's suburbs, **Spandau** retains the strongest individual identity. Older than Berlin itself, it was granted its charter in 1232 and kept its status as a separate town until 1920 when it was forced to become an administrative district of the capital. The move met with fierce local opposition at the time, though it was in fact fortuitous, as Spandau would have been incorporated into the GDR after World War II had it lain outside Berlin. In general layout and appearance, Spandau resembles scores of medium-sized towns throughout western Germany, with a compact historic centre, carefully restored following extensive war damage and ringed by residential and industrial suburbs.

The Altstadt (old town) occupies an island location at the confluence of the Spree with the Havel. At its heart is the 15th-century **Nikolaikirche** (St Nicholas' Church), a typical example of the Gothic brick architecture of the Brandenburg region. Externally, it is dominated by its massive west tower; the interior is in the favourite German format of a hall-type church, with nave, aisles and chancel all of similar height.

Spandau, the old city

The rich furnishings include the elaborate limestone Renaissance high altar, which was donated in 1582 by the Italian-born Count Rochus Guerini zu Lynar. He is portrayed with his family on either side of the central scene of *The Last Supper*, above which is a blazing depiction of *The Last Judgment*. Other notable items are the late 14th-century bronze font, a 16th-century polychrome wooden crucifix, and a florid baroque pulpit originally made for the chapel of the Stadtschloss in Potsdam.

The **Rathaus** (Town Hall), That essential secular complement to the parish church, was built just outside the southern confines of the Altstadt in the years immediately preceding World War I. Its massive scale was a brazen but ultimately unsuccessful declaration of municipal independence; aesthetically it is undistinguished and notable only for the unusual solution of having a freestanding belfry placed in the courtyard, rather than in its more logical position atop the main block.

The rest of the Altstadt is something of a compromise between old and new, with a modern pedestrian shopping precinct coexisting with plenty of historic buildings. Remnants of the medieval **Stadtmauer** (City Wall) can be seen on Kinkelstrasse, while the **Gotisches Haus** (Gothic House) at Breite Strasse 32, which dates back to around 1500, is reckoned to be the oldest surviving secular structure in Berlin. The quiet northern tip of the island, separated from the rest by the busy boulevard of Am Juliusturm, encapsulates the most atmospheric street of all, known simply as **Kolk**. Near its eastern end is a balcony offering a fine view of the **Spandauer Schleuse** (Spandau Lock) through which all boats must pass in their journey from the upper to the lower stretches of the Havel.

A few minutes' walk further east is Spandau's main attraction, the **Zitadelle** (Citadel), again occupying an island site, though linked to the mainland by a short causeway. Of the original 12th-century castle of Albert the Bear nothing survives save the round **Juliusturm** (Julius Tower). Following damage in the Napoleonic Wars, this was restored and prettified by Schinkel, who added the crown-shaped mock battlements. The tower later gained national celebrity as the treasury containing the reparations payments extracted from France after the Franco-Prussian War of 1870–1. Alongside, the **Palas** (Palace), now the local history museum of Spandau, was built by the Hohenzollern family as their main residence soon after their appointment as hereditary margraves of Brandenburg in 1415. It lost this role in 1451, when they moved their base to the twin town of Berlin-Cölln, and instead became the home for widowed margravines. Embedded in the walls are a number of Jewish tombstones, which provide telling evidence of medieval pogroms.

Spandau

© The Guidebook Company

The distinctly Mediterranean appearance of the rest of the citadel is the result of a remodelling carried out in the second half of the 16th century for the Elector Joachim II by the Venetian military architect Francesco Chiaramella Gandino, and completed by Rochus Guerini zu Lynar, the donor of the Nikolaikirche altar. This replaced the old German system of rounded bastions with the new Italian format of high-walled, sharply pointed constructions set at each of the four corners. By allowing for perfect visibility in encountering besiegers, and by giving the defenders two layers of cover against attack, the bastions were widely believed to have rendered the fortress impregnable. The northwestern bastion, known as **Kronprinz** (Crown Prince), also served as a jail: its inmates included Benjamin Raule, admiral to the Great Elector, and the physical fitness guru Friedrich Ludwig Jahn, who was imprisoned for participating in the 1848 Revolution.

East of the Zitadelle is **Siemensstadt** (Siemens City), the satellite town of the giant Siemens electronics company, which was founded in Spandau in 1897. During the interwar period, some 60,000 people were employed at the factory; as many of these had to commute a considerable distance, it was decided to construct custombuilt homes alongside. Many of Germany's leading architects, including Hans Scharoun, Walter Gropius and Otto Bartning, were commissioned to provide the designs, but the end result, as the management doubtless intended, still bears the definite stamp of corporate uniformity. The company remains an important local employer to this day, though the headquarters have been moved to Munich and only 20,000 now work at the Spandau plant.

THE LONE PRISONER OF SPANDAU

The name of Spandau gained worldwide familiarity through the Allied military prison on Wilhelmstrasse. Although capable of accommodating some 600 inmates, it was given over to the seven senior Nazis who were found guilty but nonetheless spared the death sentence at the Nuremberg Trials. These were Rudolf Hess, former deputy Führer; Walter Funk, Minister of Economics and President of the Reichsbank; Erich Raeder, one-time head of the Navy; Albert Speer, Hitler's favourite architect and the Minister for Armaments; Baldur von Schirach, Gauleiter of Vienna and founder of the Hitler Youth movement; Konstantin von Neurath, first Nazi Foreign Minister, later head of the Reich Protectorate in Prague; and Karl Dönitz, commander-in-chief of the U-boats and, for the last days of the Third Reich, Hitler's successor as Führer. After the release of Speer and Schirach in 1966, the only prisoner was Hess, who remained incarcerated at enormous expense, guarded in turn by the Americans, British, French and Russians, the last of whom persistently vetoed moves to release him on humanitarian grounds. In 1987, when he was aged 93, his body was discovered hanging from a piece of lamp flex and a verdict of suicide was recorded. To prevent the prison developing into a neo-Nazi shrine, it was torn down soon after and replaced by a shopping centre for British soldiers and their families.

A host of colourful conspiracy theories surrounded Hess, one of the most fanatical yet also most mysterious of all the leading Nazis. He grew up in Egypt, the son of a German wholesale merchant, only coming to Germany at the age of 14. Twice wounded in World War I, he qualified as a pilot and enrolled as a student of economics at Munich University on the cessation of hostilities. He quickly fell in with right-wing elements, joining the fledgling Nazi Party in 1920 and becoming a close friend of Hitler. When the latter was imprisoned for the failed Beer Hall Putsch, Hess visited him faithfully to take down the dictation of his autobiography-cum-manifesto, *Mein Kampf*.

Thereafter, Hess always ranked among the most prominent Nazis, even if his official position as Hitler's second-in-command exaggerated his actual status. His fall from grace came as a result of his bizarre decision to make a solo flight to Scotland on the evening of 19 May 1941. Bailing out of his Messerschmidt just south of Glasgow, he landed safely by parachute, gave himself up and announced that he was on a special mission to see the the Duke of Hamilton, whom he had met at the 1936 Olympic Games in Berlin and whom he believed was a confidant of both Churchill and King George

VI. Hess explained to the duke that he had come to negotiate peace with Britain, so saving the latter from certain defeat: in return for allowing Germany a free hand in Europe, the British Empire would remain intact. Churchill was immediately informed of the unexpected guest but was unimpressed: 'Hess or no Hess, I'm going off to see the Marx brothers,' he retorted, and duly set off for the cinema. The deputy Führer was treated as a prisoner-of-war and his proposals dismissed out of hand; his flight was presented to the public as a manic private initiative that stood no chance of acceptance by either side. Hitler responded by stripping his old friend of all his offices, explaining to the German public that Hess had suffered from hallucinations as a result of his war wounds.

The first conspiracy theory concerning the Hess episode came from Stalin, who believed it was part of an Anglo-German plot, reasoning that the proposals would allow the Nazis the same freedom to attack the Soviet Union as he had granted them to attack the West two years earlier. In Britain, suspicions were inevitably cast on the role of the Duke of Hamilton, with many believing he was part of a group within the British establishment who were determined to make peace with the Nazis. A similar line was taken by Hess's son, Wolf Rüdiger Hess, whose book *My Father Rudolf Hess* portrayed its subject, completely implausibly, as a heroic figure bent on staving off the catastrophe of global warfare. An alternative theory suggested that there was no plausible reason why an eminent Nazi should have undertaken such a hazardous assignment, and that the man held as Hess was an impostor despatched by Hitler himself.

The recent release of classified British documents under the new policy of government openness seem, in any event, to put all the conspiracy theories to rest. It is probable that Hess's action was a simple miscalculation, the last desperate gamble of a man who had seen his power and influence wane as a result of the war, which had diminished his role as head of the Nazi Party organization in relation to colleagues such as Göring, Himmler and Goebbels, who were all directly involved in the conflict. Only by pulling off a spectacular diplomatic coup did he see a chance of re-establishing his position with the Führer he served so devotedly: he undoubtedly believed Hitler's pronouncements that an influential coterie in Britain wanted to make peace, a view that turned out to be no more than propaganda. The role of the Duke of Hamilton, it would now appear, was entirely innocent: his political clout had been represented to Hess in a wildly exaggerated form by his foreign affairs advisor, Albrecht Haushofer, who was later executed for his role in the July Bomb Plot of 1944.

The Northern Suburbs

The suburbs of former West Berlin are extremely heterogeneous in character, reflecting their diverse origins: some grew up as adjuncts to the city centre during the 19th-century boom; others were separate towns in their own right until the great municipal reform of 1920, and still do their utmost to preserve their identity; while several of the outer districts are groupings of old rural communities, usually interspersed with modern housing developments. With the exception of Zehlendorf, which is described in the next chapter, and Spandau, described inthe previous chapter, the suburbs are not generously endowed with obvious tourist attractions. Nonetheless, each has at least one or two sights that warrant a detour and others deserve more detailed exploration.

Reinickendorf

The administrative district of **Reinickendorf** is a federation of several disparate communities spread amongst large tracts of forest and open countryside. They include Reinickendorf itself, an old village centred on a 15th-century fieldstone church; the farming community of Lübars; densely-populated Wittenau, which incorporates the Märkisches Viertel, a 1960s estate for 50,000 people which is now recognized as West Berlin's worst planning disaster; and Frohnau, an earlier and far more successful example of a planned satellite town.

The only part of the district well known to outsiders is **Tegel**: indeed, this is where most visitors to Berlin arrive, as it is the location of the city's main airport, the **Flughafen Otto Lilienthal**, named in honour of the city's own aviation pioneer. First used by airships in 1900, it was only developed at the time of the Berlin Blockade to provide relief for Tempelhof, which was subsequently used for charter flights, later taking over all scheduled passenger services as well. A hexagonal-shaped terminal, opened in 1974, was specially designed to cope with the swift processing of arrivals, checking-in and customs, cutting the normally tedious waiting times for passengers to an absolute minimum. Throughout the years of a divided Berlin, it was easily capable of handling all the air traffic into West Berlin. Reunification, however, has led to such a vast increase in demand, above all for inter-German services, that it is almost certain that a new airport will be built further away from the city centre.

The original village, now known as **Alt-Tegel**, is situated well to the north of the airport, near the head of the isle-strewn Tegeler See, the largest of the lakes formed by the River Havel. Several companies run pleasure cruises from the **Seepromenade**.

A popular short excursion is the round trip along the length of the lake, then up the Havel to Heiligensee and back again. However, it is far more enticing to take a longer voyage down to Spandau, then along the length of the Grunewald to Wannsee and Potsdam.

Across the water from the jetty is the neobaroque **Villa Borsig**, built for the eponymous locomotive manufacturer, whose name has become synonymous with Tegel. Having outgrown its premises at Oranienburger Tor and Moabit, Borsig relocated at the end of last century to a new factory complex on Berliner Strasse, just south of Alt-Tegel. This is entered via a mock-medieval gateway, behind which stands Berlin's oldest high-rise building, the **Borsigturm** (Borsig Tower), built between 1922 and 24 by the Expressionist architect Eugen Schmohl to provide much-needed extra floor area. Ironically, modern production methods have relieved the pressure for space to such an extent that the tower has become redundant and is now let to another company.

At the edge of the forest to the north of Alt-Tegel stands **Schloss Tegel**, a manor house dating back to the mid-16th century which has been in the possession of the Humboldt family since 1765. In 1820, the great scholar and educational reformer Wilhelm von Humboldt asked his friend Schinkel to remodel the house according to the modern Romantic fashion. The architect preserved most of the original façade with its distinctive oriel windows, but designed a new garden front and added sturdy towers to the four corners of the building, each adorned with a relief by Christian Daniel Rauch based on those of the Tower of the Winds in Athens. Schinkel reserved his most audacious touches for the interior, and in particular the magnificent Doric entrance hall, in which Humboldt's collection of antique sculpture and casts were given full pride of place, instead of being tucked away in a side wing. When Humboldt's wife died in 1829, Schinkel was commissioned to construct a small mausoleum for the park outside; this bears a copy of a statue named *Hope* by the Danish neoclassical sculptor Bertel Thorwaldsen.

Wedding

At the southeast corner of Reinickendorf is the inner city suburb of **Wedding**. Long known as 'Red Wedding' because of its left-wing political culture, it was one of Berlin's earliest working-class districts, a character it retains to this day. It is almost entirely devoid of tourist sights, the only exceptions being two skilfully contrasted little churches by Schinkel. The **Nazarethkirche** (Nazareth Church) on Leopoldplatz, which evokes the Romanesque style of northern Italy, is the architect's only ecclesiastical design to survive in something like its original form, notwithstanding the fact that it is now divided into upper and lower storeys. Currently, it houses the Anti-Kriegs-Museum (Anti-War Museum), a longstanding Berlin institution, albeit an incongruous one in light of the city's history. The **Paulskirche** (St Paul's Church) at the junction of Badstrasse and Pankstrasse was the parish church of Gesundbrunnen, a one-time spa (the name literally means 'Health Springs') that was subsequently submerged into Wedding. Its exterior, in which pilasters replace the usual columns, is suggestive of a classical temple; the interior was a casualty of wartime bombs and has been rebuilt in an uncompromisingly modern manner.

Plötzensee

Berlin's most potent reminder of the Third Reich's murderous brutality is the **Gedenkstätte Plötzensee** (Plotzensee Memorial), situated at the extreme north-eastern edge of Charlottenburg. The former prison now serves as a young offenders' institution and within its grounds, entered from a discrete gateway on Huttigpfad, is a shady garden with an innocuous looking brick building that served as an execution chamber for some of Nazism's main political opponents. Suspended from the ceiling is a massive iron beam embedded with eight hooks on which prisoners were hanged, often simultaneously; there was also a guillotine but this has been removed. Some 2,500 people of various nationalities were murdered in the room, which is now permanently strewn with flowers in their memory. The most notorious killings were those following the abortive 1944 July Bomb Plot, when relatives and acquaintances of the conspirators were rounded up and sentenced to death, no matter how tenuous the evidence against them. Hitler ordered that they be strung up with piano wire so that the strangulation process was as slow as possible; he then had the proceedings filmed in order that he could wallow in their suffering over and over again. In the forecourt is an urn containing earth from all the main concentration camps—a salutary reminder that Plötzensee was just one small element in a state-run apparatus of mass murder that claimed millions of lives.

About twenty minutes' walk to the west is the **Kirche Maria Regina Martyrium** (Church of Mary, Queen of Martyrs), built in the early 1960s to serve as both permanent monument to all victims of the Nazi years and a Catholic parish church; it has subsequently become a convent for Carmelite nuns as well. The architect Hans Schädel, who had gained an international reputation for his avant-garde church designs in the diocese of Würzburg in northern Bavaria, was commissioned to create a suitably symbolic plan. He laid out a vast courtyard in front of the church, capable of accommodating 10,000 worshippers at open-air masses. In a deliberate evocation of a prison, the courtyard is enclosed by walls of sombre basalt slabs, the easternmost of which is lined with abstract sculptures of the Fourteen Stations of the Cross by Otto Herbert Hajek. Adorning the façade of the church is a gilded bronze representation of the *Woman of the Apocalypse* by Fritz König; the same sculptor also made the *Pietà* which forms the centrepiece of the lower church's memorial to the martyrs for freedom of faith and conscience. Alongside are tombstones of three prominent members of the Catholic resistance to Hitler, though only Erich Klausener, who was assassinated in 1934 on Göring's direct orders, is actually buried here. On the altar wall of the main upper church is a huge abstract mural by Georg Meistermann evoking the apocalyptic vision of the New Jerusalem.

Hotel Sorat, Tegel

A Little Tale of Insurance

A financier by the name of Kückelmann who had been on the verge of bankruptcy for years was eventually forced by the wolves baying at his heels to take a week off and try his damnedest to boost his sagging morale and come up with a money-making idea. By the end of the said week he had put the bar at the Adlon Hotel, the Bristol Bar and a number of other establishments behind him for ever, without having the slightest result to show for his efforts. He had stimulated the old brain with stiff American drinks here and soothed it with incomparable coffee there, he had whipped up his flagging vitality with all kinds of jazz, he had rushed to the Kabarett der Komiker, he had sought mental fecundation in every musical in town, and from morn to midnight twixt heaven and earth had come up with nothing that would yield the slightest profit unless you owned it before you started. He ended up in Aschinger's beer bar.

Here he had an obscure urge to tap vital springs among the common folk whose struggle for existence still took the form of actual work, to draw strength, so to speak, like Antaeus from contact with mother earth. After two exhausting hours of just sitting around, his eye lit on a beggar with a glass of beer at the next table, nothing else seemed worthy of note.

The look of this beggar was quite horrifying. Kückelmann, whose sensitivity to pictures of misery was particularly acute at that time, distinctly felt a shiver go through his bones. The man bore the mark of death. His thinness was absurd. He seemed to have been fed from childhood on no more than two water biscuits a day. Overcome by a heroic desire to confront utter poverty eyeball to eyeball, Kückelmann sat down in desperation at this fellow's table. From a safe distance behind his newspaper he examined this walking, beer-swilling skeleton with growing dismay, ordered pease pudding for him as if in a dream, and then, while the man's strength revived with surprising alacrity, engaged him in conversation. And what can one say? Kückelmann ended up taking the beggar Joseph Kleiderer to his hotel for the night.

The beggar had told him that he was in the best of health, though just a little starved; and between a greasy waiter and a silver cash-register Kückelmann saw a sudden vision in the air.

From now on he had his meals sent up to his room and shared them with Joseph Kleiderer, who, preserved for the world in all his filth, was completely restored at the end of three weeks and indeed presented an appearance of blooming health. People who had known the old Kleiderer now said they could not recognize him; that he was so fat you were bound to drink a schnaps to his health. Kückelmann wanted nothing from him in return for all this, only a chance to take him to an insurance office since his, Kleiderer's, life was so dear to him, Kückelmann, that he wanted it to be covered for all eventualities—and Kleiderer saw the point. So Kückelmann insured Kleiderer for 100,000 marks and paid the first premium with most of the ready cash he had left. On the way home he told Kleiderer he had to buy some cigars and disappeared into a tobacconist's from which he never re-emerged. Understandably deep in the dumps, Kleiderer went to the hotel, and there, and later at the beer bar, he waited in vain.

Thereafter Kleiderer waited often in the beer bar for his benefactor who had gone to ground, and now that he had no funds his physical decline was rapid. His robust bloom lasted a few days, then he lost weight, and before five weeks had passed he was once again the same walking, beer-swilling skeleton, sitting in the beer bar, when Kückelmann appeared behind a newspaper just as he had done the last time.

Kückelmann still showed a great interest in Kleiderer, immediately ordered him something to eat, and even asked him to go along to his bank with him—wherewith Kleiderer complied.

In his banker's office Kückelmann produced Kleiderer's insurance policy, introduced Kleiderer as his brother-in-law, and asked the banker to buy the policy from him, Kückelmann. Since he was momentarily in financial straits he couldn't pay the premiums, though it could be seen at a glance that Joseph Kleiderer would not live a week, being all skin and bones, and the sum for which he was insured, 100,000 marks, would then be paid to the policy holder.

Kückelmann, looking ostentatiously downcast, sighed as he put the banknotes into a morocco leather case, steered his 'dying' brother-in-law carefully out of the door, helped him into a hansom and invited him to dine at Lauer's. In the next few days they dined either at Lauer's or at Kempinski's or at the Bristol Bar.

Kückelmann took a childish delight in Kleiderer's second blooming, and among other things proved conclusively to him that listening to classical music over coffee and imported cigars leads one to put on weight.

At the end of two amply filled weeks Kleiderer, on whom Kückelmann could now afford to lavish more than on the first occasion, was fully restored, and one day Kückelmann went along with him to his banker.

The man was aghast. Later on Kückelmann assured his business friends that no one else would have recognised the 'skeleton' in the fat, smiling Joseph Kleiderer, but the banker took in the situation at a glance. He had the keen eye of a man who has laid out 40,000 marks.

Kückelmann said excitedly that his brother-in-law had pulled through better then anyone had expected, and that a remarkable vitality seemed to run in the family. As things now stood, he could of course not expect anybody to pay premiums for thirty or forty years—for a man's life is three score years and ten, or at best four score. He fully wished to do the decent thing and, at a reasonable price, would buy back the policy, whose value had been drastically reduced by such a happy turn of events. The price which he felt he could reasonably offer was 2500 marks. The banker totted up in his mind the legal costs he would face if he yielded to his urge to smash Kückelmann in the teeth, but decided to forget it, since his birthday only came around once a year. He accepted the 2500 marks for the insurance policy and contented himself with reviewing his estimate of his own fitness for this life.

Kückelmann put the insurance policy in his morocco leather brief case and walked through the glass door in front of Joseph Kleiderer, then tilted his Borsalino slightly forward and, before Joseph Kleiderer's eyes, vanished into a taxi as into a cloud.

Kleiderer, whose second bloom was therewith at an end, did not even look for him again. A sullen uneasines took possession of the simple soul, who failed to understand the surprising but seemingly lucrative behaviour of his quarterly benefactor. He declined speedily, and when Kückelmann quite predictably turned up, asked him to dinner again, took him to see a banker where he again sold the same insurance policy, stowed the money in his morocco leather brief case and proceeded yet again to eat with him, a mad rebellion rose within him. As he was hungry, he could not turn the food down, but he ate only enough to stave off the pangs. He ate, as it were, absently, even with a slight disgust. He listened to Kückelmann's praise of his improved appearance (for food is food and makes you fat) with a sidelong glance from beneath his eyebrows, and walked past mirrors quickly, averting his gaze. And one day when he was still far from fat he started, to Kückelmann's complete astonishment, making the rounds of newspaper offices looking for a job. He picked the profession of a newsvendor. The job was meagrely paid but it enabled him to climb countless stairs. However, before the exercise stopped him gaining weight, Kückelmann cunningly showed him the insurance policy in the course of a meal to which he allowed himself to be seduced, and Joseph Kleiderer with eyes betraying an ocean of slimy vengeful notions, watched Kückelmann, with a look of disappointment, make a mental estimate of his, Kleiderer's, girth and then take out his leather case again.

It was in those days that Kückelmann founded the celebrated Kückelmann Jam Factory. His ship had come in, and he had little time to concern himself with Kleiderer who naturally went into total decline. Still, he looked him up, though many months later, but only because it was his principle to finish any job he started. And when he found Kleiderer, who had now sunk totally into the morass, he was in for a surprise. The man whom he had repeatedly dragged out of that morass, whom he had clothed and fed, not to say stuffed—this man, who should have thanked him for the few moments in his poor and uneventful life in which his health and fortunes had bloomed— had the gall to respond to his friendly invitation to a meal for old time's sake with a negative and quite unprintable answer.

Bertolt Brecht, 'A Little Tale of Insurance',
Short Stories, 1923–1946

Chiefly a poet and a dramatist, Bertolt Brecht (1898–1956) also wrote a number of short stories. Two set in Berlin are Hook to the Chin *about boxing (one of Brecht's passions) and* A Little Tale of Insurance, *written in his archetypal anti-capitalist vein. Exiled by the Nazis in 1933, he returned to East Berlin in 1949.*

The Southern Suburbs

Wilmersdorf

Wilmersdorf, which lies immediately south of Charlottenburg (see page 190), was for centuries an insignificant village. Under the Second Reich, its population grew tenfold as it quickly took on the role of a residential satellite town of Berlin, before becoming an inner city suburb as part of the 1920 municipal reorganization.

Being primarily residential, the built-up part of Wilmersdorf is decidedly thin on sights. However, three contrasting places of worship, all dating from the interwar years, can be seen on or near Hohenzollerndamm, the diagonal boulevard cutting right through the heart of the district. The **Russische Kirche** (Russian Church), built in the traditional Orthodox style, is the main visual legacy of the short time when Berlin served as one of the main havens for those dispossessed by the Bolshevik Revolution of 1917. This period has a major literary monument in Vladimir Nabokov's novel *The Gift*, the last he wrote in his native tongue before switching to English. Oddly enough, the church was not built until 1937–38, by which time the Nazis were firmly ensconced and the local Russian population, which had at one time numbered over 100,000, was already in sharp decline. Although the community subsequently dwindled to 2,000, this little church has retained its status as the seat of a bishop whose diocese covers the whole of central Europe. On Briener Strasse, a block to the east, a different spritual world is evoked by the **Moschee** (Mosque) of the Pakistani Ahmadiyya sect, built in 1928 in imitation of the Indian Mogul style and featuring an onion dome and two minarets.

Further north is the Protestant **Kirche am Hohenzollernplatz** (Church on Hohenzollernplatz), a bravura Expressionist structure erected during the last years of the Weimar Republic by Fritz Höger, who had previously gained an international reputation for his startlingly unconventional office buildings in Hamburg and Hanover. Here, he successfully utilized a number of medieval features and techniques in a design that nonetheless manages to be both modern and original. The exterior, crafted of traditional north German brickwork, features a strikingly angular tower and a fortress-like façade which exploit the visual possibilities of the site to the full with their bold geometric rhythms. Concerts of sacred music are regularly held in the whitewashed interior, whose thirteen small bays offer a fantastical, dream-like reinterpretation of the Gothic style.

Another Expressionist masterpiece is the **Schaubühne am Lehniner Platz** (Show Theatre on Lehniner Platz), which stands on the Wilmersdorf stretch of the Ku'-damm. Built by Erich Mendelsohn in the late 1920s as the Universum Cinema, it fell

Russische Kirche, Wilmersdorf

The Southern Inner Suburbs

N

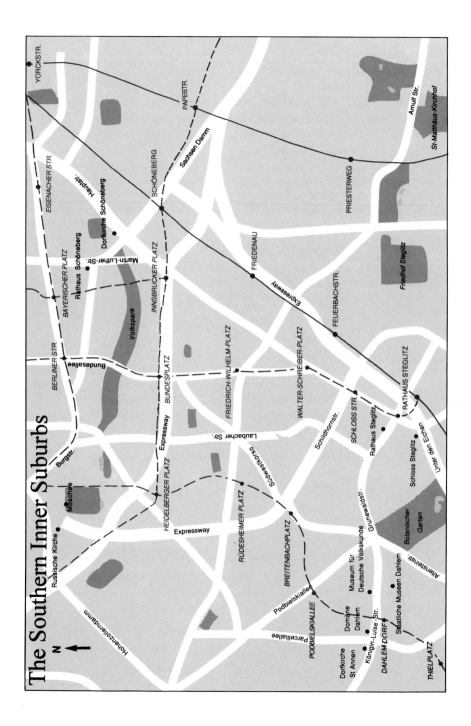

YORCKSTR.

PAPESTR.

Arnulf Str.

St-Matthäus-Kirchhof

Sachsen Damm

SCHÖNEBERG

EISENACHER STR.

Hauptstr.

Dorfkirche Schöneberg

PRIESTERWEG

Rathaus Schöneberg

Martin-Luther-Str.

BAYERISCHER PLATZ

INNSBRUCKER PLATZ

FRIEDENAU

Friedhof Steglitz

FEUERBACHSTR.

Expressway

Volkspark

BERLINER STR.

Bundesallee

FRIEDRICH-WILHELM-PLATZ

WALTER-SCHREIBER-PLATZ

RATHAUS STEGLITZ

BUNDESPLATZ

Expressway

Burgstr.

Laubacher Str.

Schildhornstr.

SCHLOSS STR.

Rathaus Steglitz

Moschee

HEIDELBERGER PLATZ

Südwestkorso

Schloss Steglitz

Unter den Eichen

Russische Kirche

RÜDESHEIMER PLATZ

Expressway

BREITENBACHPLATZ

Grunewaldstr.

Botanischer Garten

Altensteinstr.

Hohenzollerndamm

Podbielskiallee

Museum für Deutsche Volkskunde

PODBIELSKIALLEE

Parcelliallee

Domäne Dahlem

Staatliche Museen Dahlem

Dorfkirche St Annen

Königin-Luise-Str.

DAHLEM DORF

THIELPLATZ

into neglect and was threatened with demolition half a century later. It was saved by being adapted to form a permanent home for the brilliant avant-garde theatrical troupe directed by Peter Stein, which had provided a formidable rival to Berlin's state-run theatres from a variety of temporary homes. Although Mendelsohn's exterior was preserved, the interior was completely remodelled to create a new departure in theatre design—an auditorium capable of serving either as a single large space or three small stages.

Schöneberg

Schöneberg, the next district to the east, had a similar pattern of development to Wilmersdorf. Almost entirely residential and these days somewhat upmarket, it has little in the way of conventional sights but is rich in reminders of Berlin's most recent history with a number of notable Anglo-American connections.

The **Rathaus** (Town Hall), situated towards the southern end of Martin-Luther-Strasse, one of Schöneberg's main latitudinal axes, is a large and rather nondescript building from just before World War I. After World War II, it was promoted from its local role to headquarters of West Berlin's city administration and a copy of the Liberty Bell was donated by the American people to hang in its tower, which was left in a truncated state following bomb damage. On 26th June 1963, at the height of Cold War tension, it was the scene of one of the most famous political speeches of modern times, delivered by President John F Kennedy to a crowd of nearly half a million people gathered in the square outside. Kennedy concluded his peroration by declaring: 'All free men, wherever they may live, are citizens of Berlin, and therefore, as a free man, I take pride in the words: Ich bin ein Berliner'. The four words uttered in German quickly gained something of an aura, partly because of the lofty sentiments they espoused and partly because they constituted an example of the spectacular gaffes that have become something of a hallmark of American presidents. To translate his intended message 'I am a Berliner', Kennedy should have said 'Ich bin Berliner'; the addition of the 'ein' meant that he actually said 'I am a jam doughnut', this being the meaning of Berliner in bakeries throughout Germany. Although his error generated much mirth, Kennedy's sentiments won him a special place in the affections of Berliners and, when he was assassinated a few months later, the square outside Rathaus Schöneberg was immediately renamed John-F-Kennedy-Platz.

Right in the heart of Schöneberg is the **Kleistpark**, which is first documented as a kitchen garden in the early 16th century and later became the site of Berlin's first Botanical Gardens before being given the manicured appearance it has today. Facing Potsdamer Strasse on the west side of the park are the monumental **Königskolon-**

naden (King's Colonnades), which were erected near Alexanderplatz in the late 1770s by Carl von Gontard and moved here in 1910.

The colonnades were put to highly effective use as a frame for the vista across the park to the **Kammergericht** (Supreme Court), which was built shortly afterwards in orthodox neobaroque style by the specialist law court architects Paul Thoemer and Rudolf Mönnich. During the Third Reich the Kammergericht became the 'People's Court' of the notorious 'hanging judge' Roland Freisler. A number of senior soldiers and civil servants arrested in connection with the failed July Bomb Plot were tried there on 8th August 1944 and executed at Plötzensee immediately afterwards. The following February Freisler's form of instant justice received a neat poetic twist when he was the only fatality in an American air attack on the building. In 1945, the Kammergericht became the seat of the Allied Control Council, which was set up to deal with matters concerning the future of Germany but rendered impotent three years later as a result of the Soviet boycott. Nonetheless, the three Western powers continued to meet there to deal with access and security issues; it was also the place where the Quadrapartite Agreement, which guaranteed the special status of West Berlin, was signed in 1971.

Southeast of the Kleistpark is **St-Matthäus-Kirchhof** (St Matthew's Churchyard), which contains the graves of a number of prominent academics and artists. Among them are the Brothers Grimm, who ended their careers as professors at the Humboldt-Universität, and the composer Max Bruch, whose Violin Concerto remains one of the favourite warhorses of the virtuoso repertoire even though the rest of his output is almost completely forgotten. There is also a memorial tablet to Claus Shenk von Stauffenberg and his co-conspirators, whose remains were brought here after they were shot, only to be exhumed and burned a few days later.

On Pallasstrasse immediately north of Kleistpark stands the **Flakturm** (Flak Tower), one of a number of such structures built by the Nazis as protection against aerial attacks. Their much vaunted impregnability would appear justified by the fact that this tower owes its preservation to having withstood postwar demolition attempts. However, a fire in one of its counterparts apparently caused the loss of many of the city's art treasures in 1945, unless this was, as has sometimes been suspected, a cover for Soviet appropriation of these as spoils of war. Almost directly opposite is the site of the **Sportspalast** (Palace of Sport), scene of many of Hitler's most frenzied speeches and the place where Goebbels responded to the debacle of Stalingrad by declaring a policy of total warfare. The building was demolished in 1974 to make way for the huge block of flats which now straddles the road with the aid of a viaduct. At the western end of Pallasstrasse, the gaunt red brick **Matthäuskirche** (St Matthew's Church) fronts **Winterfeldtplatz**, the site of one of Berlin's best open-air food markets, held every Wednesday and Saturday morning. The area around is crammed with bars, cafés and restaurants patronized by the radical and bohemian chic.

Just to the north is **Nollendorfplatz**, dominated by the hefty bulk of the **Metropol**, which served successively as a theatre and a cinema before taking on its present role as one of the largest discotheques in Europe. During the Weimar Republic Nollendorfplatz was the hub of Berlin's large homosexual and lesbian community, who enjoyed freedoms unparalleled in Europe. These swiftly came to an end with the advent of the Third Reich, which made a brutal attempt to eradicate all intimate relationships between members of the same sex by outlawing the practice and deporting convicted offenders to concentration camps. The pink triangle on the square's U-Bahn station reproduces the symbol homosexuals were forced to wear and serves as a memorial to all those who were murdered in the camps.

Among the foreigners drawn to Berlin in the 1920s and early 1930s by the climate of homosexual liberty was the English novelist Christopher Isherwood, who lived in the tenement block at **Nollendorfstrasse 17** (see pages 309–315). That Isherwood's stories have been largely responsible for fixing Berlin's image in the Anglo-American consciousness is rather ironic: although they are heavily autobiographical, with only minimal fictional embroidering, they purge all references to the homosexuality that drew the writer to the city and underpinned most of his experiences there. Isherwood's spectacular success has spawned a stream of imitators anxious to capture the city's transition from division to reunification in the same way as he chronicled the shift from democracy to Nazism. They do not, however, live in Schöneberg, which has become too genteel and expensive, preferring neighbouring Kreuzberg or, better still, a rundown suburb of former East Berlin, such as Prenzlauer Berg.

The elevated section of the U-2 line from Nollendorfstrasse runs east to **Bülowstrasse U-Bahnhof**, a palatial *Jugendstil* station that was disused from 1961 to 1993 due to interception of services along this track as a result of the Berlin Wall. In the opposite direction, the railway descends to street level and below en route to **Wittenbergplatz U-Bahnhof**, built between 1911 and 1913 as the very first terminal of the underground railway, though neither its grand neoclassical architecture nor its prominent location in the middle of a square were ever repeated.

On Tauentzienstrasse, just across from the station, is the **Kaufhaus des Westens** (Department Store of the West). Universally known as the KaDeWe, this is Berlin's largest and most famous shop, the equivalent of Harrod's in London or Macy's in New York. First built between 1906 and 1907, it was taken over by Hermann Tietz of the Hertie chain in 1927; though almost totally destroyed by bombs in World War II, it managed to reopen in 1950. As something of a symbol for the consumerism championed by West Berlin, it was an obligatory place of pilgrimage for the East Germans who streamed into the city immediately after the fall of the Wall—not so much to buy, as to gaze transfixed at what had been denied them for so long. The food department on the sixth floor, with its whole carcasses of wild game, its tanks of live fish, its 1,700 cheeses and 800 different kinds of bread, is understandably the store's chief pride and joy.

On Kleiststrasse, on the opposite side of Wittenbergplatz, is the **Urania**, the headquarters of a large, privately run scientific and cultural institute. Housed within the complex is the **Postmuseum Berlin**, which was established as a Western answer to its counterpart in the Mitte district, with which it is now united. It has the benefit of far more modern display techniques to explain the history of the German postal service, but the exhibits themselves are far less interesting than those of its erstwhile rival.

Kreuzberg

Immediately east of Schöneberg lies **Kreuzberg**, the Berlin suburb which has gained the greatest international renown, thanks to its indelible association with the legendary alternative lifestyle of the bohemian intellectuals, draft dodgers, squatters and immigrant *Gastarbeiter* (guest workers), mostly Turks, who flocked to West Berlin during the Cold War. As a result of reunification, it has lost some of its reputation as a 'happening' place to emergent suburbs in former East Berlin but remains the most densely inhabited part of the city, despite a population figure that has fallen to well below half its prewar level. Kreuzberg is divided horizontally by the Landwehrkanal, whose course is paralleled to the north by a long elevated section of the U-2 line; inevitably nicknamed the 'Orient Express', this provides an excellent overview of the gaunt tenements which characterize the district. A more fundamental division is the vertical one between West and East Kreuzberg, known respectively as '61' and 'SO36' after their old postcodes. The former, which contains nearly all the worthwhile tourist sights, is becoming increasingly gentrified and yuppified; the latter is the Kreuzberg of popular imagination.

Kreuzberg only came into existence in 1920 as part of the major administrative reform that turned Greater Berlin into the largest city on the continent. It was formed from the union of three former suburbs: Südliche Friedrichstadt, Tempelhofer Vorstadt, which together comprise 61, and Luisenstadt, which became SO36. There was considerable debate as to what name the new district should take. At first the intention was to call it Hallesches Tor after the now vanished gateway whose existence is commemorated in a U-Bahn junction. Instead, it was named after its most prominent landmark, the hill at the extreme southeast corner of the quarter. This is now the central feature of **Viktoriapark**, one of the most pleasant areas of greenery in the built-up part of the city.

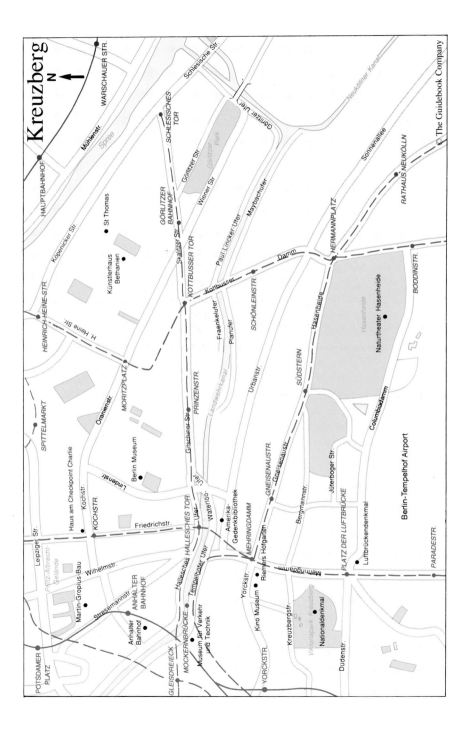

Kreuzberg

N

© The Guidebook Company

Formerly, the '**Kreuzberg**', as Viktoriapark is popularly called, was known as the Runder Weinberg (Round Vineyard): grapes were cultivated there until the mid-18th century, a practice that has recently revived, enabling it to stake a disputed claim to the title of Europe's most northerly vineyard. The present name, which literally means 'Hill of the Cross', comes from the **Befreiungsdenkmal** (Liberation Memorial) which crowns its summit. This huge cast iron spire, topped with the Iron Cross, the highest Prussian military honour, was constructed in 1821 and is the only part of Schinkel's ambitious scheme for a series of monuments in honour of Prussia's victory over Napoleon to get further than the drawing board. Its unambiguously neo-Gothic appearance, a reflection of the cherished belief of the German Romantic movement that the Gothic style was indigenous to Germany, seems very ironic now that it is known to have been a French invention. The twelve heroic statues adorning the monument were designed by Rauch and Tieck, among others; below them are plaques with the names of the decisive battles in the campaign, culminating in Belle Alliance, the alternative name for Waterloo. Immediately below the memorial, and forming a spectacular backdrop to it, is an artificial waterfall designed at the end of last century in imitation of the Zackelfall in the Riesengebirge.

Just to the north, straddling the junction of Yorckstrasse and Grossbeerenstrasse, is Kreuzberg's most exclusive tenement, **Riehmers Hofgarten**. This extravagant neo-Renaissance development, forming a compact mini-city laid out around landscaped courtyards, is named after Wilhelm Riehmer, who built it in the 1880s as an antidote to the soulless, dingy blocks then springing up all over the district. Also on Grossbeerenstrasse is the **Kinomuseum** (Cinema Museum), which screens silent and slapstick film classics and has exhibitions of old posters, programmes, cinematic equipment and photographs.

A block to the east is the axial boulevard of **Mehringdamm**, off which lie a series of interconnected cemeteries in which are buried a number of eminent Berlin personalities, including the writers E T A Hoffmann and Adalbert von Chamisso, the composer Felix Mendelssohn, the painter Adolf von Menzel and the historians Leopold von Ranke and Theodor Mommsen. A little further north, on Blucherplatz, is the **Amerika-Gedenkbibliothek** (American Memorial Library), Berlin's main public library, which was set up by a foundation in expression of gratitude for the role of the US in beating the Soviet blockade of 1948–49.

Westwards down Tempelhofufer, the **Museum für Verkehr und Technik** (Museum of Transport and Technology) has taken over the premises of the former **Anhalter Güterbahnhof** (Anhalt Station Goods Depot). It is a fast-growing collection, likely to expand into one of the largest technical museums in the world during the coming decade. In the meantime, the rail exhibits rightly have pride of place, with the station sheds forming an ideal setting for the display of original locomotives and rolling stock from 1835 to the present day. The entrance hall contains aeroplanes and motorized transport vehicles, only a selection of which can be shown at one time for reasons of space. Other departments illustrate water transport, scientific instruments, stereo photography, the textile industry, printing technology and paper manufacture, and regularly feature practical demonstrations of historic equipment. To the rear of the main complex is an open-air section with two fully functioning windmills and a smithy. The former railway administrative building at the far end is occupied by a department called Spectrum, which presents a series of hands-on displays enabling visitors to carry out their own basic scientific experiments.

On the opposite side of the Landwehrkanal is the site of the **Anhalter Bahnhof** (Anhalt Station), which was once the largest and most impressive passenger terminal in Berlin, catering for international services to southern Europe and the domestic links to Leipzig and Dresden. It was regularly used for the ceremonial arrivals of visiting heads of state. Built in the 1870s by Franz Schwechten, architect of the Kaiser-Wilhelm-Gedächtniskirche, it boasted a 62.5-metre-broad glass and steel roof that was widely regarded as one of the major engineering accomplishments of the day. Because the area behind it lay in GDR territory, the station was not restored after suffering extensive bomb damage during World War II. Despite much protest, it was demolished in 1961, leaving only a fragment of the façade as a memento, with the rest of the station grassed over as a park.

Facing it across Stresemannstrasse is the **Hebbel-Theater**, a *Jugendstil* gem by the specialist theatre architect Oskar Kaufmann. The dramatic gestures of the exterior form a striking contrast with the intimacy of the auditorium, one of the city's most prestigious theatrical venues. On the next block to the north is the **Deutschlandhalle** (German Hall), which is devoted to the 'lost territories'—those parts of the German Reich that were confiscated in 1945. From the point of view of West Germany and West Berlin, this was taken to include all the GDR as well as the lands east of the Oder-Neisse line allocated to Poland and the Soviet Union, and the displays still reflect this interpretation, with anomalous results. Nonetheless, there is a good deal of interesting archive material, particularly on such once-great German cities as Danzig (now Gdansk), Breslau (now Wroclaw) and Königsberg (now Kaliningrad), whose loss has been part of the price the nation has had to pay for its espousal of Nazism.

A little further up the street is the **Martin-Gropius-Bau** (Martin Gropius Building), named after its architect, the great-uncle of the founder of the Bauhaus (see page 170). Built between 1877 and 1881 to serve as the first home of the Kunstgewerbemuseum, its strikingly geometric design and rich terracotta decoration were both modelled on Schinkel's Bauakademie. The central *Lichterhalle*, the finest of its kind in the city, is regularly used for international art exhibitions. Three other institutions occupy the rest of the building. The **Berlinische Galerie** (Berlin Gallery) is

Façade paintings, Kreuzberg

devoted to 20th-century artists with a Berlin connection, including Otto Dix, George Grosz and the Jewish painter Felix Nussbaum. Among the works of the last-named are *Wonderful Pariser Platz*, which depicts the prewar appearance of the now desolate square beside the Brandenburger Tor, and *Concentration Camp*, a gloomy reminder that the artist himself was murdered at Auschwitz. In the gallery's sculpture section, the constructivist creations of George Rickey, an American based in Berlin since 1967, are displayed alongside those of his predecessors, Naum Gabo and Hans Uhlmann, while the photography collection is dominated by a large group of works by Heinrich Zille. Also in the building are the **Werkbund-Archiv**, which displays its holdings on the everyday designs of the 20th century in a series of changing exhibitions, and a part of the **Jüdisches Museum** (Jewish Museum), which it is hoped will relocate to its own custom-built home at a later date.

On the north side of the Martin-Gropius-Bau, a small section of the Berlin Wall has been preserved complete with its Death Strip. To the east, the desolate **Prinz-Albrecht-Gelände** (Prince Albert Estate) has an even more sinister history, as it was the very nerve centre of the Nazi's machinery of state-run terror. Housed in a series of buildings, whose presence is now marked only by explanatory boards, were the headquarters of Heinrich Himmler's SS and its various offshoots: the Gestapo (secret police), the Kripo (the criminal investigation division) and the SD (the security service). A chilling documentary exhibition on their activities, entitled **Topographie des Terrors** (Topography of Terror), has been installed in a pavilion built over the excavated cellars of a Gestapo building constructed by prisoners from Sachsenhausen, the nearest concentration camp to Berlin.

A few minutes' walk east along Kochstrasse is the junction with Friedrichstrasse, site of one of the most famous names of the Cold War era, the **Checkpoint Charlie** crossing point. With its dramatic sign proclaiming 'You are now leaving the American Sector' and its forbidding frontier installations of wire fences, guardtowers and no man's land, it became a standard setting for spy novels and films as well as the scene of many all-too-real border incidents. The control point was demolished in 1991, its place being taken by a small open-air museum comprising a section of the Wall, a replica of the famous sign, part of a watchtower, a tank trap and a number of avant-garde sculptures inspired by the site.

Just to the south is the **Haus am Checkpoint Charlie** (House at Checkpoint Charlie), which claims to be the most visited museum in Berlin but which, like so many other institutions spawned by the Cold War, is having difficulty redefining itself to take account of reunification. Its documentation, most of which looks distinctly dated, concentrates on the theme of non-violent resistance, linking the story of divided Berlin into a world perspective embracing Gandhi's India, the US Civil Rights movement and the Solidarity trade union in Poland. Far more interesting is

Six-year-old boy jumping from his house window over the Berlin Wall, 13th August 1961.
The child was caught unharmed in the jumping sheet but both his parents were seriously injured
though expressed no regrets. Four other would-be escapers died as a result of missing the sheet.

Museum Haus am Checkpoint Charlie,
Berlin's most visited museum

the specific material on the Berlin Wall, which is generously illustrated with archive photographs. Also on display are the originals of some of the often basic but ingenious inventions used in successful escape attempts, such as the car with adaptable back seat, the dummy motorbike tank and the pair of suitcases, all of which could conceal a human being.

Further along Kochstrasse is the **Springerhaus**, headquarters of the newspaper empire of Axel Springer. Built in the early 1960s, it was intended as an ideological and visual retort to the Berlin Wall and for several years it dominated the view from many parts of central East Berlin, before being shut off by the construction of high-rise flats along Leipziger Strasse. The building represented a firm commitment to West Berlin on behalf of Springer, one of the most controversial figures in modern German history. A man of deep morality and the very epitome of an enlightened employer, he nevertheless owed much of his commercial success to taking the gutter press to its most extreme, notably in the luridly sensationalist *Bild Zeitung*, Germany's most popular daily tabloid.

On Lindenstrasse, a few minutes' walk south, the stately baroque **Altes Kammergericht** (Old Supreme Court), which was built in the 1730s by Philipp Gerlach, looks somewhat incongruous in its modern surroundings. It is best known as the place where E T A Hoffmann earned the money that enabled him to be a writer of short stories in his spare time, having abandoned his earlier career as a full-time composer and theatre director (see pages 109 and 112). When the court moved to a new location in Schöneberg in 1913, the premises were taken over by the Consistory of the Evangelical Church, which in turn gave way to the **Berlin Museum**, the West Berlin rival to the Märkisches Museum.

On the ground floor, a series of maps, prints and models illustrates the city at various stages of its development, while the small Jewish department displays a roomful of liturgical treasures. The **Weissbierstübe**, a re-creation of an old Berlin tavern, must be the most imaginative museum restaurant anywhere in the world, and one which is deservedly popular for its salad buffet. Upstairs, the collection of 19th-century paintings of Berlin views is dominated by Eduard Gaertner's two-part *Panorama from the Friedrichswerdersche Kirche*, a fascinating variant of the hexagonal version in the Schinkel-Pavillon. Another room features the city as seen by 20th-century artists, with Max Beckmann, Ernst Ludwig Kirchner, Ludwig Meidner and Lyonel Feininger among those represented. Of the museum's many period interiors the most notable is that from the Charlottenburg villa of the Belgian artist and architect Henry van de Velde, featuring furniture he designed along with murals painted by Curt Herrmann, a leading light in the Berlin Secession movement.

A little to the south is the circular **Mehringplatz**, in the centre of which stands the **Viktoriasäule** (Victory Column), topped with a bronze statue by Rauch. This is a rare reminder of the prewar appearance of the plaza, which was redesigned as a major inner-city housing development in the early 1970s by Werner Düttmann to plans by Hans Scharoun. The format chosen is unusual, to say the least, with an inner ring of three-storey blocks of flats and an outer ring of five storeys.

East Kreuzberg is centred on the huge open space of **Mariannenplatz**, which was originally laid out by Lenné. Its western side is occupied by the Künstlerhaus Bethanien, an arts centre complete with studios, exhibition spaces, an archive and Berlin's only Turkish library; the building formerly a hospital, was designed by Ludwig Persius, a pupil of Schinkel. Another Schinkel protégé, Friedrich Adler, built the historicist Thomaskirche (St Thomas' Church) which closes off the north side of the square.

Nowadays, a substantial part of East Kreuzberg's population consists of Turks, who make up nearly half the total immigrant population of Berlin. The original settlers, mostly from poor villages in Anatolia, came in the early 1960s to do the menial jobs Germans were reluctant to undertake; they settled mainly in the part of the city where accommodation was most plentiful and rents lowest. The city has a higher population of Turks than anywhere outside Turkey, earning East Kreuzberg the nickname of 'Little Istanbul'. The community seems firmly entrenched, even though it is beset by problems: Turkish nationals still do not have proper citizenship rights in Germany; there is a gap in outlook between the older and younger generations, with the former still adhering strictly to traditional Muslim tenets, while the latter are increasingly adopting German values and outlooks; the issue of racial prejudice is on the increase, largely due to the unemployment that has resulted from German unification, leading to irrational claims that the Turks are depriving locals of work. The area around the Kottbusser Tor U-Bahn station encapsulates the flavour of the district; the best times to visit are Tuesday and Friday afternoons when the **Türkenmarkt** (Turkish Market), an array of foodstuffs and other goods specially imported from Turkey, is held along Maybachufer on the southern side of the Landwehrkanal.

Neukölln

Neukölln, the eastern of the two elongated suburbs stretching south from Kreuzberg to the city's extremity, is primarily residential. At its northwestern edge, however, is the **Hasenheide**, whose literal meaning, 'Hare Heath', is an indication of its original function as a place where the Brandenburg Electors hunted for small game. The educational theorist Friedrich Ludwig Jahn established Prussia's first public athletic field there in 1811, insisting that the army needed to improve its standards of physical fitness in order to reverse the series of defeats suffered at the hands of Napoleonic France. In recognition of the success of this policy, he is commemorated by a statue carved by Erdmann Encke, the sculptor who made the tombs to Kaiser Wilhelm I and his wife in the Charlottenburg Mausoleum.

The **Rixdorfer Höhe** (Rixdorf Height) in the middle of the heath is a fine vantage point: Rixdorf was the original name for Neukölln, which adopted its present designation (which means 'New Cölln') in 1912 in order that the name of Berlin's original twin town be permanently preserved on the map.

In the heart of Neukölln lies **Britz**, an old village that has, rather remarkably, managed to protect its rural identity and appearance, with an ensemble of church, manor house, estate buildings, communal pond and landscaped park that seems totally at odds with its position as part of a great metropolis.

The **Dorfkirche** (village church) dates back to the 13th century and is crafted mainly from fieldstone, a building material characteristic of the area. **Schloss Britz**, as the manor house is rather grandly called, preserves its early 18th-century kernel behind a showy exterior of the 1820s. Its elegantly furnished interior is occasionally open for guided tours and chamber music concerts.

On Fritz-Reuter-Allee, a short walk to the east, is the very different world of the **Hufeisensiedlung** (Horseshoe Settlement). Built in the mid-1920s by Bruno Taut, this development marked a sharp change in Berlin tenement design, away from the traditional method of high-rise structures clustered around dank courtyards to much lower blocks grouped in rows, which allowed for a far greater penetration of air and light.

Whereas Taut's solution has generally been deemed a success, controversy has always surrounded the **Gropiusstadt** (Gropius City) to the south. This gigantic project of the 1960s, now home to over 50,000 people, is the fulfilment of the planning ideals of Bauhaus founder Walter Gropius (see page 170), who was responsible for the overall layout, though most of the buildings were designed and executed by other architects. The areas of greenery separating the housing blocks are indicative of the thought given to creating a pleasant environment, while the provision of a large shopping centre, schools and churches are indicative of the attempt to foster a sense of community. Unfortunately, as so often is the case, the practice has not lived up to the theory, with the result that this satellite city suffers from all the usual modern urban social problems.

Tempelhof

Adjoining Neukolln to the west is **Tempelhof**, whose name indicates its 13th-century origins as a foundation of the Order of Knights Templars. Within the administrative district are four Romanesque churches, simple rough-hewn granite structures built by the Knights. These are in **Alt-Tempelhof**, the village from which the district takes its name, **Alt-Mariendorf**, **Alt-Lichtenrade** and **Alt-Marienfelde**. The last of these, set on a green and surrounded by rustic farm buildings, dates back to around 1220 and is thus probably the oldest extant building within Berlin's current city boundaries.

However, the name of the district is far less associated with churches than with the **Flughafen Tempelhof** (Tempelhof Airport) at its northwestern edge. Formerly a military parade ground, its aviation connection began in 1909 when Orville and Wilbur Wright used it to demonstrate their motorized aircraft. In 1923, it was the scene of the birth of German commerical aviation, when the rival companies Aero Lloyd and Junkers began operations, merging three years later to form Deutsche Lufthansa, which remains Germany's national airline today. During the Third Reich, a vast new airport complex was planned in line with the key role that air transport played in Nazi ideology, but this was never completed and suffered severe damage in Allied bomb raids. The fact that Tempelhof fell within the American sector in the postwar division of Berlin was of crucial importance to the history of the city, as it was only through airlifts that the Western powers were able to beat the Soviet Blockade of 1948–49, which aimed at starving West Berlin into submission. Thereafter, Tempelhof fell into decline: its inner city location meant that it had insufficient room to expand to meet the growing demand for air travel; passenger services were gradually transferred to Tegel, while it was used primarily for US military purposes. Since reunification, however, it has made a modest comeback with the reintroduction of a fair number of domestic German services, plus a few international ones.

On Platz der Luftbrücke outside the airport is the **Luftbrückendenkmal** (Air Lift Monument), dedicated to the airmen and ground staff who died during the relief of the Blockade. Shaped like a half-bridge with three arcs projecting westwards, it has earned the nickname of the 'hunger claw'. In reality, the arcs symbolize the only three air corridors the Allies were able to use—to Hamburg, Hanover and Frankfurt. The other half of the bridge is located outside the airport of the last-named.

Steglitz

Steglitz, the next suburb to the west, is altogether more upmarket than Neukölln and Tempelhof but is likewise thin on tourist sights. One of the few historic buildings is

Flughafen Tempelhof, the setting for the Allied airlift which beat the Berlin Blockade of 1948–9

Schloss Steglitz, a neoclassical manor house designed by David Gilly and Heinrich Gentz, known as the Wrangelschlösschen in honour of Field Marshal von Wrangel, who often stayed there. Alongside stands the **Schlosspark Theater**, an intimate little auditorium by Gentz, still in regular use as an outpost of the Schiller Theater.

A few minutes' walk to the southwest is Steglitz's one major attraction, the **Bota-nischer Garten** (Botanical Garden). Its relocation from Kleistpark was a direct result of Germany's belated acquisition of African colonies at the end of last century: this meant that research into tropical crops had to be undertaken and therefore more space was needed to construct hothouses. While their function soon changed to an academic one as a result of the premature end of German colonialism in 1918, they remain one of the prominent features of the garden, displaying some of the most spectacular plants on view, such as palm trees, giant bamboos, cacti, orchids and giant water lilies. Out of doors, the main part of the garden is laid out geographically, with flowering species drawn from all over the world; although attractive at any time of the year, it is best seen in spring. In addition, there is an arboretum, grouped sys-tematically by genus, and a special section for the blind with plants that can be iden-tified by touch and smell. By the Königin-Luise-Strasse entrance is the **Botanisches Museum** (Botanical Museum), which contains a herbarium of over two million speci-mens, plus a number of curiosities, including plants discovered in Ancient Egyptian tombs.

Zehlendorf

Immediately before the municipal boundary with Potsdam at the southwestern extremity of Berlin is the leafy suburb of **Zehlendorf**, the richest and most exclusive district of the German capital and location of most of the spacious luxury villas of the city's élite. Little more than a quarter of its total area is built up; the rest consists of forests (including the southern half of the Grunewald, see page 264), parks and lakes. In terms of attractions, it far surpasses all of Berlin's other outer districts and contains enough to warrant several days' sightseeing.

DAHLEM

The best known part of Zehlendorf is **Dahlem** at its northeastern end, which still retains much of its village appearance and atmosphere, though since 1948 it has combined this with the role of Berlin's main academic quarter. As the prewar setting for several research organizations of the Max-Planck-Institut, it became the obvious base for the Freie Universität, which was set up in response to the compulsory Marxist dogma taught at the Humboldt-Universität in East Berlin.

Dahlem is also renowned for its part in the resistance to Nazism: in 1933, a local clergyman, Martin Niemoller, in collaboration with the theologian Dietrich Bonhoeffer, founded the Pastors' Emergency Association in protest against the creation of Hitler's bogus Reich Church, which most Protestants were hounded into joining. A year later it became the Confessing Church, which adhered rigorously to the ideals of Luther.

Dahlem's two churches, plus the Pfarrhaus (Vicarage) at Parcelliallee 1–3 and the Gemeindehaus (Congregational House) at Thielallee 61 became centres of open opposition to the regime, resulting in Niemoller's arrest in 1937 and subsequent incarceration in the concentration camps of Sachsenhausen and Dachau. He survived to become a leading international churchman and pacifist after the war, though Bonhoeffer was not so fortunate—arrested in 1943, he was murdered in Flossenbürg concentration camp two years later.

From a tourist's point of view, Dahlem's main attraction is the **Staatliche Museen** (State Museum), which has entrances on Arnimallee and Lansstrasse. One of the great museums of the world, it is also one of the most improbable: the majority of its contents were formerly housed on Museumsinsel, but happened to be stored during the war in territory liberated by the British or Americans, who refused repeated requests to return the objects to their former homes. Instead they were put on 'temporary' display in Dahlem in a building conceived in 1914 as a museum of Asian art, but which was instead used as a store for the ethnographical collections. Even before the fall of the Wall, there were plans to transfer some of the seven separate museums in the Dahlem building to purpose-built premises in the Tiergarten Kulturforum; the opportunity to reunite the collections artificially divided by the Cold War has necessitated a more radical rethink.

In the near future, Dahlem will lose the **Gemäldegalerie** (Picture Gallery), which is due to move to the new Museum der europäischen Kunst. One of the most comprehensive arrays of old master paintings in existence, it has been primarily responsible for bringing many foreign visitors to the suburb. Its displays start on the ground floor with the Italian School. Pick of the early works are Giotto's *Dormition of the Virgin*, his largest surviving panel painting, and, in contrast, the tiny *Lamentation over the Dead Christ* by Simone Martini. The Florentine Renaissance is introduced by a number of small works by Massacio, including five panels from a dismembered altarpiece and a painted disc, *The Confinement Room of a Florentine Lady*, which served as a congratulatory gift to a mother who had just given birth. His contemporary Fra Angelico is represented by a triptych of *The Last Judgment,* a glorious Dantesque vision. From the next generation of Florentine painters come the sumptuous tondo of *The Adoration of the Magi*, one of the rare surviving works of Domenico Veneziano; the brashly modelled *Assumption of the Virgin* by Andrea del Castagno; and the mystical *Virgin Adoring the Child in the Forest* by Fra Filippo Lippi. Antonio del Pollaiuolo's *A Young Woman in Profile* is a consummate example of Early Renaissance portraiture, while his brother Piero's *The Annunciation* is a virtuoso exercise in one-point perspective. Botticelli is represented by a string of masterpieces, of which the finest is the large altarpiece of *The Madonna and Child Enthroned with the Two St Johns*. A trio of works by Mantegna, dominated by the strikingly linear *Presentation in the Temple*, makes a satisfying contrast with the altogether softer compositions of his brother-in-law Giovanni Bellini, whose art is shown at its best in *The Resurrection*. By Raphael are no fewer than five variants of his favourite *Madonna and Child* theme, all painted within six years of each other. Highlights of the Venetian High Renaissance section are Giorgione's *Portrait of a Young Man*, Titian's *Venus and the Organist* and Tintoretto's *Madonna and Child Adored by St Mark and St Luke*. Correggio's *Leda and the Swan,* one of the most sensual creations of the Renaissance period, brings the Italian section to a fitting conclusion; its survival is something of a miracle, as it was slashed to pieces by a French religious fanatic and had to be painstakingly restored.

The earliest works of the German school, which occupy the next suite of rooms, are by anonymous 14th-century masters from the main artistic centres of the time—Cologne, Westphalia and Bohemia. In the early 15th century, recognizable artistic personalities appear. Among the first was Conrad Witz, a Swabian who worked mainly in Switzerland; his panels of *The Queen of Sheba before Solomon* and *The Resolution of Redemption* both come from a large altarpiece made for a church in Basel. His contemporary, the Ulm sculptor Hans Multscher, ran a large workshop which produced the huge *Wurzach Altar,* whose violent expressiveness, harsh colouring and exaggerated gestures were to become hallmarks of German painting. The nation's most brilliant artistic period occurred in the late 15th century and early 16th century, the father figure being Martin Schongauer, best known as an engraver but represented here by one of his rare panels, *The Nativity.* There are eight examples of Albrecht Dürer, Germany's most famous artist. Italian Renaissance influence is clearly apparent in *The Virgin and Child with the Siskin* and *Frederick the Wise of Saxony,* a portrait of the powerful prince whose decision to back the rebellious monk Martin Luther against the might of the Empire and the Papacy made the Reformation possible; a more personal idiom characterizes the two late portraits, *Hieronymus Holzschuher* and *Jacob Muffel,* both of whom became mayor of the artist's home city of Nuremberg. Sharing a room with Dürer is his contemporary Albrecht Altdorfer, whose love of lush landscapes and exotic buildings—he was the municipal architect of Regensburg—are combined in such works as *The Nativity, The Rest on the Flight into Egypt* and the mercurial *Allegory of Beggary sitting on the Train of Pride.* Dürer's pupil Hans Baldung, one of art history's great eccentrics, is represented by several of his best works, with the rarely depicted mythological scene *Pyramus and Thisbe* showing his talent for simple, sharply outlined effects, while the *Altarpiece of the Three Magi* is in his most extravagant style. An entire room is devoted to Lucas Cranach the Elder, court painter to Frederick the Wise. *The Rest on the Flight into Egypt,* set in a verdant Danube landscape, is his earliest known composition but clearly the work of an accomplished master. His prodigiously original talents, however, are best illustrated by his hilarious late masterpiece *The Fountain of Youth,* which shows haggard old crones being borne to a spring where they are magically transmogrified into gorgeous maidens, while their male companions undergo the same rejuvenation by associ-ation. There are five portraits by Hans Holbein the Younger, last of the brilliant family of German painters. Of these, *The Danzig Merchant Georg Gisze* shows the dazzling bravura of the artist's early style, in which the still life component, incorporating all the attributes of the sitter's occupation, assumes an importance comparable with that of the depiction of the man himself.

In the side wing of the ground floor are the holdings of the early Netherlands School, in which the gallery is especially rich; alongside are a few rare 15th-century French panels, including two outstanding masterpieces in Jehan Fouquet's *Etienne Chevalier with St Stephen* and Simon Marmion's *St Omer Retable.* Jan van Eyck's tiny panel of *The Madonna and Child in Church* has long been one of the most copied and admired of all Flemish paintings, as much for the intense spirituality it exudes as for its miraculous technical precision. By the same artist are two outstanding portraits— *Giovanni Arnolfini* (whose wedding Van Eyck depicted in the celebrated painting in

London's National Gallery) and *Baudouin de Lannoy*. Rogier van der Weyden is represented by a superb ensemble of works, including two triptychs: the *Miraflores Altar*, dedicated to the Virgin and one of his most important early commissions, and the *Bladelin Altar*, dedicated to the mysteries of Christ's Incarnation, a masterpiece of his middle period. *The Raising of Lazarus* is the only extant painting by Aelbert van Ouwater, an influential artist in his day. One of his pupils was Geertgen tot Sint Jans, represented by a contemplative depiction of *St John the Baptist in the Wilderness*.

Among the gallery's most prized possessions are two of the few surviving altarpieces by Hugo van der Goes, who paid due respect to the traditional qualities of Flemish painting while giving it a monumental sense it had previously lacked. The two works are very different in approach: *The Adoration of the Magi* shows a detached sense of realism characteristic of his mature style, while *The Adoration of the Shepherds*, painted at the end of his life when he was suffering from mental instability, displays an exalted sense of religious fervour, especially in the dramatic and original technique of two Old Testament prophets drawing back a curtain to reveal the scene. *St John the Evangelist on Patmos* is a typically unorthodox interpretation by Hieronymous Bosch, with the bonus of a monochrome reverse side featuring scenes of Christ's Passion arranged in a mysterious circular shape. Of the 16th-century paintings, pride of place goes to Pieter Bruegel the Elder's *Netherlandish Proverbs*, which mercilessly lampoons the diverse follies of mankind in its depiction of over a hundred different maxims in the setting of a contemporary village.

Upstairs, most of the display area is given over to 17th-century Flemish and Dutch paintings. There is a good cross section of work by Rubens, ranging from the intimate charm of *Child with a Bird,* a portrait of the artist's nephew, to the exotic evocation of classical mythology in *Perseus and Andromeda.* Van Dyck is represented by several majestic full-length portraits of the Genoese nobility, all executed with the brash self-confidence of a youthful genius. There are two exquisite Vermeers, *The Glass of Wine* and *Lady with a Pearl Necklace*, and several notable portraits by Hals, among them the satirical *Malle Babbe*. Until a few years ago, the gallery boasted 25 paintings by Rembrandt, the largest collection anywhere in the world. In light of recent research, a number of these have been reattributed, including the most famous of the lot, the enigmatic *Man with the Golden Helmet*, which is probably an allegorical representation of Mars, the god of war. As its thick impasto technique was uncharacteristic of Rembrandt, it had long puzzled scholars, though the accusation that it was a forgery has now been superceded by the theory that it was painted by one of the many talented but obscure pupils who successfully imitated the master's style. The works definitely by Rembrandt himself range from the very early *Parable of the Rich Man*, via the luxuriantly baroque *Rape of Prosperine*, to such visionary late masterpieces as *Jacob Wrestling with the Angel* and *Moses Destroying the Tables of the Law*.

Finest of all is the middle-period *The Mennonite Preacher Anslo and his Wife*, a peerless example of the inherently problematic art of the double portrait.

Other 17th-century paintings occupy part of the first floor side wing: from Spain there are examples of El Greco, Velásquez, Murillo and Zurbarán; from France, Georges de La Tour, Poussin and Claude; from Italy, Caravaggio, Carracci and Guercino. The only two German artists of this period of comparable stature are represented by one work each—Adam Elsheimer's *The Holy Family with Angels* and Johann Liss's *The Ecstasy of St Paul*. In the following rooms are 18th-century Italian paintings, in which canvases by Tiepolo and Canaletto dominate. Back on the ground floor, at the end of the German section, are the rest of the 18th-century holdings, including three Watteaus formerly in the collection of Frederick the Great and an unexpectedly fair representation of British portraits by Gainsborough, Reynolds, Lawrence and Raeburn, among others.

The **Skulpturensammlung** (Sculpture Collection), housed on both floors around the central courtyard, is due to join the Gemäldegalerie in the Museum der europäischen Kunst. It is far less comprehensive than its neighbour, as it is almost entirely devoted to Italian and German works. One of the earliest examples of the former is a polychrome *Madonna and Child* especially notable for its invaluable documentation: it is signed by one Presbyter Martinus and dated 1199. Among the Renaissance pieces those by Donatello stand out, in particular the relief known as the *Pazzi Madonna*. Also of note is *Flora*, one of the rare carvings associated with Leonardo da Vinci, about whose sculptural activity little is known: the style is unmistakably his, though it is unlikely that he had any part in its execution. The collection's main strength, however, is the group of masterpieces from the golden period of German sculpture in the late 15th and early 16th centuries. Particularly worth seeking out are Nicolaus Gerhaert's *Dangolheimer Madonna*, Michel Erhart's *Madonna of Mercy*, Hans Leineberger's *Man of Sorrows*, and a glorious group of woodcarvings by Tilman Riemenschneider, including a relief of *Christ Appearing to Mary Magdalene*.

Recently, the **Museum für Spätantike und Byzantinische Kunst** (Museum of Late Antique and Byzantine Art) was detached from the Skulpturensammlung with a view to its future linkup with its much larger counterpart in the Bodemuseum. One of the most important pieces in this small but exquisite collection is a symbolic stone monument, made in Constantinople in around AD 400, showing the vacant throne of Christ surmounted by the heavenly coat and diadem. Other highlights are a 5th-century wooden relief from Egypt depicting a town under siege; a 6th-century ivory diptych of Christ and the Virgin; a 10th-century ivory plaque of *The Entry into Jerusalem*; and a 12th-century mosaic icon, *Christ of Mercy*.

Of Dahlem's three Asian collections by far the most significant is the **Museum für Indische Kunst** (Museum of Indian Art). Its name is something of a misnomer, as only the first two rooms are devoted to the subcontinent. Beginning with the Mohenjo-Daro culture of the second millennium BC, the exhibits range over the entire gamut of Indian civilization, featuring sculptures of Hindu, Jainist and Buddhist deities; handicraft objects in wood, ivory and jade; and a selection of illuminated manuscript miniatures. The following rooms contain objects from Nepal, Tibet, Burma, Thailand, Cambodia, Indonesia and Afghanistan. Finally, there are the mu-seum's most valuable possessions, a large group of Buddhist cave paintings from the famous Silk Road in China's present day Xinjiang Autonomous Region. Dating from the 5th to the 11th century, they were excavated by German archaeologists in several expeditions just before World War I, and are now superbly displayed with the aid of spotlights.

The emphasis of the **Museum für Islamische Kunst** (Museum of Islamic Art) is on the decorative arts of calligraphy and book illumination, carpet-making, ceramics, glassware, metalwork, woodcarving and jewellery. In due course, these will be moved to the Pergamonmuseum, where they will form a perfect complement to the predominantly architecture-based exhibits already there. The **Museum für Ostasiatische Kunst** (Museum of East Asian Art), on the other hand, has already been reunited, with Dahlem as its permanent home. It has a beautiful array of Chinese handscrolls and Japanese coloured woodcuts and screens, though for conservation reasons it is only possible to display these in rotation, for periods of three months at a time.

Once the Gemäldegalerie and the Skulpturensammlung are transferred to the Tiergarten, the **Museum für Völkerkunde** (Museum of Ethnography) will really come into its own. For the time being only the two most prestigious of its nine departments are displayed in anything like their entirety, with the rest of the space taken up by sections from three of the others. Highlights of the Ancient America collection are eight carved 5th–9th century stone steles from Cozumalhuapa in Guatemala, a group of 15th-century Aztec stone sculptures, and hordes of Inca gold and jewellery. The Oceania displays include a number of sailing craft (some original, others reconstructions), a complete clubhouse building from Palau, several totem poles and a vast array of masks, weapons, tools and cult objects. From the other departments, Africa is represented by bronzes from Benin and woodcarvings from Cameroon; South Asia by items from shadow-puppet and marionette theatres; and East Asia by artefacts of Mongolian nomads and religious objects from China.

About five minutes' walk from the Staatliche Museen, on the opposite side of Königin-Luise-Strasse, is the **Museum für Volkskunde** (Museum of Folklore), which extends the ethnological theme to Germany itself, displaying everyday objects drawn from all over the country. The most interesting sections are on costume, including the outrageous headgear worn at popular fesivals in the Black Forest region, toys and games, particularly dolls' houses and playing cards, and baking, notably the moulds used to make fancy designs. Furniture, jewellery, agriculture and a host of other trades and crafts are also featured. Formerly, the museum building was an annexe of Prussia's **Geheimes Staatarchiv** (Secret State Archive), whose files are now freely accessible to the general public.

Back on Königin-Luise-Strasse is the **Dahlem-Dorf U-Bahnhof**, one of the most ingenious stations in the city, designed in the shape of a thatched-roof barn in order to dovetail with the rural character of the area. The railway line has been placed with exceptional discretion: although not actually in an underground tunnel, it runs below street level, causing a minimal amount of visual and aural disturbance. Further down the street is the **Domäne Dahlem** (Dahlem Domain), a working farm and handicrafts centre in which a variety of traditional agricultural skills are demonstrated. Beyond is the village green, complete with a historic inn, the Alter Krug. At the far end, set in its own quiet close with graveyard, is the **Annenkirche** (St Anne's Church), which dates back to the 13th century, though it has been much altered in the interim, as is evident from the brickwork and half-timbering that have replaced most of the original fieldstone construction.

The Baptism of a Jewish Heiress

Sarah was seeing Julius that afternoon, and they had a talk which drove her to dine at Voss Strasse.

'It might be advisable not to broach anything until afterwards, ma'am,' Gottlieb said to her in the hall.

Sarah ignored him, but not his warning. Edu had left for London; Jules had felt entitled to excuse himself that night; she sat almost silent through the cream of chicken, the crayfish in aspic, the vol-au-vent, the calf's tongue and currants in Madeira, the chartreuse of pigeon, and the mousseline of artichokes, and it was only after the Nesselrode pudding and Mélanie sent upstairs that she disclosed that Jules Felden appeared to think it necessary for his wife to share his religion.

'He wants her to get baptized.'

'The young man with the monkeys wants our daughter baptized.'

'Who does he think we are?'

'Even Max never suggested anything of the kind!'

'I told you he was a Goy in disguise.'

'The poor child.'

'Please, Emil—'said Sarah.

'Well,' he said, 'of all the cold-blooded, ungentlemanly suggestions—'

Sarah, deciding to let it blow over, had gone home. Next morning she saw Julius again, then Friedrich, then the old man. She had asides with Markwald. The Merzes were glad to vent their feelings but refused to discuss the subject, and during the week that followed nobody budged an inch.

'It's like fighting feather-beds,' Sarah said to Jeanne. 'And it shows how wrong one can be. The old lady and Jules. I never expected any trouble from those two; they're the worst. Jules finds it odd that Mélanie wasn't christened, it alarms him. Just says he couldn't marry someone who wasn't a Catholic—it wasn't done—nobody did. Over and over again. Just sticks to that. He might have thought of it before. Really now, I'm going to wash my hands. I can see the Merzes' point. Do you understand him at all?'

'Oh quite,' said Jeanne.

'It's isn't as though he'd ever showed himself the least bit pratiquant.'

'Nor do the Merzes for that matter. Friedrich goes to nothing—except funerals—and there isn't even the pretence of keeping the Sabbath at Voss Strasse, or not eating lobsters or ham—'

'It is peculiar,' Sarah said; 'theological dead-lock between non-practising members of two religions.'

Edu returned from Epsom and heard some hard words. Jules no longer lunched at Voss Strasse; Sarah talked of summer plans. One evening Mélanie put on a thick veil and slipped out with her maid, Hedwig. They entered the Matheus Kirche by a side-door. Hedwig was a well-known face in the congregation; Mélanie carried a small purse with gold; Pastor Völler was aged. So it was after only a brief interview that she was led into the empty church where water was sprinkled on her forehead and she spoke the words taught to her by Gottlieb, signed the register, and was received a member of the Reformed Evangelical Church of Germany.

She returned to Voss Strasse, late, in high excitement, two red circles burning on her cheeks.

The family was worried but already in the dining-room. She faced them.

'It is done,' she announced: 'I am Jules's.'

'The cad,' said Markwald.

'What?' said Grandmama.

'Nothing can separate us now.'

'Have they eloped?' said Grandmama.

'Worse,' said Markwald and her husband.

'Worse!' said Emil.

'Our treasure has been baptized,' said Gottlieb.

The same night Edu and Friedrich called at the Kaiserhof demanding immediate marriage. Julius was sitting up, puzzling over the hotel charges. Edu was embarrassed, and spluttered; Friedrich was grim.

He spoke about dishonour.

Julius found his attitude most Prussian, but he consented and the two men withdrew.

A date was fixed for the end of June. The old Merzes, unwilling to see their daughter deprived of pin-money as well as Christian, stated that they would make her an annual allowance of fifty thousand marks.

Sybille Bedford, *A Legacy*, 1956

The Eastern Suburbs

Few former East Berlin suburbs lay on any tourist trail, and while practical considerations were partly to blame, another reason was the relative dearth of historical monuments and other obvious sights. While it would be idle to pretend that reunification has rendered these districts much more visually pleasing than they previously were, they do, at least for the time being, offer a wealth of insights into a society that has now been well and truly confined to the dustbin of history.

Pankow

Prior to the creation of their own exclusive custom-built settlement at Wandlitz, a lakeside town in the Schorfheide north of Berlin, most members of the GDR's élite chose to reside in the comfortable villas of the northern district of **Pankow**, one of Berlin's most prosperous residential quarters in prewar days, and in the process bestowed a certain notoriety on its name. This ruling class, while consisting primarily of politicians and diplomats, included among its co-opted membership writers, artists, musicians, scientists and sportsmen—in short, anyone whose name could add lustre to the regime. The pampered lifestyle they enjoyed was readily justified by reference to Marxist-Leninist theory: as it would take a long time for the state to wither away and produce a truly classless society, the Communist Party had to play a leading and directing role towards that end, which of necessity involved its most senior members enjoying privileges denied to most other citizens.

Wilhelm Pieck, the first and only president of the GDR, chose Pankow's principal historic monument, **Schloss Niederschönhausen**, as his official residence. After his death, the palace served as the state accommodation for visiting VIPs, the last being Mikhail Gorbachev, who stayed there during his fateful attendance at the country's ill-starred fortieth anniversary celebrations (see page 40). The building, one of the best-preserved royal palaces in Berlin, currently lacks a role, but in due course it is hoped to make it accessible to the public. Its early history in many ways resembles that of Schloss Charlottenburg: designed by Johann Arnold Nehring in the 1690s on the foundations of an existing manor house for Elector Friedrich III, it was extended by Johann Eosander von Göthe after Prussia was raised to the rank of a kingdom. A further rebuild was carried out under Frederick the Great, whose consort Elisabeth Christine passed much of her life there, safely out of the way of her misogynous husband.

Close to the Schloss is the elliptical **Majakowskiring**, where several members of the first generation of GDR leaders had their main dwellings. Pieck's private home was at No 29, while Otto Grotewohl, the man who led the Social Democrats of the Soviet-occupied sector into their shotgun marriage with the Communists, thus earning himself the office of Prime Minister, lived at No 46. The residence at No 34 of Johannes R Becher, poet turned Minister of Culture, later became a literature museum and arts centre, but forsook this role after reunification of the city.

Pankow's other sights are somewhat scattered. Along the border with Reinickendorf is the **Volkspark Schonhölzer Heide**, in which stands the **Sowjetisches Ehrenmal** (Soviet War Memorial), a typically heroic-style complex whose main features are a commemorative obelisk and a bronze sculpture of a mother mourning her son. Several blocks north of the Schloss is the Roman Catholic **Marie-Magdalenen-Kirche** (Church of St Mary Magdalene). Constructed in the late 1920s by Felix Sturm, this boasts a strikingly original tower-façade which ranks among the most impressive pieces of Expressionist architecture in the city.

A few blocks south of the Schloss is Breite Strasse, Pankow's main street, on which stand the turn-of-the-century **Rathaus** (Town Hall) and the **Pfarrkirche** (Parish Church). The latter dates back to the 13th century, but has been repeatedly altered and extended, with Schinkel and Stüler among the architects who have contributed to its present appearance. Further south, Pankow's S-Bahn station is the starting-point for what used to be one of the world's oddest rail journeys: en route to Bornhomer Strasse, the train travelled through the Death Strip dividing the two parts of the city and was the closest most East Berliners ever got to venturing into the forbidden territory of the West.

Weissensee

Weissensee, which adjoins Pankow to the east, takes its name from the **Weisser See** (White Lake), a popular boating and recreational area. It is primarily a residential district, incorporating a number of old villages plus several modern housing estates. Nowadays, it is chiefly famous for the **Jüdischer Friedhof** (Jewish Cemetery), the largest in Germany, which is located at its southernmost extremity on the district boundary with Prenzlauer Berg. Some 115,000 people are buried there, among them Herbert Baum, the leader of the Jewish resistance to Hitler, and Berlin's two most famous retailers, Adolf Jandorf and Hermann Tietz, the respective founders of KaDaWe and Hertie. The cemetery entrance has a number of imitation Renaissance and Moorish buildings by Hugo Licht and a simple circular memorial to the victims of the Holocaust, with tablets bearing the names of each of the main Nazi death camps.

Jüdischer Friedhof, Weissensee

Hohenschönhausen, **Marzahn** and **Hellersdorf**, the next three districts on Berlin's eastern boundary, were established in the 1970s and 80s out of territory ceded from Weissensee and Lichtenberg. Characterized by bleak modern high-rise apartment blocks, they serve as a salutary reminder of the desolate existence still endured by a large percentage of the population of a city whose name is all too often glibly equated with rampantly hedonistic lifestyles.

Prenzlauer Berg

Like Wedding to the west, **Prenzlauer Berg** is predominantly a working-class district of tenement blocks that sprang up in the second half of the 19th century to accommodate the city's burgeoning population. Relatively little damaged in World War II, it was allowed to fall into neglect by the GDR authorities, who preferred to build new housing schemes adhering to their own docrinal theories than to restore what were seen as hangovers of the worst excesses of capitalist exploitation. One consequence of this was that the district became the favoured home for noncomformists rebelling against the constraints of GDR society. For years, their activities were muted, confined to little more than occasional underground concerts and exhibitions and the flying of white flags from car aerials—a signal that the owner had officially applied to emigrate. The true extent of their opposition was, however, clearly manifested in the dramatic events of 1989, after which the neighbourhood began to develop a distinctive new role for itself within the reunited city. In scenes reminiscent of those in Kreuzberg in the late 1960s and early 70s, squatters began to occupy the thousands of empty properties, while the cheap rents that were legally available acted as a stimulus to others to relocate their homes or businesses from West Berlin. The result is that Prenzlauer Berg has now replaced East Kreuzberg as the heart of Berlin's *Szene*—an untranslatable word that denotes the trendiest place of the moment, frequented by those who aim to set current modes and fashions.

While there is little doubt that Prenzlauer Berg's main appeal lies in the bars, cafés, boutiques and galleries that have recently sprung up, the gaunt appearance of its massively solid tenements, with their flaking façades and crumbling balconies, do lend it a certain visual distinctiveness. Like Kreuzberg, the best overview can be had from the train, as the U-2 line emerges from **Senefelderplatz** onto an elevated stretch, locally dubbed the 'magistrate's umbrella', that cuts right down the middle of **Schönhauser Allee**, the central axis of the quarter, leaving much of it permanently in shadow.

Senefelderplatz itself makes the best starting point for a walking tour of what Prenzlauer Berg has in the way of sights; it is named in honour of Alois Senefelder, the inventor of lithography, who is commemorated by a statue on the square with his name, as in a lithographic block, appearing in mirror script. A little further up Schönhauser Allee is the entrance to the **Jüdischer Friedhof** (Jewish Cemetery), a smaller and rather more exclusive burial ground than its counterpart in Weissensee. Even so, it contains the remains of some 20,000 people, buried before the end of the Third Reich, of whom the best known are the operatic composer Giacomo Meyerbeer and the painter Max Liebermann. The Nazis uprooted many of gravestones and desecrated their inscriptions; many remain in this state, though substantial sums have recently been spent on repositioning and restoration.

In the maze of rundown streets east of Schönhauser Allee is the **Synagoge Rykestrasse** (Rykestrasse Synagogue), whose location in the heart of a bastion of left-wing radical politics explains why it was the only Jewish place of worship in the city to escape extensive damage on *Kristallnacht*. An unassuming brick structure from the early years of the century, its occupies the traditional position at the back of a courtyard, rather than having the impressive street frontage characteristic of the more important Berlin synagogues. On Knaackstrasse just to the south is the circular red brick **Wasserturm** (Water Tower), built in 1875 to provide fresh water for the district, replacing a structure of a few decades earlier which can be seen on the wooded hill just to the south. Used as a torture chamber by the Nazis, the decomposed bodies of 28 victims were later discovered in the sewers. Having outlasted its original function, the tower now serves as Prenzlauer Berg's most eccentric apartment block.

North of the synagogue is the triangular-shaped **Kollwitzplatz**, named in honour of the sculptress and graphic artist Käthe Kollwitz, who is commemorated by a statue based on one of her own very unflattering self-portrait etchings. A copy of her sculpture *The Mother* stands on the site of the house at No 25 on nearby Kollwitzstrasse, where she lived for over fifty years until its destruction in an air raid. That the best collection of Käthe Kollwitz's work is located near the brash consumerism of the Ku'damm, rather than in the deprived quarter she resided in by choice, is rather an unfortunate irony (see pages 159–161). Nonetheless, there are two worthwhile museums on Husemannstrasse immediately to the north on a block that was immaculately cleaned and repainted for Berlin's 750th anniversary in 1987, and now stands out like a gleaming jewel among the unkempt scruffiness of the neighbouring streets. The **Friseurmuseum** (Hairdressing Museum) is a quirky collection devoted to hair culture, which pays due respect to its barber-dentist origins and shows the evolution of tools, accessories and ornaments through the centuries. A couple of doors away, the **Museum Berliner Arbeiterleben** (Museum of Berlin Working-Class Life) re-creates the appearance of a furnished turn-of-the-century tenement dwelling and features documentary material on various aspects of working-class life of the time.

On Stargarder Strasse, a block south of Schönhauser Allee's combined S- and U-Bahn station, is the **Gethsemanekirche** (Gethsemane Church), a bloated red brick historicist extravaganza from the end of last century. Despite its attempt to imitate the architectural forms of the great medieval basilicas of the Rhineland, the church has no aesthetic appeal but denotes a place of major historical significance as the fountainhead of the Berlin resistance to the Communist GDR dictatorship. Like Neues Forum, the opposition group that was constituted there, the Gethsemanekirche has been unable to sustain the momentum of the crucial role it played in 1989, the attempts to introduce a moral and spiritual dimension to life in the eastern part of the city having been swamped by the triumph of rampant commercialism. Peace vigils inspired by various world events are still held in the church, but attract the merest trickle of worshippers compared to the crowds who flocked there during *Die Wende* ('The Change', or reunification).

Immediately beyond the junction of Stargarder Strasse and Prenzlauer Allee is the silvery dome of the **Zeiss-Planetarium**, one of the last prestige projects of the GDR. A short walk to the northeast, laid out between Gubitzstrasse and Sültstrasse, is the **Flamensiedlung** (Flemish Settlement), a model housing development by Bruno Taut dating from 1929–30 that marks a distinctive break with the previous dank and crowded apartment blocks of Prenzlauer Berg. Its principles are similar to those of his Hufeisensiedlung of a few years before (see page 234), while showing clear evidence of architectural influence from the De Stijl movement in the Netherlands, particularly in the provision of corner windows and balconies which impart a distinctive rhythmic touch.

Further east is **Ernst-Thälmann-Park**, a landscaped housing scheme of the 1980s, most of whose flats were allocated to card-carrying members of the ruling SED. Presiding over the development is a huge bronze head of prewar Communist leader Ernst Thälmann by the Russian sculptor Lew Kerber; completed in 1985, it was the last monumental sculpture commissioned by the GDR regime. It stands a better chance of long-term survival than most other memorials of this type, largely because Thälmann was an anti-Nazi martyr who died at Buchenwald concentration camp in 1944 after a decade of imprisonment. Though eulogized by the GDR authorities, he was not particularly distinguished or successful as an active politician: he was widely regarded within Germany, not least by the Social Democrats, as a stooge of the Soviet Union and he never attracted more than a small hard core of support, coming a very distant third to Hindenburg and Hitler in the 1932 presidential election.

Friedrichshain

Occupying an area of just under ten square kilometres, **Friedrichshain** is Berlin's smallest administrative district. Most of it having been flattened in World War II, it was rebuilt along Stalinist lines to form an extension to the city centre of East Berlin. Inevitably, the fall of the Wall led to the removal of certain key features of its landscape, notably the gigantic statue of Lenin which presided over Leninplatz, thereafter renamed Platz der Vereinten Nationen (United Nations Square). However, preservation orders have been slapped on other historical monuments of the GDR era—an encouraging sign that the authorities are not trying to sweep all traces of the GDR's existence out of sight.

Friedrichshain is bisected horizontally by a vast showpiece boulevard, laid out during the 1950s, which continues onwards into Lichtenberg, with a later, much more modest western extension to Alexanderplatz. Until 1961, the street was known as Stalinallee, but when this designation was dropped throughout the Soviet bloc, the eastern part was renamed Frankfurter Allee (signifying that it marks the start of the road to Frankfurt an der Oder at the modern border with Poland), while the western section became known as **Karl-Marx-Allee**, a name that the post-unification authorities have decided to retain. The boulevard, which has been claimed as the most important new street built anywhere in Europe this century, exemplifies the modernistic form of neoclassicism championed by the Soviet Union and its satellites. This is, for the most part, less chillingly antiquarian than the Nazi variant, though the two towers by the Frankfurter Tor, which are clearly modelled on those on Gendarmenmarkt, mark an attempt to forge a link with the city's past. Ironically enough, it was the imposition of increased production norms on building labourers engaged in

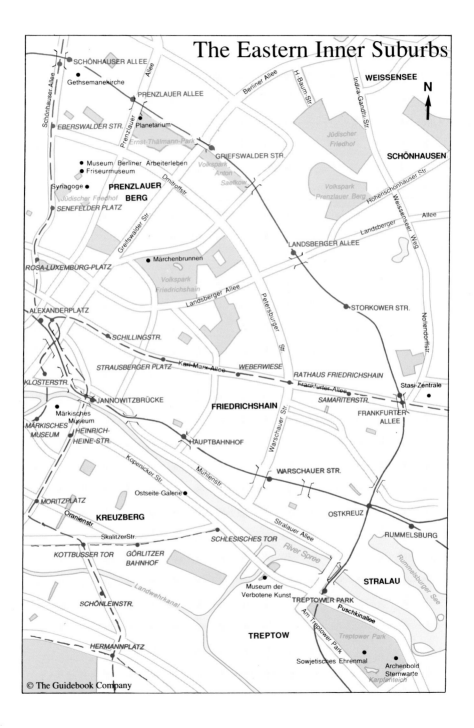

The Eastern Inner Suburbs

WEISSENSEE

N

● SCHÖNHAUSER ALLEE

Gethsemanekirche ●

Berliner Allee

H.-Baum-Str

Indira-Gandhi-Str

Jüdischer Friedhof

SCHÖNHAUSEN

● PRENZLAUER ALLEE

Prenzlauer Allee

EBERSWALDER STR. ● Planetarium

Ernst-Thälmann-Park

GRIEFSWALDER STR.

Volkspark Anton Saefkow

● Museum Berliner Arbeiterleben
● Friseurmuseum

Dimitroffstr.

Volkspark Prenzlauer Berg

Hohenschönhauser Str.

Weissenseer Weg

Synagoge ●   PRENZLAUER
Jüdischer Friedhof   BERG
SENEFELDER PLATZ

Greifswalder Str.

Allee

LANDSBERGER ALLEE

Landsberger

● Märchenbrunnen

ROSA-LUXEMBURG-PLATZ

Volkspark Friedrichshain

Landsberger Allee

Petersburger Str.

Nollendorfstr.

ALEXANDERPLATZ

● STORKOWER STR.

● SCHILLINGSTR.

STRAUSBERGER PLATZ   Karl-Marx-Allee   WEBERWIESE

RATHAUS FRIEDRICHSHAIN

KLOSTERSTR.

Frankfurter Allee

Stasi-Zentrale ●

● JANNOWITZBRÜCKE

FRIEDRICHSHAIN

SAMARITERSTR.

● Märkisches
MÄRKISCHES Museum
MUSEUM   HEINRICH-
HEINE-STR.

Warschauer Str.

FRANKFURTER ALLEE

● HAUPTBAHNHOF

Kopenicker Str.

Mühlenstr.

● WARSCHAUER STR.

Ostseite-Galerie ●

● MORITZPLATZ

KREUZBERG

Oranienstr.

SkalitzerStr.

Stralauer Allee

OSTKREUZ

RUMMELSBURG

SCHLESISCHES TOR

River Spree

Rummelsburger See

KOTTBUSSER TOR   GÖRLITZER
BAHNHOF

STRALAU

Landwehrkanal

Museum der
Verbotene Kunst ●

TREPTOWER PARK

Puschkinallee

SCHÖNLEINSTR.

Am Treptower Park

Treptower Park

HERMANNPLATZ

TREPTOW

Sowjetisches Ehrenmal ●

● Archenbold
Sternwarte
Karpfenteich

© The Guidebook Company

the Stalinallee project that sparked off the 1953 uprising. This quickly spread from a dispute about pay and conditions into one of full-scale opposition to the GDR, whereby the Communist regime revealed its true colours by resorting to the ideologically impure solution of calling on foreign tanks to crush a working-class rebellion.

North of Karl-Marx-Allee is a reminder of the district's prewar quarter in the shape of the **Volkspark Friedrichshain**. Established in 1840 to mark the centenary of Frederick the Great's accession to the Prussian throne, it was landscaped in the manner of Lenné, though its appearance was much altered by a number of additions. Prominent among these is the **Märchenbrunnen** (Fairy Tale Fountain) at the far western end of the park, an elaborate arcaded structure built in 1913 by Ludwig Hoffmann and named after its statues of characters from the stories collected by the Brothers Grimm. Further east are two artificial hills, the **Grosser Bunkerberg** and **Kleiner Bunkerberg**, which are made from the rubble of bomb-damaged buildings dumped on top of a pair of wartime bunkers. At the southeastern extremity of the park is a cemetery containing the remains of those who fell in the revolutions of 1848 and 1918. Another graveyard, for German members of the International Brigade who died in the Spanish Civil War, lies further west.

The demise of the GDR has brought Friedrichshain a new tourist attraction in the shape of the **Ostseitegalerie** (East Side Gallery), which consists of the section of the Berlin Wall running alongside the River Spree on Muhlenstrasse. It was placed under a preservation order and a number of local and international artists were allocated a section each and invited to paint an appropriate subject on it. The result evokes the flavour of the Wall in the spray can era, though it is unauthentic in two senses: the original paintings were, by necessity, on the west-facing side only and were almost entirely the work of spontaneous graffiti dabblers rather than highly finished compositions by serious artists. Nonetheless, there are some arresting images inspired by the Wall's symbolism, particularly one showing Honecker and Brezhnev indulging in a passionate French kiss, which is accompanied by the witty caption 'Release me from this deadly embrace' (see page 90). At the eastern end of the gallery is the rickety Oberbaumbrücke, now restored to its traditional function of pedestrian link between Friedrichshain and Kreuzberg, having been a restricted border crossing point throughout the Wall years.

Lichtenberg

Lichtenberg, which lies north of Treptow and east of Friedrichshain, has a fair sprinkling of industrial concerns, but is primarily a working-class residential district with a mixture of traditional tenements and postwar state-housing apartment blocks.

THE STASI

Of all the world's secret police forces, the Stasi came nearest to fulfilling the Orwellian nightmare of a society under absolute surveillance, one that had its own, all too real Big Brother in the person of Erich Mielke, a life-time Communist of unflinching devotion to the cause. Born in 1907 to an impoverished Berlin working-class family, Mielke first came to prominence in 1931, when he organized and helped carry out the assassination of two police captains known for their brutality towards left-wing political demonstrators. Resisting arrest, he fled to the Soviet Union, where he remained, apart from a spell fighting in the Spanish Civil War, until 1945. While there, he became a fanatical admirer of the counterinsurgency techniques pioneered by Felix Dzerzhinsky, and, by becoming a specialist in security matters, ensured a senior position for himself in this field on his return to the Russian-occupied sector of Germany in 1945.

Having helped establish the GDR's Ministry of State Security, initially as a branch of the Ministry of the Interior, then as a separate government department in its own right, he served successively as deputy to its first two heads, Wilhelm Zaisser and Ernst Wollweber, both of whom were purged. On the fall of the latter in 1957, Mielke took over as departmental chief, remaining until the ministry was wound up in November 1989. He also served as a member of the ruling Politburo from 1971 onwards in reward for his role in the plot that enabled Honecker to oust Ulbricht from the position of General Secretary of the SED.

Just as the fall of the Berlin Wall accounted for the Stasi's demise, so its construction, by sealing off the GDR from most outside influences, enabled Mielke to transform what had previously been a relatively modest organization into one of the key instruments of state power. Its foreign intelligence network, directed by the legendary spymaster Markus Wolf, one of Mielke's four deputies, had the highest profile, achieving a number of spectacular successes that hit the world headlines. The penetration of West German ministries by its agents culminated in the appointment of Günter Guillaume as Private Secretary to Chancellor Willy Brandt, his unmasking causing the latter's downfall in 1974.

However, operations abroad, plus surveillance of diplomats, journalists, businessmen and other foreign nationals visiting the GDR accounted for well under ten per cent of the Stasi's budget, the rest being spent on an obsessive search for opponents within the country itself. As Mielke believed that every citizen presented a potential security hazard, he believed it was his duty as a good Communist 'to know everything, everywhere', and duly set about trying to achieve this impossible goal. The Stasi eventually came to employ 85,000 permanent staff, with 33,000 based in the Normannen-strasse complex alone. In all, it owned 2,000 buildings and had a fleet of 23,000 vehicles and an arsenal of over 250,000 weapons, plus its own hospital, law school and sports teams, among them Dynamo Berlin, the virtually perpetual winners of the rigged professional football league.

In addition, the Stasi had a network of informers known as MIs whose number has been variously estimated at between 150,000 and 500,000. Based in every town, village and workplace, their function, for which their actual employment was no more than a cover, was to snoop on their neigh-bours and colleagues by compiling dossiers about their activities, down to the most trivial matters such as when and what they ate. The information was stored in six million files, suggesting that around half the adult popu-lation of the country was subject to detailed monitoring. Even the most trusted members of society, such as border guards and army officers, were spied on, while Mielke's personal paranoia also led him to monitor the movements of his closest colleagues, including Wolf. Although apparently a loyal acolyte of Honecker, he kept a file containing damning material on the GDR dictator himself, notably evidence that he had informed on fellow Communists while held as a Nazi prisoner.

Ironically, this vast supply of information proved to be of very little practical application. Hardly any evidence was corroborated, and doubtless much of it was fabricated, though this hardly mattered, as most of it was simply stored in the appropriate file and never again consulted. The sheer pointlessness of the whole Stasi set-up was ruthlessly exposed during the final year of the GDR's existence. Mielke's spies had made him fully aware of the discontent simmering throughout the country over the lack of politi-cal freedom, the restrictions on travel, the dearth of consumer choice, and a host of other matters. Yet, despite repeated warnings to the Politburo about the danger of a popular revolution, he was unable to do anything whatso-ever to forestall it.

Compared with the Gestapo, the Cheka and the KGB, or with the Securitate in Romania, the Stasi was in many ways a relatively benign organization, one that only occasionally indulged in the murder or physical torture of its opponents. However, it succeeded in inflicting a form of all-pervasive mental torture on the entire fabric of society, creating a climate of distrust that will long survive its demise. In many ways, this actually increased after the fall of the Wall, as it was only then that the full extent of the Stasi's operations became publicly known.

Despite the widespread destruction of files on collapse of the Wall by Stasi agents determined to cover their own tracks, enough remain to stretch

The Forschungs- und Gedenkstätte Normannenstrasse; the office of Erich Mielke, including the now-open safe where he kept his deadliest secrets, such as damning material on the country's dictator, Erich Honecker

for 202 kilometres if placed end to end. This legacy has proved a sticky problem for the new unified German government, which placed the entire archive in the care of a commission headed by the Lutheran pastor Joachim Gauk, himself a Stasi victim. Some 1,000 staff are employed to sift through the documents, a task that will take at least a decade; among them are a number of low-level former Stasi employees, whose knowledge of its systems is deemed essential to the project.

As from May 1991, every GDR citizen has been granted the right to apply to see his own file, though so far relatively few, other than well-known former dissidents, have actually man-aged to gain access. The clear intention of the government is to let time take its course in healing the legacy of bitterness, and to avoid acts of instant justice based on the unreliable evidence contained in the files.

Nonetheless, the Stasi heritage continues to have a life beyond the grave. A number of erstwhile East German opposition leaders have been discredited by rumour and innuendo, most notably Lothar de Mazière, the country's first and last democratic Prime Minister, who was forced to resign his cabinet post in the unified German government because of alleged links with the Stasi. Even at the time, the evidence, which has since been confirmed, suggested that these were no more than routine contacts necessitated by his work as a lawyer acting on behalf of political dissidents, but the mere suspicion of collaboration was sufficient to end his political career.

The fate of Mielke provided the authorities with another headache, not least in view of his advanced age. In December 1989, he was expelled from the SED and arrested on corruption charges. Having served only a few months in prison, he was released on health grounds, only to be rearrested shortly afterwards. By then, he had lapsed into insanity—or had decided to feign madness—and his guards responded by giving him an unconnected telephone in which he could continue to issue a relentless flow of commands to imaginary subordinates. His real-life former staff, meanwhile, suffered a variety of different fates: the tabloid press eagerly reported on instances of once mighty grandees reduced to taking menial jobs, yet there were also cases where ex-Stasi employees were able to profit from the extensive range of contacts they had built up over the years to obtain plum sinecures for themselves in the new democratic order.

While not one of the more obvious tourist destinations in the Berlin, such attractions as it has provide a nicely varied perspective on the history of the city.

Just north of Frankfurter Allee, the eastern continuation of Karl-Marx-Allee, is the grim looking mini-city occupied until 1989 by the GDR's world-famous secret police force, euphemistically known as the **Ministerium für Staatssicherheit** (Ministry of State Security) but generally referred to as the Stasi (see page 254). The site, bounded by Ruschestrasse to the west, Magdalenenstrasse to the east, and Normannenstrasse to the north, was comparable in size to London's Whitehall, yet housed just over a third of the office-based staff of this single parasitic ministry. Since its dissolution, several of the buildings have been put to other uses—the canteen, for example, is now a public bar, while the Department of Counterespionage has been taken over by Deutsche Reichsbahn, the national railway company.

The main administration block, however, has been preserved as the **Forschungs- und Gedenkstätte Normannenstrasse** (Normannenstrasse Research Centre and Memorial), entered from Ruschestrasse. In the entrance hall is documentary material on Erich Mielke, who headed the Stasi for over thirty years, and his hero, Felix Dzerzhinsky, the Polish-born founder of the Soviet Union's Cheka, forerunner of the KGB. On the first floor, Mielke's own suite of offices, all furnished with highly polished stained wood which gleams a yellow-orange colour under the fluorescent lights, have been preserved virtually as he left them. Black and white telephones are ranged on his desk, and a made-up bed lies ready in the adjoining room in case his insatiable demand to keep abreast of events should preclude him returning home to his luxury villa in Wandlitz. The second floor displays focus on some of the Stasi's victims; examples of the surveillance equipment used against them are also on view.

At the eastern end of Frankfurter Allee, Gudrunstrasse leads northeast to the vast **Zentral-Friedhof** (Central Cemetery). Just within the entrance is the **Gedenkstätte der Sozialisten** (Memorial to the Socialists), a red porphyry slab surrounded by the tombs of most of East Germany's pantheon of heroes, beginning with the martyred Communist Party founders Karl Liebknecht and Rosa Luxemburg, continuing via the artists Käthe Kollwitz and Otto Nagel to such stalwarts of the GDR as Wilhelm Pieck and Walter Ulbricht. The memorial was erected in 1951 as a replacement for its considerably more distinguished predecessor designed by Mies van der Rohe in 1926 and destroyed by the Nazis nine years later.

Further east, set in an English-style park laid out by Lenné, is one of the finest buildings in the eastern suburbs, **Schloss Friedrichsfelde**. The central section of the palace was built in the 1690s by Johann Arnold Nering for Benjamin Raule, head of the Prussian navy; two decades later it was expanded by Martin Böhme. After it came into the possession of Prince Ferdinand, younger brother of Frederick the Great, it was transformed once more, gaining the tympanum above the entrance doorway and some splendid neoclassical interiors designed by some of Berlin's leading architects of the day, including Johann Boumann, Carl von Gontard and Carl Gotthard Langhans. A number of the ground floor rooms are adorned with fine painted wallhangings, though the most imposing part is the Great Hall upstairs, which these days makes an opulent setting for chamber music concerts.

Part of the Schloss grounds are now occupied by the **Tierpark** (Animal Park), established in 1954 as East Berlin's answer to West Berlin's Zoologischer Garten. Inevitably, it is overshadowed by its illustrious counterpart and still relies quite heavily on old-fashioned caging methods. Nevertheless, it remains a pleasant place to visit, its speciality being a number of rare hoofed animals that are kept and bred in the outdoor enclosures. These include takins from Southeast Asia, kiangs from Tibet and white-lipped deer from China.

South of Friedrichsfelde, right on the border with the neighbouring district of Köpenick, is **Karlshorst**. Its barracks were the scene of the signing of the unconditional surrender of the German *Wehrmacht* to the Red Army on 8th May 1945, whereupon Karlshorst was virtually taken over by the occu-

Sowjetisches Ehrenmal, Treptow

pying forces to serve as the Soviet residential quarter of Berlin throughout the history of the GDR. For the time being it remains one of their last major bases in the country. A Soviet perspective on World War II is presented in the **Gedenkstätte Karlshorst** (Karlshorst Memorial) on Rheinsteinstrasse. Ominously subtitled the 'Museum of the Unconditional Surrender of Fascist Germany in the Great Patriotic War of 1941–5', it remains to be seen whether it will survive the official withdrawal of the Soviet troops.

Treptow

Had there been any logic whatsoever in the division of Berlin, the elongated district of **Treptow** would have lain in the Western sector: the River Spree forms a natural barrier separating it from Friedrichshain, Lichtenberg and Köpenick, with all but a short southern stretch of its land border falling within Neukölln.

As it is, the name of the district, which is a mixed concentration of housing and industry, has become synonymous with the **Treptower Park** (Treptow Park), laid out starting in 1876 by Gustav Meyer, Berlin's first Superintendent of Parks and a pupil of the great Lenné. The park in turn is indelibly associated with what posterity is likely to regard as the most significant visual reminder of the decades of Communist rule, the **Sowjetisches Ehrenmal** (Soviet War Memorial). This immense monument is dedicated to the members of the Red Army who fell in the final assault on Berlin in 1945 in the culmination of what the Soviets regarded as the 'Great Patriotic War' against Nazi Germany, a struggle that cost the country some 20 million lives. Following the fall of the Wall, there was talk of dismantling the memorial and shipping it to Russia, but this caused such an outrage that a guarantee of its continued existence was made part of the German reunification package.

The memorial, which was inaugurated on the fourth anniversary of the Nazi capitulation, employs a battery of symbolist techniques in order to fulfil its twin objectives of commemoration of the dead and re-education of the populace on whose soil it lies. For all the crudity of its socialist realism, there can be no denying its emotional impact, which remains undiminished by the passage of time. Much of the iconography is Christian in inspiration, subtly adapted to the atheistic demands of Communist ideology; the symbolism even extends to the materials used in the construction, which include masonry from Hitler's demolished Reichskanzlei, and blocks of Swedish red granite which the Nazis had imported for the triumphal monuments they intended to erect in celebration of their subjection of the rest of Europe. Forming a prelude to the complex is a statue known as *The Motherland*, showing a woman mourning her dead sons. From there, a path leads to two huge pylons shaped in the manner of lowered flags, below each of which is the statue of a kneeling soldier. Beyond is the sunken graveyard, in which around 5,000 Soviet troops are buried; it is laid out in a rigorous geometric pattern, with the sides of the sarcophagi carved in heroic style with scenes from the war. At the far end, in a clear portent of the launch of the German Democratic Republic later the same year, is a hillock crowned with a twelve-metre-high bronze statue of a Soviet soldier cradling a German child in his arms, while crushing a swastika with his sword. The plinth underneath forms a crypt adorned with a mosaic showing citizens from the various strata of the Soviet Union lining up to pay their respects to the fallen.

To the rear of the memorial is the **Archenhold-Sternwarte** (Archenhold Observatory), built for the Berlin Industrial Fair of 1896 and named after its founder, the astronomer Friedrich Simon Archenhold. Its 21-metre-long refractor, which is still among the largest in the world, is its main attraction and is regularly demonstrated for the benefit of the public. The institute is now mainly concerned with researching the history of astronomy, which is the main focus of its permanent exhibitions. Nearby lies the **Hain der Kosmonauten** (Cosmonauts' Grove), with busts of Yuri Gagarin and the first GDR spaceman, Sigmund Jahn.

Over the road is the **Gasthaus Zenner**, built in 1822 by Carl Ferdinand Langhans, son of the architect of the Brandenburger Tor. To its rear, a footbridge leads to the tiny **Insel der Jugend** (Island of Youth), a popular recreational spot complete with clubhouse and open-air theatre. A little further round the shore is the beginning of the **Plänterwald**, the seamless continuation of the Treptower Park. At its extreme northeastern corner is the inappropriately titled Kulturpark (Culture Park), a funfair with a roller coaster and giant ferris wheel. In the opposite direction, just before the S-Bahn station Treptow, is a departure jetty for cruises on the Havel.

At the far end of the tree-lined Puschkinalle, which bisects the park and then continues northwards under the railway track, is the only watchtower of the Berlin Wall to survive in its original location, now looking rather forlorn in its isolated position among cleared wasteland. It houses what is over dramatically known as the **Museum der verbotenen Kunst** (Museum of Forbidden Art), featuring changing displays of contemporary paintings and photographs. The main attraction, however, is the opportunity to climb up to the frontier guards' outlook point, which has been left furnished as though it were still operational.

Köpenick

Once a small medieval town wholly separate from Berlin, **Köpenick** has compensated for being swallowed up by the capital by expanding outwards to become its largest administrative district. With much of it taken up by lakes, forests and parks, Köpenick is also one of the more attractive parts of former East Berlin, even though it contains some of the most extensive concentrations of industry in the whole of the city.

There is one major tourist attraction in the shape of **Schloss Köpenick**, which stands on an island at the confluence of the Spree and Dahme, a site known to have been occupied by a Slav castle in the 12th century. The present baroque palace was built between 1677 and 1683 for the Great Elector Friedrich Wilhelm by the Dutch architect Rutger van Langevelt. Johann Arnold Nering subsequently completed the ensemble by adding the south wing, the ceremonial entrance gateway, and the chapel, which stands across the courtyard from the main block. Pride of the Schloss' interior is the Armorial Hall on the second floor, richly decorated by the Italian stuccoer Giovanni Carove with pairs of caryatids bearing the coats-of-arms of each of the territories, scattered all over the map of the fragmented Holy Roman Empire, that were then in the possession of Brandenburg-Prussia's ruling Hohenzollern dynasty. Other areas of the palace are used to display those parts of the **Kunstgewerbemuseum** (Museum of Applied Art) that ended up in East Berlin after World War II. The room adjoining the Armorial Hall is arranged in imitation of the Knights' Hall in the demolished Stadtschloss, in order to display the Berlin Silver Buffet to best advantage. Created for the Elector Friedrich III, this masterpiece of baroque craftsmanship was designed by Andreas Schlüter and worked by the Brill family of silversmiths in Augsburg; its value is all the greater for being one of the few tangible survivals of the magnificent interior decoration of the Hohenzollerns' main palace. Other highlights of the museum's diverse collections are the so-called Giselaschmuck, a dazzling horde of late 10th-century jewellery found in Mainz in the Rhineland, and an ornate mid-16th century panelled room from Schloss Hardenstein near Chur in Switzerland.

Just north of the Schloss is the compact Altstadt (Old Town). It has no monuments of special note, though the elaborate neo-Gothic **Rathaus** (Town Hall) that forms its centrepiece was the scene for an incident which made Köpenick famous throughout Europe. In 1906, an unemployed cobbler and former prisoner named Wilhelm Voigt acquired the uniform of an army captain, then commandeered a dozen infantrymen from the barracks at Plötzensee. He marched them to Köpenick, where he ordered them to confiscate the contents of the municipal safe and arrest the mayor and the treasurer. His charges were then despatched with their prisoners to the Neue Wache on Unter den Linden, while Voigt himself made off with the spoils. Although he was caught soon afterwards, news of his act spread quickly, causing a great deal of merriment in the telling evidence it provided of the inbuilt Prussian propensity to obey instructions, no matter how absurd, when they came from someone in uniform. Carl Zuckmayer immortalized the event in his play *The Captain of Köpenick*, which he subtitled *A German Fairy Story in Three Acts*.

Schloss Pfaueninsel, with the peacocks

On Puchanstrasse, about halfway between the Altstadt and Köpenick's S-Bahn station, is the **Gedenkstätte Köpenicker Blutwoche** (Memorial to the Köpenick Blood Week). This commemorates the other event with which the district's name is associated—the incarceration and torture of some 500 Socialists and Communists by the Nazis in June 1933, 91 of whom were murdered. The memorial is on the site of the prison where they were held, now part of the Amtsgericht (District Court).

A short distance northwest of the Altstadt is the **Wulheide**, a large tract of woodland incorporating an amusement park whose main attraction is a seven-kilometre-long miniature railway operated almost entirely by children. On An der Wulheide facing the entrance to the park is the **Bootshaus** (Boat House), built in 1910 by Peter Behrens for the electronics giant AEG. The same architect was responsible for the **NAG-Fabrikgebäude** on Ostendstrasse to the west, constructed during World War I as the headquarters of the national automobile company, and for the postwar **AEG-Siedlung**, a housing development for factory workers on Zeppelinstrasse.

East of the Altstadt is the **Grosser Müggelsee**, the largest lake within the municipal boundaries of Berlin. It is a popular recreational spot, not only for summer water sports: it frequently freezes over for long periods in winter and can thus be used as a giant skating rink. The sleepy old towns of **Friedrichshagen** and **Rahnsdorf** lie respectively on its northern and eastern shores. Just outside the former is the **Wasserwerk** (Waterworks), an imposing Neo-gothic complex which once supplied much of Berlin's running water and is now open to the public as a technical monument. To the south of the lake are the **Müggelberge** (Muggel Hills), one of which is crowned by the **Müggelturm** (Muggel Tower), a functional 1960s replacement for its burnt-out 19th-century wooden predecessor whose observation platform offers a fine view over the area. The other focus of interest is the **Teufelssee** (Devil's Lake), the starting point for a number of nature trails.

The Forests and Lakes

Grunewald

The best known of the many forests encirling Berlin, the Grunewald (literally 'Green Wood') is divided between Wilmersdorf to the north and Zehlendorf to the south, accounting for about half the former's total area. Bound to the west by an abnormally wide stretch of the River Havel, the Grunewald was for a long time the private game reserve of the Hohenzollern dynasty from which the public were excluded. However, when it came under the control of the municipal authorities early this century, it quickly developed into one of Berlin's most popular recreational areas. Once predominantly of oak and beech, it later became a managed forest in which pine, birch and poplars were planted. Most of the trees were cut down after World War II to provide desperately needed fuel; the subsequent replanting aimed at returning the forest to a semblance of its original character, complete with stocks of red and fallow deer, wild boar and moufflon. Certain sections have been designated as nature reserves and these offer a tantalizing glimpse of how the pre-urban Berlin landscape must once have looked.

Despite this, the forest has many man-made imprints, none more prominent than the 120-metre-high **Teufelsberg** (Devil's Hill) at the northern end, which was constructed from 25 million cubic metres of rubble cleared from bomb-damaged buildings after World War II. For the meantime, the hill is crowned by a US radar and signals base, which used to monitor Warsaw Pact networks but is now redundant and scheduled to be demolished. Otherwise, the Teufelsberg functions as an area for leisure pursuits, with skiing and tobogganing in winter, hang-gliding and kite-flying in summer.

Immediately below the hill is the **Teufelssee**, the first of a trio of small lakes. The others, which both lie in secluded parts of the forest to the southwest, are the Pechsee and the Barssee, the latter being more reminiscent of a swamp. Two larger lakes, the **Hundekehlesee** and the **Grunewaldsee**, both at the extreme eastern edge of the forest, attract plenty of bathers and boaters in summer. Another favourite excursion destination is the **Grunewaldturm** (Grunewald Tower) at the opposite end of the forest. This was built at the very end of last century as a memorial to Kaiser Wilhelm I by Franz Schwechten, architect of the Kaiser-Wilhelm-Gedächtniskirche, who again utilized a mock medieval imagery, this time of the defensive towers which guarded the city walls. At the base of the monument are statues of the Kaiser and his leading ministers; steps lead up to a platform commanding a fine panorama over the Grunewald and the Havel.

Cutting a dead straight line through the forest is the nine-kilometre-long highway known as the **AVUS** (an acronymn for Automobil Verkehrs- und Übungstrasse). Opened in 1921 as Germany's first motor racing circuit, it was frequently used for speed record attempts, with 400 kilometres per hour the highest achieved. After the war, the AVUS became a normal public access road to the southwest, albeit one with the full status of an autobahn, including the obligatory German characteristic of no speed limit, which is regarded, somewhat bizarrely, as an essential symbol of a free society. The AVUS lost this designation, after strong lobbying from environmental groups, in 1990, when a top speed of 100 kilometres per hour was introduced except, of course, for the sports car races periodically held there.

Just to the northwest of Dahlem, right on the edge of the Grunewald, is the **Brücke-Museum**, dedicated to the artistic group known as *Die Brücke* ('The Bridge'), one of two rival movements that together created the uniquely German artistic style known as Expressionism, which was in part a reaction against the artistic hegemony then enjoyed by France. *Die Brücke* was founded in Dresden in 1905 and its initial personnel comprised three architecture students: Ernst Ludwig Kirchner, Erich Heckel and Karl Schmidt-Rottluff. Frustrated by the fact that their subject was inimical to the immediate freshness of inspiration, they turned to painting, and were joined shortly afterwards by Max Pechstein and Otto Mueller. They placed great emphasis on colour, both as a component in its own right and as an enhancement of surface effect. Their devotion to Germany's artistic heritage—and in particular the work of the old masters of the 15th and 16th centuries—was shown in the emphasis they placed on feeling and on their revival of the woodcut as an alternative to oils. In 1911, *Die Brücke* moved to Berlin and turned away from its original preoccupation with landscapes to the depiction of city life, becoming increasingly influenced by the art of tribal peoples, which was then being appreciated in Europe for the first time. The group broke up in 1913 and thereafter each artist pursued an independent career, though they remained true to at least some of its ideals.

Included in the museum's permanent collection, which is periodically supplanted by special thematic exhibitions, is a generous selection of the work of each member of *Die Brücke*. Kirchner, who served as the unofficial leader, now appears by far the most accomplished and versatile artist of the group, equally at home in decorative design or abstraction as in his more familiar landscapes and cityscapes. Heckel is fairly close in style, but preferred a greater sense of realism, particularly in his later work. Pechstein, who was the most loyal to naturalistic representation, was regarded during his lifetime as the most important Expressionist of all, but has suffered from a slump in his posthumous reputation. Mueller's work is now chiefly of interest for its documentation of gypsy culture, with which he had a genuine affinity, as he spent much of the 1920s travelling among Balkan communities. Schmidt-Rottluff, who

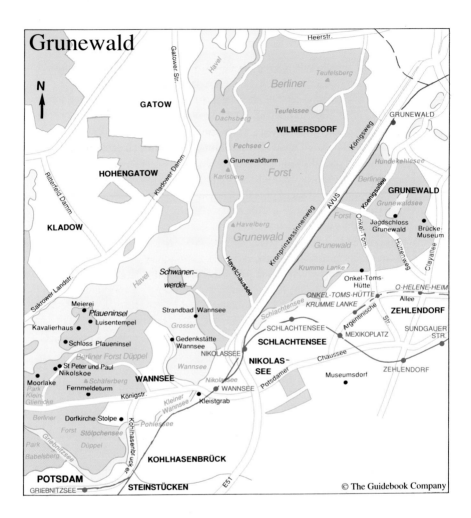

Grunewald

founded the museum in 1966 and donated much of its original collection, had the brightest palette and was the most prone to abstraction, and thus seems the most modernistic of the group. Also on view are a number of works by Emil Nolde, an artist of comparable statue to Kirchner, but who was only briefly a member of *Die Brücke* as he was far too solitary and indivualistic a figure to operate happily within its confines. His landscapes depict the rugged North Sea coastline that was his home-land, vividly conveying its harsh and forbidding nature. Flowers and garden scenes provide a lighter note within his oeuvre, but he also revived the somewhat lost art of religious painting, in which he aimed to unite the intensity of medieval German masters with the simple devotion found in primitive art.

About fifteen minutes' walk west along a forest path is the **Jagdschloss Grune-wald** (Grunewald Hunting Lodge), set overlooking the Grunewaldsee, which lies in the adjoining district of Wilmersdorf. The original whitewashed lodge stands in a courtyard surrounded by various later additions, including a magazine added by Frederick the Great which now serves as a museum of hunting equipment. Above the main entrance doorway is a relief of deer, including two rutting stags, along with a description declaring that the foundation stone was laid in 1542 by Elector Joachim II. The design is attributed to Caspar Theyss, who also rebuilt the Stadtschloss according to the Renaissance tastes of the day, and the plaque in the vestibule is thought to represent the architect in the company of his assistant Kunz Buntschuh and the sculptor Hans Schenk.

Though somewhat presumptuously titled, the Great Hall on the ground floor is the most impressive part of the interior. Its walls are lined with portraits of members of the Hohenzollern dynasty, among them one of Joachim II by Lucas Cranach the Younger, who took over the large and highly successful workshop established by his father, faithfully continuing his style. In the hall's alcove is a typical product from the shop while it was still run by Cranach the Elder—a set of nine scenes of *The Passion*, painted for the now demolished Dominican convent that formerly stood on Schloss-platz.

A number of portraits and mythological scenes from Cranach's own hand hang in the upstairs room, which is laid out as a picture gallery. Its most important and unusual possession, however, is a set of portraits, commissioned by the House of Orange, of the first twelve Roman emperors. Although the project was conceived as an entity, each portrait was painted by a different artist. Rubens' *Julius Caesar*, based on an antique model, rather steals the show by the sheer vivacity of its handling, though several others are of high quality, especially Hendrik Terbrugghen's *Claudius*, which effectively conjures up its subject's despotic personality, and Hendrik Goltzius' *Vitellius*, the work that provided the inspiration for the rest of the series.

Wannsee

Further south, still at the eastern fringe of the Grunewald, lie two more large lakes, **Krumme Lanke** and the **Schlachtensee**, whose shorelines are popular destinations with weekend ramblers. The best known lake in the area, however, is the **Grosser Wannsee**, which is formed by the River Havel. At its northeastern extremity is one of Berlin's most exclusive addresses, the **Schwanenwerder** peninsula. Beyond is the kilometre-long **Strandbad Wannsee**, Europe's largest inland beach, which was laid out as a bathing resort in the late 1920s for the benefit of tenement dwellers who were unable to afford a holiday away from home.

Across the lake is the **Gedenkstätte Haus der Wannsee-Konferenz** (Memorial House of the Wannsee Conference), a residential villa that was the setting for the fateful meeting of 20th January 1942 convened by Reinhard Heydrich, head of the Reich Central Security Office. This decided on the organization and implementation of one of the Nazi Party's most cherished ambitions, euphemistically referred to as the 'Final Solution'—the attempted genocide of European Jewry, whose population was then estimated at some 11 million. Minutes of the meeting kept by Adolf Eichmann were used as key evidence at the Nuremberg Trials, thereby refuting the testimony of many defendants who had falsely claimed to have been ignorant of the true nature of the policy. It was decided to round up all Jews in occupied countries, whether by force or by promise of resettlement, and to deport them to concentration camps, where they would be worked to death or systematically exterminated. To cut down on the transportation costs, the camps were primarily concentrated in Poland: in the wake of the country's defeat in 1939, its Jewish population, the largest in Europe, had already been forcibly segregated into urban ghettos and thus formed ready-made fodder for the first death camps. The rooms of the villa are now given over to a chilling photographic record of the tragic fate of the Jews at the hands of the Nazis, beginning with the initial repressive measures taken in Germany before the war to render it *Jüdenfrei* (free of Jews) to the mass murders at Auschwitz, which—following various exaggerated estimates and understated counterclaims—are now thought by reputable historians to have accounted for around 1.5 million Jewish lives.

On Bismarckstrasse, just to the rear of the Wannsee S-Bahn station, the **Kleist-grab** (Kleist tomb) marks the spot of the bizarre double suicide on 22nd November 1811 of the great writer Heinrich von Kleist, aged just 34, and Marianne Vogel, a 31-year-old married woman dying of cancer. This act stirred the Romantic imagination, not only because the pair approached their deaths with a feeling of triumph, but also because of the air of mystery surrounding their exact relationship, which evidence suggests was almost certainly not that of lovers. An intensely ambitious man who was nevertheless unsure of his gifts, Kleist had been driven to despair by the failure of his contemporaries to comprehend his works, even though his literary career had already been marked by more than a few successes. Kleist's output was astonishingly varied, and speaks far more forceably to the modern reader—or at least those outside the German-speaking world—than that of any of his contemporaries. His short stories, all narrated with detatched objectivity, are often set in exotic locations, such as Chile and Santo Domingo; they are characterized by dramatic twists of plot, and scenes of lyrical intensity alternate with episodes of savage brutality. The plays, which are more emotional in tone, range from *The Broken Jug*, a hilarious comedy during which a corrupt village judge tries a case in which he is the actual culprit, via *Penthesilea*, a tragicomic mythological spoof, to *Prince Frederick of Homburg*, in which Prussia's Great Elector appears as justice and mercy personified. The last of these caused a sensation for daring to suggest that the eponymous hero, a Prussian soldier, reacted less than stoically to his impending death. One of its most celebrated lines, 'Now, oh immortality, you are wholly mine!', is the epitaph on the tombstone.

Kohlhasenbrück, Steinstücken and Düppel

A couple of kilometres to the south, past the lakes of Kleiner Wannsee, Pohlersee and Stolpchensee, is **Kohlhasenbrück**, the setting for the beginning of Kleist's longest prose work, *Michael Kohlhaas*. Based on the true story of a 16th-century horse dealer whose passion for justice made him 'one of the most honourable as well as one of the most terrible men of his age', the novella focuses on the uncomfortable theme of the outsider in German society, a role Kleist himself knew only too well.

South of Kohlhasenbrück lies the small village of **Steinstücken**, which throughout the Cold War period was one of Europe's most curious corners. Although it adjoins Potsdam, it was incorporated into Berlin in 1920, and therefore lay in the Western sector of the divided city despite being an enclave within the GDR. Notwithstanding its lack of strategic value, the Soviets at first attempted to seize it, but eventually had to accede to the American demand for the opening of a restricted access road from Kohlhasenbrück. When the Berlin Wall went up, it had to be built down both sides of the road and all round the village, lending it an anomalous fortress-like appearance. This is still hinted at, if somewhat vaguely, by the patches of cleared wasteland that have succeeded the Wall.

East of the Wannsee S-Bahn station is **Düppel**. The original village, which was set on a marsh known as Krummes Fenn, was abandoned in 1220. It has since proved a fruitful hunting ground for archaeologists, who are carrying out a full-scale conjectural reconstruction of the settlement. Known as the **Museumsdorf Düppel** (Düppel Museum Village), this is open to the public a couple of days a week in summer, when there are also demonstrations of handicrafts and agricultural methods of the time.

The **Forst Düppel** (Duppel Forest) stretches from the Grosser Wannsee to the municipal border with Potsdam. Set within it, on a terrace overlooking the Havel, is the **Nikolskoe**, one of the best of the *Ausflugsgaststätten* ('excursion restaurants') in the Berlin suburbs. The building itself, a Russian-style log cabin constructed in 1819 by the military architect Hauptmann Snethlage, was commissioned by King Friedrich Wilhelm III as a retreat for his daughter, Charlotte, and her husband, the future Czar

Nicholas I—hence its name, which means 'Nicholas's own'. Some fifteen years later, it was granted an appropriate pendant in the shape of the **Kirche St Peter und Paul** (Church of SS Peter and Paul), designed by Friedrich August Stüler. He was instructed to give the church a Russian flavour but was allowed no more than one tower and onion dome instead of the traditional five; as a result, this is the only unusual touch on what is otherwise a typical example of Prussian yellow brick architecture of the period, with the early Christian basilicas of Italy the chief source of inspiration. Inside, the main feature of note is the pulpit, which stretches all the way up to the gallery and is adorned with ancient Roman mosaics of the church's two patron saints, presented to Frederick the Great by Pope Clement XIII.

Pfaueninsel

A ferry departs from the jetty below Nikolskoe for the two-minute crossing to **Pfaueninsel** (Peacock Island), the prettiest park in Berlin seen at its most glorious in springtime. For the most part, it presents an artificial landscape that was an integral part of the planned garden scheme of Potsdam, the intended embarkation point for visitors to the island, which was purchased by King Friedrich Wilhelm II in 1783. In accordance with Romantic notions then in vogue at courts throughout Europe, he set about transforming it into an evocation of an exotic, idyllic world untouched by civilization, one that would serve as a hideaway for himself and his mistress Wilhelmine Encke, whom he elevated to the title of Countess Lichtenau. In the event, the king died before his paradise was completed, but work continued under Friedrich Wilhelm III and his wife Queen Luise, who spent a great deal of time on the island. At first, the new monarch introduced a practical element by establishing a working farm, but the increased prosperity that followed victory in the Napoleonic Wars enabled him to dispense with this. Peter Joseph Lenné was then commissioned to landscape the island, planting new trees and relaying the paths in order to present as many varied vistas as possible. A menagerie of wild animals, later to form the core of Berlin Zoo, was set up; to complete the sense of bizarre curiosity, a Sandwich Islander, a negro, a giant and two dwarfs were brought to live on Pfaueninsel, which was opened to the public twice a week and quickly established itself as the best day outing from the city.

Virtually abandoned by the royal family after the death of Friedrich Wilhelm III and undamaged by war, the Pfaueninsel is now a nature reserve in which strict by-laws are enforced to maintain its restful tranquillity. Grouped along its quayside are a number of rustic buildings, including the **Schweizer Haus** (Swiss House) to the extreme left, which was designed by Schinkel. A bit further along the shore is the covered **Fregatta-Hafen** (Frigate Harbour), which was built to shelter a miniature frigate donated by King George IV of Britain.

Schloss Pfaueninsel is a true Romantic folly, a point underlined by the fact that it was designed not by a professional architect but by the court carpenter, Johann Gottlieb Brendel. He chose to build it in the form of a ruined medieval castle, concentrating on producing a striking silhouette that could be seen from afar. The fake doorway in the middle of the façade is painted with a *trompe l'oeil* portcullis with a landscape background, as though it were offering a view across the island. Linking the two towers, whose function is purely decorative, is an impressive wrought-iron balcony, made in 1807 as one of the first products from the Berlin Iron Foundry to replace its fire-damaged wooden predecessor. The interiors, which preserve almost all their original furniture and decoration, demonstrate the varied preoccupations of the Romantic mind. Particularly intriguing is the Tahiti Cabinet in the northern tower, which is painted to resemble the interior of a bamboo hut and has palm trees and tropical flowers and plants intruding on the otherwise topographically accurate scenes of the Pfaueninsel. The southern tower is entirely taken up with a spiral stairwell shaped like a huge rosette, while other rooms are variously intended to evoke India, China and Ancient Rome.

In the heart of the island is the **Kavalierhaus** (Gentleman's House), which was originally built at the beginning of the 19th century to house the farm workers. Two

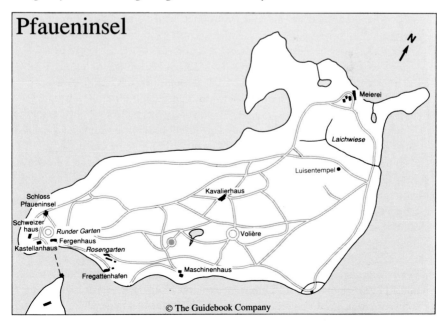

decades later it was completely remodelled by Schinkel, who reused the six-storey façade of a demolished Late-Gothic patrician mansion from Danzig that had been saved by the Crown Prince, the future Friedrich Wilhelm IV. He attached this to the south tower and redesigned the rest of the front to harmonize with it. In a neat twist, the Schinkel sandstone portico built for the Mausoleum in Charlottenburg was salvaged for the **Luisentempel** (Temple of Queen Luise) at the eastern end of the island, the original being supplanted by one of granite.

Further north is the other significant building on the island, the **Meierei** (Dairy), again by Brendel in the manner of an artificial ruin, this time aping the architecture of the brick Gothic churches of northern Germany. To the rear of the Kavalierhaus is the circular **Volière** (Aviary), whose birds are, with the exception of the sixty-odd peacocks that freely roam the island, the only surviving reminder of the menagerie.

Park Klein-Glienicke

Back on the mainland, at the westernmost end of the Forst Düppel, is another beautifully crafted landscape, the **Park Klein-Glienicke**. This property was acquired by Prince Karl, third son of Frederick Wilhelm III, who was determined to transform it into a splendid memorial to his Italian journey of 1822–3 and a fitting home for the collection of antiquities he had amassed there. Schinkel was commissioned to carry out modifications to the existing buildings on the site and to add a series of whimsical new structures to the pleasure ground that Lenné had laid out around the original 18th-century country house for the previous owner, the Prussian Chancellor Prince Karl August von Hardenberg.

The architect began with the **Casino**, converting the old billiard room on a terrace overlooking the River Havel into an Italianate villa, complete with two long side loggias. He imparted a similar touch to **Schloss Glienicke**, altering its exterior and adding a side wing with tower to the U-shaped courtyard. A few rooms have recently been made accessible to the public and serve as a gallery for temporary exhibitions of modern art; it is intended to open the rest of the house at a later date. Schinkel also created the gilded **Löwenfontäne** (Lion Fountain) outside, modelled on that of the Villa Medici in Rome, and rebuilt the so-called **Kleine Neugierde** ('Small Curiosity'), a teahouse in the form of an antique temple. His most inventive contribution, however, was the **Grosse Neugierde** ('Large Curiosity') at the extreme southwestern edge of the garden. This circular pavilion, resting on 18 Corinthian columns, is surmounted by an imitation of the famous Monument to Lysikrates in Athens; its main

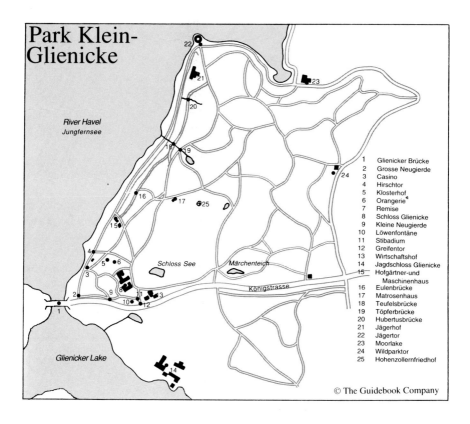

Park Klein-Glienicke

River Havel
Jungfernsee

Schloss See

Märchenteich

Königstrasse

Glienicker Lake

1	Glienicker Brücke
2	Grosse Neugierde
3	Casino
4	Hirschtor
5	Klosterhof
6	Orangerie
7	Remise
8	Schloss Glienicke
9	Kleine Neugierde
10	Löwenfontäne
11	Stibadium
12	Greifentor
13	Wirtschaftshof
14	Jagdschloss Glienicke
15	Hofgärtner-und Maschinenhaus
16	Eulenbrücke
17	Matrosenhaus
18	Teufelsbrücke
19	Töpferbrücke
20	Hubertusbrücke
21	Jägerhof
22	Jägertor
23	Moorlake
24	Wildparktor
25	Hohenzollernfriedhof

© The Guidebook Company

function was as a belvedere, offering a sweeping view of Potsdam and Babelsberg, as well as over the park, the Havel and its lakes. Various other garden structures were subsequently added by followers of Schinkel; the most notable is Ferdinand von Arnim's **Klosterhof** (Monastery Courtyard), which serves to display the Byzantine section of Prince Karl's art collection.

The prince also commissioned Lenné to landscape the extensive wooded tracts that comprise the rest of the estate. Dotted throughout are many features which echo the whimsy of the pleasure garden, including several grandiose entrance gateways and a number of eccentric little bridges, among which Ludwig Persius's **Teufelsbrücke** (Devil's Bridge) serves as part of a charming miniaturization of an alpine gorge. The same architect built the **Hofgärtner- und Machinenhaus** (Court Gardener's and Machine House), which is in the style of a fortress in Italy's Abruzzi region, while Schinkel's **Jägerhof** (Hunter's Courtyard) further north breaks with the Italian theme by mimicking the architecture of Tudor England. Just beyond the latter is the **Jägertor** (Hunter's Gate), which offers the best view in the park, notably of the Pfaueninsel to the east and of Persius's grandly isolated **Heilandskirche** (Church of

Statues at Glienicke Palace

the Saviour) a short hop across the water. The church, which can only be reached by road by means of a 20-kilometre journey via Potsdam, was such a tempting launch pad for anyone hoping to make an acquatic exit from the GDR that the authorities sealed it off and left it to crumble, though it has now been restored.

Just beyond the Grosse Neugierde is one of the most famous symbols of the Cold War era, the **Glienicker Brücke** (Glienicke Bridge), which links Berlin with Potsdam across the divide between the Jungfernsee and the Glienicke Lake. The first bridge here, erected during the reign of the Great Elector, was replaced by one designed by Schinkel, which in turn gave way to a cast-iron construction of 1908–09; this was blown up in World War II, but faithfully rebuilt. In the Cold War period, when the normal public access to Potsdam from West Berlin was via East Berlin, the bridge was used only by Allied officers and accredited GDR diplomats. It was the setting of several much-publicized spy exchanges, initiated in February 1962 with the swap of the American U-2 pilot Gary Powers for the double agent Rudolf Ivanovich Abel, and continued up to 1986 with the release of the Russian Jewish dissident leader Anatoly Sharansky. From the bridge, which swiftly regained its original role on the fall of the Berlin Wall, paths lead south to the **Jagdschloss Glienicke** (Glienicke Hunting Lodge), a huge neo-Renaissance structure that now serves as an international conference centre.

Potsdam

The thousand-year-old city of **Potsdam**, the favourite residence of Frederick the Great and other Prussian kings, presents a dazzling triumph of Man over Nature: the original swampy marshland of the site formed by the River Havel and its lakes have been transformed into a glorious planned townscape replete with palaces, parks and gardens. It forms a virtually seamless whole with the westernmost suburbs of Berlin, but remains fiercely defensive of its status as a city independent of its much larger, yet less venerable neighbour. Indeed, despite its modest population of 150,000, it is the capital of the revived Land of Brandenburg, one of five states which replaced the former GDR in Germany's federal political structure. Potsdam is an easy excursion from the metropolis, though it is so rich in sights (there are at least as many outstanding buildings as in Berlin itself) that several days' exploration are needed for more than a superficial impression. Thankfully, it is once more readily accessible—a far cry from the Cold War years, when the city was little visited by Westerners. At that time the city was out-of-bounds to those visiting East Berlin on normal day visas, and was approachable from West Berlin only by an absurdly contorted route.

Nonetheless, hangovers from Communism, which, as in the rest of the former GDR other than East Berlin itself, are still clearly in evidence (despite the departure of last remaining soldiers of the Red Army in September 1994), only add to Potsdam's fascination. Previously, the soldiers' all-too-visible presence had imparted a genuine sense of menace. Post-unification, hopelessly demoralized by the utter pointlessness of their presence here, they seemed mere figures of fun. Yet the locals continue to cling to many of the most irritating rituals of the old regime. Queues form outside shops, including supermarkets, as customers wait patiently for one of the insufficient supply of trolleys or baskets to become free. Heavily over-manned restaurants continue to insist that patrons yield up their coats and bags at the entrance, charge for the use of the toilet, make them wait for a table, serve up stodgy institutional food, and regard a tip, always included in the price in western Germany, as obligatory. The general air of neglect, whereby historic buildings were left to crumble, is accentuated by the amount of scaffolding which will be in evidence for some time to come. As the organizers of the 1993 millennium celebrations were only too ready to admit, it is a pity that the city is not a few years younger than it is.

The basis for these celebrations was the oldest documented reference to Potsdam. This mentioned that the settlement of Poztupimi (a name suggesting a Slav rather than a Germanic origin) was a gift from the Holy Roman Emperor Otto III to his aunt, the Abbess Mathilde of the wealthy imperial convent at Quedlinburg. Potsdam probably only became a fully fledged town in the 14th century, when a castle is known to have existed. It remained a modest place for several centuries more and the Thirty Years' War of 1618–48, which devastated much of Germany, saw its population shrink to a mere 79 households. In 1660, the town's big breakthrough came when Friedrich Wilhelm, the Great Elector, chose it as one of his residences and began the construction of the city's first palace. Early the following century, his namesake, the Soldier King, characteristically made it into a garrison town, a function it has retained ever since.

The real transformation of Potsdam's role and appearance, however, was due to that ultimate practitioner of enlightened despotism, Frederick the Great. Soon after acceding to the Prussian throne in 1740, he arranged for Potsdam to supplant Berlin as his principal residence and serve as a place where he could wrap himself up in musical, artistic and literary interests, unburdened by the affairs of state. The name he chose for his palace and its park was the French term *sans souci* (literally 'without cares'), reflecting both its function and his near-fanatical Francophilia. Huge teams of craftsmen, led by the leading German architects, sculptors, painters, decorators and landscape gardeners of the day, were employed to turn the monarch's whims into the reality of a complex of baroque and rococo masterpieces. Although Frederick's immediate successors added nothing of significance—and were less than entranced by his legacy—his ideals were taken a step further in the 1820s by the future Friedrich Wilhelm IV, then still a crown prince, who began adding neoclassical and Romantic palaces and gardens to complement the original ensemble.

Potsdam's status as the embodiment of the finest achievements of the royal Prussian state befell a series of unfortunate twists in the present century, tarnishing its name incalculably. The rot started on 21st March 1933, when the Reichstag was reconvened here, on the anniversary of Bismarck's opening of the first-ever Reichstag of the newly united Germany in 1871, in the wake of the mysterious burning of its Berlin headquarters. Carefully stage-managed by Nazi propaganda supremo Josef Goebbels, the proceedings climaxed with the notorious 'Potsdam handshake' between Adolf Hitler, the new Chancellor of Germany, and Paul von Hindenburg, the Federal President and retired Field Marshal who had appointed him to the position. This powerful visual symbol linked the regime of terror, mass genocide and indoctrination about to be introduced by the Nazis with the most glorious episodes of Prussia's past.

A heavy price was to be paid for this. In April 1945, Potsdam was devastated by RAF bombers; though the palaces and parks miraculously suffered little damage, the city centre was reduced to a heap of smouldering ruins. Three months later, the 'Big Three' of the United States, the Soviet Union and the United Kingdom held their victorious conference in the city, another symbolic gesture proving that the German Reich was utterly defeated (see page 296). The national humiliation was further confirmed by the official announcement of the loss of East Prussia, plus nearly all of Silesia and most of Pomerania, including the city of Stettin, Berlin's own port. Equally significantly, the agreement to divide Germany into zones of occupation laid the foundation for the partition of the country into two hostile states four years later.

Potsdam's discomfiture continued under the Communists: although the city was one of the GDR's star attractions, they were never happy with its imperialistic and militaristic associations. The most drastic consequence of this was that a number of key buildings damaged in the war were razed completely, and that parts of the centre were rebuilt according to the Stalinist preference for soulless highrise blocks. Some restitution was made from the 1970s onwards, in accordance with a reassessment of the country's past undertaken to try to foster a stronger sense of national identity. Preposterously, this included reinterpreting Frederick the Great, along with Luther, Bismarck and other historical figures with an east German connection, as 'progressive' forces, and thus precursors of Communism. Considerable sums of money were spent on restoration work in the city, though this was still pitifully insufficient. The far more ambitious programmes started since the fall of Communism will be a long time in progress, and it remains to be seen whether the town centre will eventually be reconstructed along its prewar lines or given a more modern, albeit this time capitalistic, face.

The most atmospheric approach to Potsdam is along the Havel on one of the *Weisse Flotte* steamers (see page 329); alternatively, bus 116 links Wannsee with the terminus of tram 93 on the Potsdam side of the famous spy-swap Glienicker Brücke. More prosaically but faster, there are S-Bahn trains (lines 3 and 5 from Zoologischer Garten, with the extra option of the less direct line 1 from Friedrichstrasse) which link the two city centres. Potsdam's parks are at their most beautiful in spring, but, although the chief monuments can be visited all year round, many others do not open until mid-May, closing again in mid-October. For more details, see the listings on page 330. Weekends are always best avoided because of the crowds: the loss of the formerly vast volume of organized tour groups from the Soviet bloc has been more than offset by the increased numbers from Western countries added to the regular influx of daytrippers from Berlin.

Park Sanssouci

Immediately to the west of central Potsdam lies the city's main attraction, **Park Sanssouci**, which was laid out from 1744 onwards, just four years after Frederick the Great's accession. Its original plan epitomizes the Age of Enlightenment, abandoning

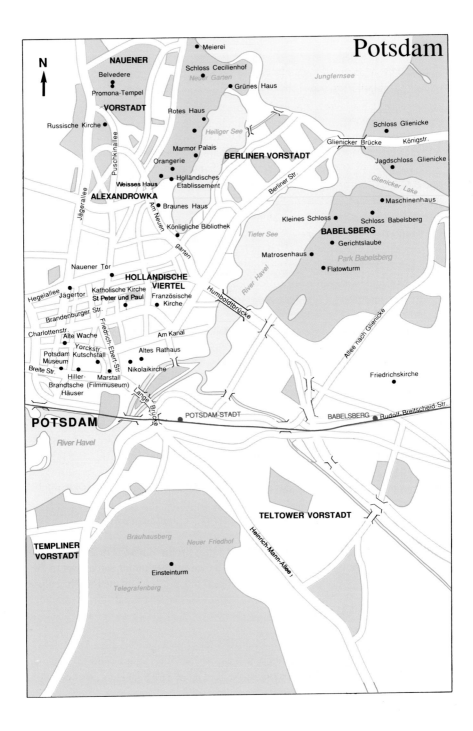

the traditional baroque format of a grandiose palace as the centrepiece. Instead, there are a host of buildings, mostly modest in scale (though this ideal was jettisoned in a couple of later additions), and the palace does not even lie on the main axis, the 2.5-kilometre Hauptweg.

The usual entry to the park is via the **Obeliskpforte** (Obelisk Gateway) at the eastern end, built in 1747 to plans by Frederick's court architect, Georg Wenceslaus von Knobelsdorff. It has a suitably impressive framework, featuring two monumental groups of four fluted Corinthian columns closely clustered together and topped by pediments bearing ornamental vase-shaped sculptures; in contrast, the gates them-selves look quite absurdly modest. On the adjoining boundary wall are statues of Flora and Pomona, the goddesses of flowers and fruit, carved by Friedrich Christian Glume, the foremost sculptor of Potsdam rococo. Just outside the park boundaries stands the **Obelisk** which gives the gateway its name. This is covered with vigorous Egyptian-style hieroglyphs, but these are purely decorative, predating the first suc-cessful modern deciphering of this script by some seven decades.

The first building of note within the park is the **Friedenskirche** (Peace Church), photogenically set beside an artificial pond. Begun in 1845 to plans by Ludwig Per-sius, it was intended as a commemoration of the centenary of Sanssouci. Modelled on the early Christian columned basilica of San Clemente in Rome, its shady atrium and seven-storey campanile readily evoke sunny Mediterranean climes. The construction history is highly unusual, as the shape and measurements were predetermined by its main adornment, the magnificent apse mosaic which Friedrich Wilhelm IV acquired from the church of San Cipriano in Murano in the Venetian lagoon. Apart from the damaged example in Berlin's Bode Museum, this is the only original Byzantine mos-aic to be found north of the Alps. Its main scene shows Christ as Judge, flanked by the Virgin, St Peter, St John the Baptist and St Cyprian, the patron of its original home; the triumphal arch displays the Agnus Dei between the archangels Michael and Raphael, each depicted as medieval heralds. To complement the mosaic, the pulpit, altar and paschal candelstick were constructed in imitation of the earlier Italian style. These are somewhat overshadowed by the large baldachin, made of Siberian jasper gifted by Czar Nicholas I, the king's brother-in-law. Friedrich Wil-helm IV and his consort, Elisabeth Luise, are buried in unassuming sarcophagi in the crypt. The church's atrium contains a copy of a statue of Christ by the Danish sculp-tor Berthel Thorwaldsen and a powerful group of Moses, Aaron and Hur, the last composition of Christian Daniel Rauch. The domed structure on the northern side is the mausoleum of Friedrich III; its echoing of the Dom in Berlin is no coincidence, being the work of the same architect, Julius Carl Raschdorf.

Beyond the church is **Marlys Garten**, a kitchen garden rearranged in the 19th century as a small *jardin anglais* by Peter Joseph Lenné. Much more characteristic of

Sanssouci is the **Neptungrotte** (Neptune Grotto), set amongst trim lawns and well-tended flower beds on the opposite side of the Hauptweg. This was Knobelsdorff's last work, completed posthumously; it marks a decisive shift away from his normally restrained, classically derived style to one of exhilarating rococo playfulness. The interior is encrusted with shells, over which spring water slowly trickles, while the parapet is crowned with statues of naiads and the sea-god Neptune, the last-named fashioned from a single block of Italian marble.

Further along the Hauptweg is the **Grosse Fontäne** (Great Fountain), a huge water jet set in a circular basin. This was a pet project of Frederick the Great, but, despite vast expenditure, one his engineers were never able to solve: it first functioned effectively in the 1840s, following the construction of the Pumpwerk. Ranged around the fountain are statues of mythological figures; some of these, notably the figures of Venus and Mercury by the distinguished French sculptor Jean Baptiste Pigalle, rank among the finest adornments of the park. To the north lies the kernel of Sanssouci, a tiered vineyard (one of the most northerly in Europe) laid out in 1744 in the form of six terraces, providing an impressively grand foreground to the main palace building.

In 1991, the uppermost of these was the scene for a bizarre midnight ceremony, attended by many prominent national figures, whereby Frederick the Great was finally laid to rest in his chosen place—alongside his beloved greyhounds. His heirs, considering this an unsuitable grave for a monarch, had defied his wishes and interred him alongside the father he hated in the Garnisonkirche in the town centre. At the end of World War II both coffins were spirited away to the family seat of Burg Hohenzollern in Swabia; only when the two German states were united was thought given to returning Frederick's remains to Potsdam. The much publicized reburial occasioned heated debate. Critics attacked it as showing tacit approval for the country's militaristic past; others, such as Federal Chancellor Helmut Kohl, who attended the ceremony, defended it as a necessary cathartic process. On the same terrace, and far more immediately noticeable, is an ornate trellis pavilion, sheltering the statue of a deity.

Schloss Sanssouci is a homely single-storey palace, constructed by Knobelsdorff from drawings by Frederick the Great himself. It was begun in 1745, the year after the vineyard, and completed just three years later. Its garden front features a curvaceously protruding domed central section and a marvellous series of 36 caryatids by Friedrich Christian Glume, each skilfully characterized. The northern façade has always been the main entrance, though the iron gate through which the original visitors would have approached its colonnaded *cour d'honneur* now fronts a sheer drop to the Maulbeerallee (Mulberry Avenue) below. From here, there is a fine view across to the Ruinenberg, a hill crowned with mock classical ruins plus the reservoir

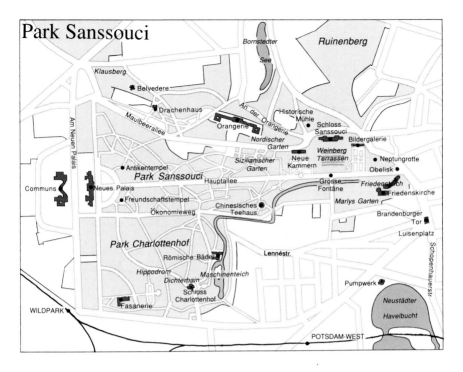

Park Sanssouci

Bornstedter
See

Ruinenberg

Klausberg

❀ Belvedere

● Drachenhaus

Maulbeerallee

An der Orangerie

Historische
Mühle

Orangerie

Schloss
Sanssouci

Nordischer
Garten

Bildergalerie

Am Neuen Palais

Sizilianischer
Garten

Neue
Kammern

Weinberg
Terrassen

Neptungrotte

● Antikentempel

Park Sanssouci

Hauptallee

Obelisk ●

Communs

Neues Palais

Grosse
Fontäne

Friedenskirch

Friedenskirche

● Freundschaftstempel

Marlys Garten

Ökonomieweg

Chinesisches
Teehaus

Brandenburger
Tor

Luisenplatz

Schopenhauerstr.

Park Charlottenhof

Römische Bäder

Lennéstr.

Hippodrom

Maschinenteich

Dichterhain

Pumpwerk ✿

Schloss
Charlottenhof

Neustädter

Fasanerie

WILDPARK

Havelbucht

POTSDAM-WEST

supplying the water to the park. Admission tickets for the interior, which can only be visited by guided tour, are sold at the window on the western side. It is advisable to get there early, particularly at weekends and in high summer: the numbers admitted daily are restricted for conservation reasons, though it is possible to book in the morning for a tour later in the day.

There are just twelve rooms in the original Schloss, all but one of which are on show; these are arranged in groups of five around the central vestibule and hall, with the king's private apartments to the east, the guest chambers to the west. The interiors are a luxuriant blend of archetypal rococo decoration, such as coloured marble, stuccowork, gilded wood, spacious ceiling frescos, specially made furniture and both genuine and ersatz antique statues. There are also a large number of ornate French paintings idealizing the carefree lifestyle of shepherdesses and dandies. The pick of these, notably several works by Watteau, were removed during the war and are currently exhibited at Schloss Charlottenburg in Berlin.

At the far end of the Schloss, approached via a narrow corridor, is the tiny circular library. Its bookcases, which are inlaid in the walls, are largely devoted to French volumes, in line with Frederick's dogmatic tastes. Next comes the king's combined study and bedroom, which were remodelled in the 1780s by Friedrich Wilhelm von Erdmannsdorff, the architect who introduced the neoclassical style of British country

Marble Gallery in the Neues Palais, Carl Graeb watercolour, 1853

houses to Germany. The Concert Chamber next door was where Frederick indulged in his passion for flute playing. Though the instrument on show is only a copy, there is a fine example of the work of one of the earliest piano manufacturers, Johann Gottfried Silbermann, who is best known as the builder of some of the world's greatest organs. The walls are adorned with murals by the court artist Antoine Pesne showing scenes from Ovid's *Metamorphoses*. Appropriately, the central ellipse-shaped Marble Hall, fashioned with marble from the quarries of Carrara, famously used by Michelangelo among others, is the most impressive room in the palace. Eight pairs of fluted Corinthian columns support the cupola, on the edge of which are sculptures representing the Liberal Arts Frederick loved so much. Of the guest rooms which follow, the first is notable for its chinoiserie, a recurrent theme in Park Sanssouci, while the fourth is named after Voltaire. The French philosopher lived in Potsdam, albeit in the Stadtschloss, for three years at Frederick's behest until the two fell out irreconcilably, exchanging insults for the rest of their lives.

Schloss Sanssouci was little used between the time of Frederick the Great's death and the accession of Friedrich Wilhelm IV. The latter was responsible for the addition of the **Damenflügel** (Ladies' Wing) to its west side in 1841, an appropriately modest looking extension for the use of ladies-in-waiting and kitchen staff.

Considerably more prepossessing are the two outlying structures which dominate their own terraces on either side of the Schloss. To the east, the **Bildergalerie** (Picture Gallery), begun in 1755 by Johann Gottfried Büring, is of special note as being the first custom-built museum in the world. Its garden front is punctuated by a series of large windows to illuminate the interior with natural light; the interior consists of a single festive hall, where the larger pictures are hung, with an intimate cabinet chamber for the smaller works at the far end. To this day, all the paintings are displayed closely packed together in the traditional but now unfashionable manner. The overall quality of the exhibited works is very variable: top-class Renaissance and baroque masterpieces of the Italian, French, Flemish and Dutch Schools intermingle with mediocre productions and copies of the same artistic schools. As the paintings are only numbered—another traditional feature—and not labelled, visitors are forced to buy a catalogue in order to appreciate the displays properly.

The most celebrated canvas is *The Incredulity of St Thomas* (No 17), which is now generally accepted as an autograph work of Caravaggio. Among the gallery's few Renaissance exhibits are *The Baptism of Fire* (No 16) by Vasari, *Noah's Thank-Offering after the Flood* (No 28) by Jacopo Bassano, and *Carnival* (No 27) by Leandro Bassano; later Italian works include several fine examples by Guido Reni, notably *The Death of Cleopatra* (No 8). Pick of the French works is the sensual and mysterious *Allegory of the Birth of a Prince of France* (No 79) by an unknown artist of the School of Fontainebleau, while the finest Dutch painting here is the dramatically realistic *Supper at Emmaus* (No 36) by Terbrugghen. The golden age of Flemish baroque is represented by a dozen canvases by Rubens and his workshop, including *Jesus and John the Baptist as Children* (No 47), *The Four Evangelists* (No 56), and *St Jerome in his Hermitage* (No 58); by Van Dyck are the large early *Descent of the Holy Ghost* (No 46) and the contrastingly small pair of devotional images, *Christ* and *The Virgin* (Nos 90 and 91).

Balancing the Bildergalerie on the west side of the Schloss is a very similar looking building known as the **Neue Kammern** (New Chambers). This was originally built by Knobelsdorff as an orangery, but was modified in the 1770s by Georg Christian Unger, who added a cupola in the centre of the building and transformed the interior into a plush guesthouse for visitors to the court. Appropriately, the rooms are slightly less striking than those of the Schloss; highlights are the Ovid Gallery, with reliefs illustrating scenes from the eponymous poet's *Elegies*, and the oval-shaped Banqueting Hall. Below the Neue Kammern is a peaceful rose garden, while directly to the west is the **Sizilianischer Garten** (Sicilian Garden), laid out by Lenné in imitation of formal Italian Renaissance models.

South of here, on the opposite side of the Hauptweg, is the kitschiest yet most endearing Sanssouci monument, the **Chinesisches Teehaus** (Chinese Tea House).

Built by Büring in the mid-1750s, it mirrors the reports of contemporary visitors to China, then regarded, with no sense of irony, as a land of peace and happiness. The tent-shaped roof has a cupola crowned with a gilded statue of a mandarin sitting under a parasol. Life-sized figures, carved with a disconcerting realism, are grouped around the entrance: some are shown drinking tea, others coffee, while yet more play a veritable orchestra of instruments. Inside, the round main hall and its three adjoining cabinets are decked out as a museum of Chinese and Meissen porcelain.

Across Maulbeerallee from the Neue Kammern is the **Historische Windmühle** (Historic Windmill), one of just two buildings in Park Sanssouci to have suffered extensive damage in the 1945 air raid. It was only restored to working order as part of the 1993 millennium celebrations and will be opened as a technical museum in due course. West of here is the **Nordischer Garten** (North Garden), another Lenné creation.

Further on, occupying a grandstand position overlooking the whole park, is the **Orangerie** (Orangery). Designed by Persius and built throughout the 1850s by August Stüler and Ludwig Hesse, it was intended as the centrepiece of a never completed triumphal way proposed as the culmination of Friedrich Wilhelm IV's additions to Sanssouci. Despite the obvious homage to Italian Renaissance models, it is a bombastically Germanic, rather monotonous-looking structure whose dimensions—the façade is 330 metres long—are wholly at odds with the original conception of the park.

The central section of the building, one of whose twin towers can be ascended during the summer months, includes the Raphael Hall, whose walls are lined with copies of Italian Renaissance masterpieces. Inspiration for this came as a result of Friedrich Wilhelm III's visit to Paris in 1813, when he saw an exhibition of paintings looted by Napoleon. He determined on acquiring a more legitimate collection by commissioning German artists to reproduce the most famous images of Raphael, then considered the greatest artist of all time. Modern scholarship has somewhat spoiled the effect of the ensemble: although Raphael's finest masterpieces, such as *The School of Athens*, *The Triumph of Galatea* and *The Sistine Madonna*, are represented, many of the works are now known to be by his master Perugino, or by pupils such as Giulio Romano. Linked by a loggia to the rear of the hall is a suite of rooms decorated in styles ranging from Regency to Empire; these were used by Czar Nicholas I and Czarina Charlotte on their frequent sojourns in Potsdam.

At the far northwestern end of Park Sanssouci is the Klausberg, a hill cultivated as a vineyard. The **Drachenhaus** (Dragon House) was built in 1770 by Carl von Gontard on the model of the Chinese pagoda in Kew Gardens in London, with a gracefully tapering three-storey tower. Originally the home of the vintner, it is now a genteel café which makes an ideal place for a rest from sightseeing. Further along is the **Belvedere**, a rococo tower which suffered a direct hit in 1945 and is currently in the process of restoration.

Due south of here, on either side of the Hauptweg, are the **Antikentempel** (Temple of Antiquity) and the **Freundschaftstempel** (Friendship Temple), both the work of Gontard. The former, a miniature version of the Parthenon in Athens, was built to house the royal collection of classical antiquities that was later moved to Berlin. The latter is a circular-shaped memorial to the Margravine Wilhelmine of Bayreuth, sister of Frederick the Great and one of the few women for whom the great misogynist showed the slightest affection. Inside the portico is a statue to the deceased, a major artistic patron in her own right; the medallions on the pillars illustrate friendships of classical antiquity.

Further west is the vast bulk of the pink **Neues Palais** (New Palace), built between 1763 and 1769 to mark the end of the Seven Years' War, which established Prussian supremacy over Austria (hitherto the dominant power in German affairs) for the first time, control of most of Silesia being transferred in the process. The scale of the palace, which marked the earliest reversal of Sanssouci's original intimate character, was a deliberately triumphalist statement demonstrating that the state coffers had been far from exhausted by the war. Plans were drawn up by Büring, but he was replaced early in the construction process by Gontard, who was enticed here from the court at Bayreuth. A huge team of craftsmen took part, with no fewer than twelve sculptors engaged to provide the rich programme of statuary on the balustrade and in the garden. In contrast to the single level characteristic of the earlier Sanssouci

Orangerie, Park Sanssouci, *Carl Graeb (1816–84)*

buildings, the Neues Palais has three storeys, the walls divided by giant pilasters stretching from the ground to the cornice. The most striking feature of the exterior, however, is the massive windowless central dome, which has smaller counterparts on each of the side pavilions.

Because of the palace's size, admission to the interior poses less of a problem than with the Schloss: visits are self-guided in summer, accompanied in winter, with tickets sold from a window on the southern pavilion. The south wing, generally not included on tours, houses another welcome café at ground floor level and a delectable rococo jewel of a theatre upstairs. Formerly only used on rare occasions for courtly entertainments, the latter is now a regular venue. Its intimate dimensions and acoustics are absolutely perfect for the performance of Mozart operas, which have been a common feature here for many years.

There could be no more singular introduction to any palace than the first room in the main block, the Grotto Hall. It is a truly extraordinary sight, the walls encrusted with striped marble, shells, fossils, precious stones, glass and corals, all dimly lit to enhance the sense of mystery. On display are a number of sleighs used by the Prussian kings for winter journeys. Next door, the Marble Gallery is no less striking. Modelled on the halls of mirrors of the French royal palaces, it features walls and floor of white Carrara marble and red jasper. The ceiling has three wonderfully ornate frescos by Christian Bernard Rode, a pupil of Pesne and director of the Berlin Academy, illustrating noon, morning and evening respectively. Of the remaining rooms on the ground floor, the Gentlemen's Bedroom is of special note for the huge, brilliantly executed documentary painting by Adolf von Menzel of the coronation of Wilhelm I at Königsberg in 1861, beside

The Chinesisches Teehaus, Potsdam

which stands a descriptive board identifying all the notables present. Directly above the Grotto Hall is the palace's principal festive chamber, the Marble Hall, which features a ceiling fresco by Charles von Loo, *The Introduction of Ganymede to Mount Olympus*, as well as four large canvases by different 18th-century French painters showing scenes from classical mythology, and eight marble statues of the Electors of Brandenburg (the ancestors of the Prussian kings) in the company of four great historic emperors. The Upper Gallery next door, corresponding to the Marble Gallery below, is hung with canvases by 17th-century Italian painters such as Guido Reni, Luca Giordano and the heroine of feminist art historians, Artemesia Gentileschi.

Facing the front entrance of the palace, and designed by Gontard to form a complimentary ensemble, are the **Communs**, twin porticoed and domed structures linked by a graceful open colonnade. Despite their majestic appearance, their functions were decidedly modest: they housed offices and servants' quarters and served to block off what would otherwise have been an unsightly view from the Neues Palais of the marshland beyond. Nowadays, they are used as classrooms by the local university.

Park Sanssouci officially ends at the Ökonomieweg, which follows a course just south of the Neues Palais, the Freundschaftstempel and the Chinesisches Teehaus to Marlys Garten. The smaller estate beyond was acquired by the future Friedrich Wilhelm IV in 1826, and laid out by Lenné, under the name **Park Charlottenhof**, in the naturalistic English style with lawns, hillocks and artificial stretches of water. For its central structure, **Schloss Charlottenhof**, Schinkel was commissioned to transform an old estate building into a villa on the ancient Roman model. He responded with a harmonious neoclassical design that respects its historical antecedents without resorting to slavish imitation. Schinkel was also responsible for planning the lakeside **Römische Bäder** (Roman Baths) just to the north, though construction was left in the hands of Persius. A typical product of the Romantic imagination, this complex incorporates a tea pavilion in the shape of an ancient temple; a Renaissance-style villa; and a suite of rooms in the manner of a Roman house, including the bathroom after which everything is named. East of the Schloss are a few other sights of more marginal interest: the Dichterhain (Poets' Grove), an open space with busts of leading German writers; the Hippodrom, an elliptical clearing; and the Fasanerie (Pheasantry), another Italianate villa.

The City Centre

The city centre of Potsdam, inevitably overshadowed by the parks, has the further disadvantage that the scars left by the war were accentuated by the ideological fixa-

Dome of the Nikolaikirche, Potsdam, which architect Karl Friedrich Schinkel dreamed of but did not live to see raised. The dome was built to his plans.

tions of Communism. Ugly highrise flats and offices stand in uncomfortable proximity to baroque and rococo masterpieces, often overshadowing them by their sheer scale. Even worse, two of the most famous showpieces, the Stadtschloss (Town Palace) and the Garnisonkirche (Garrison Church), both damaged in the war, were erased completely due to their historical connotations. The Stadtschloss was the remodelled original Potsdam residence of the Hohenzollerns, while the Garnisonkirche was the original burial place of Frederick the Great and his father, the Soldier King, and the setting for the 'Potsdam handshake' (see page 276). Since unification, town planners have had a field day trying to decide how to advance from this sorry past. There has been talk of trying to re-create the prewar appearance of the city, including resurrecting the Stadtschloss, but this seems even more of a pipe-dream than the ideas touted about its Berlin counterpart, and it is more likely that town planning here will evolve as a compromise between respecting the past and thinking ahead to the needs of the future.

Thankfully, the Communists were unable to oust the magnificent domed **Nikolaikirche** (St Nicholas' Church) from its dominant position on the skyline, visible from miles around. One of the few unquestionably great churches of 19th-century Europe, it was built on the north side of the Alter Markt (Old Market Square) from 1830 onwards under the patronage of the future Friedrich Wilhelm IV as a belated replacement for its predecessor, which had burnt down in 1795. In addition to providing the architectural plans, Karl Friedrich Schinkel also designed every detail of the decoration; the church can thus be regarded as his testament in ecclesiastical building. It is all the more ironic, therefore, that he took no part in its construction, leaving this to such followers as Ludwig Persius and Friedrich August Stüler. Nor did Schinkel live to see the completion of his great church: the dome, one of his most daring ideas for all its obvious debt to St Paul's Cathedral in London, was not raised until after his death. The four slender corner towers were added to offset the otherwise unsustainable pressure the dome exerts on the main body of the church. Externally, the only counterpoint to the dome and the towers comes from the Grecian-style entrance portico.

The dome's massive space is every bit as impressive from inside as from out. High up, it is adorned with 14 statues of Old Testament figures carved in the workshop of Christian Daniel Rauch, while its squinches have gigantic paintings of the four great prophets: Isaiah, Jeremiah, Ezekiel and Daniel. Other monumental murals, inspired by Raphael and showing Christ in Judgment, the Evangelists and the Apostles, cover the apse. In front, a ciborium crowns the main altar, while to the side the pulpit bears reliefs by August Kiss showing the Sermon on the Mount, Christ in the Garden of Gethsemane, and the Resurrection. Both side galleries are borne by coolly fluted columns topped with statuettes of angel musicians.

In front of the church is the **Obelisk** by Knobelsdorff. Formerly, it bore relief portraits of four of the Hohenzollerns, but the Communists replaced these with likenesses of some of the architects who created the face of Potsdam: Knobelsdorff, Gontard, Schinkel and Persius. The eastern side of the Alter Markt is dominated by the **Altes Rathaus** (Old Town Hall) by another of Frederick the Great's favourite builders, Johann Boumann, a Dutchman who, before coming to Potsdam, had worked more as a carpenter and shipbuilder than as an architect. For this key civic institution he chose an unbuilt design by the guru of the Late Italian Renaissance, Andrea Palladio. The cupola, astride which stands a gilded statue of Atlas bearing the world on his shoulders, was formerly the local gaol; nowadays, the building serves as a cultural complex. A rude interruption to the harmony of the square comes with the starkly avant-garde **Hans-Otto-Theater** on the south side. Although intended by the Communist authorities as the city's great modern prestige project, work was interrupted in 1989 by *Die Wende* ('The Change') and the theatre has been built in a simplified form. Even so, its future remains in doubt and it would certainly have to be demolished if the Stadtschloss, which stretched south from here, were to be reinstated.

Another ghastly example of GDR planning is the skyscraper-like **Hotel Potsdam** opposite, which again occupies part of the Stadtschloss site, offering unwelcome competition to the Nikolaikirche for the title of the most conspicuous building in town. The so-called 'socialist hotel' ironically catered almost entirely to Western businessmen, in imitation of the corporate chains they were used to staying in, and charged comparable prices, payable in hard currency only. Relocated to the banks of the Havel below the hotel is the only surviving part of the Stadtschloss, an elegant colonnade by Knobelsdorff.

The hotel marks the beginning of Breite Strasse, Potsdam's main thoroughfare in prewar days, later partially transformed into a typical Communist-style boulevard. Despite the depredations, it boasts many fine old buildings, and in particular the **Marstall** (Stables) immediately opposite. This is the only surviving monument from the first phase of the baroque town, having been built as an orangery in 1685 by Johann Arnold Nering, architect of Schloss Charlottenburg and the Berlin Zeughaus (Arsenal). Its lopsided dimensions—it is 130 metres long, but only 10 metres wide— meant that there were few alternative functions for it, but it proved eminently suitable for conversion to stables some six decades later. Knobelsdorff provided the de-signs for this, adding central projections with attics adorned with vivacious carvings of horses and riders by Friedrich Christian Glume. Nowadays, it houses the **Filmmuseum**, which documents the distinguished cinematic history of the studios in the Babelsberg suburbs (see page 306), plus the most innovative cinema in town.

Further along the street, at the corner of Dortustrasse, stands the **Militärwaisen-haus** (Military Orphanage), a four-storey, four-winged construction built by Gontard in the 1770s. Its sheer size—it was then the largest building in Potsdam after the Stadtschloss—serves as a telling reminder of the number of children left fatherless by warfare or by the temporary illicit unions that were an inevitable feature of a garrison town. On the same block, the Ständehaus (Registry Office), a more modest baroque mansion, is home to the local history collections of the **Potsdam Museum**. Across the street, the brightly coloured **Hiller-Brandtsche Häuser** (Hiller's and Brandt's Houses) make a spectacular impression, being free reinterpretations of Inigo Jones's façades for the now vanished Whitehall Palace in London. The three-storey end-structures, topped with a balustrade bearing statues of mythological figures, were intended as mansions for the eponymous merchant and tailor; they are connected by a lower central section, where members of the garrison could be billeted. On the southern half of Dortustrasse and on Kiezstrasse just off it, once the heart of an independent fishing settlement, baroque and rococo town houses, though less ornate, have been well restored.

At the western end of Breite Strasse is Potsdam's most curious and arguably most photogenic building, the Dampfmaschinenhaus (Steam Engine House) or **Pumpwerk Sanssouci** (Sanssouci Pump Works) by Persius. In true Romantic manner, this adopts all the characteristics of an oriental mosque, including the tower with minaret, the central dome and the contrast of glazed black bricks and varnished white stonework. However, it is far from being yet another folly: its inauguration in 1842 solved the previously intractable problem of Sanssouci's water supply, enabling the Grosse Fontäne to function properly at last. The main chamber mirrors the Moorish forms of the exterior, but most of the space is taken up by a giant steam-engine built by the prestigious firm of Borsig. This was electrified a few years ago and its workings are demonstrated to visitors in the course of the short guided tours of the interior.

A few minutes' walk along Zeppelinstrasse is Luisenplatz, on whose western side is one of the entrances to Park Sanssouci. Opposite stands the **Brandenburger Tor** (Brandenburg Gate), one of three of the six original gateways of the 1730s fortification system to have survived. Its appearance was sharply modified four decades after its construction by Gontard and Unger, who festooned it with cheery rococo decoration in the manner of a Roman triumphal arch.

Immediately east of here is the second baroque extension of the city, laid out on a grid plan in the 1730s. Sober in style, with only slight variations in design and colouring, the buildings suffered little damage in the war and are now mostly occupied by retail outlets.

Just to the south of the grid, at the junction of Lindenstrasse and Bäckerstrasse, is the **Alte Wache** (Old Guard House), built by Andreas Ludwig Krüger at the end of the 18th century as one of the town's first neoclassical structures. The open colonnades of the two main street façades show strong Mediterranean influence, but an authentically Prussian note is struck by the sculptured groups of the trophy-bearing gods of war Mars and Bellona, accompanied by their followers. Yorckstrasse, east of here, is the best preserved street from the 1720s, the last phase of the first baroque extension to the town; this was where many ministers and senior civil servants chose to live.

To the south is the now somewhat decrepit Neuer Markt (New Market Square). The large mansion here was once the home of Friedrich Wilhelm II when he was a crown prince, and also the birthplace in 1767 of the celebrated scholar-statesman Wilhelm von Humboldt. On the western side is the royal **Kutschstall** (Coach Stables), entered via an imposing gate designed by Krüger which bears a sculptural group depicting Frederick the Great's own coachman at the helm of the four-horse chariot of the sun-god Helios, with his stableboys at work on either side. Off the east side of the square, at the junction with Friedrich-Ebert-Strasse, is Gontard's **Acht-Ecken-Haus** (Eight-Sided House), though the name is now a misnomer: until 1945, there were similar houses at each of the other three street ends, all of which likewise had indented niches, thus making eight corners instead of the usual four.

Friedrich-Ebert-Strasse leads north to the spacious Platz der Einheit (Unity Square), dominated by the historicist mass of the post office; the site of the synagogue, razed by the Nazis, is marked by a plaque. Further north is a yet larger square,

Potsdam Public Transport System

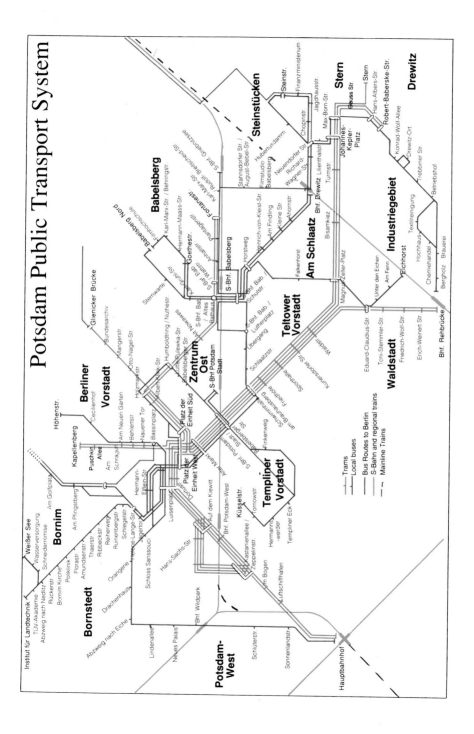

Legend:
- Trams
- Local buses
- Bus Routes to Berlin
- S-Bahn and regional trains
- Mainline Trains

Bassinplatz, whose proportions are ruined by the planting of the main bus terminal right in the middle, but which is of note for a couple of well-contrasted churches. The oval **Französische Kirche** (French Church) at the eastern end is a gem, built in the 1750s for the by then well-established Huguenot community by Boumann from plans by Knobelsdorff; oddly enough, it seems to have been modelled on the Catholic St-Hedwigs-Kathedrale in Berlin. Its refined sculptural decoration by Friedrich Christian Glume includes allegorical statues of the Christian Virtues and two reliefs of monetary themes from the Bible: The Tribute Money and Christ Driving the Money-changers from the Temple.

The much larger **Katholische Kirche St Peter und Paul** (Catholic Church of SS Peter and Paul) dates from just over a century later and was the first major place of worship for the Catholics in this staunchly Protestant city. Uncompromisingly historicist in outlook, it imitates the forms of two of the world's most famous churches— the Byzantine Hagia Sophia in Constantinople for the main body, and the Romanesque San Zeno Maggiore in Verona for the tower.

Immediately north of Bassinplatz is the first of several ethnically inspired pieces of town planning in Potsdam, the **Holländisches Viertel** (Dutch Quarter). This was Boumann's first major commission on his arrival from Amsterdam in 1732 and he kept faith with the forms and materials of his native city, choosing brick instead of the locally favoured stone, and building terraces of elaborately gabled dwellings, 134 in all, each conforming to one of three models. The effect is uncanny, though the underlying idea of being a home from home for Dutch settlers was never fully realized, as insufficient numbers of immigrants were enticed by the scheme. Extensive damage from World War II has still not been completely repaired and many houses remain derelict. However, a restoration programme had been initiated even before the fall of the Berlin Wall, and the central Mittelstrasse, in particular, has become a prime location, with many of the premises taken over by trendy boutiques, wine bars and the offices of leisure businesses.

At the edge of the quarter, bisecting Friedrich-Ebert-Strasse, is the extravagantly grandiose **Nauener Tor** (Nauen Gate), a 1750s replacement for its counterpart of two decades earlier. Resplendent with twin round towers, battlements and open arcades, it marks the German début of the English Gothic style, which restored to architectural practice the pointed arch, out of favour since the Renaissance. Further west along Hegelallee is the **Jägertor** (Hunter's Gate), the only one of the gateways to have survived in its original form, albeit stripped of its guardhouse and customs post. It takes its name from its carved decoration, which depicts a stag grounded by hounds, with hunting trophies on either side.

Adolf, the Superman *by John Heartfield (1891–1968)*,
from the famous photomontage Swallows gold, talks rubbish,
first published in Berlin's Arbeiter-Illustrierte-Zeitung *on 17th July 1932*

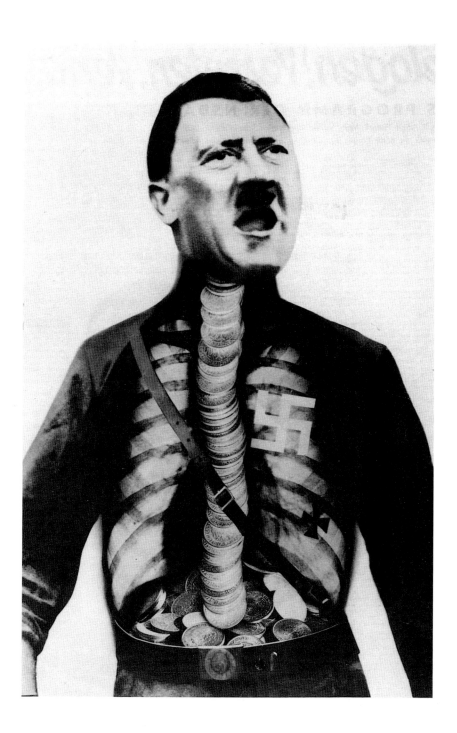

The Potsdam Conference

The **Potsdam Conference** of 17th July to 2nd August 1945 marked the
third and last of the conferences between the 'Big Three' of the anti-Hitler
coalition. Code-named 'Terminal', it followed earlier meetings at Teheran
and Yalta between Franklin D Roosevelt, President of the USA, Josef Stalin,
Chairman of the Council of People's Commissars of the USSR, and Winston
Churchill, Prime Minister of the UK. On this occasion, the deceased
Roosevelt was replaced by his successor, Harry S Truman, while Churchill
was accompanied by the Labour Party leader, Clement Attlee, who supplanted him mid-conference: a general election had been held in Britain
earlier in the month, but its results were not announced until 26th July.
These unstable circumstances could hardly have been more fortuitous for
Stalin, who was untroubled by democratic considerations and thus had a
free hand to pursue and enforce his goals, which were in any case far clearer
than those of his counterparts.

In order to emphasize the totality of German defeat, the Allies chose to
hold the victory conference in the very heart of the Reich. Berlin's
devastation was so vast that it had to be ruled out, but Potsdam's proximity
made it a more than acceptable substitute, particularly given its stock of
suitable palaces and villas. Nonetheless, a great deal of building work had to
be undertaken: in addition to renovations to Schloss Cecilienhof itself,
groups of houses around the Griebnitzsee in Babelsberg were refitted as the
main headquarters for each of the three delegations, repairs were made to
15 kilometres of road, which was extended a further 7 kilometres and a
pontoon bridge was laid across the Havel.

There remained some unfinished war business, namely the defeat of
Japan. A declaration was issued to the Japanese people warning them of the
occupation and loss of colonies that would ensue if they did not surrender.
America's successful testing of the atom bomb, later to be crucial in
bringing Japan to heel, was revealed to Stalin for the first time.

However, the main item on the agenda was the future of Germany.
Earlier conferences had toyed with the idea of breaking it up into a number
of separate states, thus returning it to its pre-1871 condition. However,
despite the powerful argument that a united Germany had consistently
threatened world peace, it was decided to preserve it as an economic unit,

divided into temporary zones of occupation. It was decreed that in due course, 'the German people would be given the opportunity to prepare for the reconstruction of their life on a democratic and peaceful basis'.

The conference also formally recognized the de facto truncation of Germany, whose eastern border was set at the so-called Oder-Neisse line, depriving it of well over 100,000 square kilometres of the prewar Reich. This was merely the logical conclusion of events set in motion at Teheran, where the Allies had accepted the Soviet Union's 1939 annexation of Poland's Eastern Territories, and continued at Yalta, where the London-based Polish government-in-exile was betrayed at Stalin's insistence that his hand-picked regime be recognized. The intention was to shunt Poland westwards across the map of Europe, gaining smaller but more valuable amounts of German territory in return for what had been lost in the east; by this means, the boundaries of the Soviet Union, and of its recognized sphere of influence, were stretched west, with the latter reaching right to the heart of Europe.

The northern half of East Prussia was allocated to the Russian Federation, giving it a strategic outlet on the Baltic. This meant that Königsberg, home city of Immanuel Kant, E T A Hoffmann and Käthe Kollwitz, one-time headquarters of the Teutonic Knights, and, above all, the place where the Prussian kings were crowned, passed to the Russians under the name of Kaliningrad. Other long-time bastions of German culture, notably Danzig and Breslau (to become Gdansk and Wroclaw respectively), were handed to Poland, with their old names banished to the history books. Most humiliating of all was the loss of Berlin's port of Stettin, whose future was in doubt until midway through the conference, when a delegation of Polish Communists, co-opted for consultation purposes, duly claimed it. These annexations added to the huge refugee problem already caused by those who had fled westwards: Poland, Czechoslovakia and Hungary were all empowered to expel their German population. They duly did as did Yugoslavia and Romania, to whom the facility was not officially extended, dumping in all 12 million displaced persons in a diminished and occupied Germany.

The Soviet Union gained permission to take over a third of Germany's naval and merchant fleet, and to extract reparations from its zones of occupation in Germany and Austria. Its hegemony over the Balkans was also recognized, albeit grudgingly and more out of acceptance for the political and military reality of what had become the status *quo*. Only in some of his more optimistic demands was Stalin disappointed, for example in his desire to annex parts of Turkey, to take over Italian colonies, to gain a voice in the Middle East discussions, and to have Franco overthrown in Spain. Stalin's policy successes made a sham of the cozy photographs fed to the world's press of the three leaders conferring and relaxing together. Among these was the famous shot of them lounging about in wicker chairs, which became the enduring image of the conference. The essential falseness of this was thrown into stark relief by the foundations for the imminent Cold War that were set in place at the Potsdam Conference.

The Northern Quarters

Potsdam is a city which rewards patient exploration and the quarters north of the centre have some of the most surprising corners. The settlement of **Alexandrowka**, a 10-minute walk north of the Nauener Tor, is one of those rare places that genuinely deserves to be classified as unique, being the only surviving example of the once common Russian military villages and the only one built outside Russia. Its origins lie in the Napoleonic Wars: in 1812, the Prussians captured some 500 Czarist soldiers, from whom 62 were selected to form a choir to entertain their captors; these men were thereby enlisted as infantry in the First Regiment. After Prussia and Russia became allies, Czar Alexander I allowed King Friedrich Wilhelm II to retain the services of the prisoners-of-war. By 1825, only a dozen of the original singers were still alive, though the choir continued to perform for another five years, with the last member surviving until 1861. To reward them for their singing, it was decided to give them a permanent home in Potsdam, and one that would remind them as much as possible of their native land.

Accordingly, Lenné was commissioned to landscape what had hitherto been a marsh, while the military architect Hauptmann Snethlage was charged with the design of the settlement. He laid out the houses in two avenues in the form of a St Andrew's cross, with the residence of the Prussian overseer in the middle and the homes of the twelve singers placed symmetrically along the axes. The occupants were provided with a comfortable lifestyle; in return, they had to keep detailed inventories of their goods. The houses, with their distinctive balconies and ornamental gables, give the appearance of authentic Russian log cabins, but this is a trick achieved by the use of facing to cover that quintessentially German method of construction, half-timbering. Each has at least one nameplate in Cyrillic script: white lettering on a black background for the name of the first occupant, the reverse for the name of the present tenant. The houses could not be mortgaged or sold; a few have passed down the generations and remain in the custody of the heirs, while the remainder have been relet.

As an adjunct to Alexandrowka, the **Russische Kirche Hl Alexander Newsky** (Russian Church of St Alexander Nevski) was built on the heights of the Kapellenberg immediately above. Plans for it were drawn up at the court in St Petersburg, though the ubiquitous Schinkel was allowed a hand in the design of the interior. This intervention, however, does nothing to alter its essential Russian flavour: the ground-plan is a Greek cross with a semicircular apse; the silhouette is dominated by a central dome surrounded by four smaller counterparts. Inside, an iconostasis divides the altar room from the congregation; some of its icons were painted in Russia while the church was under construction, others were added a couple of decades later. The church has remained in constant use by the émigré community (nowadays mainly consisting of White Russians), and in 1986 won back the right to have its own priest after a gap of many years. He lives in the parish house immediately opposite; this originally doubled as a royal tearoom, and serves as the temporary church during the current restoration programme.

North of the Kapellenberg lies another hill, the Pfingstberg, on which stand some of the city's most neglected sights, whose current dereliction is a shameful testimony to the smug complacency of four decades of Communist rule. On the brow of the hill is the **Jüdischer Friedhof** (Jewish Cemetery), a walled graveyard with numerous impressively carved tombstones. Until the Nazi takeover, Potsdam was home to a substantial number of Jews, but the community has never revived and the cemetery now has to compete for grants for its upkeep with other far more prestigious heritage sites. Guided tours are occasionally run by the tourist information office; otherwise the cemetery's gates are normally locked, though access is easy enough by scrambling over one of the lower stretches of wall.

At the top of the hill is the **Belvedere**, a Romantic-style, Italianate folly whose walkways and towers were designed to provide sweeping views over Potsdam, the Havel and its lakes. As the last thing the GDR authorities wanted was to give its citizens a bird's-eye vista over the barbed-wire frontier that separated them from the West, the building was allowed to fall into rack and ruin. It remains in a highly dangerous condition and should on no account be entered. Eventually, when funds permit, it will be restored, as is already the case with the little **Pomona-Tempel** alongside. This mock antique temple was Schinkel's first architectural design to be built, at

Frederick the Great at Sanssouci, Potsdam

When his present Majesty is at 'Sanssouci,' he is unattended by any regular guard. A corporal and four soldiers are sent there from Potzdam towards evening, and they withdraw at daybreak. Indeed, their presence is not meant for the protection of the King's person; but merely to secure his peaches and apricots from devastation, to which they might otherwise be liable. He reposes in perfect security, if not on the affections, on the obedience, subjection, and admiration of his subjects. His table, as well as his dress, are subjected to certain rules, which mark his character, and which become interesting on that account. No Prince is better served, though without any splendour or magnificence. He is, indeed, by no means insensible to the physical pleasure of eating, considered as distinct from the conviviality of the table; but as he does not like to eat alone, a small number of persons, usually officers of rank, are every day invited to his dinner. The Emperor Gallienus was not a more accurate proficient in the science of cookery, than is Frederic. He has, it is true, only eight dishes generally served; but each is dressed by a separate cook, and each is excellent in its kind. Four are French, two Italian, and the remaining two are accommodated to his Majesty's particular taste. It must be admitted that so much attention to the gratification of appetite, favours more of the school of Epicurus, than of Zeno. Philosopher as he is, the Father of the Portico is not his model.

In his dessert the King is expensive and splendid, sparing neither endeavours nor money in order to procure the most delicate fruits in abundance. The productions of the tropical, as well as temperate climates, are heaped before him. He eats plentifully, and drinks gaily as well as freely of his favourite wines, which are Burgundy and Champagne. I am assured that he commonly swallows near a bottle of the former, and of the latter some glasses every day. In 'liqueurs' he rarely indulges, and he touches no supper. He sleeps without either a night-cap, or any covering about his head. When he rises, his first operation is to pull on his stockings before he quits the bed, and then his boots over them. His hair and beard are dispatched in a few minutes, by the first valet or footman who presents himself. The Princess Amelia his sister, used formerly to make his shirts; but as she has of late years become incapable, from disease and infirmity, of continuing the practice, he is obliged to receive them from other hands.

The appropriation of his time, his occupations, and amusements, is regulated with scrupulous accuracy, and never varies except when he is absent from 'Sanssouci.' 'My uncle,' said Prince Frederic of Brunswic to me, 'rises in summer at four in the morning, and even in winter at five, or soon afterwards. He breakfasts quite alone on chocolate; and till ten o' clock he is entirely occupied in transacting affairs of state, which he dispatches in person with rigorous exactitude. From that hour till near noon he goes first to the parade, then walks, or as is more commonly his custom, rides, if his health permit. He returns to the Palace of Potzdam, or to 'Sanssouci,' before twelve, and sits down to dinner precisely at noon. After the repast he usually remains some time at table, where he unbends himself in conversation with those about him. His afternoon is divided between books and music, in the latter of which he is a connoisseur and a performer. At six, one of his secretaries enters, and reads to him such letters as are addressed to him upon literary subjects, or any intelligence relative to that line of correspondence. He dictates his replies immediately. The King eats no supper, but retires to his chamber at nine, and goes directly to bed. Such is his constant mode of life.

Sir Nathaniel Wraxall, Memoirs of the Courts of Berlin,
Dresden, Warsaw and Vienna, 1799

Nathaniel Wraxall (1751–1831) was a Bristol merchant turned adventurer. His first major journey, described in A Tour Round the Baltic, took him to the courts of Copenhagen, Stockholm and St Petersburg; this was followed by one to Berlin, Dresden, Warsaw and Vienna. On his return, he was elected as a Member of Parliament, serving for 14 years before belatedly writing up the account of the latter trip. The rest of his life was spent in obscurity, though he was created a baronet, wrote an unfinished three-volume history of France and bequeathed a historically valuable set of memoirs which were published posthumously.

a time when he was a student aged 19.

East of the Pfingstberg is the **Neuer Garten** (New Garten), another of the city's great parks. It was laid out from 1786 onwards by order of Friedrich Wilhelm II, successor to Frederick the Great, along the banks of two of the city's chain of lakes, the Jungfernsee and the Heiliger See. As an antidote to the geometric formality of Sanssouci, the Neuer Garten marked the Potsdam début of the English style of land-scape gardening, which aimed at a naturalistic effect through artificial means. A number of existing buildings, known as the White House, the Brown House, the Red House and the Green House, were incorporated into the designs, while some new structures were added.

One of these, the **Molkerei** (Dairy), is set at the northernmost tip of the park in an area out of bounds in GDR days. This was built at the end of the 18th century by Carl Gotthard Langhans, designer of the Brandenburg Gate in Berlin, as a farmhouse with cowsheds and a workshop. Persius rebuilt it half a century later, giving it its present castellated form; it was subsequently converted into Potsdam's second unu-sual pump station, in order to connect the water supply to the Neuer Garten. Badly damaged in the 1945 air raid, it still awaits proper restoration.

A short walk to the south is **Schloss Cecilienhof**, setting of the fateful postwar conference (see page 296). Built between 1913 and 1917, it was the last palace com-missioned by the imperial Hohenzollern family. In view of the fact that Germany was at war with Britain for most of this period, it is ironic that the architect's inspiration stemmed from the English country house. Named after the crown princess and de-signed for year-round use, it mimics the half-timbered Tudor style with extravagant pepperpot chimneys and creeping ivy. In 1923, the deposed Crown Prince Wilhelm returned from his Dutch exile with his family to live here, abandoning it towards the end of World War II.

Much of the palace is given over to what was one of the flagships of the GDR's state-run hostel system, but the principal reception rooms are open as a conference memorial museum. Despite the epic events that were enacted here, the rooms retain a modest, homely feel. The white and red parlours, the first of which was originally the music room, were used by the Soviet delegation. Beyond these is the entrance hall, with a resplendent imitation Danzig baroque staircase. This was where the main sessions of the conference were held, around the Russian-made table which has been left in place. The former smoking and living rooms which follow were allocated to the Americans, while the British occupied the library and reading room at the far end.

All the other notable structures in the Neuer Garten lie further south, beginning with the first of two fantasies inspired by Ancient Egypt, the **Pyramide** (Pyramid), which functioned as an ice cellar. Further on, directly beside the Heiliger See is the **Marmor Palais** (Marble Palace), built by Gontard in the late 1780s for Friedrich

Wilhelm II. Its name is rather a misnomer, brick being far more prominent than marble in a surprisingly unassuming neoclassical structure that seems more reminiscent of the architecture of colonial America than of Prussia. In GDR days, it served as a propagandist army museum; this did not survive the regime, and the palace is currently undergoing long-term restoration and will be closed for several years yet.

The houses of the palace servants, the **Holländisches Etablissement**, form Potsdam's second Dutch-style settlement, this time modelled on Holland's distinctive almshouses. Behind them is the **Orangerie** (Orangery) by Langhans, notable chiefly for its façade, which mixes Greek and Egyptian motifs with a sphinx seated atop a portico of Doric columns. By the same architect is the **Königliche Bibliothek** (King's Library) at the southern tip of the Heiliger See. This is a highly distinctive design, neoclassical in feel with the addition of a Gothic pointed arch, and featuring two single-room storeys, the smaller upper tier surrounded by a viewing platform. Reduced to a weed-infested shell, it is the most disgracefully neglected and abandoned monument in a city which would otherwise have plenty of other contenders for that role.

Between here and the Glienicker Brücke lies the **Berliner Vorstadt**, one of five suburbs created outside the town walls from the mid-18th century onwards. It had a predominantly residential function, featuring not only luxury villas for the most prosperous citizens, but also specially designed barracks for the military garrison in place of the former billeting. The finest building is the battlemented Leibgardehusaren Kaserne (Life Guards' Barracks) at No 27 on the main part of Berliner Strasse, built after designs by Schinkel.

South of the Havel

Facing the city centre across the River Havel is the hilly suburb known as the **Teltower Vorstadt**. Heinrich-Mann-Allee leads up from the Potsdam-Stadt S-Bahn station to the Alter Friedhof (Old Cemetery) and the Neuer Friedhof (New Cemetery). A narrow road skirts the latter in ascending the Telegrafenberg, a hill which takes its name from the fact that in 1832 it became the site of a telegraph station which relayed messages along a route from Berlin to Koblenz in the Rhineland. Three decades later, other scientific institutes were set up here, notably the **Astrophysikalisches Observatorium** (Astrophysics Observatory). The main building, right on the summit, is a triple-domed structure of brickwork interspersed with ceramic tiles; each dome contains a refractor which can be turned and opened to observe the heavens. At the very end of the century a building with a double refractor complete with camera was added alongside; this remains one of the largest pieces of photographic equipment in the world.

These buildings, however, are overshadowed by the extraordinary **Einsteinturm** (Einstein Tower) to the rear. Only its dilapidated condition belies the fact that it is not a product of the space age: the startlingly three-dimensional form and near surrealist shape look so uncompromisingly modern that it is hard to believe the tower was built as long ago as 1920 and ranks as the supreme and most influential masterpiece of the short-lived and uniquely German architectural style that is Expressionism. Its existence is due to a chance meeting between its architect, Erich Mendelsohn, and the astrophysicist Erwin Finlay-Freundlich, who later became an assistant to Einstein. The latter commissioned an observatory to test Einstein's theory of relativity by means of practical experiments, which involved breaking down a beam of sunlight focused into the tower along spectral lines. From a scientific point of view the results were inconclusive and thus something of a failure, but the observatory quickly became both a classic of modern design and a triumphant example of the use of concrete, for all that bricks were needed for reinforcement. Long neglected, it is now back in practical use for research into the sun's magnetic field. Signs warn visitors not to walk on the ground around it, to avoid disturbing current experiments.

East of the Teltower Vorstadt lies the former town of **Bablesberg**, now incorporated into Potsdam. Just north of the S-Bahn station, one stop on the line back towards Berlin, is the settlement of **Nowawes**, yet another intriguing piece of urban planning. It was established by Frederick the Great in 1750 as a home for Protestant weavers and spinners fleeing religious persecution in Bohemia, who were encouraged to come here to boost a population depleted by war. A decade later, the township was extended to the northwest to accommodate craftsmen from southern Germany and Switzerland who came to work on the Neues Palais. The houses built around the triangular-shaped Weberplatz were all single-storey semi-detached dwellings; unfortunately none survives in its original state, though many give a fair enough impression. More obviously authentic is the **Friedrichskirche**, the rustic-looking parish church in the centre of the square named in honour of the king and built by Johann Boumann. Its interior, designed for services in which preaching was the key component, features a two-tiered horseshoe-shaped gallery.

Beyond the built-up area north of here stretches **Park Babelsberg**, the last of Potsdam's wonderful open spaces. Even in such a patently Anglophile city, there is no more obvious debt to Britain than this park, which imitates English-style landscaping in the architecture of its main palace, as well as in the smaller buildings and follies dotting its hillsides. The whole complex was created for Friedrich Wilhelm IV's younger brother Wilhelm, who was to succeed him as King of Prussia, later becoming, upon unification of Germany in 1871, the first Kaiser of the Second Reich. Initial landscaping was carried out by Lenné, but the major role was taken by the second great landscape architect of 19th-century Germany, Prince Hermann von Pückler-Muskau, who had first developed his skills on his own Saxon estate.

Despite the modest yellow bricks used in its construction, **Schloss Babelsberg** is an aggressively picturesque creation, bristling with towers, turrets, balconies and oriel windows, all grouped round a solid central octagon. The well-proven team of Schinkel and Persius was entrusted with the designs, the main source of inspiration being the recent extension to Windsor Castle; the contrast in architectural style with the Nikolaikirche, under construction at the same time, could hardly be more stark. Long closed to the public, with the furnishings kept in storage, the Schloss has recently been opened, though only the basement plus half a dozen upstairs rooms can be visited. The first three of these were the private apartments of Princess Augusta, consort of the future Kaiser Wilhelm I; they are intimate in scale and furnished and decorated in a style reminiscent of earlier palaces. More fashionably up to date are the three rooms that follow: the Tea Salon, with its star-shaped ceiling; the Library, featuring the distinctively English fan vault; and the two-storey Dance Hall set inside the great octagon. The last-named was the main reception room of the Schloss and

Shooting a film at Studios Babelsberg

illustrates the historicist tastes of the time in its truly spectacular star vault, elaborately frescoed in High Gothic manner.

Below the main Schloss, right beside the Havel, is the whitewashed **Kleines Schloss** (Small Palace), formerly the quarters of the ladies-in-waiting but now a restaurant. Also by the waterside are Persius's **Maschinenhaus** (Machine House) to the north, from where the park's water supply was controlled, and the **Matrosenhaus** (Sailors' House) to the south, a gabled dwelling for the crew of the royal boats. On the hill above the latter is the **Flatowturm**, a guesthouse and look-out tower which copies the extravagant forms characteristic of its medieval German predecessors. The **Gerichtslaube** (Court House), a partially original building from this time, dominates the hill opposite, its open-arcaded lower storey giving it a distinctive touch. Though it now seems hard to credit, this little building was once the main town hall of Berlin. It was demolished to make way for the Rotes Rathaus, but the bricks were preserved, enabling it to be re-erected here.

On August-Bebel-Strasse, about ten minutes' walk southwest of the Griebnitzsee S-Bahn station (the stop between Babelsberg and Wannsee) lies the most exciting new tourist attraction of the Berlin area, the **Studios Babelsberg**. A huge complex of 430,000 square metres, it is the nearest European equivalent to Hollywood, being designated a Mediastadt (Media City). Production began here in 1912 with Guido Seeber's Deutsche Bioscop Gesellschaft, which made silent films in a studio made of glass to receive the sunlight, this technique predating proper artificial lighting techniques. Asta Nielsen was the first actress to appear before the cameras, inaugurating a distinguished tradition of screen goddesses. Later, the Tonkreuz, a complex of four sound studios, was added, enabling early talkies to be produced. The halcyon days of Babelsberg came in the interwar years when it produced over a thousand films under the name of UFA (Universum-Film AG). These included such classics as Fritz Lang's futuristic *Metropolis,* whose studio of 5,300 square metres remains in use to this day, and Josef von Sternberg's *The Blue Angel*, an adaptation of Heinrich Mann's novel *Professor Umraut*, which catapulted the hitherto unknown Marlene Dietrich to instant international stardom, largely as a result of the song *Falling in Love Again.*

Under the Third Reich, UFA was taken over by Goebbels' Ministry of Propaganda, whose most notorious creation, Jew Süss, corrupted Lion Feuchtwanger's pro-Jewish novel into an anti-Semitic tirade. During World War II, the studios' artistic status was further undermined by the constant production of patriotic material designed to fool the population into believing events were going well. However, at least one masterpiece was also made: the notoriously hard-to-film *Baron Münchhausen*, in which Gerd Albers gave a lolloping, virtuoso performance as the 18th-century German 'King of Liars' to a battery of truly visionary special effects. Renamed DEFA in 1946, the studios were thereafter used for the very different propaganda requirements of the GDR, though some excellent children's films were made, such as the internationally acclaimed *Little Muck*. With the demise of Communism, there were fears that the studios would have to close for want of funds, but they were saved by a French organization, the Compagnie d'Aménagement et de Développement. The popular actor Volker Schlondorff has been installed as managing director, parts of the complex have been thrown open to the public, attracting vast crowds, and production schedules are as busy as ever, indicating a rosy future.

Although visitor facilities are still far from fully developed, with as yet few concessions to non-German speakers, there is enough to make a good day out, with four hours the minimum time to take in all the attractions. These include an English-language film about the history of the studios; a guided visit to see some of the indoor sets; a demonstration of the art of film cutting, editing and mixing; a chance to see the unique collection of spotlights; and a rehearsal with actors, stuntmen and extras, in which some of the secrets behind filming are revealed. Highlight of the set-piece attractions is a visit to the props department, which numbers well over a million items, by far the largest in the world and an asset which was of crucial importance in guaranteeing the studios' future. A team of craftsmen is employed to forge anything needed to give a film the authentic touch, from jewellery to old master paintings. The collection of carriages and the outdoor sets can be visited at leisure. The latter include a farm village, a pirate town, a witches' house (from the film *Sherlock Holmes and the Seven Dwarfs*), and a reproduction of a 1920s Berlin street. Incorporated in the last of these is a make-up department where visitors can model and be photographed in historical costumes.

Potsdam's last and most unassuming palace is the **Jagdschloss Stern** (Star Hunting Lodge), which lies southeast of the Studios Babelsberg in the grim industrial suburb of Drewitz, until recently a separate town. Its name is derived from its position at the epicentre of eight hunting trails cut through a heath known as the Parforceheide by order of Friedrich Wilhelm I. A simple piece of brick architecture with only a gable for decoration, the lodge marked the Potsdam début of the Dutch style, seen at its most effective in the Holländisches Viertel built immediately afterwards (see page 294). Inside, the star motif is continued in the ceiling of the main hall, painted to resemble the sky at night.

(following page) *Façade painting, Charlottenburg*

Berlin Cabaret

Through his stories of the raunchy twilight years of the Weimar Republic, Christopher Isherwood has been responsible, far more than any other writer, for shaping the English-speaking world's perception of Berlin. Like many of his generation at Oxbridge, he had first been attracted to Germany as an antidote to Britain, which he hated for its snobbishness and class-consciousness. However, he did not visit the city until 1929, by which time he was aged 24, had dropped out of university and medical school, and had already published his first novel, *All the Conspirators*. He returned to settle in the city late the same year, and stayed until just after the Nazi assumption of power in 1933. It was his intention to make his experiences the basis of an epic entitled *The Lost*, but found the task beyond his creative abilities. Instead, he repackaged the material as a brief novel, *Mr Norris Changes Trains*, first published in 1935, and a collection of six short stories, *Goodbye to Berlin*, which appeared four years later.

These books revolved around the lives of a series of classic Berlin types. Isherwood himself appears as narrator: he adopted the guise of William Bradshaw (his two middle names) in the novel, but rejected this as artificial and reverted to his real name for the later stories. The central character in each book is likewise an English émigré—the adventurer and swindler Arthur Norris, and the cabaret singer Sally Bowles; both are amoral, duplicitous, frivolous and fundamentally weak human beings, yet are sympathetically drawn. Around them are a richly varied group of locals—the elderly landlady Fräulein Lina Schroeder, with her dubious lodgers Bobby the bartender, Fräulein Kost the prostitute and Fräulein Mayr the music-hall *jodlerin*, or yodeller; the Nowaks, a poor working-class family displaced from their home in the Polish Corridor and now cramped into a small damp tenement; and the Landauers, a wealthy Jewish family of retailers who reside in a fabulous lakeside villa. Woven into the background to the stories are taut descriptions of the rise of the Nazis that clearly demonstrate the narrator's understanding of the reasons behind the movement's political success and his early awareness of the full extent of its evil, not least in the key role of anti-Semitism.

The two books gained Isherwood instant fame and led to extravagant expectations of him: Somerset Maugham went so far as to declare, 'That young man holds the future of the English novel in his hands'. In 1951, the stories were brought to a wider public by the hugely successful Broadway play *I am a Camera*, which was filmed four years later; this took its title from the opening sequence of *Goodbye to Berlin*, where the narrator compares his role to that of a camera recording events. In 1966, the stories were transformed into an even bigger smash-hit, the musical *Cabaret*, which in 1972 was made into the spectacular film, starring Liza Minelli and Joel Grey. By this time, Isherwood's characters, and in particular Sally Bowles, had undergone radical transformations. As the author himself wryly remarked in a foreword to a reissue of his books as *The Berlin of Sally Bowles*, the vulnerable would-be-singer-actress, desperately trying to carve out a career in pitiful nightclubs, had instead become the star of 'a show which would have been the wonder of its epoch and drawn crowds from all over Northern Europe'.

Although he lived to a ripe old age, Isherwood dismally failed to live up to the early promise of his Berlin stories. Having emigrated to the United States in 1939 because of his pacifist leanings, he worked as a Hollywood scriptwriter, but later became totally obsessed with Indian mysticism and his own homosexuality, themes which pervade all his later writings. One of the books which best illustrates the alarming decline of his powers is *Christopher and his Kind*, published in 1977 as a memoir of the years when he researched and wrote the Berlin novels. This mawkishly subjects the behaviour of his younger self, referred to throughout as 'Christopher', to retrospective self-examination, and gives full and often embarrassing details of his endlessly promiscuous homosexual affairs.

Despite its considerable deficiencies, the book nonetheless gives fascinating insights into the background and creative process of the Berlin stories which turn out, like all of Isherwood's output, to be largely autobiographical. Each of the characters was based on a real-life prototype and most of their adventures were likewise true stories, albeit subject to a certain amount of imaginative reordering. The only major difference from Isherwood's actual experiences was in his editing out of all references to homosexuality. Yet this was of the profoundest significance, as he chose to live in Berlin precisely because of its atmosphere of sexual tolerance. The city then had at least 170 male brothels; thus, as he states baldly at the beginning of *Christopher and his Kind*, to him 'Berlin meant Boys'. Similarly, homosexuality underpinned the real-life events and characters—with the notable exception of Sally Bowles—that formed the basis for his stories, and it was the Nazi categorization of it as an eradicable disease that was ultimately responsible for his departure from the city.

Exactly why Isherwood so completely expunged all homosexual references from his two early Berlin books is unclear. In part, it was to protect the people who served as the models for his characters, and in part because to have done otherwise he would have risked alienating most of his potential readership, given the social mores of the time. Purely artistic considerations were also involved: making the narrator a homosexual, for example, would have been to deflect attention away from his intended role as a neutral 'camera' recording what he saw.

While it remains an enormous irony that one of the most famous and enduring literary portraits of Berlin should be based so clearly on a deliberate distortion of reality, it is a matter of great good fortune that the young Isherwood—for all the discomfiture it caused his older self—chose to write the books as he did. Rich in characterization, subtle in tone, entertaining in anecdote and profound in political analysis, the stories are a masterly evocation of a city at a crucial period in its history which gain immeasurably from the self-effacement of an author who was normally self-obsessed. Having found his ideal subject, Isherwood wrote about it brilliantly. In so doing, he gained a place in literary history that remains assured, regardless of the feebleness of so much of his later work.

I am a camera with its shutter open, quite passive, recording, not thinking. Recording the man shaving at the window opposite and the woman in the kimono washing her hair. Some day, all this will have to be developed, carefully printed, fixed.

Christopher Isherwood, 'A Berlin Diary, Autumn 1930', Goodbye to Berlin, *1939*

The Cabaret Singer

One afternoon, early in October, I was invited to black coffee at Fritz Wendel's flat. Fritz always invited you to 'black coffee', with emphasis on the black. He was very proud of his coffee. People used to say that it was the strongest in Berlin.

Fritz himself was dressed in his usual coffee-party costume—a very thick white yachting sweater and very light blue flannel trousers. He greeted me with his full-lipped, luscious smile:

'lo, Chris!'

'Hullo, Fritz. How are you?'

'Fine.' He bent over the coffee-machine, his sleek black hair unplastering itself from his scalp and falling in richly scented locks over his eyes. 'This darn thing doesn't go,' he added.

'How's business?' I asked.

'Lousy and terrible.' Fritz grinned richly. 'Or I pull off a new deal in the next month or I go as a gigolo.'

'Either . . . or . . . ' I corrected, from force of professional habit.

'I'm speaking a lousy English just now,' drawled Fritz, with great self-satisfaction. 'Sally says maybe she'll give me a few lessons.'

'Who's Sally?'

'Why I forgot. You don't know Sally. Too bad of me. Eventually she's coming around here this afternoon.'

'Is she nice?'

Fritz rolled his naughty black eyes, handing me a rum-moistened cigarette from his patent tin:

'Mar-vellous!' he drawled. 'Eventually I believe I'm getting crazy about her.'

'And who is she? What does she do?'

'She's an English girl, an actress: sings at the Lady Windermere—hot stuff, believe me!'

'That doesn't sound much like an English girl, I must say.'

'Eventually she's got a bit of French in her. Her mother was French.'

A few minutes later, Sally herself arrived.

'Am I terribly late, Fritz darling?'

'Only half an hour, I suppose,' Fritz drawled, beaming with proprietary pleasure. 'May I introduce Mr Isherwood—Miss Bowles? Mr Isherwood is commonly known as Chris.'

'I'm not,' I said. 'Fritz is about the only person who's ever called me Chris in my life.'

Sally laughed. She was dressed in black silk, with a small cape over her shoulders and a little cap like a page-boy's stuck jauntily on one side of her head:

'Do you mind if I use your telephone, sweet?'

'Sure. Go right ahead.' Fritz caught my eye. 'Come into the other room, Chris. I want to show you something.' He was evidently longing to hear my first impressions of Sally, his new acquisition.

'For heaven's sake, don't leave me alone with this man!' she exclaimed. 'Or he'll seduce me down the telephone. He's most terribly passionate.'

As she dialled the number, I noticed that her fingernails were painted emerald green, a colour unfortunately chosen, for it called attention to her hands, which were much stained by cigarette-smoking and as dirty as a little girl's. She was dark enough to be Fritz's sister. Her face was long and thin, powdered dead white. She had very large brown eyes which should have been darker, to match her hair and the pencil she used for her eyebrows.

'Hilloo,' she cooed, pursing her brilliant cherry lips as though she were going to kiss the mouthpiece: 'Ist das Du, mein Liebling?' Her mouth opened in a fatuously sweet smile. Fritz and I sat watching her, like a performance at the theatre. 'Was wollen wir machen, Morgen Abend? Oh, wie wunderbar . . . Nein, nein, ich werde bleiben Heute Abend zu Hause. Ja, ja, ich werde wirklich bleiben zu Hause . . . Auf Wiedersehen, mein Liebling . . . '

She hung up the receiver and turned to us triumphantly.

'That's the man I slept with last night,' she announced. 'He makes love marvellously. He's an absolute genius at business and he's terribly rich—' She came and sat down on the sofa beside Fritz, sinking back into the cushions with a sigh: 'Give me some coffee, will you, darling? I'm simply dying of thirst.'

And soon we were on to Fritz's favourite topic: he pronounced it *Larv*. 'On the average,' he told us, 'I'm having a big affair every two years.'

'And how long is it since you had your last?' Sally asked.

'Exactly one year and eleven months!' Fritz gave her his naughtiest glance.

'How marvellous!' Sally puckered up her nose and laughed a silvery little stage-laugh. 'Doo tell me—what was the last one like?'

This, of course, started Fritz off on a complete autobiography. We had the story of his seduction in Paris, details of a holiday flirtation at Las Palmas, the four chief New York romances, a disappointment in Chicago, and a conquest in Boston; then back to Paris for a little recreation, a very beautiful episode in Vienna, to London to be consoled and, finally, Berlin.

'You know, Fritz darling,' said Sally, puckering up her nose at me, 'I believe the trouble with you is that you've never really found the right woman.'

'Maybe that's true—' Fritz took this idea very seriously. His black eyes became liquid and sentimental: 'Maybe I'm still looking for my ideal . . . '

'But you'll find her one day, I'm absolutely certain you will.' Sally included me, with a glance, in the game of laughing at Fritz.

'You think so?' Fritz grinned lusciously, sparkling at her.

'Don't you think so?' Sally appealed to me.

'I'm sure I don't know,' I said. 'Because I've never been able to discover what Fritz's ideal is.'

For some reason, this seemed to please Fritz. He took it as a kind of testimonial: 'And Chris knows me pretty well,' he chimed in. 'If Chris doesn't know, well, I guess no one does.'

Then it was time for Sally to go.

'I'm supposed to meet a man at the Adlon at five,' she explained. 'And it's six already! Never mind, it'll do the old swine good to wait. He wants me to be his mistress, but I've told him I'm damned if I will till he's paid all my debts. Why are men always such beasts? Opening her bag, she rapidly retouched her lips and eyebrows: 'Oh, by the way, Fritz darling, could you be a perfect angel and lend me ten marks? I haven't a bean for a taxi.'

'Why, sure!' Fritz put his hand into his pocket and paid up without hesitation, like a hero.

Sally turned to me: 'I say, will you come and have tea with me sometime? Give me your telephone number. I'll ring you up.'

I suppose, I thought, she imagines I've got cash. Well, this will be a lesson to her, once for all. I wrote my number in her tiny leather book. Fritz saw her out.

'Well!' He came bounding back into the room and gleefully shut the door: 'What do you think of her, Chris? Didn't I tell you she was a good-looker?'

'You did indeed!'

'I'm getting crazier about her each time I see her!' With a sigh of pleasure, he helped himself to a cigarette: 'More coffee, Chris?'

'No, thank you very much.'

'You know, Chris, I think she took a fancy to you, too!'

'Oh, rot!'

'Honestly, I do!' Fritz seemed pleased. 'Eventually I guess we'll be seeing a lot of her from now on!'

When I got back to Frl. Schroeder's, I felt so giddy that I had to lie down for half an hour on my bed. Fritz's black coffee was as poisonous as ever.

Christopher Isherwood, 'Sally Bowles', Goodbye to Berlin, 1939

Resident in Berlin from 1929–1933, Christopher Isherwood is certainly the best known English writer about Berlin. He abandoned his planned epic on the city, publishing instead a novel and a book of short stories which draw on his time there in the years leading up to Hitler's rise to power.

Practical Information

Useful Addresses

Some useful emergency numbers are:

Police	110
Fire and ambulance	112
Directory enquiries	011 88
International directory enquiries	001 18
Medical	31 00 31
Wake-up call	11 41

TOURIST INFORMATION OFFICES
■ IN BERLIN

Europa-Center
Budapester Strasse
Mon–Sat 8 am–10.30 pm, Sun 9 am–9pm
Tel 2 62 60 31

Bahnhof Zoo
Mon–Sat 8 am–11 pm. Tel 3 13 90 63

Flughafen Tegel
Daily 8 am–11 pm. Tel 41 01 31 45

Alexanderplatz
Daily 8 am–8 pm. Tel 2 42 46 75

■ IN THE UK
German National Tourist Office
65 Curzon Street, London W1Y 7PE
Tel 071 235 5033

■ IN THE US
German National Tourist Office
122 E 42nd Street, New York NY 10017
Tel 212 661 7200

German National Tourist Office
11766 Wilshire Boulevard
Suite 750, Los Angeles CA 90025
Tel 310 575 9799

EMBASSIES AND CONSULATES
■ IN BERLIN
Australia
Uhlandstrasse 181–183. Tel 23 82 20 41

Canada
Friedrichstrasse 95. Tel 2 61 11 61

Ireland
Ernst-Reuter-Platz 10. Tel 3 48 00 80

United Kingdom
Unter den Linden 32–34. Tel 2 20 24 31

United States
Clayallee 170. Tel 8 32 40 87

■ IN THE UK
German Embassy
23 Belgrave Square, London SW1X 8PZ
Tel 071 235 5033

■ IN THE US
German Embassy
4645 Reservoir Road NW, Washington DC 20007
Tel 202 298 4000

AIRLINES
■ IN BERLIN
Air Canada
Kurfürstendamm 209. Tel 8 82 58 79

American Airlines
Bundesallee 213. Tel 2 11 00 32

British Airways
Europa-Center. Tel 69 10 21

Conti-Flug
Flughafen Tempelhof. Tel 69 09 858

Lufthansa
Kurfürstendamm 220. Tel 88 75 88

TWA
Europa-Center. Tel 8 82 70 96

United Airlines
Flughafen Tegel. Tel 41 01 34 35

■ IN THE UK
British Airways
156 Regent Street, London W1R 5TA
Tel 081 897 4000

Conti-Flug
602 Kingston Road, London SW20 8DN
Tel 0293 568885

Fashion shoot in east Berlin

Lufthansa
23–26 Piccadilly, London W1V 0EJ
Tel 081 750 3500

■ IN THE US
Toll-free Airline Numbers

American Airlines	800/433-7300
Air Canada	800/776-3000
British Airways	800/247-9297
Delta	800/241-4141
Lufthansa	800/645-3880
TWA	800/221-2000
United Airlines	800/241-6522

SPECIALIST TRAVEL AGENCIES
■ IN THE UK
DER
18 Conduit Street, London W1R 9TD
Tel 071 499 0577

German Travel Centre
8 Earlham Street, London WC2
Tel 071 836 4444

GTF Tours
182–186 Kensington Church Street,
London W8 4DP
Tel 071 792 1260

■ IN THE US
DER
9575 W Higgins Road, Rosemont IL 60018
Tel 800/937-1234

CULTURAL INSTITUTES
■ IN BERLIN
Amerikahaus
Hardenbergstrasse 22–24. Tel 3 10 00 10

British Council
Hardenbergstrasse 20. Tel 31 10 91 10

FINANCIAL CENTRE
■ IN BERLIN
American Express
Kurfürstendamm 11. Tel 8 82 75 75

BOAT TRIPS
■ IN BERLIN
Kultur-Kondor
Savignyplatz 9–10. Tel 31 08 88

Reederei Spreefahrt Horst Duggen
Regensburger Strasse 8. Tel 2 18 99 33

Reederei Georg Krüger
Grünhofer Weg 33. Tel 3 31 36 59

Reederei Siegfried Pfeifer
Waldkauzstrasse 42. Tel 4 31 87 16

Reederei Heinz Riedel
Planufer 78. Tel 6 91 37 82

Reederei Werner Triebler
Johannastrasse 24. Tel 3 31 54 14

Reederei Vogt
Steinadlerpfad. Tel 4 31 05 65

Reederei Bruno Winkler
Levetzowstrasse 12a. Tel 3 91 70 10

Stern und Kreisschiffahrt
Sachtlebenstrasse 60. Tel 8 10 00 40

Weisse Flotte
Treptower Hafen. Tel 2 71 23 27

LOST PROPERTY OFFICES
■ IN BERLIN
BVG Fundbüro (items lost on public transport network)
Lorenzweg 5. Tel 7 51 80 21

Zentrales Fundbüro
Platz der Luftbrücke 6. Tel 69 90

Accommodation

One of the problems thrown up by the reunification of Berlin and its reinstatement as capital of Germany is that it has an insufficient supply of hotel beds to cope with the hugely increased flow of both business and holiday visitors. It is therefore advisable to book a room as far in advance as possible, regardless of the time of year: winter trade fairs are responsible for filling up scores of hotels for days on end. In case of difficulty, contact the tourist office, which has access to otherwise unavailable private rooms in cases of emergency.

HOTELS

■ DE LUXE (SINGLES OVER DM250)

Bristol Kempinski
Kurfürstendamm 27
Tel 88 43 40 Telex 185 651 Fax 8 83 60 75

Grand Hotel
Friedrichstrasse 158–164
Tel 2 32 70 Telex 115 197 Fax 23 27 33 62

Grand Hotel Esplanade
Lützowufer 15
Tel 26 10 11 Telex 185 986 Fax 2 62 91 21

Inter-Continental
Budapester Strasse 2
Tel 2 60 20 Telex 184 380 Fax 26 02-8 07 60

Schweizerhof
Budapester Strasse 21–31
Tel 26 96-0 Telex 185 501 Fax 26 96-900

■ SUPERIOR (SINGLES DM150–DM250)

Am Zoo
Kurfürstendamm 25
Tel 88 43 70 Telex 183 835 Fax 88 43 7-714

Forum
Alexanderplatz 8
Tel 23 89 43 33 Telex 114 111-13 Fax 23 89 43 05

Luisenhof
Kopenicker Strasse 92. Tel 2 79 11 09

Riehmers Hofgarten
Yorckstrasse 83. Tel 78 10 11 Fax 7 86 60 59

Unter den Linden
Unter den Linden 14
Tel 2 20 03 11 Telex 112 109 Fax 2 29 22 62

■ MODERATE (SINGLES DM85–DM150)

Bogota
Schlüterstrasse 45
Tel 8 81 50 01 Telex 184 946 Fax 8 83 58 87

Charlot
Giesebrechtstrasse 17
Tel 3 23 40 51 Fax 3 24 08 19

Dittberner
Wielandstrasse 26. Tel 8 81 64 85

Heidelberg
Knesebeckstrasse 15. Tel 31 01 03 Fax 3 13 58 70

Meineke
Meinekestrasse 10. Tel 8 82 81 11 Fax 8 82 57 16

■ BUDGET (SINGLES UNDER DM85)

Alpenland
Carmerstrasse 8. Tel 3 12 48 98 Fax 3 13 84 44

Arka
Kurfürstendamm 103–104
Tel 8 92 98 88 Fax 8 91 97 83

Centrum Pension Berlin
Kantstrasse 31. Tel 31 61 53

Grossbeerenkeller
Grossbeerenstrasse 90. Tel 2 51 30 64

Pension Kreuzberg
Grossbeerenstrasse 64. Tel 2 51 13 62

MITWOHNZENTRALEN (PRIVATE LETTING AGENCIES)

An attractive alternative to staying in a hotel is to book either a room in a private house or a complete flat via one of the many Mitwohnzentrale agencies, which always have large numbers of short-term lets available. The flats in particular can be extraordinarily good value, particularly for families or for stays of upwards of two weeks, and cost a mere fraction of the price of even the cheapest hotels.

■ RECOMMENDED AGENCIES

Erste Mitwohnzentrale
Sybelstrasse 53. Tel 3 24 30 31

Mitwohnzentrale Ku'damm Eck
Kurfürstendamm 227–228 (3rd floor)
Tel 88 30 51

Mitwohnzentrale Kreuzberg
Mehringdamm 72. Tel 7 86 60 02

Zeitraum Mitwohnzentrale
Horstweg 7. Tel 3 25 61 81

Where to Eat

RESTAURANTS

■ TRADITIONAL BERLIN GASTSTÄTTEN (INNS)

Altberliner Bierstuben
Saarbrückerstrasse 16. Tel 2 82 89 33

Alter Krug
Königin-Luise-Strasse 52. Tel 8 32 77 49

Blockhaus Nikolskoe
Nikolskoer Weg. Tel 8 05 29 14

Ermeler Haus
Märkisches Ufer 10. Tel 2 79 36 17

Goethe Eck
Leibnitzstrasse 81. Tel 3 12 12 12

Grossbeerenkeller
Grossbeerenstrasse 90. Tel 251 30 64

Hardtke
Meinickestrasse 27a. Tel 8 81 98 27

Historische Weinstuben
Poststrasse 23. Tel 24 31 31 48

Lothar und Ich
Dominicusstrasse 46. Tel 7 84 41 42

Zum Nussbaum
Am Nussbaum 3. Tel 21 71 33 27

Zum Paddenwirt
Nikolaikirchplatz 6. Tel 24 31 32 31

Zur Letzten Instanz
Waisenstrasse 16. Tel 2 42 55 28

■ GASTSTÄTTEN WITH HOUSE BREWERY

Brauhaus Johann Albrecht
Karolinenstrasse 12. Tel 4 34 10 97

Luisenbrau
Luisenplatz 1. Tel 3 41 93 88

Rixdorfer Brauhaus
Glasower Strasse 27. Tel 6 26 88 80

■ SOUTH GERMAN AND AUSTRIAN

Heinrich (Baden)
Sophie-Charlottenstrasse 88. Tel 3 21 19 48

Kellerrestaurant im Brechthaus (Viennese)
Chausseestrasse 125. Tel 2 82 38 43

Kulisse (Swabian)
Friesenstrasse 4. Tel 6 92 65 06

Tegernsee Tönnchen (Bavarian)
Mommsenstrasse 34. Tel 3 23 38 27

■ NEUE DEUTSCHE KÜCHE (NEW GERMAN CUISINE)

Alt Luxemburg
Pestalozzistrasse 70. Tel 3 23 87 30

Französischer Hof
Jägerstrasse 56. Tel 2 29 39 69

Frühsammer's Gaststätte
Matterhornstrasse 101. Tel 8 03 27 20

Hasenburg
Fichtestrasse 1. Tel 6 91 91 39

Königin Luise
Opernpalais, Unter den Linden 5. Tel 2 00 22 69

Restaurant im Logenhaus
Emser Strasse 12–13. Tel 87 63 26

Rockendorf's Restaurant
Dusterhauptstrasse 1. Tel 4 02 30 99

■ INTERNATIONAL

Anteo
Joachimstaler Strasse 31. Tel 8 83 44 07

Florian
Grolmanstrasse 52. Tel 3 13 91 84

Hemingway's
Hagenstrasse 18. Tel 8 25 45 71

Lutter und Wegner
Schlüterstrasse 55. Tel 8 81 58 01

Mundart
Muskauer Strasse 33–34. Tel 6 12 20 61

Offenbach-Stuben
Stubbenkammerstrasse 8. Tel 4 48 41 06

■ FRENCH

Bamberger Reiter
Regensburger Strasse 7. Tel 24 42 82

Le Paris
Kurfürstendamm 211. Tel 8 81 52 42

Petite France
Damaschkestrasse 20. Tel 3 24 64 87

Reste Fidele
Bleibtreustrasse 41. Tel 8 81 16 05

■ ITALIAN
Anselmo
Damaschkestrasse 17. Tel 3 23 30 94

Castel Sardo
Hagenstrasse 2. Tel 8 25 60 14

Cristallo
Teltower Damm. Tel 8 15 66 09

Peppino
Fasanenstrasse 65. Tel 8 83 67 22

Ponte Vecchio
Spielhagenstrasse 3. Tel 3 42 19 99

■ OTHER CUISINES
Angkor (Cambodian)
Seelingstrasse 34–36. Tel 3 25 59 94

Borriquito (Spanish)
Wielandstrasse 6. Tel 3 12 99 29

Carib (Caribbean)
Motzstrasse 30. Tel 2 13 53 81

Der Ägypter (Egyptian)
Kantstrasse 26. Tel 3 13 92 30

Jüdisches Gemeindehaus (Jewish)
Fasanenstrasse 79. Tel 88 42 03 39

Kashmir Palace (Indian)
Marburger Strasse 14. Tel 2 14 28 40

Kopenhagen (Danish)
Kurfürstendamm 203. Tel 8 81 62 19

Kurdistan (Kurdish)
Kaiser-Friedrich-Strasse 41. Tel 31 70 21

Lusiada (Portuguese)
Kurfürstendamm 132a. Tel 8 91 58 69

Merhaba (Turkish)
Hasenheide 39. Tel 6 92 17 13

Ming's Garden (Chinese)
Tauentzienstrasse 16. Tel 2 11 87 28

Moskau (Ukrainian)
Karl-Marx-Allee 34. Tel 2 79 16 70

Samowar (Russian)
Luisenplatz 3. Tel 3 41 41 54

Tadschikische Teestube (Russian, Tadzhik)
Palais am Festungsgraben 1. Tel 2 08 08 43

Tres Kilos (Mexican)
Marheinekeplatz 3. Tel 6 93 60 44

Udagawa (Japanese)
Feuerbachstrasse 24. Tel 7 92 23 73

Wein-ABC (Bulgarian)
Schiffbauerdamm 8. Tel 2 82 39 65

Zorbas (Greek)
Zossener Strasse 25. Tel 6 91 94 34

■ VEGETARIAN
Das Abendmahl
Muskauer Strasse 9. Tel 6 12 51 70

Hakuin
Martin-Luther-Strasse 1. Tel 2 18 20 27

Thürnagel
Gneisenaustrasse 57. Tel 6 91 48 00

CAFÉS
Café Hardenberg
Hardenbergstrasse 10. Tel 3 12 33 30)

Café Kranzler
Kurfürstendamm 18–19. Tel 8 82 69 11

Café Möhring
Kurfürstendamm 213. Tel 8 82 38 44
Kurfürstendamm 234. Tel 8 82 38 44
Gendarmenmarkt. Tel 20 90 22 40

Café Richter
Giesebrechtstrasse 22. Tel 3 24 37 22

Café Savigny
Grolmanstrasse 53. Tel 3 12 81 95

Café Übersee
Paul-Lincke-Ufer 44. Tel 6 18 87 63

Café Westphal
Kollwitzstrasse 64. Tel 4 48 32 89

Leysieffers
Kurfürstendamm 218. Tel 8 82 78 20

Operncafé
Opernpalais, Unter den Linden 5
Tel 2 00 22 69

Shops

BOOKSHOPS
Bücherbogen am Savignyplatz
Savignyplatz S-Bahn, Bogen 593. Tel 3 12 19 32

British Bookshop
Mauerstrasse 83–84. Tel 238 46 80

Herder Buchhandlung
Tauentzienstrasse 13. Tel 21 24 40

Kiepert
Hardenbergstrasse 4–5. Tel 3 11 00 90

Marga Schoeller
Knesebeckstrasse 33–34. Tel 8 81 11 12

DEPARTMENT STORES
Hertie
Wilmersdorfer Strasse 118. Tel 31 10 50

KaDeWe
Tauentzienstrasse 21. Tel 2 12 10

Karstadt
Wilmersdorfer Strasse 109. Tel 3 18 90

Kaufhof
Alexanderplatz 9. Tel 2 46 40

Wertheim
Kurfürstendamm 234. Tel 88 20 61

FASHION STORES
Blue Moon
Wilmersdorfer Strasse 80. Tel 3 23 70 88

Durchbruch
Schlüterstrasse 54. Tel 8 81 55 68

Evento
Grolmanstrasse 53–54. Tel 3 13 32 17

Fantazzi
Urbanstrasse 65. Tel 6 91 94 12

Hallhuber
Kurfürstendamm 237. Tel 8 81 44 77

Kramberg
Kurfürstendamm 56. Tel 3 23 60 58

Mey & Edlich
Kurfürstendamm 217. Tel 8 85 43 75

Molotow
Gneisenaustrasse 112. Tel 6 93 08 18

INTERNATIONAL NEWSAGENTS
Internationale Presse
Joachimstaler Strasse 1. Tel 8 81 72 56

Internationale und Berliner Presse
Kurfürstendamm 206–209. Tel 8 81 33 96

JEWELLERS
Astoria
Bleibtreustrasse 50. Tel 3 12 83 04

Rio
Bleibtreustrasse 52. Tel 3 13 31 52

Wempe
Kurfürstendamm 215. Tel 8 82 68 78

PORCELAIN MANUFACTURERS
Königliche Porzellan-Manufaktur (Royal Porcelain
Manufactory)
Kurfürstendamm 26a. Tel 8 81 18 02
Wegelystrasse 1. Tel 39 00 90

Meissen Porzellan, Unter den Linden 39b
Tel 229 26 91

SHOE SHOPS
Budapester Schuhe, Kurfürstendamm 199
Tel 8 81 17 07

Schuhtick
Savignyplatz 11. Tel 3 12 49 55

Zapato
Maassenstrasse 14. Tel 2 15 20 27

Markets

FLEA MARKETS

Fehrbelliner U-Bahn
Sat and Sun 8 am–3 pm

Kreuzberger Krempelmarkt
Am Reichpietsufer
Sat and Sun 9 am–3 pm

Pariser Platz
Daily until dusk

Strasse des 17 Juni
Sat and Sun 8 am–3.30 pm

FOOD MARKETS

Markthalle
Martheinkeplatz
Mon–Fri 8 am–5 pm, Sat 8 am–1 pm

Türken Markt (Turkish Market)
Maybachufer
Tues and Fri noon–6 pm

Winterfeldplatz
Wed and Sat 8 am–2 pm

Wittenbergplatz
Tues and Fri 8 am–2 pm

Arts Venues

BALLET, OPERA AND DANCE

Deutsche Oper Berlin, Bismarckstrasse 35
Tel 3 41 02 49

Deutsche Staatsoper Berlin
Unter den Linden 7. Tel 2 00 47 62

Komische Oper
Behrenstrasse 55–57. Tel 2 29 25 55

■ CONTEMPORARY DANCE

Tanzfabrik Berlin
Möckernstrasse 68. Tel 7 86 58 61

Theater am Halleschen Ufer
Hallesches Ufer 32. Tel 2 51 09 41

Theater unterm Dach
Dimitroffstrasse 101. Tel 4 20 06 10

CABARET

■ POLITICAL SATIRE

Die Distel
Friedrichstrasse 101. Tel 2 00 47 04

Kartoon
Französische Strasse 24. Tel 2 29 93 05

■ VARIETY

Berliner Kabarett Anstalt
Mehringdamm 32–34. Tel 2 51 01 12

Chamäleon Varieté
Rosenthaler Strasse 40–41. Tel 2 82 71 18

Wintergarten-Das Varieté
Potsdamer Strasse 96. Tel 2 62 70 70

THEATRES

■ CLASSICAL AND MODERN DRAMA

Berliner Ensemble
Bertolt-Brecht-Platz 1. Tel 2 82 31 60

Deutsches Theater Berlin
Schumannstrasse 13. Tel 2 84 41-225

Deutsches Theater Kammerspiele
Schumannstrasse 13a. Tel 2 84 41-226

Hebbel Theater
Stresemannstrasse 29. Tel 2 51 01 44

Maxim-Gorki-Theater
Am Festungsgraben. Tel 2 08 27 83

Schaubühne am Lehniner Platz
Kurfürstendamm 153. Tel 89 00 23

Schiller Theater
Bismarckstrasse 110. Tel 3 12 65 05

Schlosspark Theater
Schloss Strasse 48. Tel 7 93 15 15

Volksbühne am Rosa-Luxemburg-Platz
Rosa-Luxemburg-Platz. Tel 3 08 74-661

■ CHILDREN'S THEATRE

Grips Theater
Altonaer Strasse 22. Tel 3 91 40 04

■ COMEDIES AND FARCES

Hansa Theater
Alt-Moabit 48. Tel 3 91 44 60

Komödie
Kurfürstendamm 206. Tel 8 82 78 93

Renaissance-Theater
Hardenbergstrasse 6. Tel 3 12 42 02

Theater am Kurfürstendamm
Kurfürstendamm 206. Tel 3 00 60 00

Tribüne
Otto-Suhr-Allee 18. Tel 3 41 26 00

■ ENGLISH-LANGUAGE DRAMA
Freunde der Italienischen Oper
Fidicinstrasse 40. Tel 6 91 12 11

■ EXPERIMENTAL DRAMA
BAT
Belforter Strasse 15. Tel 4 48 28 57

Frei Theateranstalten
Klausenerplatz 19. Tel 3 21 58 89

Vaganten Bühne
Kantstrasse 12 a. Tel 3 12 45 29

■ MUSICALS
Metropol-Theater
Friedrichstrasse 101. Tel 2 03 64-117

Theater des Westens
Kantstrasse 12. Tel 3 19 03-193

■ PUPPETS
Berliner Figurentheater
Yorckstrasse 59. Tel 7 86 98 15

Fliegendes Theater
Hasenheide 54. Tel 6 92 21 00

■ REVUES
Friedrichstadtpalais
Friedrichstrasse 107. Tel 28 36-0

La Vie en Rose
Europa-Center. Tel 3 23 60 06

■ YOUTH THEATRE
Berliner Kammerspiele
Alt-Moabit 99. Tel 3 91 55 43

CONCERT HALLS
Philharmonie
Matthäikirchstrasse 1. Tel 2 54 88-132

Philharmonie Kammermusiksaal
Matthäikirchstrasse 1. Tel 2 54 88-232

Schauspielhaus (Grosses Konzersaal)
Gendarmenmarkt. Tel 20 90-21 56

Schauspielhaus (Kammermusiksaal)
Gendarmenmarkt. Tel 20 90-21 22

CINEMAS
Arsenal
Welserstrasse 25. Tel 2 18 68 48

Babylon
Rosa-Luxemburg-Strasse 30. Tel 2 42 50 76

Eiszeit
Zeughofstrasse 20. Tel 6 11 60 16

Movimiento
Kotbusser Damm 22. Tel 6 92 47 85

Notausgang
Vorbergstrasse 1. Tel 7 81 26 82

Sputnik 1
Reinickendorfer Strasse 13. Tel 4 65 87 69

Sputnik 2
Hasenheide 54. Tel 6 94 11 47

Museums and Galleries

Abguss Sammlung antiker Plastik
Schloss Strasse 69b
Thurs–Sun 2–5 pm.

Ägyptisches Museum
Schloss Strasse 70
Mon–Thurs 9 am–5 pm, Sat and Sun 10 am–5 pm.
(See also Bodemuseum)

Akademie der Künste
Hanseatenweg 10
Mon 1–7 pm, Tues–Sun 10 am–7 pm.

Altes Museum
Bodestrasse 1–3
Tues–Sun 10 am–7 pm

Antikensammlung
Schloss Strasse 1

Mon–Thurs 9 am–5 pm, Sat and Sun 10 am–5 pm.
(See also Pergamonmuseum)

Anti-Kriegs Museum
Müllerstrasse 158
Daily 4–8 pm.

Bauhaus-Archiv
Klingelhöferstrasse 14
Daily except Tues 10 am–5 pm, Thurs till 8 pm.

Berlin Museum
Lindenstrasse 14
Tues–Sun 10 am–8 pm.

Berliner Handwerksmuseum
Mühlendamm 5
Tues–Fri 9 am–5 pm, Sat 9 am–6 pm, Sun 10 am–
5 pm.

Bertolt-Brecht-Haus
Chausseestrasse 125
Guided tours Tues–Fri 10 am–noon, Thurs also
5–7 pm, Sat 9.30 am–noon and 12.30–2 pm.

Bodemuseum
(Ägyptisches Museum, Gemäldegalerie,
Münzkabinett, Museum für Spätantike und
Byzantinische Kunst, Skulpturensammlung)
Museumsinsel, entrance Monbijoubrücke.
Wed–Sun 9 am–5 pm.

Botanisches Museum
Königin-Luise-Strasse 6–8
Tues–Sun 10 am–5 pm.

Brücke-Museum
Bussardsteig 9
Wed–Mon 11 am–5 pm.

Deutsches Historisches Museum
Unter den Linden 2
Thurs–Tues 10 am–6 pm.

Deutsches Rundfunk-Museum
Messedamm
Wed–Mon 10 am–5pm.

Deutschlandhaus
Stresemannstrasse 90
Mon–Fri 9 am–7 pm, Sat and Sun 2–6 pm.

Documenta artistica
Inselstrasse 7

Wed–Sun 10 am–6 pm.

Ephraim-Palais
Poststrasse 16
Tues–Fri 9 am–5 pm, Sat 9 am–6 pm, Sun 10 am–
5 pm.

Friseurmuseum
Husemannstrasse 8
Mon–Thurs 10 am–6 pm, Sun 10 am–4 pm.

Galerie der Romantik
Knobelsdorff-Flügel, Schloss Charlottenburg
Tues–Fri 9 am–5 pm, Sat and Sun 10 am–5 pm.

Gemäldegalerie
See Bodemuseum and Staatliche Museen Dahlem

Georg-Kolbe-Museum
Sensburger Allee 25
Tues–Sun 10 am–5 pm.

Haus der Kulturen der Welt
John-Foster-Dulles-Allee 10
Tues–Sun 10 am–8 pm.

Heinrich-Zille-Museum
Bahnhof Friedrichstrasse S-Bahn Bogen 201
Wed–Mon 11 am–6 pm.

Huguenotten-Museum
Gendarmenmarkt (in the Turmbau of the Franzö-
sische Kirche)
Wed–Sat noon–5 pm, Sun 1–5 pm.

Käthe-Kollwitz-Museum
Fasanenstrasse 24
Wed–Mon 11 am–6 pm.

Knoblauchhaus
Poststrasse 23
Tues–Sun 10 am–6 pm.

Kunstgewerbemuseum
Matthäikirchstrasse 10
Tues–Fri 9 am–5 pm, Sat and Sun 10 am–5 pm.
(See also Schloss Köpenick)

Kupferstichkabinett
Matthäikirchstrasse 30
Tues–Fri 9 am–5 pm, Sat and Sun 10 am–5 pm.

Märkisches Museum
Am Köllnischen Park 5
Wed–Sun 10 am–6 pm.

Münzkabinett
See Bodemuseum

Museum Berliner Arbeiterleben
Husemannstrasse 12
Tues–Thurs 10 am–6 pm, Fri 10 am–3 pm.

Museum der Verbotenen Kunst
Puschkinallee, corner with Schlesische Strasse
Sat and Sun 3–6 pm.

Museum für Indische Kunst
See Staatliche Museen Dahlem

Museum für Islamische Kunst
See Pergamonmuseum and Staatliche Museen
Dahlem

Museum für Naturkunde
Invalidenstrasse 43
Tues–Sun 9.30 am–5 pm.

Museum für Ostasiatische Kunst
See Staatliche Museen Dahlem

Museum für Spätantike und Byzantinische Kunst
See Bodemuseum and Staatliche Museen Dahlem

Museum für Verkehr und Technik
Trebbiner Strasse 9
Tues–Fri 9 am–5.30 pm, Sat and Sun 10 am–6 pm.

Museum für Völkerkunde
See Staatliche Museen Dahlem

Museum für Volkskunde
Im Winkel 6
Tues–Fri 9 am–5 pm, Sat and Sun 10 am–5 pm.

Museum für Vor- und Frühgeschichte
Langhansbau, Schloss Charlottenburg
Mon–Thurs 9 am–5 pm, Sat and Sun 10 am–5 pm.

Museumsdorf Düppel
Clauertstrasse 11
Easter–Sept Thurs 3–7 pm, Sun 10 am–5 pm.

Musikinstrumentenmuseum
Tiergartenstrasse 1
Tues–Fri 9 am–5 pm, Sat and Sun 10 am–5 pm.

Nationalgalerie
Museumsinsel, entrance Bodestrasse.
Wed–Sun 9 am–5 pm.

Neue Nationalgalerie
Potsdamer Strasse 50
Tues–Fri 9 am–5 pm, Sat and Sun 10 am–5 pm.
Otto-Nagel-Haus
Märkisches Ufer 16
Sun–Thurs 9 am–5 pm.

Pergamonmuseum
(Antikensammlung, Museum für Islamische
Kunst, Vorderasiatisches Museum)
Museumsinsel, entrance Am Kupfergraben
Daily 9 am–5 pm; on Mon and Tues, only main
halls with architectural exhibits are open.

Postmuseum
Leipziger Strasse 16
Tues–Sat 10 am–6 pm.

Postmuseum Berlin
An der Urania 15
Mon–Thurs 9 am–5 pm, Sat and Sun 10 am–5 pm.

Schinkel-Museum
See Friedrichswerdersche Kirche

Skulpturensammlung
See Bodemuseum and Staatliche Museum Dahlem

Staatliche Museum Dahlem
(Gemäldegalerie, Museum für Indische Kunst,
Museum für Islamische Kunst, Museum für
Ostasiatische Kunst, Museum für Spatantike und
Byzantinische Kunst, Museum für Völkerkunde,
Skulpturensammlung)
Arminallee 23–27 and Lansstrasse 8
Tues–Fri 9 am–5 pm, Sat and Sun 10 am–5 pm.

Vorderasiatisches Museum
See Pergamonmuseum

Zeughaus
See Deutsches Historisches Museum

Sights

Aquarium
Budapester Strasse 32
Daily 9 am–6 pm, last Sat of month until 9 pm.

Archenhold-Sternwarte
Alt-Treptow 1
Wed–Sun 2–4.30 pm

International Congress Centre

Belvedere
Schlossgarten Charlottenburg
Tues–Fri 9 am–5 pm, Sat and Sun 10 am–5 pm.

Berliner Panoptikum
Ku'damm Eck, Kurfürstendamm 227
Daily 10 am–11 pm.

Berlin-Pavillon
Strasse des 17 Juni 100
Tues–Sun 10 am–7 pm.

Domäne Dahlem
Königin-Luise-Strasse 49
Wed–Mon 10 am–6 pm.

Dorotheenstädtischer Friedhof
Chausseestrasse 126
Daily 8 am–4/8 pm according to season.

Dreifaltigkeits-Kirchhof I
Mehringdamm corner with Zossener Strasse
Daily 8 am–5/8 pm according to season.

Dreifaltigkeits-Kirchhof II
Bergammstrasse 39–41
Daily 8 am–5/9 pm according to season.

Fernsehturm
Alexanderplatz
Daily 9 am–midnight.

Forschungs- und Gedenkstätte Normannenstrasse
Ruschestrasse 59
Tues–Fri 11 am–6 pm, Sat and Sun 2–6 pm.

Funkturm
Messedamm
Daily 10 am–11 pm.

Gedenkstätte Deutscher Widerstand
Stauffenbergstrasse 13
Mon–Fri 9 am–6 pm, Sat and Sun 9 am–1 pm.

Gedenkstätte Haus der Wannsee-Konferenz
Am Grossen Wannsee 56–58
Tues–Fri 10 am–6 pm, Sat and Sun 2–6 pm.

Gedenkstätte Köpenicker Blutwoche
Puchanstrasse 12
Mon 10 am–4 pm, Tues and Thurs 10 am–6 pm,
Fri 10 am–2 pm.

Gedenkstätte Plötzensee
Huttigpfad
Daily 8 am–6 pm.

Glockenturm am Olympia-Stadion
Friedrich-Friesen-Allee
Daily 9.30 am–5.30 pm.

Grunewaldturm
Havelchaussee
Daily 10 am–9 pm.

Haus am Checkpoint Charlie
Friedrichstrasse 44
Daily 9 am–10 pm.

Huguenotten-Friedhof
Chausseestrasse 127
Daily 8 am–4/7 pm according to season.

Huguenotten-Friedhof
Wöhlertstrasse
Daily 8 am–4/7 pm according to season.

Jagdschloss Grunewald
Hüttenweg, am Grunewaldsee
Tues–Sun 10 am–1 pm and 1.30–6 pm.

Martin-Gropius-Bau
Stresemannstrasse 110
Tues–Sun 10 am–8 pm.

Rathaus Schöneberg
John-F-Kennedy-Platz
Wed and Sun 10 am–4 pm.

Reichstag
Platz der Republik
Tues–Sun 10 am–5 pm.

Rotes Rathaus
Rathausstrasse, corner with Jüdenstrasse
Mon–Fri 10 am–6 pm, Sat 9 am–3 pm.

Schinkel-Pavillon
Schlossgarten Charlottenburg
Tues–Fri 9 am–5 pm, Sat and Sun 10 am–5 pm.

Schloss Britz
Alt-Britz 73
Guided tours Wed 2–6 pm.

Schloss Charlottenburg Nering-Eosanderbau
Luisensplatz
Guided tours Tues–Fri 9 am–5 pm, Sat and Sun
10 am–5 pm.

Schloss Charlottenburg Knobelsdorff-Flügel
Luisenplatz
Tues–Fri 9 am–5 pm, Sat and Sun 10 am–5 pm.

Schloss Friedrichsfelde
Am Tierpark 125
Guided tours Tues–Fri at 1 pm, Sat and Sun at
2 pm.

Schloss Glienicke
Königstrasse 36
Tues–Fri 2–6 pm, Sat and Sun 10 am–6 pm.

Schloss Köpenick Kunstgewerbemuseum
Schlossinsel
Wed–Sun 9 am–5 pm.

Schloss Pfaueninsel
Pfaueninsel
Guided tours April–Oct Tues–Sun 10 am–12.30
pm and 1.30–4.30pm.

Schloss Tegel
Adelheidallee 19-20
May–Sept Mon 10 am–noon and 3–5 pm.

Siegessäule
Strasse des 17 Juni 30–31
Tues–Sun 9 am–6 pm.

Spandauer Zitadelle
Am Juliusturm
Tues–Fri 9 am–5 pm, Sat and Sun 10 am–5 pm.

Tierpark Friedrichsfelde
Am Tierpark 125
Daily 9 am–dusk.

Topographie des Terrors
Stresemannstrasse 110
Tues–Sun 10 am–6 pm.

Churches and Cemeteries

Alter St-Matthäus-Kirchhof
Grossgörschenstrasse 12
Daily 8 am–5.30 / 8 pm according to season.

Berliner Dom
Lustgarten
Mon–Sat 9 am–5 pm, Sun noon–5 pm.

Nikolaikirche
Nikolaikirchplatz
Tues–Fri 9 am–5 pm, Sat 9 am–6 pm, Sun 10 am–
5 pm.

Nikolaikirche, Spandau
Reformationsplatz
Sat 11 am–3 pm, Sun 2–4 pm.

Französische Kirche
Gendarmenmarkt 5
Tues–Sat noon–5 pm, Sun 1–5 pm.

Französische Kirche Turmbau
Gendarmenmarkt 5
Mon–Sat 10 am–4 pm.

Friedrichswerdersche Kirche
Werderstrasse
Wed–Sun 9 am–5 pm.

Jerusalem und Neue Kirchengemeinde III
Mehringdamm
Daily 8 am–5/8 pm according to season.

Jüdischer Friedhof (Prenzlauer Berg)
Schönhauser Allee 23
Mon–Thurs 8 am–4 pm, Fri 8 am–1 pm.

Jüdischer Friedhof (Weissensee)
Herbert-Baum-Strasse
Sun–Thurs 8 am–5 pm, Fri 8 am–3 pm.

Kaiser-Wilhelm-Gedächtniskirche
Breitscheidplatz
Tues–Sat 10 am–6 pm.

Kirche Maria Regina Martyrum
Heckerdamm 232
Daily 9 am–4.30 pm.

Kirche St Peter und Paul
Nikolskoer Weg

Daily 11 am–4 pm.

Marienkirche
Kalr-Liebknecht-Strasse 8
Mon–Thurs 10 am–noon and 1–4 pm, Sat noon–4 pm.

Matthäuskirche
Matthäikirchplatz
Wed–Sun noon–6 pm.

Mausoleum
Schlossgarten Charlottenburg
April–Oct Tues–Fri 9 am–5 pm, Sat and Sun 10 am–5 pm.

St-Hedwigs-Kathedrale
Bebelplatz
Mon–Sat 10 am–5 pm, Sun 1–5 pm.

Other

SHOWPIECE FACTORIES
Brotfabrik
Prenzlauer Promenade 3. Tel 4 71 40 02

UFA-Fabrik
Viktoriastrasse 13. Tel 75 50 30

PARKS AND GARDENS
Botanischer Garten
Königin-Luise-Strasse 6–8
Daily 9 am–5 pm, increasing progressively to 8 pm in summer.

Zoologischer Garten
Hardenbergplatz and Budapester Strasse
Daily 9 am–5/6.30 pm according to season.

EXHIBITION HALL
Deutschlandhalle, Messedamm. Tel 30 38-44 44

OPEN-AIR EVENTS
Waldbühne, Am Glockenturm. Tel 3 04 06 76.

SPORTS FACILITIES
Olympia-Stadion, Olympischer Platz
Daily 9 am–5 pm.

Potsdam Practical Information

Note that when calling from outside Potsdam, all telephone numbers are preceded by the code 0331.

USEFUL ADDRESSES
■ **TOURIST OFFICE**
Potsdam-Information
Friedrich-Ebert-Strasse 5. Tel 2 11 00
April–Oct Mon–Fri 9 am–8 pm, Sat and Sun 10 am–6 pm, Nov–March Mon–Fri 10 am–6 pm, Sat and Sun 11 am–3 pm

■ **CRUISES**
Weisse Flotte
Lange Brücke. Tel 2 15 27

HOTELS
Hotel Schloss Cecilienhof, Neuer Garten
Tel 2 31 41
Hotel Potsdam
Lange Brücke. Tel 46 31

Tourisen- und Congresshotel
Saarmunder Strasse 60. Tel 860

Hotel Bayrisches Haus
Im Wildpark 1. Tel 97 23 29

RESTAURANTS
Altes Jadgschloss Stern
Kohlhasenbrücker Strasse 31
Tel 62 13 44

Badische Weinstube
Gutenbergstrasse 90. Tel 2 61 70

Kleines Schloss
Park Babelsberg. Tel 7 51 56

Pegasus
Schloss Strasse 14. Tel 7 51 56

Terrassenrestaurant-Minsk
Max-Plank-Strasse 10. Tel 2 36 36

THEATRES
Hans-Otto-Theater
Theaterhaus am Alten Markt
Tel 28 00 693

Schlosstheater
Neues Palais. Tel 28 00 693

■ CABARET
Kabarett am Obelisk
Schopenhauerstrasse 27. Tel 2 17 38

MUSEUMS AND GALLERIES
Bildergalerie
Park Sanssouci
Mid-May–Mid-Oct daily 9 am–noon and 12.45–
5 pm, closed every fourth Wed of the month.

Filmmuseum
Schloss Strasse 1
Tues–Sun 10 am–5 pm.

Potsdam-Museum
Breite Strasse 13
Tues–Sun 9 am–5 pm.

Neue Kammern
Park Sanssouci

Guided tours Sat–Thurs 9 am–noon and 12.30–
3/5 pm according to season.

Dampfmaschinenhaus
Breite Strasse
Guided tours Mid-May–Mid-Oct Wed–Sun 9 am–
5 pm, Mid-Oct–Mid–May Sat and Sun 9 am–4 pm.

SIGHTS
Altes Rathaus
Am Alten Markt
Daily 10 am–6 pm.

Chinesisches Teehaus
Park Sanssouci
Mid-May–Mid-Oct daily 9–11.45 am and 12.30–
5 pm.

Jagdschloss Stern
Am Stern
Mid-May–Mid-Oct Sat and Sun 10 am–5 pm.

Neues Palais
Park Sanssouci
Daily 9 am–12.45 pm and 1.15–3 / 5 pm according
to season; closed every second and fourth Mon of
the month.

Orangerie
Park Sanssouci
Daily Mid-May–Mid-Oct 9 am–noon and 1–5 pm,
closed every fourth Thurs of the month.

Römische Bäder
Park Charlottenbof
Daily Mid-May–Mid-Oct 9 am–noon and 12.30–5
pm, closed every third Mon of the month.

Schloss Babelsberg
Park Babelsberg
Wed–Sun 9 am–5 pm.

Schloss Cecilienhof
Neuer Garten
Daily 9 am–5pm, closed every fourth Mon of the
month.

Schloss Charlottenhof
Park Charlottenhof
Guided tours daily Mid-May–Mid-Oct 9 am–12.30
pm and 1–5 pm, closed every fourth Mon of the
month.

Schloss Sanssouci
Park Sanssouci
Guided tours daily 9 am–12.30 pm and 1–3/5 pm
according to season; closed every first and third
Mon of the month.

Schloss Sanssouci Damenflügel
Park Sanssouci
Mid-May–Mid-Oct Wed–Sun 9–11.45 am and
12.30–5 pm.

Studios Babelsberg
August-Bebel-Strasse 26
Daily 10 am–6 pm.

CHURCHES
Friedenskirche
Marlygarten, Am Grunen Gitter
Mid-May–Mid-Oct Mon–Sat 10 am–6 pm,
Sun noon–6 pm.

Nikolaikirche
Am Alten Markt
Mon–Sat 2–5 pm, Sun 11.30–5 pm.

Bismarck monument in Grosser Stern

German Glossary

Frustrated at his difficulties in coming to grips with 'this fearsome tongue', Mark Twain wrote the hilarious essay 'The Awful German Language', which he inserted as an appendix to *A Tramp Abroad*, a book about his travels in southern Germany and Switzerland. Even if Twain exaggerated more than a little, German is undoubtedly an extremely complex language, one full of idiosyncrasies, but as a result capable of great precision of expression. It cannot be mastered in a short time, which makes it all the more fortuitous that English is very much a second language throughout Germany.

Be warned, however, that people's ability of to speak fluent English is as yet not as common in Berlin as in most other parts of the country: in East Berlin, as throughout the former GDR, it has only recently supplanted Russian, while the West Berliners' island mentality made them less prone to learn other languages than their West German counterparts. In any event, learning a little German can only contribute towards the enjoyment of a visit.

There are a number of linguistic peculiarities to observe. All nouns are shown with capital letters. Compounds, made up of several words joined together without hyphens, are very popular and often of a seemingly daunting length. Plurals are formed very irregularly by the addition of one of a variety of different letters. The Scharfes s, written ß, usually substitutes for ss in a word. There are three genders—masculine, feminine and neuter—which each have their own ending and a corresponding ending for attached adjectives. The designation of these can appear very illogical: for example, a girl is neuter, a cat (including a tom-cat) is feminine, while a train is masculine.

Pronunciation

For all its grammatical complexities, German is a phonetic language presenting few pronunciation difficulties. Most syllables are pronounced exactly as they are written: the trick is learning how to place the stresses in the notoriously lengthy German words.

VOWELS
a as in m*a*tter
e as in p*e*t or *ay* in s*ay*
i as *ee* in sh*ee*p
o as in c*o*tton or d*o*se
u as *oo* in f*oo*t

In addition, an umlaut can appear above the letters a, o and u, substituting for a displaced e.
ä can be like *e* in m*e*t, or like *ai* in m*ai*d
ö is like the French *eu*
ü is a sharper sounding version of *ue* as in bl*ue*

VOWEL COMBINATIONS
ai as *ie* in p*ie*
au as *ou* in m*ou*se
ie as *ee* in tr*ee*
ei as *i* in d*i*ne
eu as *oi* in b*oi*l

CONSONANTS
Consonants are pronounced as they are written,
with no silent letters. The ones that differ from the English are as follows:
j is pronounced like an English *y*
r is given a dry, throaty sound, similar to French
s is pronounced similar to but slightly softer than an English *z*
v is pronounced somewhere between an English *f* and *v*
w is pronounced the same way as an English *v*
z is pronounced *ts*

Vocabulary

BASIC WORDS

ja	yes
nein	no
bitte	please, you're welcome
danke (schön)	thank you (very much)
hier	here
da	there

jetzt	now		sechszig	60
später	later		siebzig	70
früher	earlier		achtzig	80
dieses	this one		neunzig	90
jenes	that one		hundert	100
gross	big		zweihundertfünfunddreissig	235
klein	small		tausend	1,000
mehr	more			
weniger	less			

wenig	a little
viel	a lot
billig	cheap
teuer	expensive
gut	good
schlecht	bad
mit	with
ohne	without
heiss	hot
kalt	cold
geöffnet, offen, auf	open
geschlossen, zu	closed
rechts	right
links	left
oben	up
unten	down

DAYS, MONTHS, SEASONS AND DATES

Montag	Monday
Dienstag	Tuesday
Mittwoch	Wednesday
Donnerstag	Thursday
Freitag	Friday
Samstag, Sonnabend	Saturday
Sonntag	Sunday
Januar	January
Februar	February
März	March
April	April
Mai	May
Juni	June
Juli	July
August	August
September	September
Oktober	October
November	November
Dezember	December
Frühling	spring
Sommer	summer
Herbst	autumn
Winter	winter
Montag, der erste April	Monday, the first of April
Der zweite April	the second of April

NUMBERS

eins	1
zwei, zwo	2
drei	3
vier	4
fünf	5
sechs	6
sieben	7
acht	8
neun	9
zehn	10
elf	11
zwölf	12
dreizehn	13
vierzehn	14
fünfzehn	15
sechszehn	16
siebzehn	17
achtzehn	18
neunzehn	19
zwanzig	20
einundzwanzig	21
zweiundzwanzig	22
dreissig	30
vierzig	40
fünfzig	50

GREETINGS AND TIMES

Guten Morgen	Good morning
Guten Tag	Good day
Guten Abend	Good evening
Gute Nacht	Goodnight
Wie geht es Ihnen?	How are you?
Heute	today
Gestern	yesterday
Morgen	tomorrow
Vorgestern	the day before yesterday
Übermorgen	the day after tomorrow
Tag	day
Nacht	night
Woche	week

Wochenende	weekend
Monat	month
Jahr	year
vormittags	in the morning
nachtmittags	in the afternoon
abends	in the evening
Mittag	Midday
Mitternacht	Midnight
drei Uhr	three o'clock
viertel nach drei	quarter past three
halbvier	half past three (ie half to four)
viertel vor vier	quarter to four

QUESTIONS, REQUESTS AND STATEMENTS

Note that all requests should be preceded by *Entschuldigen Sie bitte* (excuse me please).

Sprechen Sie Englisch?	Do you speak English?
Ich spreche kein Deutsch	I do not speak German
Sprechen Sie bitte langsamer	
	Please speak more slowly
Iche verstehe	I understand
Ich verstehe nicht	I do not understand
Wo ist . . . ?	Where is . . . ?
Wie komme ich zur/zum . . . ?	
	How do I get to . . . ?
Ich hätte gern dieses	I would like this one
Wieviel kostet das?	How much does this cost?
Haben Sie etwas billigeres?	
	Have you anything cheaper?
Wann fährt der nächste Zug?	
	When does the next train leave?
Um wieviel Uhr?	At what time?
Wieviel Uhr ist es?	What time is it?
Sind die Plätze noch frei?	
	Are these places free?
Die Speisekarte, bitte	The menu, please
Die Rechnung, bitte	The bill, please
Haben Sie Zimmer frei?	Are there rooms available?
Ich hätte gern ein Zimmer für zwei	
	I would like a room for two
Ich hätte gern ein Einzelzimmer	
	I would like a single room
Hat es Dusche, Bad, Toilette?	
	Has it got a shower, bath, toilet?
Wie sagt man das auf Deutsch?	
	How do you say that in German?
Ich komme aus England	I come from England
Schottland	Scotland

Wales	Wales
Irland	Ireland
die Vereinigten Staaten	the United States
Kanada	Canada
Australien	Australia
Neuseeland	New Zealand

SIGNS

Abfahrt	departure
Achtung	attention
Ankunft	arrival
Ausgang	exit
Baustelle	building works
Besetzt	engaged
Damen, Frauen	women's toilets
Drücken	push
Eingang	entrance
Frei	vacant
Herren, Männer	men's toilets
Kasse	cash desk
Kein Eingang	no entrance
Krankenhaus	hospital
Nicht rauchen	no smoking
Notausgang	emergency exit
Polizei	police
Privat	private
Rundgang	way round
Verboten	forbidden
Vorsicht	beware
Ziehen	pull
Zoll	customs

TRANSPORT

Auto	car
Bahnhof	station
Bus	bus
Fahrkarte, Fahrschein	ticket
Fahrplan	timetable
Fahrrad	bicycle
Flughafen	airport
Gleis	platform
Haltestelle	stop
Platz	seat
S-Bahn	overground munici- pal railway
Schiff	ship, boat
Taxi	taxi
U-Bahn	underground railway
Zug	train

SHOPS

Antiquitätengeschäft	antique shop
Antiquariat	second-hand bookshop
Apotheke	chemist
Bäckerei	baker
Bioladen, Reformhaus	health food shop
Blumenhändler, Florist	florist
Buchhandlung	bookshop
Delikatessen, Feinkost- geschäft	delicatessen
Drogerie	drugstore
Eisdiele	ice-cream parlour
Eisenwarenhandlung	ironmonger
Fischgeschäft	fishmonger
Fotowarenladen	photography shop
Galerie	commercial art gallery
Glaswaren	glassware shop
Haushaltgeschäft	household goods store
Herrenausstatter	gents' outfitter
Juwelier, Schmuckhändler	jeweller
Kaufhaus, Warenhaus	department store
Keramikwaren	ceramic goods shop
Konditorei	confectioner
Lebensmittelhändler	grocer
Lederwaren	leather goods shop
Markthalle	farmers' market hall
Metzgerei	butcher
Modegeschäft, Modesalon	female fashions
Modernes Antiquariat	discount bookshop
Molkerei	dairy
Obst- und Gemüsehandlung	greengrocer
Optiker	optician
Parfümerie	perfume and cosmetics shop
Pelzwarenladen	fur goods shop
Reisebüro	travel agency
Schallplattenhandlung	record shop
Schreibwarenhändler	stationer
Schuhgeschäft	shoe shop
Schuhmacher	cobbler
Spielwarenladen	toy shop
Supermarkt	supermarket
Uhrmacher	watchmaker
Wein- und Spirituosen- handlung	off-licence
Zeitungshändler	newsagent

SIGHTSEEING

Allee	avenue
Auskunft	information
Ausstellung	exhibition
Bank	bank
Berg	hill
Bezirk	district
Bibliothek	library
Brücke	bridge
Damm	embankment
Denkmal, Gedenk- stätte	memorial
Friedhof	cemetery
Fussgängerzone	pedestrian precinct
Garten	garden
Gaststätte	restaurant
Gemäldegalerie	picture gallery
Hof	courtyard
Insel	island
Kino	cinema
Kirche	church
Kneipe	bar, pub
Markt	market square
Mauer	wall
Museum	museum
Palais, Palast	palace, mansion
Platz	square
Rathaus	town hall
Sammlung	collection
Schloss	castle, palace
See	lake
Strasse	street
Theater	theatre
Tor	gate, gateway
Turm	tower
Ufer	quay
Viertel	quarter
Wald	forest
Wechselstube	currency exchange shop

Recommended Reading

Art and Architecture

Adam, Peter, *The Art of the Third Reich* (Thames and Hudson, London, 1992). The first book in English to tackle a subject far more worthy of attention than is generally supposed, especially as Hitler, having once been an artist, took an uncommon interest in the medium for a political leader.

Dube, Wolf-Dieter, *The Expressionists* (Thames and Hudson, London, 1972). General introduction to the most distinctive movement of German 20th-century art, one of whose two main groups, *Die Brücke*, was latterly based in Berlin.

Friedrich, Thomas, *Berlin: A Photographic Portrait of the Weimar Years* (Tauris Parke, London, 1991). Wonderful collection of archive photos, showing all classes of society at work and play during one of the most exciting epochs in Berlin's history.

Pachnicke, Peter and Honnef, Klaus (ed.), *John Heartfield* (Harry Abrams, New York, 1991). Of unusually luxurious quality for an exhibition catalogue, this hefty volume has full-page reproductions of the artist's best work, including many examples of photomontage, a medium he invented and used to devastating satirical effect.

Schinkel, Karl Friedrich, *Architectural Drawings* (Butterworth-Heinemann, Oxford, 1989; first pub. 1866). Intended as a source book for practising architects, this tome features reproductions of Schinkel's working drawings, but the consumate draughtsmanship is worthy of a far wider audience.

Snodin, Michael (ed.), *Karl Friedrich Schinkel: A Universal Man* (Yale University Press, London, 1991). The best general introduction to Schinkel's diverse genius. In addition to reproducing and describing all the paintings and drawings at the exhibition it originally accompanied, it contains coloured shots of his surviving buildings, archive pictures of those destroyed during and after World War II, and several scholarly essays.

Vaughan, William, *German Romantic Painting* (Yale University Press, London, 1980). Introduction to the main tendency in 19th-century German painting, including many artists with a specific Berlin connection.

Waldenburg, Hermann, *The Berlin Wall Book* (tr. Thames and Hudson, London, 1990;). Photographs, with a short accompanying text, of the paintings and graffiti that adorned the West-facing side of the Wall. Now something of an unintentional memorial, given that most of these were lost when the Wall was pulled down.

Watkin, David and Mellinghoff, Tilman, *German Architecture and the Classical Ideal, 1740–1840* (Thames and Hudson, London, 1987). Comprehensive scholarly study of neoclassicism, one of the most distinguished periods of German architectural history; includes a chapter on Schinkel.

Whitford, Frank, *Bauhaus* (Thames and Hudson, London, 1984). Concise account of the most influential architectural school of the 20th century, which was based for a time in Berlin.

Willett, John, *The Weimar Years* (Thames and Hudson, London, 1984). Visual and descriptive round-up of the short-lived but heady period of creativity that immediately preceded the cultural collapse that occurred under the Nazis.

Biography

Bullock, Alan, *Hitler, A Study in Tyranny* (Penguin, London, 1990; first pub. 1952). The classic biography, both scholarly and readable, of the former corporal and failed artist who hoodwinked a great nation and caused the death of millions. See also *Hitler and Stalin* (Fontana, 1993; first pub. 1991), in which the author compares and contrasts Hitler's career with that of his equally evil contemporary and discovers many unnerving parallels.

Jewish monument at the Auschwitz deportation point

Duffy, Christopher, *Fredrick the Great, A Military Life* (Routledge, London, 1985). As the title suggests, this focuses on the military aspects of the career of the greatest of the Prussian kings.

Mitford, Nancy, *Frederick the Great* (Hamish Hamilton, London, 1988; first pub. 1970). A more general portrait, told with a true novelist's elegance, of the flute-playing philosopher whose army made Prussia into a major European power.

Taylor, A J P, *Bismarck: The Man and the Statesman* (Hamish Hamilton, London, 1985; first pub. 1955). The most controversial British historian describes the life of the political and diplomatic manipulator *par excellence* who—reluctantly, in Taylor's view—finally forged a united Germany after a millennium of division.

Current Affairs

Ardagh, John, *Germany and the Germans* (Penguin, London, 1991; first pub. 1987). Wide-ranging journalistic survey of all aspects of modern German culture and society, including plenty of material pertinent to Berlin. The second edition reprints a couple of historic chapters about the GDR from its predecessor, in addition to discussing present and future consequences of reunification.

McElvoy, Anne, *The Saddled Cow* (Faber and Faber, London, 1993; first pub. 1992). Retrospective journalistic examination of the final years of the GDR, featuring extensive interviews with its former citizens.

Miller, Peter, *Tomorrow Belongs to Me* (Bloomsbury, London, 1992). Subtitled *Germany Through the Extraordinary Lives of Ordinary People*, this is a marvellous series of improbable but true stories collected by the author during his time as the only English-language journalist, other than a political defector, based in the GDR.

Schneider, Peter, *The German Comedy* (tr., I B Tauris, London, 1992; first pub. 1990). Stimulating discussion of the myriad problems caused by German reunification, with many wry descriptions and observations on some of the bizarre contradictions and anomalies that ensued.

Smith, Ken, *Berlin: Coming in from the Cold* (Penguin, London, 1991; first pub. 1990). By far the best of the instant histories inspired by the fall of the Berlin Wall, with a series of detailed first-hand accounts of life in the city before, during and after the big event.

Fiction (English-Language and Foreign)

Bedford, Sybille, *A Legacy* (Picador, London, 1992; first pub. 1956). Semi-autobiographical novel about two German families, one Berlin, Jewish and mercantile, the other provincial, Catholic and aristocratic, improbably united by marriage. Full of sparkling dialogue and richly comic episodes, particularly in the run-up to the wedding.

Boyd, William, *The New Confessions* (Penguin, London, 1988; first pub. 1987). This supposed autobiography of a self-appointed but failed Scottish genius includes among its many settings the Berlin cinema world of the 1920s and Berlin in the aftermath of its wartime devastation.

Deighton, Len, *Winter: A Berlin Family 1899–1945* (Grafton, London, 1988; first pub. 1987). Saga of an upper middle-class family passing through two world wars and three very different political regimes. The author is better known for his Cold War spy thrillers, which include *Funeral in Berlin* (Grafton, London, 1978; first pub. 1964) and *The Berlin Game* (Grafton, London, 1984; first pub. 1983).

Feinstein, Elaine, *Loving Brecht* (Sceptre, London, 1993; first pub. 1992). Highly plausible piece of 'faction' based around the magnetic personality of Bertolt Brecht and its effect on his theatrical entourage.

Hamilton, Hugo, *Surrogate City* (Faber and Faber, London, 1990). The strikingly individualistic prose style and vivid evocation of the Turkish and alternative communities of early 1980s West Berlin compensate for the less than fully convincing handling of the main plot about a love affair between two Irish émigrés.

Harris, Robert, *Fatherland* (Arrow, London, 1993; first pub. 1992). Rings the changes on the conventional thriller by being set in a 1960s Nazi Berlin that dominates Europe and is waging a Cold War against the United States.

Higgins, Aidan, *Lions of the Grunewald* (Secker & Warburg, London, 1993). Firmly rooted in the great Irish literary tradition, this richly crafted and densely written novel, set in West Berlin in the late 1960s and early '70s, describes the rivalry between the wife and mistress of a visiting Irish writer. The subsidiary characters include a number of real-life authors and celebrities.

Isherwood, Christopher, *Mr Norris Changes Trains*, (Methuen, London, 1987; first pub. 1935), *Goodbye to Berlin* (Minerva, London, 1989; first pub. 1939). It was the author's intention to produce a huge episodic saga of Berlin life in the closing years of the Weimar Republic, but instead he wrote only a shortish novel centred on the roguish Arthur Norris and a collection of stories about such other memorable characters as Sally Bowles, the Nowaks and the Landauers. Together with the films they inspired, *I am a Camera* and *Cabaret*, these books have provided the English-speaking world with its most enduring definition of Berlin—a highly-charged city of seedy nightclubs, rotting tenements and luxury suburban villas.

Jerome, Jerome K, *Three Men on the Bummel* (Penguin, London, 1983; first pub. 1900). This sequel to the more famous *Three Men in a Boat* features the same trio of feckless English tourists on a cycling trip through Germany. The few pages on Berlin paint an unflattering but laconically accurate picture of the turn-of-the-century city, narrated with the author's customary gentle humour.

Kerr, Philip, *March Violets*, *The Pale Criminal*, *A German Requiem* (Penguin, London, 1990, 1991, 1991 respectively; first pub. 1989, 1990, 1991 respectively). Trilogy of high-class, fast-moving thrillers with well-researched historical detail, all featuring the detective Bernie Gunther on the prowl in Berlin during and after the Nazi epoch.

Le Carré, John, *The Spy who came in from the Cold* (Coronet, London, 1990; first pub. 1963). The ultimate classic of Cold War fiction, describing the fateful last mission of the British spy Alec Leamas before his intended retirement. Twists and turns through a variety of locations, but begins and ends at the then recently built Berlin Wall.

Levi, Primo, *The Sixth Day* (tr., Abacus, London, 1991; first pub. 1966). Best known for his disarmingly humane recollections of Auschwitz concentration camp, in this volume of fantastical short stories the author drew heavily on his working background as a scientist. Of the two set in Berlin, 'Angelic Butterfly' utilizes the backdrop of the postwar occupation, while 'The Sleeping Beauty in the Fridge' offers a chilling foretaste of the year 2115.

Mosley, Nicholas, *Hopeful Monsters* (Minerva, London, 1991; first pub. 1990). This huge experimental novel, which begins in Berlin, is a major, if highly untypical, accomplishment of English postwar fiction.

Nabokov, Vladimir, *The Gift* (tr., Penguin, London, 1981, first pub. 1938). The author's last novel in his native Russian before switching to writing in English is the supposed autobiography of a writer living in the closed world of the community of Russian émigré intellectuals in Berlin just after World War I.

Wendorf, Patricia, *Peacefully: in Berlin* (Futura, New York, 1988; first pub. 1983). The story of a problematic Anglo-German marriage, told in a series of flashbacks in the course of a train journey to Berlin.

Fiction (German, in Translation)

Brecht, Bertolt, *Collected Short Stories* (Methuen, London, 1983; first pub. 1921–46). This little known but rewarding area of the author's output includes a collection entitled *Berlin Stories*, though only a couple are actually set in the city: 'Hook to the Chin' reveals Brecht's passion for boxing, while 'A Little Tale of Insurance' is in his archetypal anti-capitalist vein.

Döblin, Alfred, *Berlin Alexanderplatz* (tr., Continuum, New York, 1992; first pub. 1929). Written under the immediate influence of James Joyce's *Ulysses*, this weighty novel about the city's underclass in the days of the Weimar Republic makes for a difficult but rewarding read. The trilogy *November 1918* (1950), published in English as *A People Betrayed* and *Karl and Rosa* (both Fromm International Publishing, New York, 1983), recounts the failed German Revolution, juxtaposing embroidered descriptions of the real-life struggle among rival left-wing political leaders with the impact this had on the lives of fictional citizens.

Fallada, Hans, *Little Man, What Now?* (tr., Academy Chicago Publishers, Chicago, 1983; first pub. 1932). A once famous but now unjustly neglected gem of German literature, describing with great style, humour and tenderness the story of a young married couple's struggle to make ends meet during the spiralling inflation of the Weimar Republic's last years. It captures the German psyche on the eve of the Nazi takeover far more effectively than any history book.

Fontane, Theodor, *Before the Storm* (tr. Oxford University Press, Oxford, 1985; first pub. 1878). Written when he was in his mid-fifties, this remarkable historical epic of the Napoleonic Wars, a German counterpart to *War and Peace*, marked Fontane's novelistic début. It was succeeded by a range of shortish novels and novellas describing with great clarity and accuracy contemporary life in the Second Reich, with its rigid social mores and diverse character types. Typically, the action shifts between Berlin and the provinces and focuses on the relationship between the sexes, with strong emphasis on the woman's predicament. The most famous of these is *Effi Briest* (tr. Penguin, London, 1967; first pub. 1894), which deals with the theme of adultery; *Cécile* (tr. Angel, 1992; first pub. 1886) likewise focuses on moral dilemmas and ends tragically. *The Poggenpuhl Family* (tr., Continuum, New York, 1989; first pub. 1896), whose wonderfully detailed descriptions circumvent the virtual absence of plot, is available in English coupled with either *Delusions, Confusions* (tr. Continuum, New York, 1989; first pub. 1887), the tale of a love affair which founders on class distinctions, or *The Woman Taken in Adultery* (tr. University of Chicago Press, Chicago, 1979; first pub. 1882), which comes to an unexpectedly happy ending. Another compilation pairs *A Man of Honour* (tr. Continuum, New York, 1982; first pub. 1883), which exposes the mores of the Prussian officer class, with *Jenny Treibel* (tr. Continuum, New York, 1982; first pub. 1893), a comedy of manners about Berlin bourgeoisie.

Grass, Günter, *Local Anaesthetic* (tr. Harcourt Brace Jovanovich, 1970; first pub. 1969). Manic satirical novel about 1960s West Berlin by Germany's most famous contemporary novelist; the themes of wartime guilt, middle-age ennui and youthful rebellion are filtered through the story of a teacher's hallucinations while under dental anaesthetics and his intervention in his star pupil's plan to shock the complacent local conscience by burning a pet dachshund outside the city's top hotel. Berlin also makes fleeting appearances in two of Grass's longer fantasies, *Dog Years* and *From the Diary of a Snail* (both tr., Picador, London, 1989; first pub. 1963 and 1972 respectively).

Hein, Christoph, *The Distant Lover* (tr., Picador, London, 1990; first pub. 1982). Written in the persona of an East Berlin woman doctor, whose apparently well-ordered lifestyle is exposed as being numbingly empty.

Heym, Stefan, *Five Days in June* (tr. Hodder and Stoughton, London, 1977; first pub. 1974). The workers' revolt of 1953 is described and analysed by the erstwhile Marxist who soon became a one-man opposition to the GDR regime, though here he tempers his criticism with accusations against the West. In *Collin* (tr. Hodder and Stoughton, London, 1980; first pub. 1979) Heym wittily recounts the tense relationship that develops in an exclusive East Berlin clinic between a top party functionary with a great deal to hide and a fêted novelist who has begun to write his memoirs.

Hoffmann, Ernst Theodor Amadeus, 'A New Year's Adventure' (tr. in *The Best Tales of Hoffmann*, Dover, Mineola, NY, 1967; first pub. 1816). A typical example of the art of the great Romantic master of the macabre, using his characteristic technique of telling two apparently different tales, one set in Berlin, the other in Italy, which turn out to be the same story told at different levels. 'My Cousin's Corner Window' (tr. in *The Golden Pot and Other Tales*, Oxford University Press, Oxford, 1992; first pub. 1822) is set in Berlin's Gendarmenmarkt, which is described in the intuitive manner of a detective story, a literary form Hoffmann himself invented.

Jünger, Ernst, *Aladdin's Problem* (tr. Quartet, London, 1993; first pub. 1983). A taut yet lusciously written and enormously profound short novel, written at the age of 85 by the most controversial German writer of the century. Its unlikely story is the tale of the manager of a Berlin funeral parlour who sets up a business empire centred on an international non-denominational necropolis in the wastelands of Turkey.

Kästner, Erich, *Fabian, the Story of a Moralist* (tr., Libris, London, 1990; first pub. 1931). Autobiographical novel set in Berlin in 1929–30 at the time of the Weimar Republic's economic collapse. The author is best known for his children's stories, particularly *Emil and the Detectives* (tr., Puffin, London, 1959; first pub. 1929), which is studded with concise descriptions that vividly sum up the essential character of the city.

Kleist, Heinrich von, 'Michael Kolhaas' (tr. in *The Marquise of O and Other Stories*, Penguin, London, 1978; first pub. 1810). This masterly Romantic novella adds a supernatural coating to the true story of a 16th-century horse dealer living on the outskirts of Berlin whose obsessive quest for justice sparked off an armed uprising.

Mann, Heinrich, *Man of Straw* (tr., Penguin, London, 1984; first pub. 1918). A searing indictment, narrated with a heavy sense of irony, of the Wilhelmine Second Reich, its corrupt commercial values and idolization of militarism and monarchy. The 'hero' Diederich Hessling, outwardly a highly successful businessman and pillar of society, is dissected as morally, emotionally and intellectually bankrupt—a man of straw.

Mann, Klaus, *Mephisto* (tr., Penguin, London, 1983; original German version banned from publication). An update of the Faust legend, one of the great themes of German literature, which tells the story of Heinrich Hoffmann, an actor who sells out to the Nazis. It is heavily based on the life of the author's brother-in-law, Gustav Gründgens; other leading artistic figures, such as Thomas Mann, Marlene Dietrich and Max Reinhardt, appear under pseudonyms, while Hermann Göring and Josef Goebbels are identified only by the offices they held. *The Pious Dance* (tr. Gay Men's Press, 1988; first pub. 1925), written while Mann was still a teenager, anticipates the writings of Christopher Isherwood in its descriptions of the interwar Berlin underworld of tacky guesthouses, transvestite nightclubs and seedy cabarets.

Plenzdorf, Ulrich, *The New Sufferings of Young W* (tr. Unger, 1979; first pub. 1973). Wickedly funny spoof reworking, in the setting of 1970s East Berlin, one of the great icons of German culture, Goethe's *The Sufferings of Young Werther.*

Schneider, Peter, *The Wall Jumper* (tr. Allison and Busby, London, 1984). A series of vignettes about the Berlin Wall, those who crossed it (in both directions) and the two different castes of mind it induced. Although billed as fiction, much of it is clearly autobiographical and factual, albeit larded with some hoaxes.

Tucholsky, Kurt, *Germany? Germany!* (tr. Carcanet, 1990; first pub. 1916–32). A reader drawn from the writings of the sharpest German satirist of the 20th century, embracing newspaper articles, essays, poems and cabaret songs with music. The outrageously witty monologues of Herr Wendriner, a complacent Jewish businessman, are chillingly prophetic, and all the more telling for having been penned by a Jew. *Castle Gripsolm* (tr. Chatto and Windus, London, 1985; first pub. 1931), though no more than a novella, is Tucholsky's only extended work, an unexpectedly optimistic story set mostly in Sweden but with plenty of examples of characteristic Berlin wit.

Wolf, Christa, *What Remains and Other Stories* (tr. Virago, London, 1993; first pub. 1990). The autobiographical title story, about the harassment of a celebrated writer by the Stasi, was not published until after reunification, though apparently drafted a decade earlier; its publication led many to deride the author as a cowardly hypocrite, given that she had openly supported, and allowed herself to be fêted by, the GDR regime. Included in the same volume is *Unter den Linden*, a highly impressionistic story set in Berlin's most famous boulevard.

History

Berghahn, Volker, *Germany and the Approach of War in 1914* (Macmillan, London, 1993). Gives an instructive general picture of the political, social and economic pressures current in Germany at the beginning of the century, with plausible explanations for why these exploded as they did.

Childs, David, *The GDR—Moscow's German Ally* (Unwin Hyman, London, 1988). Best of the academic studies of the GDR, fully revised the year before *Die Wende* when the regime still seemed secure. Though now obviously dated, it is of interest as a historical portrait.

Farr, Michael, *Berlin! Berlin!* (Viking Penguin, London, 1992). General history of the city, including not only the expected descriptions of its political, social and economic development, but also detailed information about the key events in its artistic and cultural life.

Fest, Joachim C, *The Face of the Third Reich* (tr., Penguin, London, 1979; first pub. 1963). Primarily of interest for its portraits of the leading members of the gallery of rogues who made up Hitler's court: Göring, Goebbels, Hess, Himmler and Speer.

Gelb, Norman, *The Berlin Wall* (Michael Joseph, London, 1986). The definitive history of the world's most hated border from its construction up to 1986, when it seemed as though it really would stand, as GDR leaders boasted, for another half-century or more.

Gill, Anton, *A Dance Between Flames* (John Murray, London, 1993). Offers a comprehensive study of cultural life in Berlin during the heady years of the Weimar Republic.

Hart-Davies, Duff, *Hitler's Games* (Coronet, London, 1988; first pub. 1986). Thoroughly researched book on the 1936 Olympiad, which started the uncomfortable but still prevalent trend of using sport in the service of politics.

Koch, H W, *History of Prussia* (Longman, Harlow, UK, 1978). Scholarly study on the life and death of the militaristic state centred on Berlin that rose from a provincial backwater to take over leadership of the previously fragmented German nation.

Kolb, Ebehard, *The Weimar Republic* (tr. Unwin Hyman, London, 1988; first pub. 1984). Thought-provoking analysis of the fascinating but fundamentally flawed state that lasted for just fourteen years and was, until 1989, the only attempt at a democratic unified Germany.

Le Tissier, Tony, *The Battle of Berlin* (Jonathan Cape, London, 1988). Immensely detailed account of the long and bloody struggle prior to the city's capitulation to the Red Army in 1945.

Middlebrook, Martin, *The Berlin Raids* (Penguin, London, 1990; first pub. 1988). Account of the RAF campaign to destroy Berlin by saturation bombing, drawing on interviews with civilian survivors and with pilots on both sides.

Read, Anthony and Fisher, David, *The Fall of Berlin* (Pimlico, London, 1993; first pub. 1992). Traces the story of Berlin from the triumphant international spotlight of the 1936 Olympic Games to the nadir of 1945, when the Soviets celebrated their capture of the city with an orgy of rape and looting; rich in the human detail so often missing from histories of the period.

Berlin, The Biography of a City (Hutchinson, London, 1994). This is now the most comprehensive history of Berlin in English, albeit one whose coverage of the present century is far more detailed than that of earlier times.

Reissner, Alexander, *Berlin 1675–1945* (Oswald Wolff, 1984). Concise survey of the city's history from its belated rise as a major capital to the end of the Third Reich.

Shirer, William, *The Rise and Fall of the Third Reich* (Mandarin, London, 1991; first pub. 1960). As an American journalist based in Berlin throughout the Third Reich, the author was ideally placed to document its history. Despite the daunting length and excessive journalese, the book is an ideal work of reference with a comprehensive index.

Simmons, Michael, *Berlin, The Depressed City* (Hamish Hamilton, London, 1988). History of Berlin in the 20th century, up to the later years of the Wall.

Tusa, Ann and John, *The Berlin Blockade* (Hodder and Stoughton, London, 1988). Recounts the epic story of the airlifts that saved the beleaguered half-city of West Berlin from falling into Communist clutches, detailing the high-level political background and individual acts of heroism.

Trevor-Roper, Hugh, *The Last Days of Hitler* (Pan, London, 1983; first pub. 1978). Painstaking re-creation of the closing chapter of the Third Reich, set in the Führerbunker on Potsdamer Platz.

Literary Criticism

Bridgwater, Patrick, *Georg Heym* (Libris, London, 1991). A biographical and critical analysis of the Expressionist poet of Berlin's Bohemian circles, who died in an accident at the age of 24. Includes many otherwise unavailable translations of his poems.

Garland, Henry, *The Berlin Novels of Theodor Fontane* (Clarendon Press, Oxford, 1980). Dissects all the novels with a Berlin setting by the city's greatest writer. Despite the continuing rise in Fontane's posthumous reputation, it is regrettable that several of these novels have yet to be translated into English.

Memoirs

Adams, Henry, *The Education of Henry Adams* (Houghton Mifflin, North York, Ontario, 1974; first pub. 1918). One of the great American autobiographies, this has only a single short chapter on Berlin, describing the author's student days there, but it contains some of the wittiest comments ever made about the city.

Bielenberg, Christabel, *The Past is Myself* (Corgi, London, 1984). This autobiography of an Anglo-Irish aristocrat married to a German lawyer who participated in the resistance to Hitler gained cult status through Dennis Potter's television serialization. The short cameo chapters are particularly fine, summing up the effects Nazism had on everyday behaviour. Her return to Berlin after the war, along with her subsequent life in Ireland, is recounted in the sequel *The Road Ahead* (Corgi, London, 1993; first pub. 1992)

Canetti, Elias, *The Torch in My Ear* (tr., Picador, London, 1990; first pub. 1980). This second part of the autobiographical trilogy of the Nobel Prize-winning novelist and social scientist includes coverage of his sojourn in Berlin, where he got to know, among others, Bertolt Brecht, Isaac Babel and the brothers Wieland Herzfelde and John Heartfield.

Clare, George, *Berlin Days 1946–47* (Pan, London, 1990; first pub. 1989). Written by an Austrian Jew who joined the British army, this is the best first-hand account of the postwar Allied occupation of Berlin, with particularly good detail on the denazification process in which the author was heavily involved.

Grosz, George, *A Small Yes and a Big No* (tr. Allison and Busby, London, 1982; first pub. 1955). Autobiography of the Dadaist artist who was one of the leading lights in the cultural life of the Weimar Republic. Illustrated with many of its own satirical drawings, it includes anecdotes on other leading figures of the time, such as Bertolt Brecht and Kurt Tucholsky.

Hellmann, Lillian, *Pentimento* (Quartet, London, 1976; first pub. 1974). Included among this series of portraits of people the playwright knew at various stages of her life is 'Julia', the story of her own part in helping a friend involved in the Berlin resistance to Hitler. Doubts have been raised as to the authenticity of the episode.

Hitler, Adolf, *Mein Kampf* (tr., Pimlico, London, 1992; first pub. 1926). Probably the most evil book ever written; a series of rambling, irrational and hysterical discourses on just about every subject in the universe, interspersed with an account of the author's own early life. Dictated to Rudolf Hess while in prison for the failed Munich Beer Hall Putsch of 1923, it effectively served as the Nazis' manifesto for power and their policy programme once this was achieved.

Isherwood, Christopher, *Christopher and his Kind* (Methuen, London, 1985; first pub. 1977). For the most part, a tiresome catalogue of the author's promiscuous homosexual adventures, showing all too clearly the self-obsessiveness that was primarily responsible for the collapse of his creative powers in the latter half of his career. However, it does offer revelatory insights into the real-life background to his Berlin stories of nearly half a century earlier.

Mann, Klaus, *The Turning Point* (Serpent's Tail, London, 1987; first pub. 1942). A hard-hitting literary autobiography, written in English as a direct result of the long-running German ban on the novel *Mephisto*, whose background is recounted here.

Rimmer, Dave, *Once Upon a Time in the East* (Fourth Estate, London, 1992). Account of life in Berlin before and after the fall of the Wall by an émigré Englishman who was careless enough to be in Czechoslovakia at the time of the great demolition.

Shirer, William, *Berlin Diary* (Little, Brown and Co, Boston, 1988; first pub. 1941). Personal reminiscences of the American journalist who chronicled the history of the Third Reich.

Spender, Stephen, *World Within World* (Faber and Faber, London, 1991; first pub.1977). Only has a short section on Berlin, which is notable mainly for anecdotes on Christopher Isherwood. It was a cooling of this friendship that led Spender to move from the city where he had originally planned to spend a much longer sojourn.

Vassiltchikov, Marie, *The Berlin Diaries* (Methuen, London, 1987; first pub. 1985). A friend of the Bielenbergs and her diaries likewise cover life in wartime Berlin and the resistance movement.

Walker, Ian, *Zoo Station* (Abacus, London, 1988; first pub. 1987). This offers a wealth of insights about life in both halves of Berlin in the 1980s, but is marred by a tedious addiction to swearwords, a pompous pretention towards rock music connoisseurship, and an embarrassing infatuation with the intimate details of the author's own love life. It would all have been so much better dressed up as a novel.

Poetry

Brecht, Bertolt, *Poems 1913–56* (tr. Methuen, London, 1987; first pub. 1913–56). This superb collection, which includes a fair number of verses with specific Berlin associations, celebrates Brecht's artistry far more effectively and consistently than do his plays, many of which now seem rather worn.

Haushofer, Albrecht, *Moabit Sonnets* (tr. Norton, London, 1978; first pub. 1945). Powerful poems in honour of the German resistance to Hitler, by a man who was executed for his part in this cause.

Travel and Description

Baedeker, Karl, *Berlin* (Baedeker, Ostfildern, Germany, first pub. 1903). The old Baedeker guides, with their wonderful pull-out maps and splendidly forthright advice, are still indispensable classics. That they are so out of date—in their opinions, as much as in the character and appearance of the city they describe—only adds to their charm.

Boswell, James, *Journal of a Tour Through the Courts of Germany, 1764* (Yale Publications, London, 1953). Full of characteristic gossip, this journal is an outstanding product of the days of the aristocratic Grand Tour. Boswell hung around both Charlottenburg and Potsdam in the hope of gaining an audience with Frederick the Great, but had to be content with a number of sightings of the king.

Wraxall, Nathaniel, *Memoirs of the Courts of Berlin, Dresden, Warsaw and Vienna* (1799). Dating from a decade after Boswell's visit, but not written up until twenty years later, this long out-of-print memoir is well worth seeking out, as the author did meet Frederick the Great. He provides many insights into the lifestyle of the king and the Prussian court, including information on the construction of the palaces in Potsdam.

Neoclassical sculpture in Olympia Stadion, one of the few remaining examples of Fascist architecture still standing in Berlin

Index